The James-Hawthorne Relation

Thaddeo K. Babiiha

The James-Hawthorne Relation

Bibliographical Essays

G. K. Hall and Company Boston, Massachusetts

Library of Congress Cataloging in Publication Data

Babiiha, Thaddeo K
The James-Hawthorne relation.

Bibliography: p.
Includes index.
1. James, Henry, 1843-1916—Criticism and interpretation—Addresses, essays, lectures.
2. Hawthorne, Nathaniel, 1804-1864—Influence—James—Addresses, essays, lectures. I. Title.
PS2124.B3 813'.4 80-12741
ISBN 0-8161-8431-3

This publication is printed on permanent/durable acid-free paper
MANUFACTURED IN THE UNITED STATES OF AMERICA

To
Hyatt H. Waggoner

I enjoyed last week the great pleasure of reading The House of the Seven Gables . . . . *It also tickled my national feeling . . . to note the resemblance of Hawthorne's style to yours and Howells's . . . That you and Howells with all the models in English literature to follow, should needs involuntarily have imitated (as it were) this American, seems to point to the existence of some real American mental quality.*

–WILLIAM JAMES

I'm glad you've been liking Hawthorne. But I mean to write as good a novel one of these days (perhaps) as The House of the Seven Gables.

Monday, 14th. With the above thrilling prophecy I last night laid down my pen.

–HENRY JAMES

Contents

Foreward

I suppose no relationship between any two American writers is more complex, more difficult to disentangle, or more important than that between Hawthorne and Henry James. None at least has been given more serious study or prompted more brief comment. Yet until the present work, it has been difficult and time-consuming to find out all that has been written, even by James himself, on the subject, with the result that discoveries have been too often rediscovered and both insights and oversights repeated.

Long after Hawthorne's importance to James was made clear by Eliot and Leavis, with their different interpretations of the nature of that importance but their agreement on the fact of it, after the detailed studies of Marius Bewley, Peter Buitenhuis, Robert Long, and others, it has seemed possible to discuss James's development without mentioning Hawthorne, or to admit the relationship but limit the influence to a few works of James's early apprenticeship. In support of such interpretations the writers could cite selected statements by James himself, who felt he had more to learn about his craft from the continental masters than from poor provincial Hawthorne, dear as Hawthorne's works were to him. Until quite late in life, when his own fame was secure, James could not bring himself to acknowledge how important Hawthorne's work had been, and continued to be, to him. Respect, tenderness, and condescension are generally mingled in James's comments on Hawthorne, as Hawthornesque touches and effects impossible to imagine Hawthorne achieving often stand side by side in James's fiction. Perhaps partly as a result of this, not even the tangled Hawthorne-Melville relationship has so invited conflicting interpretations.

Interpretations will continue to differ no doubt, but with the appearance of this work there is no longer any excuse for judgments based on only part of the evidence, or for the continued discovery of relations long seen. Thaddeo Babiiha has made it possible for each of us, without making a major project of it, to isolate the questions that are still really open and concentrate on them. There is no longer any need to waste our time reading through unconvincing, ill-informed, or repetitious treatments of the subject.

For anyone seriously interested in the influences that affected James's development, or in those aspects of our literary history illuminated by the relations between these two great writers, Babiiha's work will be indispensable. A work of immense labor, scrupulous scholarship, and critical intelligence, it makes a major contribution.

HYATT H. WAGGONER

Preface

There are many studies of the ways in which the fiction of Henry James was strongly influenced by that of Nathaniel Hawthorne. But there is no single work which brings together and evaluates the various findings in all these studies. The main purpose of this study is to fill this gap.

The text is made up of six essays. The first essay considers forty-one separate items in which James wrote about, or directly referred to, Hawthorne and/or his works; it also reviews the explanations which critics have given for James's shifting attitudes–throughout his writing career–toward his predecessor. The second essay reviews those works in English–including unpublished doctoral dissertations–which have considered, either exclusively or in part, the *general* relationship between the two authors and their fiction. The last two sections of this essay are addressed to two particular aspects which have received much critical attention: the relation of the artist to society as revealed in Hawthorne's and James's works; and the heroines the two writers created, as well as the attitudes of these writers towards their women characters. The last four essays evaluate those items which have focused on the *specific* influence of, respectively, *The Scarlet Letter, The Blithedale Romance, The Marble Faun,* and Hawthorne's other works, on James's various novels and tales. Each of these four essays is introduced by a summary of James's comments, in his critical biography of Hawthorne (1879), on that particular work. In most cases, the items in all the essays except the first are reviewed in their descending order of significance. In the other cases they are reviewed chronologically.

In his Foreword to *American Literary Scholarship: An Annual, 1972* (Durham, N.C.: Duke University Press, 1974), p. vii, J. Albert Robbins noted that many "*ALS* contributors treat ill-formed and shallow articles by not mentioning them at all." It is felt, however, that the purpose of the present study is best served by comprehensiveness, not selectivity. Unfortunately, some of the more recent items reviewed are further evidence of what one *ALS* contributor, quoted by Robbins in the same Foreword, complained of:

"the lamentable tendency toward repetitiveness" (vi). This is nowhere more disturbing than in the unpublished dissertations.

In his article entitled "In Memory of Henry James" (*The Egoist*, January 1918, pp. 1-2), T. S. Eliot observed that "to be influenced by a writer is to have a chance inspiration from him; or to take what one wants; or to see things one has overlooked." The items reviewed in all the essays except the first include all those which consider specifically the influence of Hawthorne's fiction on James's, as well as those which examine such topics as the two authors' use of similar techniques–without necessarily implying influence–their treatment of similar themes, their preoccupation with similar problems, or their position in the general development of American literature. Almost all these items were published between 1918 and 1973; only a few appeared before 1918. (For the first essay, the period covered is from 1865 to 1917.)

In addition to Professor Hyatt H. Waggoner, to whom this study is dedicated, I want to thank three people who helped me in various ways while I was working on this project at Brown: Professor George Monteiro, Professor Edward A. Bloom, and (Mrs.) Nearlene J. Francis, who was then adviser to foreign students and faculty at Brown.

Chapter 1

Henry James on Hawthorne, 1865-1917

> I speak of him . . . as a man of his own craft, an emulous fellow-worker, who has learned from him more of the lessons of the engaging mystery of fiction than from any one else, and who is conscious of so large a debt to repay that it has had positively to be discharged in instalments; as if one could never have at once all the required cash in hand.
>
> –JAMES, "The Lesson of Balzac"

In "Henry James on Hawthorne," *New England Quarterly,* 32 (June, 1959), 207-25, Peter Buitenhuis notes that not only did James read Hawthorne from his childhood days, but that, as "a young reviewer, he referred repeatedly to Hawthorne's work and often used him as a standard by which to judge other novelists." Earlier critics had made the same observation, and many others have echoed it since. But no one has attempted a more exact estimate of how pervasive this habit was, for James referred repeatedly to Hawthorne and his work, not only as a young reviewer, but throughout his entire writing career. Between the publication of his unsigned critical notes on Mary Elizabeth Braddon in 1865 and the posthumous publication of *The Sense of the Past* in 1917, James wrote about, and made direct reference to, Hawthorne in not less than forty-one separate items that have been published. These range in length from one-line references in various reviews, essays, letters and notes, to the book-length biography of the author. Undoubtedly, what James said of Balzac in 1905 is equally applicable to Hawthorne: James was "conscious of so large a debt to repay [Hawthorne] that it . . . had positively to be discharged in instalments; as if one could never have at once all the required cash in hand."[1]

To facilitate the handling of this material, the forty-one items considered here have been divided into three periods: those between 1865 and 1878, that is, before the publication of *Hawthorne*; those between 1879 and 1899; and those during the twentieth century. In addition to restating one of

Buitenhuis's findings—that these periodic assessments by James reveal considerable changes in his opinion of Hawthorne—this section will provide more evidence of the diversity of the authors to whom James applied the Hawthorne standard, and the variety of situations in which he reverted to the Hawthorne condition which he knew so well.

Items between 1865 and 1878

In January, 1855, Hawthorne expressed a fear that "America is now wholly given over to a d--d mob of scribbling women, and I should have no chance of success while the public taste is occupied with their trash."[2] Ten years later, James wrote about one of these scribbling women, whose popularity he felt was greatly disproportionate to her merits. In "Miss Braddon," *Nation,* 1 Nov. 9, 1865), 593-94, James stated that Braddon's novels have no purpose, are of little originality, and reveal no imaginative content. For contrast, one of the "great authorities" he mentioned was Hawthorne. The public which reads Miss Braddon, he wrote, "is that public which . . . reads neither George Eliot, George Sand, Thackeray, nor Hawthorne." It is a public made up of "very poor critics of human nature," whose main desire is for color, action, and detail. "With people who are not particular, therefore, as to the . . . intellectual strength" of their author, "Miss Braddon is very naturally a favorite." Thus this early James placed Hawthorne in the company of George Eliot, George Sand, and Thackeray, all authors of "intellectual strength."

In his favorable review of Howells's "Italian Journeys," *North American Review,* 106 (January, 1868), 336-39, a minor fault James mentioned was Howells's lack of judicial rigor, his being more generous than just. Among his literary merits, James emphasized his keen observation and his descriptions of the Italian people, their manners and morals. However, even here Howells related merely "what he saw with his own eyes, and what he thereupon felt and fancied, and his work has thus a thoroughly personal flavor." This comes out more strongly when he is contrasted with Hawthorne:

> Mr. Howells is, in short, a descriptive writer in a sense and with a perfection that . . . can be claimed for no American writer except Hawthorne. Hawthorne, indeed, was perfection, but he was only half descriptive. He kept an eye for an unseen world, and his points of contact with this actual sphere were few and slight. One feels through all his descriptions . . . that he was not a man of the world . . . But Hawthorne cannot be disposed of in a paragraph, and we confine ouselves to our own author. (339)

James was to make an important "prediction" before he got an opportunity to devote more than a paragraph to Hawthorne.

During 1869-1870, James made a tour of Europe, and wrote frequently to his brother William. On January 19, 1870, William's reply included the following:

> I enjoyed last week the great pleasure of reading *The House of the Seven Gables*. . . . It made a deep impression on me and I thank Heaven that Hawthorne was an American. It also tickled my national feeling . . . to note the resemblance of Hawthorne's style to yours and Howells's . . . That you and Howells with all the models in English literature to follow, should needs involuntarily have imitated (as it were) this American, seems to point to the existence of some real American mental quality.[3]

In his reply on February 13, 1870, James prophesied thus:

> I'm glad you've been liking Hawthorne. But I mean to write as good a novel one of these days (perhaps) as *The House of the Seven Gables*.
> Monday, 14th. With the above thrilling prophecy I last night laid down my pen. I see nothing left but to close my letter.[4]

With James's admission above, it would be difficult to deny that from his earliest, James emulated Hawthorne as the American writer to equal–and perhaps surpass.

James's "Hawthorne's French and Italian Journals," *Nation*, 14 (March 14, 1872), 172-73, is one of his five long estimates of Hawthorne which Buitenhuis examines in detail (*New England Quarterly*, 1959, pp. 207-10). Buitenhuis points out, quite appropriately, that at the time of writing this review, James was yearning for Europe, and was actually preparing to take another trip there. This may explain why his tone remains patronizing even when he praises Hawthorne or expresses his "tender personal regard" for him.

James found the journals superficial, diffuse, and shallow; they are "a record of things slight and usual," and represent Hawthorne as "uninformed, incurious, inappreciative." They lack any intimacy, and reveal Hawthorne's detachment from, and his mistrust of, everything foreign. James dwelt at length on Hawthorne's lack of robust taste, and the "rich simplicity" of his frank, unsophisticated mind.

Despite all their shortcomings, James found an irresistible charm in these journals. But, as Buitenhuis once again points out, "James found it highly difficult (as he did to the end of his career) to say *why* he found Hawthorne's work" both "charming" and "distinguished." He praised his predecessor's "fundamental wisdom," his "moral integrity," his delightful style, and his "finest and firmest" perception as revealed in the people he sketches. Above all, he found the journals "interesting from their strong national flavor. Exposed late in life to European influences, Mr. Hawthorne was superficially affected by them . . . We seem to see him strolling through churches and galleries as the last pure American—attesting by his shy responses . . . his loyalty to a simpler and less encumbered civilization." It was these virtues, Buitenhuis indicates, that must have seemed to James "both desirable and yet completely unattainable by him."

Another observation Buitenhuis makes is that "the young Henry James often compared his European experiences with that of Hawthorne." In two of his essays on Italy, James actually mentioned Hawthorne. In "A Roman Holiday," *Atlantic Monthly,* 32 (July, 1873), 1-11, James found that the carnival in secularized Rome did not live up to the picture the daydreams of his infancy had built up. Its "elements of picture and colour and 'style'" are gone; gone too from the city streets is the splendor of the Pope, the cardinals and all their coaches. Looking for compensation elsewhere James was rewarded by the view from the Forum. "Nowhere in Rome," he declared, "is more colour, more charm, more sport for the eye." Viewing the "loungers and knitters . . . seated round the massively inscribed base of the statue of Marcus Aurelius," James found that he could not express better than Hawthorne the feeling evoked by the statue:

> Hawthorne has perfectly expressed the attitude of this admirable figure in saying that it extends its arm with 'a command which is in itself a benediction.' I doubt if any statue of king or captain in the public places of the world has more to commend it to the general heart. (4)

James was also amazed that "in the capital of Christendom the portrait most suggestive of a Christian conscience is that of a pagan emperor."

One of the cities James described in "A Chain of Italian Cities," *Atlantic Monthly,* 33 (February, 1874), 158-64, is Perugia. It seems more than likely that James reread chapter 34 of *The Marble Faun* ("Market-Day in Perugia") while writing this essay. His description of Perugia's landscape features (pp. 161-62) is not unlike that by Hawthorne, especially in the first two paragraphs of that chapter. There is a consistency as well in the other aspects they both point out: Perugino's frescoes in the Exchange, the statue of Pope Julius III, the cathedral; and, just as Kenyon and Donatello "loitered" and "wandered to and fro" in the city, James advises the visitor to Perugia to avoid haste, to walk "everywhere very slowly and very much at random." This may seem stretching the parallel, but a better way to judge is to read over both Hawthorne's chapter and James's passages. More specifically, of course, James does mention Miriam and Kenyon's rendezvous at the base of the statue of Pope Julius III (chapter 35: "The Bronze Pontiff's Benediction"). After advising the reader to visit the huge Palazzo Pubblico and the Etruscan Gate, James continues:

> He must uncap to the picturesque statue of Pope Julius III., before the cathedral, remembering that Hawthorne fabled his Miriam to have given rendezvous to Kenyon at its base. Its material is a vivid green bronze, and the mantle and tiara are covered with a delicate embroidery, worthy of a silversmith. (162)

When this essay was reprinted in *Italian Hours* (1909; reprinted N.Y.: Grove Press, 1959), pp. 228-45, James substituted another phrase for the word "picturesque," and added a qualifying phrase about Hawthorne. The added phrases are emphasized below:

> He must uncap to the *irrevocable, the inimitable style of the* statue of Pope Julius III. before the cathedral, remembering that Hawthorne fabled his Miriam, *in an air of romance from which we are well-nigh as far to-day as from the building of Etruscan gates,* to have given rendezvous to Kenyon at its base. (238)

James's review of Turgenev, also published in 1874, contained another mention of "our own Hawthorne." In "*Frühlingsfluthen. Ein König Lear des Dorfes.* Zwei Novellen. Von Iwan Turgěniew. Mitau. 1873," *North American Review,* 108 (April, 1874), 326-56, James called Turgenev "the first novelist of the day." He pointed out that all of Turgenev's themes are Russian; that it is "the Russian type of human nature that he depicts," and that his "works savor strongly of his native soil, like those of all great novelists." (James had made a similar observation in 1872 when admiring the "strong national flavor" in Hawthorne's *French and Italian Notebooks.*) Of Turgenev's private personality, James explained that one might consider him a "cold-blooded pessimist" who cares "for nothing in life but misery." All his tales are gloomy with "unrelieved sadness"; there is nothing cheerful in them. But such pessimism can be beneficial to an artistic imagination. For a short illustration, James naturally reverted to Hawthorne. Turgenev is "a man disappointed . . . in the land which is dear to him," he wrote:

> Driven back, depressed and embittered, into his imagination for the edification which the social spectacle immediately before him refuses him, and shaped by nature to take life hard and linger among its shadows, our observer surrenders himself . . . to a shaded portrayal of things. An imaginative preference for dusky subjects is a perfectly legitimate element for the artistic temperament; our own Hawthorne is a signal case of its being innocently exercised; innocently, because with that delightfully unconscious genius it remained imaginative, sportive, inconclusive, to the end.

Whereas Turgenev's pessimism at times became morbid, Hawthorne's was always spontaneous.

In "A Chain of Italian Cities," James had referred to chapters 34 and 35 of *The Marble Faun.* In "Mr. Tennyson's Drama," *Galaxy,* 20 (September, 1875), 393-402, he referred to chapter 10 of the same romance ("The Sylvan Dance"). In this review of *Queen Mary,* James's verdict is that Tennyson is not a dramatic poet. He represents "not the action itself," but "his complex perception of it" (a "charge" similar to that sometimes leveled against the later James). He is not a natural chronicler of movement; what he represents best is "repose and stillness, and the fixedness of things." His scenes of violence are always "singularly limited and compressed":

> There are, for example, several descriptions of tournaments and combats in the 'Idylls of the King.' They are all most beautiful, but they are all curiously delicate. One gets no sense of the din and shock of battle; one seems to be looking at a bas relief of two contesting knights in chiselled silver, on a priceless piece of plate. They belong to the same family as that charming description, in Hawthorne's 'Marble Faun,' of the sylvan dance of Donatello and Miriam in the Borghese gardens. Hawthorne talks of the freedom and frankness of their mirth and revelry; what we seem to see is a solemn frieze in stone along the base of a monument. These are the natural fruits of geniuses who are of the brooding rather than the impulsive order. (395)

Clearly, then, by 1875 James had already recognized, in writing, Hawthorne as a great authority, "the last pure American," a literary genius whose work breathes a "strong national flavor." But it is a brooding, "delightfully unconscious genius."

In 1876, James said of Hawthorne what he would say again many times later: that Hawthorne had a very strong sense of evil. In "Charles Baudelaire," *Nation,* 22 (April 27, 1876), 279-81, an unsigned review of *Les Fleurs du Mal,* James had very little to commend the author for. He recognized the charm of his verses–if one ignored the subject matter. Baudelaire had a "natural sense of the superficial picturesqueness of the miserable and the unclean," but this sense was more "for how things looked" than "for what they meant." But what James objected to most was Baudelaire's superficial sense of evil. In 1874, James had written of Turgenev's pessimistic preference for "dusky subjects," and pointed to Hawthorne as an example of how this might be used imaginatively. Baudelaire's imagination too was "melancholy and sinister"; "his fancy was of a dusky cast." Had he always plunged into this "darkness and dirt" disinterestedly, he might have become a great poet. But for him, evil always began outside. "He knew evil not by experience, not as something within himself, but by contemplation and curiosity, as something outside of himself." To put it succinctly, James once again recalled the example of Hawthorne:

> A good way to embrace Baudelaire at a glance is to say that he was, in his treatment of evil, exactly what Hawthorne was not—Hawthorne. who felt the thing at its source, deep in the human consciousness. Baudelaire's infinitely slighter volume of genius apart, he was a sort of Hawthorne reversed. (280)

His "treatment of his favorite subjects" lacked any metaphysical quality.

"Daniel Deronda: A Conversation," *Atlantic Monthly,* 38 (December 1876), 684-94, has only a passing reference to Hawthorne. Pulcheria, whose favorite novelists, like James's, are Thackeray, Jane Austen, Balzac, and George Sand, objects very strongly to George Eliot's novel, for she finds it "protracted, pretentious, pedantic." Theodora, on the other hand, finds George Eliot extremely pure, and the world of her creation vast and all-embracing. Constantius, less dogmatic than Theodora, admits that *Daniel Deronda* is the weakest of Eliot's novels, but feels that Eliot nevertheless "gives us something that is strikingly . . . characteristic of human life." Pulcheria remains unconvinced, and maintains that *Daniel Deronda* is a failure, especially when measured against the work of the greats. "All that is very fine," she says,

> but you cannot persuade me that Deronda is not a very awkward and ill-made story. A silly young girl and a heavy, overwise young man who *don't* fall in love with her! That is the *donnée* of eight monthly volumes. I call it very flat. Is that what the exquisite art of Thackeray and Miss Austen and Hawthorne has come to? (693)

Theodora may consider "spirit" higher than "form," and Constantius may call Pulcheria "sadly aesthetic," but Pulcheria would agree with James that "it is art that *makes* life, makes interest, makes importance."[5]

In "George Sand," *Galaxy,* 24 (July, 1877), 45-61, James grouped Hawthorne among those "leading English novelists" who treat only virtuous love (and even then only to a point, preferring to leave most things unsaid) and shy away from the portrayal of such "ardent forces of the heart" as passion and vicious love. George Sand, on the other hand, was "curious about all things, open to all things," and accessible to all experience. She drew no hard distinction between virtuous and vicious love. "In her view love is always love, and is always of divine essence and of ennobling effect." But this is not the case with most English novelists:

> Miss Austen and Sir Walter Scott, Dickens and Thackeray, Hawthorne and George Eliot have all represented young people in love with each other; but no one of them has . . . described anything that can be called a passion—put it into motion before us, and shown us its various paces. (55)

Compared with George Sand, therefore, most of these writers "appear to have ommitted the erotic sentiment altogether." (James himself, of course, has sometimes been accused of shying away from "this improving passion.")

In 1877, James referred to Hawthorne's sketch, "About Warwick," which first appeared in *Atlantic Monthly*, 10 (December, 1862), 708-20, and was reprinted in *Our Old Home* (1863; reprinted Columbus: Ohio State University Press, 1970), pp. 65-89. At the beginning of "In Warwickshire," *Galaxy*, 24 (November, 1877), 671-80, James observed that when he was lately in Warwickshire, he felt as if he "were at the grassy centre and core of the English world" (671). He commented on "Kenilworth castle," "the charm of an English country church," "some of the features of an English rural Sunday," and the soft, shy, charming "faces of the English young people." He wrote also on the "ancient charities" in "the picturesque old towns of Coventry and Warwick": the almshouses, the asylums, the infant schools, and, especially, "Leicester's hospital at Warwick." As he had earlier referred to Hawthorne while writing about Perugia, he now once again referred to his predecessor:

> The American tourist usually comes straight to this quarter of England—chiefly for the purpose of paying his respects to Shakespeare's birthplace. Being here, he comes to Warwick to see the castle; and being at Warwick, he comes to see the odd little theatrical-looking refuge for superannuated warriors which lurks in the shadow of one of the old gate-towers. Every one will remember Hawthorne's charming account of the place, which has left no touch of fancy to be added to any reference to it. (675-76)

Apparently Hawthorne had said all there was to say about Warwick. After describing Leicester's hospital and its twelve "old hospitallers," James went on in the next paragraph to recount his visit to Coventry. In *Portraits of Places* (1883; reprinted New York: Lear Publishers, 1948), pp. 273-95, James changed the word "fancy" in the above indented quotation to "charming taste." "Shakespeare's birthplace" was also changed to "the birthplace of Shakespeare." Hawthorne too, of course, wrote at length about "Leycester's Hospital" and its "twelve brethren."

Items between 1879 and 1899

Between 1879 and the end of the century, James wrote two extended evaluations of Hawthorne, in addition to many other references to the author in essays, letters, notes and reviews. In the critical biography, *Hawthorne* (London: Macmillan, 1879), James evaluated the cultural conditions that shaped Hawthorne and made critical observations on the author's specific works. So as to more readily correlate James's assessment of Hawthorne's various works and the influence of those works on his own fiction, his specific comments on each of Hawthorne's works will be summarized at the beginning of the essay on the influence of that particular work on James's fiction. Given below, therefore, are mostly the general observations that various critics have made on the biography.

One of James's main theses, of course, was that Hawthorne was a victim of a provincial country, with little past and little social texture. As such, Hawthorne's condition points "a valuable moral. This moral is that the flower of art blooms only where the soil is deep, that it takes a great deal of history to produce a little literature, that it needs a complex social machinery to set a writer in motion" (*Hawthorne,* chapter 1). But James's most controversial statement—and one which, like many others in the biography, reveals as well his own attitude toward nineteenth-century America— was in chapter 2 of the biography, where he enumerated "the items of high civilisation . . . which are absent from the texture of American life":

> No State . . . No sovereign, no court, no personal loyalty, no aristocracy, no church, no clergy, no army, no diplomatic service, no country gentlemen, no palaces, no castles, nor manors, nor old country-houses, nor parsonages, nor thatched cottages, nor ivied ruins; no cathedrals, nor abbeys, nor little Norman churches; no great Universities nor public schools—no Oxford, nor Eton, nor Harrow; no literature, no novels, no museums, no pictures, no political society, no sporting class—no Epsom nor Ascot!

There is a similar passage in *The Notebooks of Henry James,* edited by F. O. Matthiessen and Kenneth B. Murdock (1947; reprinted New York: Oxford University Press), p. 14.

> In a story, some one says—'Oh yes, the United States—a country without a sovereign, without a court, without a nobility, without an army, without a church or a clergy, without a diplomatic service, without a picturesque peasantry, without palaces or castles, or country seats, or ruins, without a literature, without novels, without an Oxford or a Cambridge, without cathedrals or ivied churches, without latticed cottages or village ale-houses, without political society, without sport, without fox-hunting or country gentlemen, without an Epsom or an Ascot, an Eton or a Rugby . . .!!' [February 21, 1897]

Hawthorne too had made a similar observation in the Preface to *The Marble Faun,* an observation which James quoted in the same paragraph where he enumerated "the items of high civilisation . . . absent from . . . American life." "No author, without a trial," Hawthorne wrote:

> can conceive of the difficulty of writing a Romance about a country where there is no shadow, no antiquity, no mystery, no picturesque and gloomy wrong, nor anything but a common-place prosperity, in broad and simple daylight, as is happily the case with my dear native land.

One should note, however, as Buitenhuis points out, that Hawthorne "wrote the preface to *The Marble Faun* in 1859, seven years after the publication of *Blithedale,* the last 'American' novel. There is little evidence to show that the difficulty of writing a romance in America had preoccupied Hawthorne before he went to live in Europe in 1853" (*New England Quarterly,* 1959, p. 212).[6]

Of all James's writings on Hawthorne, this biography has been the one most frequently discussed. There are introductions to its various reprints, and other comments ranging in length from mere passing remarks to multiparagraph passages in a host of books and articles. Two general observations have often been made. First, that throughout his assessment of Hawthorne's works, James found it difficult to appreciate objectively artistic techniques different from those he himself was trying to master as a writer of realism. Thus in chapter 3 he termed allegory "one of the lighter exercises of the imagination," not "a first-rate literary form." Secondly, many critics have found that James's criticism in this biography is often marred by his condescension. In this respect, it is interesting to recall Julian Hawthorne's differing opinion on the matter. "When the Macmillans asked [James] to write the sketch of Nathaniel Hawthorne," Julian wrote (*The Memoirs of Julian Hawthorne,* edited by Edith G. Hawthorne [New York: Macmillan, 1938], p. 127):

> he came from London to see me in Hastings, and he was in doubt and distress. . . . "I don't want to do it," he said again and again. "I'm not competent: and yet, if I don't, some Englishman will do it worse than I would. Your father was the greatest imaginative writer we had, and yet, I feel that his principle was wrong. . . . Imagination is out of place; only the strictest realism can be right. But how can a barely known scribbler like me offer criticism on him?"
>
> The book was written, and the shyness that pervades it, obvious to me, was interpreted by many as arrogance. It is an honest and painful piece of work, and will endure.

In his review, "James's Hawthorne," *Atlantic Monthly,* 45 (February, 1880), 282–85, William Dean Howells raised a number of issues that have been repeated over and over again. He recognized that James was writing for an English audience, and, as such, his observations were likely to displease many of his countrymen. But Howells objected strongly to James's having repeatedly called Hawthorne and the societies of Salem and Concord provincial. "If it is not provincial for an Englishman to be English," he wrote, "then it is not so for an American to be American" (282). Americans are not at all provincial, and Hawthorne had more universality than almost any Londoner of his time. Provinciality is a state of mind, Howells asserted, not a matter of experiences.

Howells further felt that James had badly propounded the theory, or illusion, "that it needs a long history and 'a complex social machinery to set a writer in motion.'" "As a romancer," he observed, "the twelve years of boyhood which [Hawthorne] spent in the wild solitude of Maine were probably of greater advantage to him than if they had been passed at Eton and Oxford." Responding specifically to "the items of high civilisation" which James found absent from American life, Howells wrote:

> After leaving out all those novelistic "properties" . . . by the absence of which Mr. James suggests our poverty to the English conception, we have the whole of human life remaining, and a social structure presenting the only fresh and novel opportunities left to fiction . . . No man would have known less what to do with that dreary and worn-out paraphernalia than Hawthorne. (284)

But Howells overstates his case when he argues that, although Hawthorne seemed to share this illusion, he "wrote *The Marble Faun,* so inferior, with its foreign scene, to the New England romances, to prove the absurdity of it." Other critics have seen the inferiority of *The Marble Faun* to Hawthorne's other romances as a result of what Howells suggests in the last sentence of the indented quotation above. As a romancer, Hawthorne worked best with a minimum of factual details, and his imagination supplied the rest of the materials needed for his fictional world. In Italy, he was completely overwhelmed by the overabundance of materials there. As Jay Bochner puts it in "Life in a Picture Gallery: Things in *The Portrait of a Lady* and *The Marble Faun*," *Texas Studies in Literature and Language,* 11 (1969), 777: "Hawthorne was so caught up with the brilliant, meaningful surfaces that he was not able to distil from them the unified meaning which can make for art."

Lastly–on the negative side–Howells censured James for having failed to distinguish clearly and consistently between the novel and the romance. He agreed that the people in *The Scarlet Letter* may be types rather than persons, conditions of the mind rather than characters, but that is precisely because the romance deals with types and mental conditions. Hawthorne's fictions are "always and essentially, in conception and performance, romances, and not novels." James, of course, totally rejected this kind of distinction–in the same paragraph in which he once again referred to Hawthorne—in his 1884 essay, "The Art of Fiction." "I can think of no obligation," he wrote, "to which the 'romancer' would not be held equally with the novelist; the standard of execution is equally high for each."[7]

Howells's greatest praise went to James's characterization of Hawthorne as "an innocent, affectionate heart," of "simple, domestic . . . qualities," with "high purposes . . . and an 'unperplexed intellect.'" He also found the chapters on Salem, Brook Farm, and Concord valuable and delightful. "Skillful and manly the whole book is," he concluded, "a miracle of tact and self-respect."

In his reply of January 31, 1880 (Percy Lubbock, ed., *The Letters of Henry James,* New York: Charles Scribner's Sons, 1920, I, 71-74), James regretted his having overused the word provincial, but stood by his conviction that it *is* "extremely provincial for a Russian to be very Russian," just as it is for an American to be very American. He found even less valid Howells's "protest against the idea that it takes an old civilization to set a novelist in motion"—a proposition James considered a truism. "It is on manners, customs, usages, habits, forms, upon all these things matured and established, that a novelist lives—they are the very stuff his work is made of;" and when these "dreary and worn-out paraphernalia" are absent, there is as much less of human life left "as these same 'paraphernalia' represent, and . . . they represent an enormous quantity of it" (*Letters,* I, 72).

The best balanced and most sustained commentary on *Hawthorne* appears in Buitenhuis's article (*New England Quarterly,* 1959, pp. 211-16). Buitenhuis first points out that at the time of writing this biography, James "was still seeking recognition and prestige in English society," and this partly accounts for his ironic or patronizing attitude towards America. He next observes that the picture James reconstructed of Hawthorne's provincial environment "bore far more resemblance to his own view of American life at the time than it did to Hawthorne's during the latter's creative American years." Buitenhuis's central and most significant observation is that whereas in his review of Hawthorne's *French and Italian Note-Books* in 1872 James had regarded Hawthorne's loyalty to a simpler civilization and his strong national flavor as "advantages," in 1879 he saw them as "limitations." It is as if in the biography James was saying that Hawthorne had "paid for being a good American by being a poorer novelist." Ultimately, of course, James blamed Hawthorne's failings almost entirely on his *milieu.*

Another observation Buitenhuis makes is that when James refers to Hawthorne's "exaggerated, painful, morbid national consciousness," he is once again "comparing his own situation with that of Hawthorne." Buitenhuis believes that the inordinate space James devotes to "tracking down the causes of this national consciousness, and . . . evaluating its effect on Hawthorne's art" indicates that James himself was perhaps searching for "Hawthorne's key to the American mind—a key which he was very conscious of not yet having found himself." If Hamlin Garland may be trusted, James may have doubted even late in life whether he had ever found that key. "If I were to live over again," Garland reports James having told him:

> I would be an American. I would steep myself in America, I would know no other land. I would study its beautiful side. The mixture of Europe and America which you see in me has . . . made of me a man who is neither American nor European. I have lost touch with my own people . . . As a man grows old he feels these conditions more than when he is young. I shall never return to the United States, but I wish I could.[8]

Buitenhuis's concluding comment on *Hawthorne* is that James, "on the eve of writing *The Portrait of a Lady,* thought . . . that Hawthorne would no longer quite do. He was interested in more solid *maîtres,* such as Balzac, Turgenev, and George Eliot."

Another fine evaluation of *Hawthorne* is in Quentin Anderson's 1962 introduction to this biography (reprinted New York: Collier Books, 1966), pp. 7-12. Anderson explains that James's overriding intention was to make plain to the English reader Hawthorne's time and place, and his cultural scene. As such, the biography is "full of excellent cultural judgements," even though many of these may not be "directly addressed to the merits of Hawthorne."

Anderson notes that for James, the "valuable moral" which Hawthorne's situation pointed was that "although the American civilization of that day was 'vast and varied and substantial' it was not ripe for treatment by its writers." For James, Europe thus offered much that was lacking in America: "the distinctions of classes, the interplay of manners . . . the presence of high artistic achievements," the interaction between writers, and an awareness of a common tradition. These were the factors which led James to settle in London. But he was also aware of what materials *were* available in America. He recognized that what Hawthorne dealt with were simply individuals and their moral relationships. James wrote at length about the importance of the individual in the American world, his sense of moral responsibility, and "the shadow of the sense of sin" under which he grows up and looks at life. Anderson finds that these observations remind one of the Wentworths of *The Europeans* (1878), and "suggest how detached Henry James, the New Yorker, felt from the spectacle of the New England conscience."

Anderson finds further that James was "quite troubled by Hawthorne." But he was "too honest with himself" to deny that his predecessor had dealt with significant issues, such as "the deeper psychology," or "the whole deep mystery of man's soul and conscience." And when in chapter 3 of the biography he called Hawthorne's sense of America's common guilt "almost exclusively imported [in] character," he was merely "trying to imagine for

Hawthorne that measure of disengagement, that aesthetic distance from his subject" which characterized for him the practice of those writers he greatly admired. Nonetheless, one may wonder how much of Hawthorne's greatness James recognized. His general remarks on Hawthorne's prose qualitites were "excellent," but his discussion of the particular works fell short. He analyzed well *The Seven Gables, The Blithedale Romance,* and some pieces in *Twice-Told Tales,* but on the greatest of the tales he was "either silent or misleading." And, although he recognized the importance of the Puritan consciousness of sin "as a fact of Hawthorne's biography," he could not acknowledge its significance to Hawthorne as an artist, for "his own ideal of fiction stood in the way." Anderson's most significant observation—addressed specifically to James's evaluation of *The Scarlet Letter,* but equally applicable to his comments on Hawthorne's other works—is that it is not in the "intensity" of his praise that James fails; it is rather "in his choice of episodes and themes for praise and dispraise that James gives himself away." In *The Scarlet Letter,* he praised Hawthorne's uses of Chillingworth as original and ingenious—he was later to create his own Chillingworths—but deplored chapter 19 of the work ("The Child at the Brook-Side"), for it struck him as "fanciful, allegorical, and only marginally successful."

Anderson's conclusion is that *Hawthorne* "is the book of a writer launched on a career in fiction" very different from Hawthorne's. He had written, and meant to write, books which would be filled by "the deepest reality of substance." He thus saw Hawthorne as a figure in the past. But Hawthorne, of course, was always to remain by his side: the remark, in chapter 5 of the biography, that the people in *The Scarlet Letter* are not characters but representatives of a single state of mind describes as well *The Golden Bowl;* in his later works, James even more than Hawthorne "mishandled his material by making it all too representative of 'a single state of mind.'"

Edwin Fussell too makes a number of significant observations on *Hawthorne.* In "Hawthorne, James and 'The Common Doom,'" *American Quarterly,* 10 (1958), 438-53, Fussell singles out as James's conspicuous virtues his ability to connect both Hawthorne's life with his work, and his life and work with his times. He also believes that James "apologizes for Hawthorne more than he ought," and he relates this "curious mixture of tenderness and condescension" to James's view that each of his parents "drew on the strength of the other . . . each battening on the other's diminution." This is the same notion that caused him to say that Minny Temple died so that he might live. "James insists on Hawthorne's innocence," Fussell explains, "because he has put Hawthorne into the same pattern with his parents and Minny Temple. For obscure reasons, it is necessary for James to figure Hawthorne as, in part, a doomed progenitor. 'He stopped short that I might go further' is close to what he is saying" (450).

With regard to James's list of the items of high civilization unavailable to Hawthorne, Fussell argues that when these things are left out, what remains to the American is—to borrow James's phrase in chapter 3 of the biography—the opportunity "to open an intercourse with the world." To James, the difference between British and American culture was in the contrast between "thick" and "thin," and he preferred the "thin," since "one may move freely from 'thin' to 'thick' (thus comprehending both), but not so easily from 'thick' to 'thin.'" This is why his American characters are "so flexibly imaginative" while his European characters are "so unimaginatively constrained." Fussell errs here, for James decided to live in Europe not because he had mastered, comprehended, or exhausted what the "thin" American culture had to offer the imagination, but rather because he found it constraining, whereas the "thick" British culture was teeming with a variety of artistic possibilities. Fussell's comment on James's American and European characters is also rather simplistic, for "thin" and "thick" here have more to do with American "innocence" as contrasted with European "corruption," with all the ambiguous connotations of both those words. Fussell does better when he extends his comments on the thinness of American life to *A Small Boy and Others,* and observes that James, like Hawthorne, concentrated first on the inward life, for he too was aware that "the world outside could be won only when the inner man gave up his extravagant self-regard" and accepted his lot with the rest of mankind. James shared this theme, Fussell says, because his early life "repeated the situations that elicited the theme in Hawthorne in the first place."

There is very little originality in Tony Tanner's introduction to *Hawthorne* (London: Macmillan, 1967), pp. 1-21. He seems almost entirely indebted to Buitenhuis's article, although he gives it only a casual reference. He follows Buitenhuis's layout, discusses the same five extended evaluations of Hawthorne by James, and many of his arguments, their phrasing, and even their very positioning, are similar to Buitenhuis's. One almost wishes he had confined himself to a discussion of the biography, for his few fresh comments are mostly there.

His discussion of James's review of Hawthorne's *French and Italian Note-Books,* for example, starts off by pointing out that James was eager to return to Europe at the time of writing this review, and that this explains its rather patronizing tone. Not only are all his subsequent remarks on this review in Buitenhuis's essay, but they are in about the same order as well. The only emphasis not in Buitenhuis is Tanner's suggestion of what James must have learned from Hawthorne's limited response to Europe. Whereas Hawthorne had been "mistrustful, shrinking, puzzled and ineffective," James would be open and eager. "It is as though by 'placing' Hawthorne, James was tentatively marking out the territory he intended to claim as his own. Hawthorne had not explored the 'complex fate' of being an American in Europe"; James would. "And of course he did."

Tanner's comments on *Hawthorne* have repetitions of Buitenhuis too. Buitenhuis had remarked that when this biography was written James "was still seeking *recognition and prestige in English society*" (*New England Quarterly,* 1959, p. 211). Tanner too indicates how James "was still very keen to gain some sort of *recognition and prestige in English society*" (Tanner, p. 4; emphases in both quotations mine). There are more repetitions, but there are also some fresh observations.

Tanner believes that James saw the invitation to write Hawthorne's biography as an opportunity "to reveal and demonstrate his own superior understanding of . . . European society [and] the traditions of European art"; to show that he, unlike Hawthorne, had transcended America's provinciality. And he praised European society not because it was morally or intellectually superior to America but because "it was more complex, more stimulating, and thus more nutritive for the aspiring novelist." His case against America was that, for a novelist, it was "comparatively empty." He was also aware that Hawthorne "had operated on quite contrary convictions." Thus, his patronizing and condescending tone, and his emphasis on the aridity of Hawthorne's environment, were in part "an indirect attempt to justify the different path he had elected to follow"; he sympathetically outlined Hawthorne's difficulties as an artist in America as an indirect justification of his own expatriation to Europe.

Tanner is rather disturbed by the "contradictions" in *Hawthorne.* He notes that whereas James put great value on Europe for the American artist, he nevertheless found half the virtue of *The Scarlet Letter* and *The Seven Gables* to reside in their local quality, their New England air, and said in chapter 6, "England and Italy," that "Hawthorne forfeited a precious advantage in ceasing to tread his native soil." "Perhaps then Hawthorne was at his best when he was most 'provincial'?" Tanner asks. But there is more of a dilemma here than simple contradiction. On the one hand, James was acutely aware of Hawthorne's strong national consciousness, of his possessing a "key to the American mind"—a virtue he always desired but never quite attained. On the other, he felt that Hawthorne had virtually "paid for being a good American by being a poorer novelist" (Buitenhuis), that his genius, to use Tanner's own words, had been "starved of adequate material to work on." James never quite resolved this dilemma until late in life, as his other assessments of Hawthorne will show.

Tanner mentions some other "contradictions" in James's evaluation of Hawthorne's work. On the one hand, he calls it charming," "soft," "natural," "childlike": epithets emphasizing that his "work was as innocent and simple as the land it emerged from." On the other, he seems aware of "the troubling depths in Hawthorne's work," his "haunting care for moral problems," and his care for "the deeper psychology"—territories surely beyond the reach of a childlike writer. And, although James "speaks disparagingly of allegory and the use of symbols," some of Hawthorne's works he praises are allegorical. But James would probably consider these exceptions rather than contradictions. Tanner also notes that James's "late work tended increasingly towards allegory and a use of symbols" very close to the way Hawthorne used them. Furthermore, it was the very same elements he considered responsible for Hawthorne's emergence as the first major American novelist—"his sense of moral guilt, his awareness of evil knowledge," his feeling for all the darkness in the world—that made James himself a great American novelist.

In his conclusion Tanner reasserts that the most important point about *Hawthorne* is James's need at the time to justify his move to Europe, for "he was aspiring to become a novelist of concrete social detail" like Balzac and Thackeray. And much of his work *is* "far more concrete than Hawthorne's." But it was Hawthorne's examples which made him a great writer, and even in 1879, he admired him perhaps more than he implied.

In his review article, "A Tanner in the Works," *Cambridge Review,* 89A (May 3, 1968), 430-31, P. R. Grover disagrees strongly with Tanner's "exposition of the essential and lasting connections between Hawthorne and James," for although James did borrow Hawthorne's "themes, situations, settings, and sometimes techniques," a comparison between his early romances and Hawthorne's novels reveals that "other very powerful influences were at work in shaping James's techniques: Mérimée, George Sand," and especially Balzac, whose lessons were more lasting for James. Grover greatly oversimplifies Hawthorne's symbolism in his attempt to suggest that the reason James's imagery and metaphor in his late novels is richer, more complex, and more suggestive is "because he had other examples to draw from, and they weren't American. They were French and Balzac was amongst the most important." Surely Hawthorne's symbolism wasn't as "transparent," with "a simple one-to-one relationship between image and idea," as Grover makes it out to be. The complex imagery and symbolism of *The Scarlet Letter,* for example, has been noted by many critics. It "is only when we isolate Hawthorne's influence from all the others that are important for James," Grover declares, "that he can seem to play the role that is so often assigned to him in James's development." Many items considered in subsequent essays in this text will dispel any such notion.

Between the publication of Howells's review (1880) and Fussell's essay (1958), two other people had commented on *Hawthorne.* In *The Thought and Character of William James,* 2 volumes (Boston: Little, Brown, 1935), I, 90n., Ralph B. Perry found a passage in chapter 4 of *Hawthorne,* where James wrote that Hawthorne "must have been struck with the glare of [Margaret Fuller's] understanding, and, mentally speaking, have scowled and blinked a good deal in conversation with her," quite reminiscent of part of a letter from James's father to Emerson expressing his impressions of Boston's

Saturday Club, after he attended a dinner there on January 26, 1861. Part of this long and fascinating letter is quoted below:

> Hawthorne isn't a handsome man nor an engaging one anyway, personally: he had the look all the time, to one who didn't know him, of a rogue who suddenly finds himself in a company of detectives. But in spite of his rusticity I felt a sympathy for him amounting to anguish and couldn't take my eyes off him all the dinner, nor my rapt attention. . . .
>
> Hawthorne, however, seemed to me to possess human substance and not to have dissipated it all away. . . . He seemed much nearer the human being than any one at that end of the table. . . . It was so pathetic to see him, contented, sprawling Concord owl that he was and always has been, brought blindfold into that brilliant daylight, and expected to wink and be lively. . . . How he buried his eyes in his plate, and ate with such a voracity that no person should dare to ask him a question!
>
> My heart broke for him as that attenuated Charles Norton kept putting forth his long antennae towards him, stroking his face, and trying whether his eyes were shut. . . . It was heavenly to see him persist in ignoring Charles Norton, and shutting his eyes against his spectral smiles: eating his dinner and doing absolutely nothing but that, and then going home to his Concord den to fall upon his knees, and ask his heavenly Father why it was that an owl couldn't remain an owl, and not be forced into the dimensions of a canary. I have no doubt that all the tenderest angels saw to his care that night, and poured oil into his wounds more soothing than gentlemen ever know. (Perry, pp. 88-90)

F. O. Matthiessen, who reprints this letter in *The James Family* (New York: Alfred A. Knopf, 1947), pp. 479-80, agrees with Perry that James does "re-echo some of the phrases in this letter" in his remark about Hawthorne and Margaret Fuller (*The James Family,* pp. 480-81). Matthiessen was also the first to observe that since James wrote the biography when he had just become an apostle of realism—which partly explains why he underrates "some of the imaginative energy in Hawthorne's romances"—it reflects more his own aims than those of Hawthorne. Lastly, Matthiessen also remarked that when James discusses the special problems faced by the artist in America, he is actually referring to himself, for his experiences in writing *The Europeans* and *Washington Square* were of this nature.

James did not make another extended evaluation of Hawthorne until 1897. Between the publication of *Hawthorne* and that date, however, there are scattered references to Hawthorne in many of his writings. The publication of the biography itself provoked a furor in the American public. On

February 22, 1880, James wrote to Elizabeth Boott expressing his surprise over this:

> The American press, with 2 or 3 exceptions, seems furious over my poor little Hawthorne. It is a melancholy revelation of angry vanity, vulgarity and ignorance. I thought they would protest a good deal at my calling New England life unfurnished, but I didn't expect they would lose their heads and their manners at such a rate. (*Notebooks,* p. 29n.)

In the winter of 1881 James returned to America after an absence of six years. In the Notebook he began on November 25, 1881, he recollected the events that had befallen him since he left the country in the fall of 1875. In 1879, he wrote, "I stayed in London during all August, writing my little book on Hawthorne." In September he traveled to Paris, but did not see as much of France as he had planned to. "But I did a good deal of work: finished the ill-fated little *Hawthorne,* finished *Confidence,* began *Washington Square,* wrote *A Bundle of Letters"* (*Notebooks,* p. 29).

In his review, "The Correspondence of Carlyle and Emerson," *Century Magazine,* 26 (June, 1883), 265-72, James made another reference to Hawthorne. Of the differences between Carlyle and Emerson, he noted that Carlyle was "a pessimist of pessimists," Emerson an optimist:

> His optimism makes us wonder at times where he discovered the errors that it would seem well to set right, and what there was in his view of the world on which the spirit of criticism could feed. He had a high and noble conception of good, without having . . . a definite conception of evil. . . . Carlyle, on the other hand . . . has a vivid conception of evil without a corresponding conception of good. (269)

I have quoted this passage at length because of the contrast James was to draw between Hawthorne and Emerson in 1887. In the present review he called Emerson "the voice of New England in those days," and found him full of "a local quality, with a narrow social horizon":

> His letters are especially interesting for the impression they give us of . . . the thinness of the New England atmosphere in those days—the thinness, and, it must be added, the purity. An almost touching lightness, sparseness, transparency marked the social scenery in those days; and this impression, in Emerson's pages, is the greater by contrast with the echoes of the dense, warm life of London that are transmitted by [Carlyle]. (270)

This seems a passage transposed almost directly from *Hawthorne.* And since Emerson was "the inventor of Transcendentalism" (266), his "great doctrine" was naturally "the importance of the individual." In the line next to the indented quotation above, James writes: "One is reminded, as we remember being reminded in the perusal of Hawthorne's 'American Notebooks', of the importance of the individual in that simple social economy." To Emerson, "the ear of the universe" was open to anything that even the humblest might have to say. (Towards the end of chapter 2 of *Hawthorne,* after remarking that Hawthorne "thought nothing too trivial to be suggestive," and calling his *Note-Books* a "minute and often trivial chronical" of "his perception of common and casual things," James had gone on to write about this same "importance of the individual in the American world.")

In "The Impressions of a Cousin," *Century Magazine,* 27 (November and December, 1883), 116-29, 257-75, James once again referred to the characters in *The Marble Faun.* After Adrian Frank, a sketcher who "has seen a great deal of the world," observes that Eunice, the narrator's cousin, is a fair, "really very pretty" woman, he asks the narrator, who also sketches, whether she thinks the realistic school is to be admired. The narrator "answered him freely":

> I declared that I held the realistic school in horror . . . that I thought the American girl the finest result of civilisation. I am sure I convinced him that I am a most remarkable woman. . . . He is a charming creature—a kind of Yankee Donatello. If I could only be his Miriam, the situation would be almost complete, for Eunice is an excellent Hilda. (121)

Of Hawthorne's characters, James may have identified most with Coverdale in *The Blithedale Romance,* but it is to Miriam, Hilda, and Donatello, and *The Marble Faun* in general, that he frequently refers directly.

In "The Art of Fiction," *Longman's Magazine,* 4 (September, 1884), 502-21, James did refer to *The Blithedale Romance* directly. In this rebuttal to Walter Besant's lecture of the same title, one of the issues James addressed himself to was the "celebrated distinction between the novel and the romance," a distinction which, as already indicated, Howells had taken him to task for not employing in his discussion of Hawthorne's works (*Atlantic Monthly,* 1880, p. 283). "There are bad novels and good novels," James argued in the present essay, "but that is the only distinction in which I see any meaning." "The novel and the romance," he continued, "the novel of incident and that of character—these clumsy separations appear to me to have been made by critics and readers for their own convenience." The same is true of Besant's other "shadowy category," namely, "that of the 'modern English novel'":

> One writes the novel . . . of one's language and of one's time, and calling it modern English will not, alas! make the difficult task any

> easier. No more, unfortunately, will calling this or that work . . . a romance—unless it be, of course, simply for the pleasantness of the thing, as for instance when Hawthorne gave this heading to his story of *Blithedale*. . . . I can think of no obligation to which the 'romancer' would not be held equally with the novelist; the standard of execution is equally high for each.[9]

This seems a direct reply to Howells's charge as well.

In 1883, James had written of Emerson's optimism and his lack of a "definite conception of evil" (*Century Magazine*, 1883, p. 269). In 1887, he returned to this "ripe unconsciousness of evil" in Emerson, and in the course of its elaboration he accorded Hawthorne the most unreserved praise he had given him as yet. In "The Life of Emerson," *Macmillian's Magazine*, 57 (December, 1887), 86-98, a review of James Elliot Cabot's *A Memoir of Ralph Waldo Emerson*, James charged Cabot with having completely neglected "the social conditions in which Emerson moved," especially since "we know a man imperfectly until we know his society." Turning to Emerson's reading, he found that although his books "were numerous and dear to him," still there was "a latent incompleteness in his own literary side." James was especially amazed by Cabot's observation that Emerson "rarely read a novel, even the famous ones," and that he "'could see nothing in Shelley, Aristophanes, Don Quixote, Miss Austen, Dickens'," an insensibility he found too large an "allowance to have to make for a man of letters." But what was the hardest to believe was the reference to Hawthorne:

> Mr. Cabot makes use of a singular phrase when he says, in speaking of Hawthorne, for several years our author's neighbor at Concord, and a little—very little we gather—his companion, that Emerson was unable to read his novels—he thought them "not worthy of him." This is a judgement odd almost to fascination—we circle round it and turn it over and over: it contains so elusive an ambiguity. How highly he must have esteemed the man of whose genius *The House of the Seven Gables* and *The Scarlet Letter* gave imperfectly the measure, and how strange that he should not have been eager to read almost anything that such a gifted being might have let fall! It was a rare accident that made them live almost side by side so long in the same small New England town, each a fruit of a long Puritan stem, yet with such a difference of taste. Hawthorne's vision was all for the evil and sin of the world: a side of life as to which Emerson's eyes were thickly bandaged. . . . He had no great sense of wrong . . . no sense of the dark, the foul, the base. There were certain complications in life which he never suspected. (97)[10]

This is high praise for Hawthorne indeed. The passage suggests as much as, if not more than, what is generally considered James's most generous tribute to Hawthorne in *Notes of a Son and Brother.* If James had had Emerson's opportunity, one can imagine what long evenings he would have spent by Hawthorne's fireside, and how eagerly he would have awaited each word that fell from Hawthorne's pen.

While writing about Warwickshire in 1877, James had referred to Hawthorne's sketch, "About Warwick." In "London," *Century Magazine,* 37 (December, 1888), 219-39, he referred to another of Hawthorne's sketches, "A London Suburb." London, he noted, is a city full of variety. She "spreads her dusky mantle over innumerable races and creeds," and whether one is a native-born or an adopted son, one feels a strong loyalty to her. And there are many "fine reasons" to support this loyalty. The primary one, of course, is that "the British capital is the particular spot in the world which communicates the greatest sense of life." For supportive opinion, James naturally turned to Hawthorne:

> I hasten to explain that if half the source of one's interest in it comes from feeling that it is the property, and even the home, of the human race,—Hawthorne, that best of Americans, says so somewhere, and places it, in this sense, side by side with Rome,—one's appreciation of it is really a large sympathy, a comprehensive love, of humanity. (225)

In "A London Suburb," which was first published in *Atlantic Monthly,* 11 (March, 1863), 306-21, and reprinted in *Our Old Home,* pp. 213-42, Hawthorne recounted one of the English summers that the family had spent in "a particularly delightful abode in the neighborhood of London." "I already knew London well," he wrote, after calling it "the central spot of all the world":

> Day after day, at an earlier period, I had trodden the thronged thoroughfares, the broad, lonely squares, the lanes, alleys. . . . I had sought all parts of the metropolis, in short, with an unweariable and indiscriminating curiosity. . . . The result was, that I acquired a home-feeling there, as nowhere else in the world; though afterwards I came to have a somewhat similar sentiment in regard to Rome; and as long as either of those two great cities shall exist, the cities of the Past and of the Present, a man's native soil may crumble beneath his feet without leaving him altogether homeless upon earth. (*Our Old Home,* p. 215)

After referring to "A London Suburb," James in the same paragraph placed Hawthorne and Emerson beside Shakespeare and Milton. It is a stroke of luck, he said, "that the capital of the human race happens to be British":

> For, after all, if the sense of life is greatest there, it is a sense of the life of people of our incomparable English speech. It is the headquarters of that inestimable tongue; and I make this remark with a full sense of the terrible way in which the idiom is misused by the populace in general, than whom if there be a race of more vulgar and abominable tone I know it not. For a man of letters who endeavors to cultivate, however modestly, the medium of Shakespeare and Milton, of Hawthorne and Emerson, who cherishes the notion of what it has achieved and what it may yet achieve, London must ever have a great illustrative and suggestive value, and indeed a kind of sanctity. (*Century Magazine,* December, 1888, p. 225)

When this essay was reprinted in *Essays in London and Elsewhere* (1893; reprinted London: James R. Osgood, McIlvaine, 1903), pp. 1-46, the phrase "our incomparable English speech" in the above passage was changed to "our consecrated English speech"; "that inestimable tongue" became "that strangely elastic tongue"; and "if there be a race of more vulgar and abominable tone I know it not" was changed to "it has been given to few races to impart to conversation less of the charm of tone."

One of the direct references to Hawthorne in James's fiction occurs in book 8 in volume II of *The Tragic Muse* (1889-1890; reprinted New York: Charles Scribner's Sons, 1908). Towards the end of chapter 49, Nick Dormer offers to paint a portrait of Gabriel Nash, "some sort of sketch of you . . . to prove to me in future that you were once a solid sociable fact" (II, 408). At first Nash consents to sit, which pleases Nick, for "he had never at all thoroughly explored his friend." But "after a few hours of the job," Nash became "uncomfortable . . . silent, restless, gloomy, dim." The next day he never returned, "and the next and the next passed, but he never came back":

> Nick had the prospect, for the future, of waiting to see, all curiously, when Nash would turn up, if ever, and the further diversion . . . of imagining in the portrait he had begun an odd tendency to fade gradually from the canvas. He couldn't catch it in the act, but he could have ever a suspicion on glancing at it that the hand of time was rubbing it away little by little—for all the world as in some delicate Hawthorne tale—and making the surface indistinct and bare of all resemblance to the model. Of course the moral of the Hawthorne tale would be that his personage would come back in quaint confidence on the day his last projected shadow should have vanished. (II, 412-13)

In *American Renaissance* (New York: Oxford University Press, 1941), pp. 299-300, 300n., F. O. Matthiessen takes this passage as one of the many instances of James's familiarity with Hawthorne's device of using a portrait—

in *The Seven Gables,* for example—to analyze character and probe beneath conventional appearances.

In both the 1892 and 1897 essays on Lowell, James once again referred to Hawthorne. In "James Russell Lowell," *Atlantic Monthly,* 69 (January, 1892), 35-50, he combined both Hawthorne's national consciousness, and his sense of evil and darkness in the world, in contrast to Lowell. Hawthorne had been "the last pure American" (*Nation,* 1872, p. 173); Lowell was "the last accomplished representative of the joy of life," "the last of the literary conservatives" (*Atlantic Monthly,* 1892, p. 42). Lowell had a "robust and humorous optimism," his poetry was patriotic and intensely moral, and he emphasized action, conduct, and decency. Most of all, he complemented Hawthorne:

> Like all interesting literary figures, he is full of . . . reference to the conditions that engendered him; he really testifies as much as Hawthorne to the New England spirit, though in a totally different tone. The two writers, as witnesses, weigh against each other, and the picture would be imperfect if both had not had a hand in it. If Hawthorne expressed the mysticism and the gloom of the transplanted Puritan, his passive and haunted side, Lowell saw him in the familiar daylight of practice and prosperity and good health. . . . If Hawthorne fairly cherished the idea of evil in man, Lowell's vision of "sin" was operative mainly for a single purpose—that of putting in motion the civic lash. (42)

If Baudelaire "was a sort of Hawthorne reversed" (*Nation,* 1876, p. 280), Lowell was a sort of Hawthorne "complementor"—a very high honor indeed.

James's third extended evaluation of Hawthorne—the earlier two being his review of the *French and Italian Note-Books* (1872), and the biography (1879)—is his introduction to the selections from Hawthorne in *Library of the World's Best Literature,* edited by Charles D. Warner (New York: R. S. Peale and J. A. Hill, 1896-1897), XII, 7053-61. The selections themselves, pp. 7061-96, are made up of four from *The Scarlet Letter* ("Salem and the Hawthornes"—from "The Custom-House" sketch—"The Minister's Vigil," "The Child at the Brook-Side," and "The Revelation of the Scarlet Letter"), and one each from *The Seven Gables* ("Hepzibah and Pyncheon"), *Mosses from an Old Manse* ("The Old Manse"), and *The Marble Faun* ("The Faun's Transformation").

James first summarized the nonliterary events of Hawthorne's life: his Puritan ancestry, his contemporaries Longfellow and Franklin Pierce, his twelve years' solitude at Salem, his appointment to the Boston Custom House, his sojourn at Brook Farm, his marriage and move to the Old Manse, then back to Salem; his seven years' residence in England and Italy, his return to America, and his death. Once again he indicated that Hawthorne's imagination worked best with "the spiritual contortions, the darkened outlook" of his community, with its "ingrained sense of sin, of evil, and of responsibility"; a community whose "great complication was . . . the restless individual conscience." With little else material to work with, Hawthorne's imagination had to look "behind and beneath for the suggestive idea," so that it made "a mystery and a glamour where there were otherwise none very ready to its hand." Thus did it end "by living in a world of things symbolic and allegoric. . . . Any figure therefore easily became with him an emblem, any story a parable, any appearance a cover" (7054).

James devoted most of the space to Hawthorne's works. In *Fanshawe* he detected "the author's beautiful touch"; in *Twice-Told Tales, The Snow Image,* and *Mosses from an Old Manse* he found "the note that was to be Hawthorne's distinguishing mark–that feeling for the latent romance of New England," an element which sprang from "the secret play of the Puritan faith." He divided Hawthorne's short fiction into three categories: the "myths and mysteries of old Massachusetts" like "The Grey Champion"; the "'moralities' without the moral" like "Roger Malvin's Burial"; and the fanciful all for fancy's sake" like "The Great Carbuncle." Of the longer romances, he found *The Scarlet Letter* the most original of his novels, and "the most distinguished piece of prose fiction that was to spring from American soil." He was impressed especially by the nobility and truthfulness of the image of Hester and Pearl, and the malignant influence of Chillingworth over Dimmesdale. *The Seven Gables* he felt reflected more closely than the others "the surface of American life," and had more elements of the novel of manners. "I am tempted," he declared, "to pronounce the book, taking the subject and treatment together . . . the closest approach we are likely to have to the great work of fiction . . . that is to do us nationally most honor and most good" (7057). And he found the character of Judge Pyncheon Hawthorne's most solidly suggested figure–with the possible exception of Zenobia.

Although Warner's *Library* contained no selections from *The Blithedale Romance,* James devoted over a page to this work. He pointed out its "value as a picture of manners," and praised Hawthorne's "appetite that could often find a feast in meagre materials." He was disappointed, however, that Coverdale let off too easily the radicals and reformers and philanthropists at Blithedale; he should have ground them in the mill of his satire. James, of course, atoned for this in *The Bostonians.* Coverdale's greatest contribution, he felt, was the idea of "the unconscious way in which the search for the common good may cover a hundred interested impulses and personal motives," and how such a search can succeed only after a total surrender of self (7058). Lastly, he praised the characterization of Hollingsworth and Zenobia.

In *The Marble Faun,* the two characters he found very striking were Donatello and Hilda. In Donatello, he indicated, Hawthorne created a literary type: the blissfully immature character who awakens to manhood "through the accidental, the almost unconscious, commission of a crime." Of Hilda's "same sad initiation," James wrote that "one of the most charming passages in the book describes how at last, at a summer's end, in sultry solitude, she stops at St. Peter's before a confessional, and Protestant and Puritan as she is, yields to the necessity of kneeling there and ridding herself of her obsession" (7059-60). This scene made a deep, lasting impression on James; he referred to it again at greater length in *The Sense of the Past* (1917), his last published reference to Hawthorne.

In his review of Hawthorne's *French and Italian Note-Books,* James had emphasized the author's excessive mistrust of and detachment from Continental life, and "the irreconcilable foreignness of his instincts" to most European things (*Nation,* 1872, p. 172). "Exposed late in life to European influences," he had concluded, "Mr. Hawthorne was but superficially affected by them" (173). In his 1897 comments on *Our Old Home,* although he found in Hawthorne's impressions of England "something of the same . . . mixture of sensibility and reluctance, of response and dissent," that had characterized his stay in Italy, the emphasis was different:

> He came to the Old World late in life . . . and with inevitable reserves, mistrusts, and antagonisms. The striking thing to my sense, however, is not what he missed but what he so ingeniously and vividly made out. If he had been, imaginatively, rather old in his youth, he was youthful in his age; and . . . we owe him, as a contribution to the immemorial process of lively repartee between the mother land and the daughter, the only pages of the business that can be said to belong to pure literature. . . . At home he had fingered the musty, but abroad he seemed to pine for freshness. In truth, for many persons his great . . . sign will have been his aloofness wherever he is. He is outside of everything, and an alien everywhere. He is an aesthetic solitary. . . . It was a faculty that gave him much more a terrible sense of human abysses than a desire rashly to sound them and rise to the surface with his report. (*Library,* XII, 7060-61)

The criticisms are still there: Hawthorne preferred to remain on "the surface of the soul" and to linger in "the thin exterior air." But, on the whole, it is evident that by 1897 James's appreciation of Hawthorne had grown considerably.

It is this growth that Buitenhuis's article delineates in the section on James's 1897 essay (*New England Quarterly*, 1959, pp. 216-20). Whereas in 1879 James had pictured Hawthorne as starved for fictional material in America, in 1897 he praised his appetite which "could often find a feast in meagre materials." This larger sympathy with Hawthorne, Buitenhuis explains, enabled James to discover many things in the American novels that he had missed in 1879. He praised the exquisite art of *The Seven Gables,* and wrote on values in *The Blithedale Romance* which he had not admitted in the earlier study. His estimation of the European books had risen too. Buitenhuis says that when James discusses Hilda's case, "we can almost see him making a mental note for the device which he was to use to such good effect in *The Ambassadors*" (218). Furthermore, although James had insisted in the biography that Hawthorne forfeited a precious advantage by being outside of everything he described in Europe, in 1897 he termed alienation the vital principle of all Hawthorne's work. "Hawthorne therefore ceased to be, in James's eyes, an underprivileged novelist and became a writer with a consistent and effective point of view." Buitenhuis notes also that when James calls Hawthorne an alien everywhere, he is once again comparing himself with Hawthorne, for like him "he was seeking to 'go behind' . . . for 'the suggestive idea, the artistic motive.' In Hawthorne he . . . found a valuable guide for his own explorations into the contortions and subtleties of the individual's psychology." Lastly, Buitenhuis indicates that the type of symbolism James adopted in his late works such as *The Wings of the Dove* and *The Golden Bowl* derives from the very aspect of Hawthorne's fiction that he had derided in 1879 (219-20).[11]

Tanner's introduction to *Hawthorne* (London: Macmillan, 1967) continues to repeat Buitenhuis. Tanner too points out the "notable changes of emphasis" in James's attitude toward Hawthorne: he praises Hawthorne's appetite that created so much out of so little, and even commends him on his surrender to the charm of Italy. Tanner believes it was James's years in Europe which "brought him to a much more sympathetic understanding of Hawthorne's complex responses. In adopting a different attitude to Hawthorne, James is also revealing changes in himself" (17). Other critics have found that, specifically, as James grew more confident of himself and his techniques, and as his literary success became more established, his responses to Hawthorne likewise became more generous. Tanner again observes, like Buitenhuis, that James no longer calls Hawthorne an outsider in Europe, but the universal alienated writer. "For James, too, often felt himself to be 'an alien everywhere', and what he says of Hawthorne's method fits his own." In a comment on the time between this 1897 essay and James's next extended evaluation of Hawthorne in 1914, Buitenhuis had written:

> As the nineteenth century drew to a close, Henry James began increasingly to feel the extent of his own alienation from his native land. The nostalgic letters that he wrote to friends and relatives in America reveal the strength of this emotion. . . . In a number of [letters published in *Literature* in 1898], James stressed that it was necessary above all things for an author to be "saturated" in his native environment. (*New England Quarterly,* 1959, p. 220)

Tanner too writes that "the fact is that towards the end of the century James was feeling that it could be a bad thing for any artist to be alienated from his native land," and one letter to his brother William in 1899 stressed the importance "for young Americans 'to contract local saturations and attachments'" (Tanner, p. 18).

James made four more references to Hawthorne before the close of the century. Volume XVI of Warner's *Library* (1897) contained selections from James Russell Lowell (pp. 9237-78), for which James wrote an introduction (pp. 9229-37). He found Russell "the American of his time most saturated with literature and most directed to criticism" (*Library,* XVI, 9229). He praised his mastery of verse, and his love of language, of expression, of style and of form. Lowell was unlike Emerson, who had "less of applied knowledge and successful form, less of the peace of art," and whose work is fragmentary and devoid of order. Neither was he like Irving or Longfellow, whose work is loose and diffuse. Of Hawthorne, James wrote:

> Hawthorne had further to wander and longer to wait; and if he too, in the workshop of art, kept tapping his silver hammer, it was never exactly the nail of thought that he strove to hit on the head. What is true of Hawthorne is truer still of Poe; who, if he had the peace of art, had little of any other. (9231)

James does not say what it was that Hawthorne's silver hammer kept striving to hit. Within the context of the essay, one may suppose that he was referring to something related to three of the observations he had made in *Hawthorne*: that Hawthorne had "a large and healthy appetite for detail," but looked in vain for subjects in the thin, blank American soil (chapter 2); that he regretted his "having laid up no treasure of pleasant memories against old age," and his having "seen so little of the world that I have nothing but thin air to concoct my stories of" (chapter 3); and that he had constantly struggled "between his shyness and his desire to know something of life; between . . . his evasive and his inquisitive tendencies" (chapter 3). Possibly this is what the indented passage above refers to, although James had just praised, in his other introduction in Warner's *Library,* Hawthorne's appetite which "could often find a feast in meagre materials."

James had frequently referred to Hawthorne's strong national consciousness (in his review of the *French and Italian Note-Books,* and in his introduction in volume XII of Warner's *Library,* for example), and asserted that most great artists are rooted in their native soil (in his 1874 review of Turgenev, for instance). There is also a sense of regret in his admission to Hamlin Garland that if he were to live his life over again, he would know no other land but America. And both Buitenhuis and Tanner have written of how, towards the end of the century, James increasingly felt the disadvantages of his own alienation from America. In "The Story-Teller at Large: Mr. Henry Harland,"

Fortnightly Review, 69 (April 1, 1898), 650-54, a review of *Comedies and Errors,* James suggested that it was perhaps time to review

> the old notion that, to have a quality of his own, a writer must needs draw his sap from the soil of his origin. The great writers of the world have, as a general thing, struck us so as fed by their native air and furnished forth with things near and dear to them, that an author without a country would have come long ago—had any one ever presumed to imagine him—to be a figure as formless as an author without a pen, a publisher or a subject. . . . As the novelist is essentially a painter we assign him his climate and circumstances. (650)

To demonstrate the veracity of this, James said, all one has to do is refer, "with a fond and loyal glance, to Dickens, to Scott, to Balzac, to Hawthorne, respectively so English, so Scotch, so French, so American, particularly in the matter of subject" (650). However, James felt the situation was changing, and argued that although it was "true earlier in the century and in a larger world" that one painted best who painted nearest home, "the globe is fast shrinking, for the imagination, to the size of an orange that can be played with," and soon it will be difficult to say what is "near" home and what is far from it.

Turning to Harland, James found in *Comedies and Errors* "not a single direct glance at American life." Its interest lay partly in the "peculiar intensity" of its acute sense of the "Europe" of the American mind, and part of James's interest in Harland was to discover what "nutrition" there was for a cosmopolitan artist who sees Europe and America as being in the process of "overlapping and getting mixed." His conclusion was that *Comedies and Errors* does not develop its material sufficiently to provide an answer. Harland is "a little too much everywhere"; it is only when "he really stops and begins to dig" deeper into his subject that it will be possible to answer "the question of soil . . . and of the possible ups and downs, as an artist, of the citizen of the world" (654). As Buitenhuis observes, this was the time when James was wondering about "the price he himself had paid for his long expatriation" (*New England Quarterly,* 1959, p. 220).

James's "American Letter," *Literature,* 3 (July 9, 1898), 17-19, discusses Charles E. Craddock's *The Juggler,* Sarah B. Elliott's *The Durket Sperret,* Mary E. Wilkins's *Silence,* and W. D. Howells's *The Story of a Play.* James first draws attention to the rise and popularity of novels portraying "the simpler folk," and the disproportionate emphasis placed on "dialect in the subject-matter of the American fiction of the day" (18). "Leaving out Hawthorne and beginning after him," he writes, "I can think of no such neat hands as the hands dealing with the orders that in other countries are spoken of as the 'lower'" (18). Both Craddock and Elliott have written about "the life and speech of the mountaineers of Tennessee"; Harriet Beecher Stowe's *Uncle Tom's Cabin* is about the life of Negro slaves; Edward Townsend's *Chimmie Fadden* reproduces "the dialect of the New York newsboy and bootblack." These are the great successes, and James predicts that, unless conditions change, this kind of portrayal will flourish in the United States, for a period, much more than "the studies of the human plant under cultivation" (18).

James's letter to Mrs. Humphrey Ward in July, 1899 (Lubbock, *Letters,* I, 320-23), contains the slightest direct reference to Hawthorne recorded. As Edel observes in *Henry James: The Treacherous Years, 1895-1901* (Philadelphia and New York: J. B. Lippincott, 1969), p. 298, Mrs. Ward had sent James proofs of *Eleanor,* and asked for his opinion on the American character in the story, Lucy Foster, and the details of the American background in which she moves. James felt that there were no "peccant particular spots" in Lucy's character that the American reader would challenge, and no false notes in her background to worry about. What needed worrying about were her untypical reactions to Rome:

> I *don't* quite think the however obscure American girl I gather you to conceive would have any shockability about Rome, the Pope, St. Peter's, kneeling, or anything of that sort . . . She would probably be either a Unitarian or "Orthodox" . . . and in either case as Emersonized, Hawthornized, J. A. Symondsized, and as "frantic" to *feel* the Papacy &c, as one could well represent her. (*Letters,* I, 321)

In the reference to Hawthorne, James was probably thinking of Hilda's reactions to Rome, Catholicism, and the papacy, especially in chapter 39 of *The Marble Faun.*

Items During the Twentieth Century

James continued to write about and make references to Hawthorne during the twentieth century. In "Honoré de Balzac," a critical introduction to *The Two Young Brides* (London: William Heinemann, 1902), pp. v-xliii, James restated that Balzac was "the first and foremost member of his craft"; that his subject was the great garden of France; and that he handled his material "as a patient historian, a Benedictine of the actual, the living painter of his living time." "All painters of manners and fashions," he continued, "are historians, even when they least don the uniform: Fielding, Dickens, Thackeray, George Eliot, Hawthorne among ourselves."[12] James is here again referring to the way most great artists are rooted in their native soil.

Four chapters in *William Wetmore Story and His Friends,* 2 volumes (Boston: Houghton Mifflin, 1903), have lengthy references to Hawthorne: chapters 2, 3, and 6 in volume I, and chapter 8 in volume II. In chapter 2, James considers at length the sculptor's father, Judge Story, a man of culture, liberality, and high distinction. James admires especially Story's statue of his father—in the memorial chapel of the cemetery of Mount Auburn—for it so completely captures the essence of this eminent man. Its very presence makes one exclaim, "What a *lovable* great man!":

> The author of these remarks is reminded by his type, and above all by . . . his amenity, of something once said to himself by an accomplished French critic . . . who, much versed in the writings of Englishmen and Americans, had been dilating with emphasis and with surprise upon the fine manner of Hawthorne, whose distinction was so great, whose taste, without anything to account for it, was so *juste*. "Il sortait de Boston, de Salem, *de je ne sais quel trou*"—and yet there he was, full-blown and finished. So it was, my friend surely would have said, with the elder Story. He came, practically, out of the same "hole" as Hawthorne, and might to the alien mind have been as great a surprise. (I,24)

The highest tribute James gives to Judge Story is to say of him what a great French critic had said of Hawthorne.[13]

In chapter 3, James considers the Storys' circle of friends in Rome. One of these friends was Margaret Fuller, who in her young years had been "a sparkling fountain to other thirsty young." But her circle represented a small stage, and "there were those on its edges to whom she was not pleasing. This was the case with Lowell and, discoverably, with Hawthorne; the legend of whose having had her in his eye for the figure of Zenobia, while writing 'The Blithedale Romance,' surely never held water" (I, 129). James had earlier dismissed this "legend" in his biography of Hawthorne. After noting that "Hawthorne does not appear to have been intimate with her," and conceding that "she was, in his imagination, the starting-point of the figure of Zenobia," he had nevertheless argued that "it is idle to inquire too closely whether Hawthorne had Margaret Fuller in his mind in constructing the figure of this brilliant" woman, "or, on the assumption that such was the case, to compare the image at all strictly with the model":

> There is no strictness in the representation by novelists of persons who have struck them in life, and there can in the nature of things be none. From the moment the imagination takes a hand in the game, the inevitable tendency is to divergence, to following what may be called new scents. The original gives hints, but the writer

> does what he likes with them, and imports new elements into the picture. (*Hawthorne,* chapter 5)

As will be shown later, when James himself was accused of having modeled the figure of Miss Birdseye in *The Bostonians* on Miss Peabody, he reacted in a similar way, and insisted that "she was not in the smallest degree my starting-point or example" (Lubbock, *Letters,* I, 115).

In chapter 6, James considers the Palazzo Barberini, Story's permanent residence in Rome. In Rome Story had "sought and found the secret of beauty, of harmony, and . . . of truth." Relating more of the history of Rome and the Palazzo Barberini, James is reminded of the sound of rain in Rome, and all the images it conjures up:

> It was always . . . but the plash of the great fountain, that babble of water from somewhere which is ever the most Roman note of all: as if, precisely, in one of the most bloodstained of cities, fate had provided for it a proportionate washing away. There is plash enough, at any rate, at the Barberini, to cleanse, for the fancy, the threshold on which poor Lady Coventry bled, and even to send up its cheer into the other wing, where generations of tourists, with Hawthorne's beautiful novel in their hand, still fancy they find in the sweet face of Guido's picture the plea of justifiable parracide. (*Story,* I, 343)

(James had earlier written, in chapter 6 of *Hawthorne,* that *The Marble Faun* "is part of the intellectual equipment of the Anglo-Saxon visitor to Rome, and is read by every English-speaking traveller who arrives there, who has been there, or who expects to go.")

One of the Storys' acquaintances in Rome was Mrs. Gaskell. James quotes from a number of her letters, many of them expressing her pleasant memories of Rome. Others recount her various activities in England:

> Writing at another time that she had been for a while at Whitby . . . she mentions that Hawthorne was at the same time, on the same coast, at Redcar, ten miles off, engaged in finishing "Transformation," the subject of which she sketches as she has heard it narrated. Then touching on that outbreak of the faun nature, the animal, in the strange hero, which moves him at a given moment to the commission of a murder: "For all of which, somehow, you like Donatello the better!"
>
> For all of which . . . we like *her,* Mrs. Gaskell, so much the better. (*Story,* I, 357)

She had a refined "sentiment of appreciation," and James's estimation of her is heightened by her favorable comments on Italy and on Hawthorne.

Soon after, he relates another of her letters to the Storys:

> After Hawthorne's romance has come out she expresses to her friends her supposition that they will have read, as every one in England had, the "Cleopatra chapter," and assures them that she is proud of being able to say to people that she had been acquainted from the first with the statue commemorated. "I feel funnily like Quin, who, when George III. made his first speech before Parliament after his accession, said, 'I taught the boy to read!'–for I come in crowing over my having seen the thing even in the clay and describing more fully what every one is asking about. I can't say, unluckily, 'I taught the boy to imagine beauty.'" (I, 358)

In chapter 8 in volume II, James considers, among other things, Story's talents as a sculptor. He praises the unsurpassed Libyan Sibyl, and correlates chapter 14 of *The Marble Faun,* "Cleopatra," with Story's sculpture of the same title, so that the brilliance of the one may illuminate the glow of the other. First, he returns to "the echo started for us, a while back, in Mrs. Gaskell's letter":

> She was full of her Hawthorne, she had been reading "Transformation," and she sets us . . . reading it again for ourselves. Then it is that a much pleasanter thing occurs . . . then it is that we are contented and charmed to be, in the matter, whatever the good Hawthorne was in the golden air of his Romanised vision; then it is, in fine, that we assist . . . at the odd, delightful business of practical *consecration* of a work of art, and are moved . . . to brood genially on the shy phenomenon. That is perhaps easier than to express it, to say exactly how it is that in such a case we are affected by the poetry of association, the beneficence of perspective, the antiquity . . . of tone. . . . The mysterious Miriam, in the novel, it will be remembered, comes, in her sad unrest, to the studio of Kenyon, the young American sculptor, and makes acquaintance there with the image of a grand seated woman, a personage royal and wonderful, who is none other than a fine prose transcript of Story's Cleopatra. Immensely impressed, she questions her host as to the source of his vision, and his admirable answer may doubtless stand for the artist's only possible account of the origin of any work. "I kindled a great fire in my mind and threw in the material–as Aaron threw the gold of the Israelites into the furnace–and in the midmost heat uprose Cleopatra as you see her." She saw her, Miriam, as romantically as the artist himself could have wished, weaving fine fancies about her in the gentle Hawthornesque way; as a result of which . . . the beautiful light mantle of the book, all loose and soft and ample,

> is thrown over the statue. It is not exactly, of course, as if the protection had, in advance, been needed, but when once the phenomenon . . . occurs–the phenomenon of a recognition, an assimilation . . . we take it in for our edification. Such is the quality . . . of the sweetness that we impute; an element that so constantly clears and disinfects Hawthorne's so-called gloom, making it light, pictorial, digestible . . . . "Transformation," in short, with its laxities of insistence, its timidities of indication, its felicities of suggestion, its sincerities of simplicity, and, most of all, its total vague intensity, so curiously composed of all these, is, more than anything, a lovable production–which, in its wandering amiability, holds up for a moment a mirror to another work, a little magic mirror from which the reflection, once caught, never fades. (II, 84-87)

James had obviously written less vaguely on Hawthorne in his previous uses of the author to define or clarify his own estimation of other artists and their work. Nevertheless, it is a tribute to Hawthorne that James reverts to chapter 14 of *The Marble Faun* as his own statement on Story's Cleopatra.

In "Henry James and the Hawthorne Centennial," *Essex Institute Historical Collections,* 92 (July, 1956), 279-83, B. Bernard Cohen prints four letters from James to the Essex Institute in connection with the centennial celebration of Hawthorne's birthday. On March 23, 1904, Robert S. Rantoul, President of the Essex Institute, wrote asking James for a contribution to this commemoration. On April 5, 1904, James replied that he had already said, more than once, *all* he wanted to say on Hawthorne. He mentioned his biography of the author, and his introduction in volume XII of Warner's *Library.* "Such tributes should be fresh and eager," he continued, "not insipid and pumped-up." He also knew of no Italian well versed in Hawthorne's work to contribute such an article. "'The Marble Faun,' though dealing with Rome, deals with it from a point of view so intensely Anglo-Saxon as to be capable of meaning almost nothing . . . to a foreign mind not extraordinarily initiated." He recalled how he had once tried to get "a very accomplished Roman friend" to read his novel, only to be told "it was not for *him.*" In *Notes of a Son and Brother* (1914), James identified this "friend" as H. B. Brewster. It is interesting to note how James recounted this incident then:

> I recall how once, in the air of Rome . . . a friend and countryman now no more, who had spent most of his life in Italy and who remains for me . . . the clearest case of "Cosmopolitan culture" . . . exclaimed with surprise on my happening to speak as from an ancient fondness for Hawthorne's treatment of the Roman scene: "Why, can you read *that* thing, and *here*?–to me it means nothing at all!" I remember well that under the breath of this disallowance

> of any possibility of association, and quite most of such a one as I had from far back positively cultivated, the gentle perforated book tumbled before me from its shelf. . . . [I was lost] in the sense that the note of harsh inquiry . . . of the stroke I had anciently wished to avert, *there* fell straight upon my ear. It represented everything I had so early known we must have none of; though there was interest [enough] . . . in an "American" measure that could so reject our beautiful genius and in a Roman, as it were, that could so little see he had done anything for Rome. H. B. Brewster in truth, literary master of three tongues at least, was scarce American at all; homely superstitions had no hold on him . . . and there would have been small use, even had there been any importance, in my trying to tell him . . . why it had particularly been . . . that I had settled once for all to take our author's case as simply exquisite and not budge from that taking.[14]

James further observed that Hawthorne had attracted little attention in France, for people there did not care about Puritan art. Guillaume Guizot, the French critic he had quoted in *Story,* I, 24, was long dead, as was Emile Montegut, who once wrote about Hawthorne.

The centennial committee made further requests to James through Joseph Hodges Choate, American ambassador to Great Britain, and on May 13, 1904, Choate wrote to Rantoul that he had "got positive promises from Henry James and James Bryce . . . to send brief tributes to Hawthorne to be read and published as part of your proceedings."[15] James mailed his contribution on June 10, 1904, with a letter to Rantoul requesting that if his remarks "are read out, instead of being only printed," they should be read as completely and intelligently as possible. On the same day he telegraphed Choate that he had mailed his comments.

James's "Letter" was delivered by proxy on June 23, 1904, and published the following year in *Essex Institute Historical Collections,* 41 (January, 1905), 55-62. He regretted his not being able to participate, in person, "in the honours you are paying . . . to the beautiful genius to whom Salem owes the most precious gift perhaps that any honest city may receive from one of her sons." But he felt the physical distance would give him the perspective and objectivity needed in expressing his admiration for Hawthorne, and even his "certain tenderness of envy."

James had always admired Hawthorne's strong national consciousness. In 1897 he had praised his "appetite that could often find a feast in meagre materials" (*Library,* XII, 7057). But he had prefaced this by suggesting that his community had so much developed the life of the spirit that it offered the artist little else to work with. Thus Hawthorne's imagination had, almost of necessity, to look "behind and beneath for the suggestive idea . . . so that it ended by living in a world of things symbolic and allegoric" (*Library,* XII, 7054). In the present "Letter," while trying to account for the universality of Hawthorne's works, James found that "the old sunny and shady Salem" was essential to his art. Whereas in 1879 he had said that the "valuable moral" which Hawthorne's situation points is that "the flower of art blooms only where the soil is deep" (*Hawthorne,* chapter 1), in 1904 he admitted—thus agreeing with Howells's 1880 observation—that as a romancer, the years Hawthorne spent in Salem were of greater advantage to him than if they had been passed in the "thick" atmosphere of Europe. In the same 1879 biography James had enumerated "the items of high civilisation" which were absent from Hawthorne's environment, partly as a justification of his own expatriation to Europe. In 1904, he saw the absence of this "paraphernalia" from American life almost as a stroke of luck for Hawthorne:

> Salem had the good fortune to assist him, betimes, to this charming discrimination—that of *looking for romance near at hand,* and *where it grows thick and true,* rather than on the other side of the globe and in the Dictionary of Dates. We see it, nowadays, more and more, inquired and bargained for in places and times that are strange and indigestible to us; and for the most part, I think, we see those who deal in it on these terms come back from their harvest with their hands smelling . . . [of] the homeliest growth of our actual dusty waysides. These adventurers bring home, in general, simply what they have taken with them, the mechanical, at best the pedantic, view of *the list of romantic properties.* (*Essex Institute Historical Collections,* 1905, p. 58; emphasis mine.)

By 1904 James may have regretted, or even felt embarrassed about, that 1879 listing of the items of high civilization absent from Hawthorne's culture. One can already see him progressing toward that revision of the "moral" in Hawthorne which he was to make ten years later; for in *Notes of a Son and Brother* (1914), he wrote that Hawthorne

> proved to what use American matter could be put by an American hand: a consummation involving . . . the happiest moral. For the moral was that an American could be an artist, one of the finest, without "going outside" about it, as I liked to say; quite in fact as if Hawthorne had become one just by being American *enough,* by the felicity of how the artist in him missed nothing, suspected nothing, that the ambient air didn't affect him as containing. Thus he was at once so clear and so entire—clear without thinness, for he might have seemed underfed, it was his danger; and entire without heterogeneity, which might, with less luck and to the discredit of

our suffering manners, have had to be his help. (*Henry James: Autobiography,* p. 480)

This is quite a different moral from that of 1879. By 1904 James had learnt that materials for "romance" are not found on some "particular spot on the map," or in any accumulation of external paraphernalia. "What was admirable and instinctive in Hawthorne," he wrote in the centenary letter, "was that he saw . . . the interest *behind* the interest, of things, as continuous with the very life" the people of Salem "were leading . . . saw it as something deeply within us, not as something infinitely disconnected from us." Of Hawthorne's works, he singled out *The Seven Gables, The Blithedale Romance,* and *The Marble Faun* as "examples of the real as distinguished from the artificial romantic note," instances of how Hawthorne "read the romantic effect into the most usual and contemporary things."

In the last section of his letter, James tried to suggest how such classics as *The Scarlet Letter, The Seven Gables,* and *The Blithedale Romance* "acquire their final value. They acquire it," he wrote, largely "by the manner in which later developments have worked in respect to them," and later developments have worked in respect to Hawthorne's romances more by *contrast* than by emulation. "The scene has changed and everything with it": pitch, tone, quantity, and quality. Here James was perhaps thinking of his own artistic methods as well, and the achievements and errors of the school of realism in general. "The grand sign of being a classic," he concluded, "is that when you have 'passed,' as they say at examinations, you have passed; you have become one once for all; you have taken your degree and may be left to the light and the ages."

Buitenhuis's comments on the centenary letter are few (*New England Quarterly,* 1959, pp. 220-21). He notes that the angle of approach here is again different from that of the 1897 article. James here says nothing of Hawthorne's "alienation," but rather concentrates on the claim that Hawthorne's relationship to his New England environment was his very making as an artist. Buitenhuis also indicates that the idea that Hawthorne "turned the bare necessities of America into artistic virtues" is of course developed from the 1897 article, where it was first mentioned. Tony Tanner too, in his introduction to *Hawthorne* (London: Macmillan, 1967), points out how James here "ascribes Hawthorne's success as a writer precisely to the fact that he stayed at home and exposed himself to the local environment." "Having once rather patronized Hawthorne for not having derived very much from coming abroad," Tanner concludes, "James now seems almost to envy him for having extracted so much out of staying at home" (18).

On July 6, 1904, George Francis Dow, Secretary of the Essex Institute, wrote to James about his contribution to the Hawthorne Centenary. In his reply on July 21, 1904, James was glad that his paper "had proved in any degree readable or helpful," and requested a printed copy of it. (In his first letter to Rantoul–*Essex Institute Historical Collections,* July 1956, p. 280–James had complained that he had never seen a printed copy of his article on Hawthorne in Warner's *Library*.)

The last letter printed in Cohen's article is addressed to Rantoul, dated September 3, 1904, when James was already in the United States. He regretted his not having been able to return the corrected proof of his centenary letter sooner; he had been too busy ever since he arrived from Europe. "I return the Proof now," he wrote, "with no alterations . . . save some small rectifications of punctuation."

James's next reference to Hawthorne was in "The Lesson of Balzac," a lecture first delivered at the Contemporary Club of Philadelphia on January 12, 1905, and reprinted in the *Atlantic Monthly,* 96 (August, 1905), 166-80. It is in this lecture, of course, that James acknowledged his having learned from Balzac "more of the lessons of the engaging mystery of fiction than from any one else" (170). He called Balzac "really the father of us all," the very model of the novelist, and quite a challenge "for any other painter of life." As he had observed in his introduction to *The Two Young Brides* (1902), he repeated that Balzac's field was the huge "picture of the life of France in his time." Detailed, specific, he reproduced "the real on the scale of the real." Turning to the question of the "spiritual presence" of the author in his works, James first set up a contrast:

> Just how, accordingly, does the light of the world . . . strike us as different in Fielding and in Richardson, in Scott and in Dumas, in Dickens and in Thackeray, in Hawthorne and in Meredith, in George Eliot and in George Sand, in Jane Austen and in Charlotte Brontë? . . . Why is it that the life that overflows in Dickens seems to me always to go on in the morning . . . Why is it that in George Eliot the sun sinks forever to the west, and the shadows are long? . . . Why is it that in Charlotte Brontë we move through an endless autumn? Why is it that in Jane Austen we sit quite resigned in an arrested spring? Why does Hawthorne give us the afternoon hour later than any one else?–oh, late, late, quite uncannily late, and as if it were always winter outside? (172-73)

The color of Balzac's air, in contrast, "is rich and thick, the mixture of sun and shade diffused through the *Comédie Humaine.*" Since James was discussing only Balzac, he excused himself from elaborating on the complex system of clocks and seasons he had set up in the indented passage above.

When James returned to the United States in September, 1904, he had been away since August, 1883. Chapter 8 of *The American Scene* (1907; reprinted New York: Horizon Press, 1967), the book that resulted from this tour, recounts his visit to Concord and Salem. Peter Buitenhuis expresses succinctly the purpose and mood of this visit:

> The return visit was a pilgrimage made to discover again the "New England homogeneous," and to demonstrate the theory advanced in his centenary letter. Perhaps [Salem], with its old houses . . . and its legacy of puritanism could, with the aid of his strenuous imagination, supply one half of the equation of Hawthorne's success as an American artist, the problem that had exercised him over so many years.
>
> The picture of Salem that James had fondly conjured up, however, like so many pictures of America that he had cherished before his return visit, proved to be hopelessly out of date. (*New England Quarterly,* 1959, p. 222)

James termed Concord "the biggest little place in America," too easily the first among places of her own size, and even of greater weight than many places fifty time her size. He reflected upon her character, her moral charm, her felicity, and her good fortune. But the real significance of Concord cannot be seen by the naked eye; one has to *know* it, has to be aware of its specific details:

> Would one know, for one's self, what had formerly been the matter here, if one hadn't happened to be able to get round behind, in the past, as it were, and more or less understand? Would the operative elements of the past—little old Concord Fight, essentially, and Emerson and Hawthorne and Thoreau, with the rest of the historic animation . . . would even these handsome quantities have so lingered to one's intelligent after-sense, if one had not brought with one some sign by which they too would know [?] (*American Scene,* p. 258)

James was glad little of Concord had changed. He thought of "the great company kept by her in the past," and of her significance in history: "Beautiful exceedingly the local Emerson and Thoreau and Hawthorne"; equally impressive the Concord River, which "had watched the Fight . . . without a quickening of its current." "I hung over Concord River then as long as I could," he wrote, "and recalled how Thoreau, Hawthorne, Emerson himself, have expressed with due sympathy the sense of this full, slow, sleepy, meadowy flood." He lingered by the bridge and took in the whole scene. "All the commemorative objects, the stone marking the burial-place of the three English soldiers . . . the intimately associated element in the presence, not far off, of the old manse, interesting theme of Hawthorne's pen, speak to the spirit, no doubt, in one of the subtlest tones of which official history is capable, and yet somehow leave the exquisite melancholy of everything unuttered." James felt that the manse had, through the passage of time,

> shaken itself a trifle disconcertingly free of the ornamental mosses scattered by Hawthorne's light hand; it stands there, beyond its gate, with every due similitude to the shrunken historic site in general. . . . [But] I was much more struck with the way these particular places of visitation resist their pressure of reference. . . . Intrinsically they are as naught—deeply depressing, in fact, to any impulse to reconstitute the house in which Hawthorne spent what remained to him of life after his return from the Italy of his Donatello and his Miriam. Yet . . . this mild monument benefits by that something in the air which makes us tender, keeps us respectful; meets, in the general interest, waving it vaguely away, any closer assault of criticism. (263-64)

In Salem, James overtook a young Italian and asked him the way to the House of the Seven Gables. The foreigner "glared frank ignorance of the monument"; but, as he was Italian, James wondered how the native estimate of the house "as a romantic ruin might strike a taste formed for such features by the landscape of Italy":

> I will not profess that by the vibration of this note the edifice of my fond fancy—I mean Hawthorne's Salem, and the witches' . . . was not rather essentially shaken; since what had the intention of my pilgrimage been, in all good faith . . . but a search again, precisely, for the New England homogeneous—for the renewal of that impression of it which had lingered with me from a vision snatched too briefly, in a midsummer gloaming, long years ago. (265-66)

James went on to recount his earlier attempt to visit this house, and recalled the "goodly Colonial habitations" that occupied the area, with nothing else in sight except "the sense of dead marine industries, that finally looked out at me . . . from the blank windows of the old Custom House of the Introduction to *The Scarlet Letter.*" That was all he had seen then:

> But the image of these things I had not lost, wrapped up as it even was, for the fancy, in some figment of the very patch of old embroidered cloth that Hawthorne's charming prefatory pages unfold for us—pages in which the words are as finely "taken" as the silk and gold stitches of poor Hester Prynne's compunctious needle. It had hung, all the years, closely together, and had served—oh, so conveniently!—as the term of comparison, the rather rich frame, for any suggested vision of New England unalloyed. (266)

On his return to Salem, he again was directed to these "goodly Georgian and neo-Georgian houses." He found them dignified, with a "thin and clear . . . boldly unspotted" tone of respectability. Their "high bland foreheads" had "no musty secrets in their eaves . . . in spite of the 'specialty,' in this respect, of the Seven Gables." But such edifices "never very curiously testify" to all the mysteries behind them—"as I was presently to learn, to my cost, from the dreadful anti-climax of the Seven Gables."

One of James's reasons for coming to Salem, of course, was to visit the House of the Seven Gables, and "the birth-place of their chronicler." When he finally found "the small stale structure that had sheltered the romancer's entrance into life," it appeared, "according to the preference of fancy, either a strange recipient of the romantic germ or the very spot to cause it, in protest and desperation, to develop." He nonetheless accepted the neighborhood as "the small original Hawthornesque world." A little American boy showed him "the window of the room in which Hawthrorne had been born," but he did not go in; and when the boy brought him to an object that was said to be the Seven Gables, all James could say was, "Dear, dear, are you very sure?" He could not take it to be the house. But the little boy somehow understood James's disappointment, "so that in short I think of him as the very genius of the place, feeding his small shrillness on the cold scraps of Hawthorne's leaving." And the fact that the shapeless object would not do for the germ of *The Seven Gables* troubled James only until he repudiated "the poor illusion of a *necessity* of relation between the accomplished thing, for poetry, for art, and those other quite equivocal things" that are supposed to have suggested it. This "weak, vague domiciliary presence . . . may have 'been' . . . the idea of the admirable book," but the book's inner force is so independent of any such origin or reference that the connection turns "a somersault into space, repudiated like a ladder kicked back from the top of a wall." (In chapter 5 of *Hawthorne,* James had made a similar observation with respect to Zenobia and Margaret Fuller.) "Hawthorne's ladder at Salem," James continued:

> has now quite gone, and we but tread the air if we attempt to set our critical feet on its steps and its rounds, learning thus as we do . . . how merely "subjective" in us are our discoveries about genius. Endless are its ways of besetting and eluding, of meeting and mocking us. When there are appearances that might have nourished it we see it as swallowing them all; yet we see it as equally gorged when there are no appearances at all . . . and we recognize ruefully that we are forever condemned to know it only after the fact. (271-72)

Buintenhuis's section on *The American Scene* (*New England Quarterly,* 1959, pp. 222-23) emphasizes James's disillusionment with Hawthorne's

"New England homogeneous," for he found that his "theories about Hawthorne's relationship to his environment . . . could not be put to the test," and the romancer's genius was "to remain as mysterious in essence for him at the end as it had been in the beginning." Throughout his career, James had tried to estimate Hawthorne's greatness; but modern Salem, far from providing an answer to this puzzle, was only another symbol of the greed and materialism that had taken over the land. All the old places had changed, and James felt there was no longer in America any viable environment for an artist. "He returned to England," Buitenhuis concludes, "convinced once again of the rightness of his original decision to live there, and sure that whatever price he might have paid for this expatriation had been well worth it."

Tanner too points out, in his introduction to *Hawthorne* (London: Macmillan, 1967), that the nostalgic feelings James expressed towards the end of the century did not survive his contact with the actual America of the twentieth century. The Salem he saw failed to "sustain the role he had claimed for it in the evolution of Hawthorne's genius"; and "the environment which he thought had produced and been responsible for Hawthorne's particular genius" had been obliterated by business and industry. Like Buitenhuis, Tanner concludes that "when James returned to Europe he felt with renewed conviction that his decision to leave America for Europe had been a wise one; that whatever the drawbacks of expatriation, what he had gained, as an artist, was well worth the price." (18-20)

Two other chapters in *The American Scene* have slight references to Hawthorne: chapter 1, "New England: An Autumn Impression," and chapter 7, "Boston." Among the things James considered in chapter 1 were the changes at Harvard University. Universities in the United States, he discovered, had gained "the character and function of the life-saving monasteries of the dark ages." They were "the place to perambulate, the place to think, apart from the crowd." In contrast to their surroundings, which James likened to "a huge Rappacini-garden [sic], rank with each variety of the poison-plant of the money-passion," they glowed, even the humblest, "with all the vividness of the defined alternative, the possible antidote," and seemed "to call on us to blow upon the flame till it is made inextinguishable" (57-58). The reference here, of course, is to Hawthorne's "Rappaccini's Daughter."[16]

In chapter 7, James considered the changes in Boston at large. Parts of the city were declining in their social scale, lapsing "into shabbiness and into bad company." The question was what would remain, intellectually, aesthetically, or even morally, of the old New England spirit. James regretted especially the disappearance of the old Museum Theatre, which had given Boston some aesthetic dignity. "I spare a sigh to its memory," he wrote, "and, though I doubtless scarce think of it as the haunt of Emerson, of Hawthorne or of Mr. Ticknor, the common conscience of the mid-century in the New

England capital insists on showing, at this distance of time, as the richer for it" (243).

There were a few aspects of Boston that had not suffered the harshness of change: Mount Vernon Street, for instance, and Charles Street. From about this point southward, however, spread "the new splendours of Boston." The city of character and genius stopped here, "and the southward, the westward territory made up . . . a platform or stage from which the other, the concentrated Boston of history, the Boston of Emerson, Thoreau, Hawthorne, Longfellow, Lowell, Holmes, Ticknor, Motley, Prescott, Parkman and the rest . . . could be seen in as definite . . . a concentration . . . as the finished background of a Dürer print" (245).[17]

James's first autobiographical work, *A Small Boy and Others* (New York: Charles Scribner's Sons, 1913), has two slight references to Hawthorne, in chapters 7 and 27. In chapters 5 and 6 James writes about, among other things, the authors and artists he knew as a child: Tom Hicks, Charles Dana, George Ripley, Washington Irving, and many others. But most of these "early indigenous vogues and literary flurries," he explains in chapter 7, did not make any strong or lasting impact on him. "The Scarlet Letter and The Seven Gables had the deep tone as much as one would; but of the current efforts of the imagination they were alone in having it till Walt Whitman broke out in the later fifties" (46). And his wanderings to the bookstore introduced him only to English authors, and this, of course, merely intensified his longing for English life.

In chapter 27, James gives his impression of "the Institution Fezandié, Rue Balzac," the "oddest and most indescribable" establishment the James children had been taken to as pupils in Paris. Their father had sent them there because, "like so many free spirits of that time," he

> had been much interested in the writings of Charles Fourier and in his scheme of the "phalanstery" as the solution of human troubles, and . . . he must have . . . heard of M. Fezandié as an active and sympathetic ex-Fourierist . . . who was embarking . . . on an experiment if not absolutely phalansteric at least inspired . . . by a bold idealism. I like to think of the Institution as all but phalansteric–it so corrects a fear that such places might be dreary. I recall this one as positively gay–bristling and bustling and resonant, untouched by the strenuous note, for instance, of Hawthorne's co-operative Blithedale. (205-206)

The whole Fezandié phase was for the James children "a brave little seeing of the world on the happy pretext of 'lessons.'"

According to Buitenhuis (*New England Quarterly,* 1959, p. 224), James's next autobiographical volume contains his most generous estimate of Hawthorne. In July, 1860, James had been moved to Germany; chapter 2 of

Notes of a Son and Brother (New York: Charles Scribner's Sons, 1914), recounts his summer activities in Bonn. He shared with his brother Wilkinson a room in "the house of our good Herr Doctor Humpert, professor at the Bonn Gymnasium." The professor's sister-in-law reminded James of a Hawthorne character:

> I seem to see the Frau Doctorin and her ancient mildly-scowling sister Fräulein Stamm, who reminded me of Hepzibah Pyncheon in The House of the Seven Gables, perpetually wiping green hock-glasses and holding them up to our meagre light, as well as setting out long-necked bottles, with rather chalky cakes, in that forward section of our general eating-and-living-room which formed our precinct of reception and conversation. (256)

That same year the Jameses returned to Newport, Rhode Island. In chapter 6 James recalls how, when they were young, the James children felt embarrassed and even humiliated because their father, unlike the fathers of other children, "was *not* in business." "What shall we tell them you *are*," they frequently asked, but his answers—"Say I'm a philosopher, say I'm a seeker for truth," or "just say I'm a Student"—would not do. James lacked even the confidence of his brother Bob, who, when challenged as to their father's occupation, readily answered that he was a writer, the very author of *Lectures and Miscellanies James*:

> I think that when we settled awhile at Newport there was no one there who had written but Mr. Henry T. Tuckerman, a genial and graceful poet of the Artless Age, as it might still be called in spite of Poe and Hawthorne and Longfellow and Lowell, the most characteristic works of the first and the two last of whom had already appeared. (279)

In the same chapter 6, James prints his father's Saturday Club letter to Emerson, in which he expressed his impressions of Hawthorne. There are a number of structural differences between James's text and the text in Perry's *The Thought and Character of William James* which was quoted in the section on *Hawthorne.* The differences, however, do not affect the essence of the letter. Below are two examples:

> James (1914): Hawthorne isn't to me a prepossessing figure, nor apparently at all an *enjoying* person in any way: he has all the while the look—or would have to the unknowing—of a rogue . . . (360)

> Perry (1935): Hawthorne isn't a handsome man nor an engaging one anyway, personally: he had the look all the time, to one who didn't know him, of a rogue . . . (I, 88)

James (1914): It was heavenly to see him persist in ignoring the spectral smiles–in eating his dinner . . . and then go home to his Concord den to fall upon his knees and ask his heavenly Father why it was that an owl couldn't remain an owl and not be forced into the diversions of a canary. (361)

Perry (1935): It was heavenly to see him persist in ignoring Charles Norton, and shutting his eyes against his spectral smiles: eating his dinner . . . and then going home to his Concord den to fall upon his knees, and ask his heavenly Father why it was that an owl couldn't remain an owl, and not be forced into the dimensions of a canary. (I, 89)

Although one hesitates to say Perry edited the text, his version sounds more literary, and James's more epistolary. There could also have been two drafts of the letter.

It is in chapter 12, of course, that James accords Hawthorne his fondest and most generous tribute. In 1864 the James family had moved to Boston, and this period bristled with events. James writes of "the last impressions of the War," its various climaxes, and "the huge national emergence." It was also during this period that he published his first article in the *North American Review.* But of greatest impact were the deaths of Lincoln and Hawthorne:

> Ashburton Place resounds for me with a wild cry, rocks as from a convulsed breast, on that early morning of our news of Lincoln's death by murder; and, in a different order, but also darkening the early day, there associates itself with my cherished chamber of application the fact that of a sudden, and while we were always . . . awaiting him, Hawthorne was dead. What I have called the fusion strikes me as indeed beyond any rendering when I think of the peculiar assault on my private consciousness of that news: I sit once more . . . on my belated bed, I say, and yield to the pang that made me positively and loyally cry. . . . To tell at all adequately why the pang was fine would nevertheless too closely involve my going back . . . on the whole rich interpenetration. I fondly felt it in those days invaluable that I had during certain last and otherwise rather blank months at Newport taken in for the first time and at one straight draught the full sweet sense of our one fine romancer's work–for sweet it then above all seemed to me; and I remember well how, while the process day after day drew itself admirably out, I found the actual exquisite taste of it, the strain of the revelation, justify up to the notch whatever had been weak in

> my delay. This prolonged hanging off from true knowledge had been the more odd, so that I couldn't have explained it, I felt, through the fact that The Wonder-Book and Twice-Told Tales had helped to enchant our childhood; the consequence at any rate seemed happy, since without it, very measurably, the sudden sense of recognition would have been less uplifting a wave. The joy of recognition was to know at the time no lapse—was in fact through the years never to know one, and this by some rare action of a principle or a sentiment . . . that placed the Seven Gables, the Blithedale Romance and the story of Donatello and Miriam (the accepted title of which I dislike to use, not the "marble" but very particularly the human Faun being throughout in question) somewhere on a shelf unvisited by harsh inquiry. The feeling had perhaps at the time been marked by presumption, by a touch of the fatuity of patronage; yet wasn't well-nigh the best charm of a relation with the works just named in the impulse, known from the first, somehow to stand in *between* them and hard inquiry? (477-79)[18]

James goes on to recall his encounter, in Rome, with the cosmopolitan H. B. Brewster, who shocked him by declaring that *The Marble Faun* meant nothing to him at all. After recounting this episode, which has been quoted at length in the section on James's contribution to the Hawthorne Centenary, James observes that it was the "ever so appreciably American" tone of Hawthorne's works which had "proved to what a use American matter could be put by an American hand," and pointed that happiest of morals: that an American could be one of the finest artists "without 'going outside' about it."[19]

In the last two pages of his article, Peter Buitenhuis points out that as James grew old, he "turned increasingly towards the past," and the results of this nostalgic return include his three autobiographical volumes. Although James had once assumed that Hawthorne's influence had operated only in his earliest writing period, he now realized it had reached over to the very latest of his books. In *Notes of a Son and Brother,* while recalling the effect Hawthorne's death had had on his sensibilities as a young man, the wheel came full circle, and its revolution—the various assessments he had made of Hawthorne's work—"reveals clearly the flexibility and adaptability, the inexhaustible curiosity of Henry James's mind":

> He had declared in his first evaluation, over forty years before, that Hawthorne had been the last pure American—so pure that he hadn't known about the artistic resources of Europe until too late to be really affected by them. In . . . 1879, he had tried to maintain that this ignorance had constricted and hampered Hawthorne's artistic development in America and made him an outsider in Europe. In

> 1897, James modified this position by asserting that Hawthorne had not only been an outsider in Europe but also "an alien everywhere," a detached and subtle observer. But in 1904 he shifted ground again to maintain that Hawthorne's genius had been a product of his vital relationship to the environment of New England. When James saw that this environment had been destroyed, he fell back on his old belief, but this time without any air of patronizing. Hawthorne had lived in a time of American innocence. Then it had been possible for an artist to be one of the greatest without going outside his environment. (*New England Quarterly,* 1959, p. 225)

Tanner too observes, at the end of his introduction to *Hawthorne* (London: Macmillan, 1967), that James's last reference to Hawthorne echoes his earliest comments on him, but without the "condescension of youth"; rather, with "the mellow sympathy and understanding of age." Just as he had earlier referred to Hawthorne as "the last pure American," he once again, at the end of his life, looked back at him "not as the total outsider but as the essential artist of an earlier America." Whereas James, with every justification, *had* left America for Europe, "for Hawthorne, in his more innocent America, that had not been necessary" (20).

Notes of a Son and Brother, however, does not contain James's last reference to Hawthorne or his works. In "Mr. and Mrs. James T. Fields," *Atlantic Monthly,* 116 (July, 1915), 21-31; *Cornhill Magazine,* NS 39 (July, 1915), 29-43, James noted that Fields of "Ticknor, Reed and Fields" was the only American publisher of the time who "had a conception of possibilities of relation with his authors and contributors." Not only did he shine "with the reflected light of Longfellow and Lowell, of Emerson and Hawthorne and Whittier," but he also returned with interest any glory borrowed from his stars. "Few were our native authors, and the friendly Boston house had gathered them in almost all." Furthermore, it was at the Fields's salon that many of the contributors to the *Atlantic* "dined and supped and went to tea," and it was there that they learned "the possible relation between such amenities and hospitalities and the due degree of inspiration." (Most "germs" for James's stories, of course, had sprung from conversations overheard in such "salons.") The *Atlantic Monthly,* he continued, was for many years practically the sole organ of Oliver Wendell Holmes, who

> had been from the first the great 'card' of the new *recueil,* and this with due deference to the fact that Emerson and Longfellow and Whittier, that Lowell himself and Hawthorne and Francis Parkman, were prone to figure in no other periodical . . . and when I ask myself what best distinction the magazine owed to our remaining hands I of course remember that . . . the impressions and reminiscences of England gathered up by Hawthorne into *Our Old Home* had

> enjoyed their first bloom of publicity . . . under Fields's protection. . . . Everything that either Lowell or Hawthorne published in those days [made] its first appearance, inveterately, in the *Atlantic* pages.

Although James considered Holmes's *Elsie Venner* inferior to *The Autocrat of the Breakfast Table,* still nothing would induce him "now to lower our then claim for this fiction as the charmingest of the 'old' American group, the romances of Hawthorne of course always excepted." (*Atlantic Monthly,* July 1915, pp. 23-26; *Cornhill Magazine,* July 1915, pp. 32-36)

Towards the end of the article, James recalled a visit paid him in England by Mrs. Fields, who brought with her "a young friend of great talent." Sarah Jewett was "mistress of an art of fiction all her own, even though of a minor compass." She was "surpasssed only by Hawthorne as producer of the most finished and penetrating of the numerous 'short stories' that have the domestic life of New England for their general and their doubtless somewhat lean subject." (*Atlantic,* p. 30; *Cornhill,* pp. 41-42)

Leon Edel's edition, *Henry James: The American Essays* (New York: Vintage Books, 1956), pp. 280-83, prints two passages from the draft typescript of the above essay. In the section on the *Atlantic Monthly,* James had planned to include the following:

> Pin on to the Fieldses the various other associations of memory, Hawthorne in fact and Hawthorne or his story or two about him—about going down to Salem the winter day and seeing him, in his poor abode, sitting by the stove with his head bound up for a toothache, or something of the sort and sadly and shyly producing the *Scarlet Letter* for Fields to take back home and see if it would do. Fields's account of reading it that night, and how I thought this more wonderful than words, etc. (281)

James, of course, had already written about this episode in chapter 5 of *Hawthorne.*

James's last reference to Hawthorne's work appears in the posthumously published *The Sense of the Past* (New York: Charles Scribner's Sons, 1917). Ralph Pendrel, the hero of the book, had encountered in a darkened room the figure of the portrait of his ancestor, and its "face—miracle of miracles, yes—confounded him as his own." (86-88) At the beginning of book 3, James considers the effect produced on Pendrel by this encounter. After three or four days, he suddenly decided to call on the ambassador:

> The idea, in coming to him, brought him ease, offered an issue to his pressing need to communicate. He had been divided between this need and the equal one . . . of silence. . . . He wished he had been a Catholic, that he might go to confession; his desire . . . being no less

> for secrecy than for relief. He recalled the chapter in Hawthorne's fine novel in which the young woman from New England kneels, for the lightening of her woe, to the old priest at St. Peter's, and felt that he sounded as never before the depth of that passage. *His* case in truth was worse than Hilda's and his burden much greater, for she had been but a spectator of what weighed upon her, whereas he had been a close participant. It mattered little enough that his sense was not the sense of crime; it was the sense . . . of something done in passion, and of an experience far stranger than a mere glimpse, or than, if it came to that, a positive perpetration, of murder. (89)

F. O. Matthiessen, while considering the question of "whether James' social and moral values were at any period as solidly based as Hawthorne's," writes of the above passage that it "does no good for James to maintain that 'it mattered little enough that his sense was not the sense of crime,' for the falsehood of the whole analogy is that Hilda was at least oppressed by her knowledge of the mortal guilt of Donatello and Miriam, whereas Ralph Pendrel is involved in nothing worse than his eerie sensation of having gained a private entrance into the past. He is an unattached young man . . . [and] his action here can hardly have great consequences for anyone save himself." (*American Renaissance,* pp. 363-64)

The foregoing discussion has considered those items in which James wrote about, or directly referred to, Hawthorne and his works. The following essays review the critical studies which have examined Hawthorne's general influence on James, and those which have found influences of Hawthorne's specific works in James's various novels, *nouvelles,* and short stories. It is in James's own fiction, ultimately, that the real proof of Hawthorne's influence is to be found.

Chapter 2

General Considerations

The James-Hawthorne Relation

In August, 1918, the *Little Review* devoted volume 5, number 4, to Henry James. The second part of T. S. Eliot's contribution, "The Hawthorne Aspect," pp. 47-53, was the first extended consideration of James's relation to Hawthorne. But Eliot was not the first to recognize an affinity between the works of the two writers. As early as January 19, 1870, James's brother William, after reading *The House of the Seven Gables,* had written to James about his discovery of a "resemblance of Hawthorne's style to yours and Howells's"; unfortunately, William did not specify any of James's or Howells's works. In his reply on February 13, 1870, James did not deny the "resemblance," but rather hoped "to write as good a novel one of these days (perhaps) as *The House of the Seven Gables*."[1] William Dean Howells, in a review of *A Passionate Pilgrim and Other Tales* in the *Atlantic Monthly,* 35 (April, 1875), 490-95, mentioned *The Marble Faun* in connection with "The Last of the Valerii" (494), but he did not draw any similarity between the two. And on June 26, 1890, William James wrote to Henry about *The Tragic Muse,* "a most original, wonderful, delightful and admirable production." "The only thing I find positively to object to in the book," he continued, "is the length of the chapter on Mr. Nash's portrait, which is a little too much in the Hawthornian allegorizing vein for you."[2] Once again William did not elaborate on his observation.

Two other people commented on the James-Hawthorne relation before Eliot. In *A Study of Prose Fiction* (Boston: Houghton Mifflin, 1904), Bliss Perry was very decided in his preference, although his judgement seems rather odd:

> Hawthorne had as good a right to construct a romance, laying the scene in Rome, as had Mr. James to set a realistic novel—or at least a chapter of a realistic novel—in Albany, or to derive his heroine

> from Schenectady; and if Mr. James who knows the theory of fiction so much better than Hawthorne, fails to make 'The Portrait of a Lady' as great a book as 'The Marble Faun,' it simply proves, not that romance is superior to realism, or that life in Albany is any less suited to the novelist's art than life in Rome, but simply that Nathaniel Hawthorne is a better story-writer than Henry James. (231)

Hawthorne may be a better story-writer than James, but one would need a very exotic category to demonstrate the superiority of *The Marble Faun* to *The Portrait of a Lady*.

Rebecca West, in *Henry James* (New York: Henry Holt, 1916), was not entirely pleased with Hawthorne's influence on James, although she recognized the earlier novelist as a valuable guide. West found that James's first stories, which appeared in the *Atlantic Monthly* and the *Galaxy,* and which were written before his visit to Europe in 1869, have little substance in them. "Where there is any richness of effect," she wrote, "as in *The Romance of Certain Old Clothes,* it comes from the influence of Nathaniel Hawthorne" (24). After crediting that one story with some "imaginative exuberance," she declared that

> Hawthorne was not altogether a happy influence—it is due to him that Mr. James' characters have "almost wailed" their way from *The Passionate Pilgrim* to *The Golden Bowl*—but he certainly shepherded Mr. James into the European environment and lent him a framework on which to drape his emotions until he had discovered his own power to build up an imaginative structure. The plot of *The Passionate Pilgrim* . . . is very clumsy Hawthorne, but in those days Mr. James could not draw normal events and he had to have some medium for expressing his wealth of feeling about England. (25-26)

It is with T. S. Eliot, however, that extended considerations of the James-Hawthorne relation begin. His contribution to the James number was in two parts. In the first part, "In Memory" (*Little Review,* August, 1918, pp. 44-47), he appraised James's significance both as a writer and as a critic of literature and of America. He found that in the best of James's works, the focus is never on one character, or a group of characters, but on "a situation, a relation, or an atmosphere, to which the characters pay tribute." This method was "partly foretold in Hawthorne, but James carried it much further." As a literary critic, however, James was not successful. "His criticism of books and writers is feeble"; "in writing of a novelist, he occasionally produces a valuable sentence out of his own experience rather than in judgement of the subject." And, in dealing with American writers, he tries to be generous, to argue that "under the circumstances this was the best possible." As a critic of America, he offended many of his countrymen by constantly pouncing on them and tracking down their vices and absurdities.[3]

In part 2, "The Hawthorne Aspect," pp. 47-53, Eliot tried to determine James's "antecedents, affinities, and 'place.'" Although James lived mostly in Europe, Eliot explained, the soil of his origin contributed a flavor that was actually improved by transplantation; and "this strong native taste" springs from Hawthorne. "The point is that James is positively a continuator" of that New England tradition associated with such writers as Emerson, Thoreau, Hawthorne, and Lowell. Eliot argued that although James's relation to Hawthorne was very "personal," there was no "consideration of influence. James owes little, very little, to anyone; there are certain writers whom he consciously studied, of whom Hawthorne was not one . . . his relation to Hawthorne is on another plane from his relation to Balzac." This has always been a debatable issue. Hawthorne's may not have been a *studied* influence, but that is because it struck a deeper root, and at that younger age when James was peculiarly susceptible. Hawthorne's influence seems as perfectly evident in some of the earlier novels as Eliot says Balzac's is, and the tone of his criticism of Hawthorne, just like the tone of his criticism of Balzac, shows how much he was moved by the earlier novelist, and how he followed him with concentrated admiration. The first essay in this text should have indicated as much. Eliot, unfortunately, drew his conclusion only from *Hawthorne,* in which he perceived, as its conspicuous quality, "the tenderness of a man who had escaped too early from an environment to be warped or thwarted by it, who had escaped so effectually that he could afford the gift of affection." This tenderness and affection always remained, but in his later writings, James accounted for Hawthorne's success as an American artist almost entirely in terms of his vital relationship to this New England environment, and he virtually envied him for having "turned the bare necessities of America into artistic virtues" (Buitenhuis, *New England Quarterly,* 32, June, 1959). Eliot's observation applies only to the biography. In 1879 James was gentle in criticizing Hawthorne, Eliot explains, because he realized "the difficult fact that the soil which produced him with his essential flavor is the soil which produced, just as inevitably, the environment which stunted him." In his subsequent writings, however, James no longer saw Hawthorne as a stunted artist, but as one whose genius was partly explainable by the very environment which James had "escaped" from.

Eliot isolated many categories within the James-Hawthorne relationship which later critics have discussed at length. One of these is the two novelists' sense of the past. "In one thing alone," he wrote, is Hawthorne "more solid than James: he had a very acute historical sense . . . . Both men had that sense of the past which is peculiarly American, but in Hawthorne this sense exercised itself in a grip of the past itself; in James it is a sense of the sense." Another category relates to James's statement in chapter 3 of *Hawthorne,* that "the fine thing in Hawthorne is that he cared for the deeper psychology, and that, in his way, he tried to become familiar with it." This "deeper psychology," Eliot noted, allies the two novelists and separates them from their English contemporaries. They both "perceive by antennae" more than by sight, and this deeper psychology was responsible for some of Hawthorne's excesses; "it was forever tailing off into the fanciful, even the allegorical." In James its dangers can be seen in *The Turn of the Screw,* which is a good example of an "attempt to get the artistic effect by meretricious means."

A third category which Eliot discussed, and one which he had already mentioned in part 1 of his contribution, was the dramatic device used by both Hawthorne and James in characterization. "Hawthorne was acutely sensitive to situation," he wrote, and he grasped "character through the relation of two or more persons to each other; and this is what no one else, except James, has done." There is the relation of Dimmesdale to Chillingworth, of Judge Pyncheon to Clifford, of Hepzibah to Phoebe. Hawthorne "is the one English-writing predecessor of James whose characters are *aware* of each other, the one whose novels were in any deep sense a criticism of even a slight civilisation."

Eliot's last general observation was that James touched Hawthorne most evidently at the beginning of his career—"simply as a New Englander of letters"—as evidenced in *Roderick Hudson*; and at the end of his course—"with almost a gesture of approach"—as shown by *The Sense of the Past.* The rest of the article dealt with specific works, and will be discussed in subsequent essays in this text. In his lifetime, Eliot concluded, James took "talents similar to Hawthorne's and made them yield far greater returns than poor Hawthorne could harvest from his granite soil." In his work we "seem to detect Hawthorne coming to a mediumistic existence again," reminding us "of what he really was, had he had the opportunity," and attesting "his satisfaction that that opportunity had been given James."

The next extended consideration of the James-Hawthorne relationship was by F. O. Matthiessen, in a section entitled "Hawthorne and James" in *American Renaissance* (New York: Oxford University Press, 1941), pp. 292-305. In addition to this section, and the section entitled "From Hawthorne to James to Eliot," pp. 351-68, there are scattered references to the relationship throughout book 2, pp. 179-368, which is devoted to Hawthorne; and in the last chapter of the volume, "Man in the Open Air," pp. 626-56. Some of these references are indicated below; others are discussed in subsequent essays.

Eliot had written that James's mind was "so fine that no idea could violate it." Hawthorne too, wrote Matthiessen, was little swayed by any one school of thought. But Eliot had further characterized James "as a metaphysical poet. This separates him sharply from Hawthorne, in whose writing there is none of the amalgamation of sense and thought" that would place him in the metaphysical strain. But there are other areas of similarity. Both writers, for instance, found their "dramatic contrasts in moments of moral crisis rather than in external events." In 1863, Hawthorne admitted that "the Present, the Immediate, the Actual" of the Civil War "had proved too potent for him"; it had taken away "even his 'desire for imaginative composition.'" During World War I, James too found it impossible to continue *The Ivory Tower.*

Eliot had further observed that the focus in James's works is usually on "a situation, a relation, or an atmosphere, to which the characters pay tribute." Matthiessen noted that in the symmetrical design of *The Scarlet Letter* Hawthorne achieved "his utmost approach to the inseparability of elements that James insisted on. . . . Of his four romances, this one grows most organically out of the interactions between the characters." And its theme allowed him to make "continual correspondences" between external events and inner significances: for example, the various interpretations of the red letter which Dimmesdale beheld in the zenith during his vigil on the scaffold. "Out of such variety of symbolical reference," Matthiessen observed, "Hawthorne developed one of his most fertile resources, the device of multiple choice, which James was to carry so much further in his desire to present a sense of the intricacy of any situation for a perceptive being."

The preceding observations are made on pp. 231-76 of the general section on Hawthorne. In the specific section entitled "Hawthorne and James," pp. 292-305, Matthiessen indicated that the factor which differentiated the early developments of Hawthorne and James was "the presence or absence of an American example to build on." Some of James's earliest works, like "The Romance of Certain Old Clothes," "The Last of the Valerii," and *Roderick Hudson,* follow very closely Hawthorne's model. What is tantalizing about *Hawthorne,* therefore, is "what it omits to say, since it was written at the very period when James was most determined to abandon all traces of romance for realism. He took generously for granted all he had learned from Hawthorne," and although his "main concern was to make an accurate tribute," he nevertheless used the book to clarify his own views and state why the new school of realism "seemed to him on much firmer ground than the provincial American had been." As a result, there was no overt sign of Hawthorne in his "realisitic" middle period. It was not until he had discovered that the possibilities of realism had ended with *Madame Bovary,* not until such late stories as those dealing with the life of the artist, that he returned to the allegory, or at least to parable. In such stories as "The Altar of the Dead," James furnished an instance of the definition of romance which he had made in the preface to *The American,* a definition which was similar to Hawthorne's. Nonetheless, Matthiessen found no specific debts to Hawthorne in James's final novels; they show only "a fundamental reassertion of kinship in moral values, which defied for both writers any merely realistic presentation."

One of the "many leads back to Hawthorne" which Matthiessen considered were the similar types of characters which both novelists conceived. Olive Chancellor in *The Bostonians* and Gilbert Osmond in *The Portrait of a Lady,* Hollingsworth in *The Blithedale Romance* and Miriam's model in *The Marble Faun* are all cold egoists who prey upon other people. Several other types of characters are repeated in both authors' fiction. Even in such heroines as Isabel Archer and Milly Theale, characters who mark James's "greatest advance beyond anything in Hawthorne's scope . . . even here his meditation over Hawthorne may have borne some fruit."

Another lead back to Hawthorne which Matthiessen discussed was James's device of a narrator through whose consciousness all the events are sifted. In this respect, Lambert Strether in *The Ambassadors* is a development from Miles Coverdale in *The Blithedale Romance,* and Coverdale's greatest fear, "that he was becoming inhuman through his analytical detachment, became the increasingly inescapable situation for James' super-subtle observers. They grew obsessed with their author's . . . scrutiny of motive for motive's sake, until," in *The Sacred Fount,* the narrator could not tell whether his inquisitiveness was good or evil, or whether he was not actually insane. Many of James's other technical developments, Matthiessen found, were likewise a direct response to his sense of Hawthorne's limitations. His dissatisfaction with Hawthorne's use of allegory, for example, stimulated him to develop his own "dense symbols," so that by the time he wrote *The Ambassadors,* "his themes themselves came to him as images," and "people or situations fixed his attention because they 'would fall into a picture or a scene.'" Again, in chapter 5 of *Hawthorne* he had expressed his dissatisfaction with the characters in *The Scarlet Letter,* who struck him as mere representatives of a single state of mind. He thus visualized his own characters "as elements of a composition," related one to another, and frequently he used the vocabulary of painting so as to catch "the color of life itself." But so had Hawthorne, in the preface to *The Seven Gables,* expressed his desire so to manage "his atmospherical medium as to bring out or mellow the lights and deepen and enrich the shadows of the picture."

Both Hawthorne and James, Matthiessen continued, also used the device of "the portrait as a means of analyzing character" and probing beneath conventional appearances: in *The Seven Gables* for Hawthorne, in *The Sense of the Past* and *The Tragic Muse* for James. However, whereas in his work

Hawthorne usually started with a dominant moral idea, which he illustrated by a picture, "James, in a sense, started where Hawthorne left off. He seized first upon a dramatic image," which he made "the concrete core of his range of feeling and thought." His frequent reiteration, "Dramatize, dramatize," was probably a response to his "sense of the inadequacy of Hawthorne's loosely finished sketches," and of the romancer's having "gained picturesque arrangements but not dynamic composition."

The last section of book 2, "From Hawthorne to James to Eliot," pp. 351-68, continues to consider the various interrelations between the master and his disciples. For Hawthorne and James, Matthiessen concentrated on their moral sense and social perception. Both authors, he explained, were indifferent to religious dogma, although they were exceptionally aware of spiritual reality. With respect to the active forces in America, although Hawthorne understood the limitations of the seventeenth century—as shown in *The Scarlet Letter*—his imagination could not leap "from his relatively simple time and province to the dynamic transformations of American society that were just beginning to emerge." Neither are there any "really integrated principles" in his various reflections on his social and economic milieu. And when he returned from Europe in 1860, what he was most conscious of "was the slow disintegration of the bases upon which the earlier moral values had depended." James's consciousness of social complexity, of course, was more developed than Hawthorne's. However, his exemptions from ordinary existence were far more sweeping than Hawthorne's, and it is questionable whether his social and moral values were at any period as solidly based as his predecessor's. His moral sense too, "exquisite as it could be, drew little nourishment from any widely accepted ethical system." In his created realm of infinite leisure, his characters finally became "breathlessly abandoned to idle curiosity." Most of them "are segregated from any but the most dimly implied connections with the social" realities of the time. Neither, in marked contrast with Hawthorne, is there an "implication of any dependence upon a world overhead. The only intrusion of a Church is through a figure like Father Mitchell, 'a good holy hungry man,' who 'prattled' undiscouraged over 'viands artfully iced' on a hot Sunday at Fawns, while Maggie Verver, from the resources of her inner reliance, knew that she had no need for him [*The Golden Bowl,* chapter 39] ."

In book 3, "Melville," pp. 371-514, Matthiessen continued to make remarks on Hawthorne and James. James had argued, in chapter 2 of *Hawthorne,* that since it takes a significant accumulation of history and custom to form a fund of suggestion for a novelist, the American writer of Hawthorne's day must inevitably have been starved. "The context of this remark," Matthiessen observed, "gives it—like so much in James's critical study—more intimate bearing upon himself than upon Hawthorne." Although in the preface to *The Marble Faun* Hawthorne had complained about "the difficulty of writing a romance about a country where there is no shadow"—a passage which James quoted in the same chapter—the romancer's view had been different when he wrote *The Scarlet Letter* and *The Seven Gables*, and James's comment, that Hawthorne's phrase "must have lingered in the minds of many Americans who have tried to write novels" indicates the center of his own interest, for he had just written a novel laid in New England, *The Europeans*, and was about to begin *Washington Square*.

The last connection between Hawthorne and James which Matthiessen discussed was their deliberate use of ambiguity. When Hawthorne suggested "several choices as to the reasons for his characters' acts," Matthiessen explained, his intention was "to heighten our sense of the complexity of human motives." And this is the one device from Hawthorne which James developed to greatest lengths. The ambiguities with which he endowed many of his characters were "not owing to any obscurantism on his part . . . but to a desire to create the dense illusion of the passage of life itself, the alternate disclosures and bafflements that you sense in your inevitably partial knowledge of any person or situation."

In "James and the Plastic Arts," *Kenyon Review*, 5 (Autumn, 1943), 533-50, Matthiessen repeated many of the observations he had made in *American Renaissance*. He again noted that one of the many devices Hawthorne taught James was "the use of a portrait to bring out character." In *The Seven Gables*, Holgrave's daguerreotype pried beneath Judge Pyncheon's smooth appearance and revealed "his real kinship to his hard and grasping ancestor." James used this device both at the beginning (in *A Passionate Pilgrim*) and at the end (in *The Sense of the Past*) of his career. However, since he felt that with Hawthorne such devices remained naked allegories, to avoid the same charge he frequently used a painter as the narrator of his stories, as in *A Landscape Painter, Travelling Companions*, and *Roderick Hudson*, the last actually an allegory of the life of an artist. "The more closely we look at James," Matthiessen concluded, "the more signs we find of Hawthorne everywhere." There is more influence of Hawthorne in James's late work than in that of his deliberately "realistic" middle period. In *The Sacred Fount*, for instance, he explored the implications of the likeness between his characters and the portrait of the pale young man; in *The Wings of the Dove* he used a Renaissance picture; and in *The Golden Bowl* the bowl itself became his most complex symbol. *The Ivory Tower* too was to have used an *object d'art* as its central symbol.

Matthiessen's *The James Family* (New York: Alfred A. Knopf, 1947) is also dotted with references to the James-Hawthorne relation, many of them previously made in his earlier publications. Matthiessen points out that although "it was not as a conscious disciple of Hawthorne's that [James] began to write"—for from the earliest he had tried to be a realist—it was nevertheless Hawthorne's moral preoccupations that were deeply interwoven with his own background. He thus "owed to Hawthorne, not an assessable sum but rather the pervasive and inescapable debt that a man owes to the largest figure in his immediate background who is devoted to the same pursuit." Throughout his career James frequently "began where Hawthorne left off, and carried his effects further." Like Hawthorne he experimented with allegory, but by 1879 he had decided that this mode of projecting spiritual truths was likely to spoil both the story and the moral, the meaning and the form. In *American Renaissance,* p. 219, Matthiessen had noted that James's prefaces "seem to have received their first hint from the laconic but devastating self-appraisal of his countryman"; in *The James Family,* p. 482, he again observed that James's "famous prefaces may well have received their first hint from Hawthorne's brief but telling discussions of his own works." He also restated that Miles Coverdale was one of the sources of James's device of a narrator who, "as a central consciousness, frames and interprets the events." "By the time of his late work," he continued, James "was no longer concerned with being a strict realist, and though he did not revert to allegory, he subordinated his immensely developed skills of representation to the inner meanings they could symbolize." In *American Renaissance,* again, Matthiessen had wondered "whether James's social and moral values were at any period as solidly based as Hawthorne's"; in *The James Family,* he restated that James's "ethical values were less firmly based in a traditional pattern than Hawthorne's, just as Hawthorne's solid grasp of New England history had been refined into HJ's [sic] somewhat attenuated 'sense of the past.'"

A few other observations on the James-Hawthorne relation in *The James Family* can also be found in Matthiessen's other works. After repeating that in his last works James moved away from strict realism to a symbolic dramatization of moral problems which stems from Hawthorne, Matthiessen indicated that both Hawthorne's and James's definition of the differences between romance and realism were actually similar. In the preface to *The American,* James declared that both were modes of apprehending truth; the only distinction is that the romance deals with "experience liberated." In the preface to *The Seven Gables,* Hawthorne too affirmed that such experience may convey "the truth of the human heart." Indeed, the later James believed that "only by breaking away from the restrictions of realism could a writer express the things 'we never *can* directly know . . . [except] through the beautiful circuit and subterfuge of our thought and our desire.'"[4]

In book 6 of *The James Family,* after explaining that James's good characters are those whose consciousness has an ethical as well as an aesthetic awareness, and his bad ones those who are unaware of the qualities and the beauty of life in others, Matthiessen nonetheless asserted that James is not a religious novelist as Hawthorne and Dostoevsky are. His characters do not wrestle with the issues of faith; "they merely hover before the altars of the dead." In addition to *American Renaissance,* where he had made a similar observation, Matthiessen had noted again, in *Henry James: The Major Phase,* pp. 148–49, that the consciousness which James depicts, "though interpenetrated with ethical values, is more of the mind than of the soul. James is not a spiritual writer in the sense that Hawthorne and Dostoevsky are."

Two other works by Matthiessen have comments on the James-Hawthorne relation. In *The Achievement of T. S. Eliot,* 2nd. edition, revised and enlarged (New York: Oxford University Press, 1947), Matthiessen summarized some of "Eliot's observations on the basic relation between James and Hawthorne" which Eliot had made in an unpublished lecture at Harvard in 1933. Eliot "perceived that James's 'real progenitor' was Hawthorne, that he cannot be understood without Hawthorne." Both writers were indifferent to religious dogma but were exceptionally aware of spiritual reality. They were also profoundly sensitive to good and evil, and conveyed horror with extraordinary power.[5] It is clear from James's presentation of evil in *The Turn of the Screw,* Matthiessen continued, that only Hawthorne, Dostoevsky, and Conrad, as Eliot has elsewhere remarked, "were comparable in their 'essential moral preoccupation.'"[6] The Puritan mind, with its consciousness of the nature of evil, is as acute in *The Turn of the Screw* as it is in "Ethan Brand" or "Gerontion"; and "The Love Song of J. Alfred Prufrock" and *The Scarlet Letter* express equally the "full understanding of the dark consequences of loneliness and repression." "Both James and Eliot, no less than Hawthorne," Matthiessen concluded, were mainly concerned with what lay "behind action and beneath appearance," and they affirmed "the value of renunciation, sympathy, and tenderness."

The last comments by Matthiessen on the James-Hawthorne relation occur in his edition, with Kenneth B. Murdock, of *The Notebooks of Henry James* (New York: Oxford University Press, 1947). In the introduction the editors explain that although most of James's ideas came to him through chance anecdotes overheard at dinner engagements, occasionally he "proceeded in the way habitual to Hawthorne"; that is, "he started with an abstraction and sought an embodiment for it," as was the case with "The Friends of the Friends," "The Beast in the Jungle," and "A Round of Visits" (xii–xiv). In Notebook I, the editors again note that the entry for January 22, 1879, about the ghostly presence behind a walled-up or locked door, although never "developed into a story, looks back to Hawthorne as well as forward to James' most characteristic handling of the ghost story" (10). They also point out that James incorporated the passage in the *Notebooks* about the United States having no sovereign almost word for word into *Hawthorne,* with only one significant alteration: "a picturesque peasantry" was dropped, and "no museums, no pictures" was added. Many critics, the editors explain, "have noted that such an enumeration throws more light on James than on Hawthorne, and that fact, as well as the [passage's] rhetoric flourish . . . seems accounted for by its having originally been conceived in terms of James' own fiction."

In Notebook III, Matthiessen and Murdock identify, in addition to the entry on p. 151, three of the phases through which James's "Hawthornesque abstraction" of a young man who has some secret trouble to tell but has no *recipient* passed before it was finally embodied in "A Round of Visits": the entries for April 21, 1894, May 7, 1898, and February 16, 1899. Finally, after recording in Notebook IV James's entry about "a man haunted by the fear . . . that *something will happen to him* . . ." and noting that James had made an earlier entry (182-84) about "the passions that 'might have been,'" the editors conclude that "James' absorption, to the end of his career, with giving embodiment to such a formalized spiritual and psychological pattern is again a token of his enduring kinship with Hawthorne." However, James "progressed beyond Hawthorne's method of presenting, as in *Ethan Brand,* an allegory of the Unpardonable Sin." In "The Beast in the Jungle," for example, he intensified his effects "through the repetition of a dominant symbol."

Following Eliot's and Matthiessen's lead, Marius Bewley published a number of articles on the James-Hawthorne question, which were later reprinted in *The Complex Fate: Hawthorne, Henry James, and Some Other American Writers* (1952; reprinted New York: Gordian Press, 1967). Two of these—"*The Blithedale Romance* and *The Bostonians*," pp. 11-30, and "*The Marble Faun* and *The Wings of the Dove*," pp. 31-54—will be discussed in subsequent essays.

The Complex Fate has one serious drawback: in all the essays on Hawthorne and James, Bewley hardly ever tells which editions his numerous quotations are taken from. With no clue even as to chapter, it is extremely difficult and frustrating to follow up the arguments Bewley establishes. I have tried, especially with his two essays on specific works, to supply at least the chapters of the novels he quotes from.

In his first essay, "Hawthorne, Henry James, and the American Novel," pp. 1-10, Bewley indicates that the largest problem which confronted Cooper, Hawthorne, Melville, and James was their "separateness," as well as their connection with European culture. All these writers had great faith in America, but they were also among its greatest critics. Out of this fatuous optimism and cynical disillusion they created the American novel. Hawthorne, Bewley argues, showed James how the facts of American life could be used *in art*; "it was through Hawthorne that James found New England artistically accessible." The earlier novelist's "methods of work, his moral preoccupations, the fundamental problems that confronted him as an artist in America, his attraction to a kind of allegory that was akin to symbolism, even . . . the actual scenes and materials and types he chose to deal with, made a deep and lasting impression on James's 'fictions.'" Many passages in James's early prose are so Hawthornesque that one can mistake the works for Hawthorne's. But Hawthorne's influence was not confined to James's earliest works; it persisted to the very end, and in some ways it grew more insistent. Even after living in Europe for many years, James never lost those moral values which the literary tradition of Hawthorne and other nineteenth-century American artists had supplied him from the earliest. In his later life, of course, this influence operated in the sensibility at levels below active consciousness. Bewley points out also that in addition to Hawthorne's immediate example, the similarity between his and James's work is due as well to "mutual proclivities of temperament and shades of value" which characterized the local scene on which both novelists drew. They both responded similarly to the same problems in the American scene. Hawthorne's influence on James, therefore, "is not merely a matter of surface similarity, but exists in the very reality with which the novelists deal."

Bewley's second general essay, "The American Problem," pp. 55-78, first appeared in *Scrutiny,* 17 (Spring, 1950), 14-37. Both Hawthorne and James, he writes, had so strong a moral bias in favor of America that their art could not perfectly discipline their partiality. Frequently they were uncertain in dealing with the issues they faced, and in the end these problems got out of hand and produced such figures as Hilda in *The Marble Faun* and Milly Theale in *The Wings of the Dove.* Basically, the problem that lies at the basis of their resemblance is that of Europe *versus* America, the past *versus* the present, and both the past and present *versus* the future. However, the conditions under which they tried to solve this conflict were different. With James, the conflict "was the wholly conscious concern of his art–almost . . . his chief incentive to work." Hawthorne, however, was not as conscious of it as James was, "and he was ill-equipped by background to handle it deliberately. It was too hot a subject for his provincial training," and he suffered intensely from the tensions it created. Although he used these tensions effectively in his earlier work, they grew increasingly intractable until they became unmanageable. His art was martyred at their hands, but the martyrdom helped James's development of the international novel.

Hawthorne, Bewley continues, was often concerned with "solitude as a 'crime.'" Because he could not function effectively as an artist in his society, he frequently withdrew from it. But this created a sense of guilt, and led him to over-emphasize American positives–of which he wasn't much convinced–simply because they were American. The sharpness of the conflict between the American and European traditions in *The Marble Faun* "is largely the result of Hawthorne's lifelong inability to adjust himself practically to the society that, as an American, he wished to believe in." On the one hand, he was attracted to solitude, appreciated Europe, and loved the past; the practice of his art and his deepest sympathies were on this side. But this "was also the side that he distrusted," the side that his American conscience could not support. Thus he denied solitude, which, "as an expression of aristocratic withdrawal sided with Europe rather than America"; affirmed the superiority of America to Europe; and championed the present and future against the past.

Bewley next discusses a number of Hawthorne's works. He calls "Ethan Brand" "an indictment of solitude in its largest social sense." As such, he finds it a failure because its villain, Ethan Brand, is the only character with any dignity or decency. Like Coverdale, another detached and analytic observer, and Holgrave, a restless analyst who ought to have been an artist, Ethan Brand has some of Hawthorne's–and James's–characteristics. And yet, none of these characters, despite their "crimes," were presented as villains. Bewley believes that this was the impossible dilemma in Hawthorne's practice which eventually ruined his art. There was an irreconcilable conflict "between the demands of his genius and the demands he deemed American society to make on the citizen." In this respect, the heavily autobiographical "The Devil in Manuscript" shows "the personal anguish, ending in frustration and social alienation," which he experienced as an American artist. In "Wakefield," however, the implication is that if one has a strong will from the beginning, one cannot lose one's active place in society. Presumably, then, it was "a deliberate effort of the will that caused Hawthorne to attempt to deal with contemporary life in his late novels." Bewley points out further that the elements in "The Devil in Manuscript," "Ethan Brand," and "Wakefield" also function in *The Scarlet Letter,* "a subtle exploration of moral isolation in America." Hester's punishment, as described in chapter 5, seems as well a commentary on the sanctions directed against the artist; her richly embroidered "A" could also stand for "Artist."

Bewley next observes that although the American scene was the main subject for both Hawthorne and James, they found it unstimulating. Thus, during the peak of Hawthorne's career, he expatriated himself in time just as James did geographically. His best work, therefore, deals with the past; it was in images of Colonial history that he most effectively dealt with his contemporary problems. Whenever he dealt with the present, his touch became unsteady. In *The Marble Faun,* for example, he handled the conflict between the American and European traditions crudely. An example of his fine historical sense occurs in his description of Governor Bellingham's garden in chapter 7 of *The Scarlet Letter,* into which he subtle introduces a contrast between the English tradition and the American modification. And the contrast in the novel is resolved artistically. As long as Hawthorne worked in this Colonial past he was at ease, for its atmosphere provided the density which he, like James, missed in the America of his day. Whenever he turned to the contemporary scene, however, the cleavage between the cultures deepened, and the tensions became unmanageable, as in *The Marble Faun,* where in the preface the only things he praised Europe for were its ruins.

"When Hawthorne deserted Colonial history for the contemporary scene," Bewley continues, "he lost, somewhat paradoxically, his grasp of contemporary problems." Although *The Seven Gables* is a contemporary novel, its success lies in the sense of the past which suffuses its pages. Unlike James, whose special province was cultural antagonisms, Hawthorne did not have the knowledge or special security to deal with such problems, and when they became the dominant theme in his work "he became confused, biased, and ineffectual." It was his fear of solitude and of the past which made him invade the modern scene, and by the time he went to Europe he was too old to benefit from its advantages as the younger James did. He was also exposed to "very little good English society." As he explains in his *English Notebooks,* edited by Randall Stewart (New York: MLA, 1941), p. 4, his consular office was "a little patch of America, with English life encompassing it on all sides." After his seven years in Europe he never "recovered the fineness of his association with the American Colonial past," and his work "became unsatisfactory in a way . . . James's would have done had he returned to America in middle life and remained there."

In Hawthorne, Bewley reiterates, the question of America *versus* Europe was intrinsically bound up with the opposition of past and present, and both Hawthorne and James dealt with this question ambivalently. "They distrusted the past, but they reached out towards it instinctively as towards a totality of experience, and the inadequacy of the American present without a sense of European tradition persisted in tormenting their consciousness." Hawthorne's feelings about his return to England in 1853 (*English Notebooks,* p. 92) became a recurrent and tormenting subject in his later work. He often portrayed a young American who returns to England and tries to claim an ancient family estate. But that's as far as he got, "breaking off each time in a confusion of floundering symbols and a despair of finishing." Possibly this incoherence resulted from the fact that the symbolism of the returned American tends to fuse the two cultures instead of "counterpointing" their separate characters. It is therefore a mark of James's skill in counterpoint that his "international novels" abound in passages similar to that describing Governor Bellingham's garden in *The Scarlet Letter.* In Gilbert Osmond in *The Portrait of a Lady* James presented a portrait of the "fused" American; in *A Passionate Pilgrim* and *The Sense of the Past* he tried to create an American who was not "merely exposed to and enlarged by the European experience, but one who returned to Europe as to his proper home." Significantly, Clement Searle in *A Passionate Pilgrim* discovers, "not that he is both American and English, but that he is neither"—which reminds one of Hamlin Garland's *Roadside Meetings,* p. 461. And in *The Sense of the Past,* although

Ralph Pendrel's double identity belongs both "to the present and the past, to America and to Europe," the portrait of his ancestor does not really integrate the two aspects, and the repeated attempts to make it do so nearly "destroy the whole structure, so that we are tempted to say that in Hawthorne's symbol James encountered Hawthorne's failure."[7]

Bewley concludes that despite their lapses and failures, Hawthorne and James "established a strategy by which the American . . . might develop a refined consciousness of that cultural . . . unity that underlies the divisions" between England and America. Both novelists had a "sympathy," rather than a "relation," between them. If James felt "tenderness" for Hawthorne it was not, as T. S. Eliot remarked, "the tenderness of a man who had escaped too early from an environment to be warped or thwarted by it"; rather, "it was the tenderness of a battle-comrade for a fatally wounded friend." And if in the end the conflict proved too much for Hawthorne, his "example helped to focus James's attention." Hawthorne kept before James the constant reminder that an American artist must be morally concerned with certain national and social problems, and this shared concern in their work unfolds "into still deeper problems and resemblances that became . . . the very texture and meaning of their art. It was Hawthorne, then, who helped make James into an American novelist, and who prevented him from becoming a 'slightly disenchanted . . .' cosmopolite."

Bewley's third general article, "Appearance and Reality in Henry James," pp. 79-113, which first appeared in *Scrutiny,* 17 (Summer, 1950), 90-114, has very few references to Hawthorne. Bewley explains that the question of appearance and reality, truth and falsehood, and evil and goodness, occupied a central position in James's work. Hawthorne too was concerned with these problems, but for him the strain between the terms was not as great as it was for James, and he did reconcile them within the framework of his orthodoxy. In a story like "The New Adam and Eve," he dealt with the problem explicitly. Other stories like "Young Goodman Brown" and "My Kinsman, Major Molineux" also deal with the conflict between appearance and reality, and the difficulty of knowing evil. Certain aspects in *The Scarlet Letter* too may be considered explorations of the relation between appearance and reality. However, unlike James, Hawthorne was not victimized by these conflicts.

Bewley next demonstrates how James's most recurrent image of the looking glass expresses "Hawthorne's concern with the distinction between appearance and reality," and how it functions as a stabilizing metaphor demonstrating simultaneously the distinctions and the intrinsic relation between the two terms. Most of James's stories, he finds, question the validity of the relation between appearance and reality. In "The Path of Duty," for example, everything points to the conflict between appearance and reality. "The Liar" too deals with "the interaction of truth and falsehood, of appearance and reality," and *The Golden Bowl* itself is "a gigantic parable" of "how truth is fabricated out of lies." Bewley notes further that in "The Liar," Oliver Lyon commits the worst crime in both Hawthorne and James: he violates the integrity of another man's personality and tries to take possession of it. In *The Turn of the Screw* too, which is mostly "a hide-and-seek game between" appearance and reality, the governess wants to possess Miles and Flora "in a way which, for both Hawthorne and James represented a violation of human personality. Westervelt, Chillingworth, Olive Chancellor, Gilbert Osmund [sic], are all guilty of this crime."

Like Hawthorne, Bewley continues, James wanted to escape from "the world's artificial system." But sometimes he inverted ordinary human values and "wrenched appearance and reality apart . . . far beyond any requirement of social criticism." *The Turn of the Screw* is a good example. In "The New Adam and Eve," Hawthorne had said that "it is only through the medium of the imagination that we can lessen those iron fetters, which we call truth and reality, and make ourselves even partially sensible of what prisoners we are." But in James's story the fetters are so much lessened "that moral action seems to lose any intelligible form." One is no longer in the world of "The New Adam and Eve," but has rather entered the world of Gervayse Hastings in "The Christmas Banquet": nothing is real, and we are sure of nothing. By contrast, in *What Maisie Knew* "appearance and reality co-exist without violence to each other." The terms appearance and reality, Bewley concludes, and "the conflict between America and Europe, and between the past and present," "illuminate still further the nature of the similarity between Hawthorne and Henry James."

In *The Eccentric Design: Form in the Classic American Novel* (New York: Columbia University Press, 1959), Bewley tries "to enlarge upon, to corroborate with additional evidence, and define more rigorously, certain general statements made in the opening chapter of *The Complex Fate*" (9). He again notes "a concealed fellowship" between Cooper, Hawthorne, Melville, and James. With Hawthorne, he discusses "the tension between isolation and sympathy which is, perhaps, the dominant theme of his work"; with James he considers mainly "the everlasting dialectic between Europe and America" in his works. Hawthorne and James, he finds, drew nearest to each other in their treatment of the American and the European ways of life, "a protracted debate between the merits of democracy and aristocracy, between the past, present, and future." They were interested especially in the way these tensions affect people's moral action and outlook. Hawthorne' approach was "impersonal and moralistic with a minimum of interest in the psychology of the individual." In James's fiction, "Europe is a symbol that acts . . . rather like Hawthorne's Great Carbuncle. It shows everybody up for what they really are."

In addition to his comments on *The Seven Gables* and *The Spoils of Poynton,* which will be discussed in a later essay, Bewley notes that "Madame de Mauves and Bernard have all the unbending puritan righteousness of Hilda and Kenyon in *The Marble Faun.*" As chapter 5 of James's story shows, even their speech accents are similar. And when Bernard returns to America, he "settles down to a life which, as the years go by, one feels will come to resemble" Coverdale's at the close of *The Blithedale Romance.* Furthermore, what James meant by "life" in his frequent dictum, "Live all you can," can be equated with what Hawthorne meant by the "inner sphere." The search for life is the most overwhelming problem most of James's characters face, "just as Hawthorne's characters are all brought up against that 'inner reality' which was 'life'" for him. But James greatly improved on Hawthorne's sense of "life," or "inner sphere." In addition to this, "Hawthorne had his conception of the magnetic chain of humanity." When that chain was broken, "men ceased to live significantly." James's international theme is "merely the magnetic chain of humanity envisaged on a trans-Atlantic scale. And just as Hawthorne's characters were always breaking the chain . . . so James's characters have abundant troubles of their own." Lastly, Bewley notes that Cooper's and James's conception of American cultural poverty were almost identical. In *The Travelling Bachelor,* Cooper's description of the deprivations facing the American novelist is remarkably similar to James's description, in *Hawthorne,* of the social and cultivated amenitites which America lacked. Because of the impoverished materials in America, Hawthorne's "great theme became that of deprivation–deprivation of life." This was a major theme in James too, "because he knew what life was, and what his characters were being deprived of." Bewley's conclusion is that "James is far greater than Hawthorne because he possessed a positive knowledge of, and a feeling for, life that eluded the older novelist" (240).

Three other people have written rather considerably on the general relation between Hawthorne and James. As indicated in the first essay, Peter Buitenhuis's main concern in "Henry James on Hawthorne," (*New England Quarterly,* 1959, 207-25) is to show how James's periodic assessments of Hawthorne reveal the different things he learned from Hawthorne at various stages of his development. In addition to his general conclusions, Buitenhuis makes a number of specific observations, although none are developed in detail. He finds that whenever James treated his European experience in fiction, he seems "to have made a conscious attempt to begin where Hawthorne left off." "A Passionate Pilgrim," for example, is based on an incident Hawthorne relates in "Consular Experiences" in *Our Old Home* (1863; reprinted Ohio State University Press, 1970), p. 23. *Roderick Hudson* too has as its inspiration and setting the Rome of *The Marble Faun.* In most of James's early stories and travel sketches, Buitenhuis notes, one can detect footprints of Hawthorne. James seems also to have felt that he appreciated Europe more than Hawthorne did. In the end, of course, he "concluded that the very conditions of the continent were necessary to his development as an artist. In 1875 he went over to live there permanently."

Buitenhuis notes further that James's debt to Hawthorne increased rather than diminished with time. "In *The Bostonians,* for instance, James not only treated the reforming crew satirically," thus profiting from *Blithedale*'s failure, "but he also learned from Hawthorne's treatment of his characters." Even *The Princess Casamassima* "may well have been influenced by Hawthorne's concern in *Seven Gables* with conservatism and radicalism. All through James's work of the 1880's and '90's Hawthorne's influence is traceable to some degree. Even *What Maisie Knew* can be traced to some of the things that Pearl knew in *The Scarlet Letter*."

In *The Grasping Imagination: The American Writings of Henry James* (Toronto: University of Toronto Press, 1970), Buitenhuis continues to comment on Hawthorne's presence in James's various works. He notes that when "A Landscape Painter" was first published, the heroine's name "was the Dickensian one of Esther Blunt." Later, "James changed it to the Hawthornesque and slightly sinister Miriam" (22). Similarly, when "Poor Richard" was first published, "Richard's second name was Clare. In the revision, James . . . changed it to Maule, perhaps in order to recall the curse placed on the Pyncheon family" in *The Seven Gables* "as an analogy of Richard's betrayal of Severn" (33). And in "My Friend Bingham," as "in Hawthorne's fiction, suffering brings about refinement of feeling and access of knowledge" (26). Later, Buitenhuis explains that Winch's suicide in "A Round of Visits" "is not the act of a man unhinged by worry and hopelessness"; it is "a considered act of resignation, even of expiation of fraudulent practices." What James is using here is Hawthorne's familiar theme of "education by sin and suffering" (236).

In chapter 3, "The Hawthorne Aspect," pp. 38–44, Buitenhuis again observes that Hawthorne's voice "is heard increasingly in the stories that James wrote from the late 1860s on." "The Story of a Masterpiece," for one, was possibly derived from "The Prophetic Pictures," the name of whose hero, Ludlow, James had earlier used in "A Day of Days." However, whereas Hawthorne's emphasis is on "the painter's ability to discover and portray characteristics invisible to unskilled eyes and on the almost magical aspects of this kind of gift," James's treatment centers on the psychological rather than the magical. Even more Hawthornesque is "The Romance of Certain Old Clothes," which "is set in one of Hawthorne's favourite milieux, colonial Massachusetts, 'toward the middle of the eighteenth century.'" The description of the scene in which Lloyd finds Viola dead "compares not unfavorably with Hawthorne's description" of Colonel Pyncheon's corpse in *The Seven Gables.* However, this conclusion is out of keeping with the rest of the story.

"Hawthorne's method was to create a warm haze of ambiguity so that there are always at least two possible explanations of mysterious events, one of them natural." In James's story, the author "simply transferred his evolving notions of psychological realism to the eighteenth century." Imbued with ideas about the necessity of realism in fiction, he was not able at this time to profit fully by Hawthorne's example. Another early story, "De Grey: A Romance," also has its origins in the "Hawthornesque idea of the hereditary curse," and its theme "is enhanced by a variation that James probably derived from . . . *Rappaccini's Daughter*."

In the other chapters of *The Grasping Imagination,* Buitenhuis comments on Hawthorne's "prominent" influence in "The Ghostly Rental," where the Gothic convention enabled James, as it had enabled Hawthorne, "to use the slender resources of American history for imaginative purposes." James "was also careful to emulate Hawthorne's example and maintain an ambiguity of meaning in the story." In "The Impressions of a Cousin," James "made a half-hearted attempt to model his situation on . . . *The Marble Faun*." As was indicated in the first essay, Miss Condit observes in this story that Adrian Frank "is a charming creature—a kind of Yankee Donatello. If I could only be his Miriam, the situation would be almost complete, for Eunice is an excellent Hilda" (*Century Magazine,* November 1883, p. 121). Buitenhuis, however, disagrees:

> Hawthorne's schema . . . is quite inappropriate for the New York situation. Adrian has none of the wild, rustic, Italianate grace of Donatello, and Miss Condit is a pretty pallid Miriam. Eunice will do well enough as Hilda, but where is the fourth member of Hawthorne's quartet, the sculptor, Kenyon, to come in? Caliph bears no resemblance to him. If anything, James transposed Miriam's exotic, passionate, and Semitic qualitites to Caliph. He then watered down Hawthorne's theme of the "unpardonable sin" into Miss Condit's interference with Eunice's affairs, and ended up with a complete botch. (Buitenhuis, p. 130)

One might point out, however, that Miss Condit says "the situation would be *almost* complete" (emphasis mine); James was surely not attempting to create a situation identical in every detail to that in *The Marble Faun.*

One of the last topics Buitenhuis discusses is James's use of symbolism in his late works. In these works, "the symbol is a means of organizing experience into complex artistic forms and of increasing the range of perception for the reader," and in this late development "Hawthorne probably influenced James more than any other writer." In his 1897 introduction to the Hawthorne selections in volume XII of Warner's *Library* (see the first essay):

> James praised Hawthorne for his ability to "go behind" the meagre facade of New England to find the suggestive idea, the artistic motive, which were far more complex things than "the mere eye of sense" could suspect. James found in his work the consistent stance of "an alien everywhere . . . an aesthetic solitary." This . . . "was a faculty that gave him much more a terrible sense of human abysses than a desire rashly to sound them and rise to the surface with his report . . . he was . . . discreetly contemplative, pausing oftenest wherever . . . there seemed most of an appeal to a sense for subtleties." In the piece . . . for the Hawthorne Centenary in 1904, he pointed out further that Hawthorne had made use of his New England materials with "an artistic economy which understands *values* and uses them."
>
> James's own stance in his later work closely resembles that which he found in his revaluation of Hawthorne. His own sense of subtleties and his fine understanding of values contribute to the remarkable detachment which is characteristic of his point-of-view technique. One of the artistic motives which James . . . found most impressive in Hawthorne's work was his use of the comprehensive titular symbol, such as is often found in the short stories and in all the novels except *The Blithedale Romance.* From *The Sacred Fount* . . . until the end of his life, James used titular symbols for his novels and many of his short stories. These comprehensive symbols [the golden bowl, the ivory tower, etc.] provide an organic structural element which binds together the characters and themes of the story. (246)

Richard Poirier, in *The Comic Sense of Henry James* (New York: Oxford University Press, 1960), pp. 33-35, writes on the similarity between Hawthorne's definition of the romance in the preface to *Blithedale* and James's in the preface to *The American.* "The equivalent in James of 'the theatre, a little removed,'" he writes, "is the society of . . . the elect, of those people of high intelligence and selflessness" of whom Rowland Mallet in *Roderick Hudson* is an example. Elsewhere, Poirier points out that in *Roderick Hudson* and in *The American* "James demonstrated how much he had assimilated Hawthorne"; that in *The Europeans* the Wentworths "are ironically the descendants . . . of the Puritans who in Hawthorne tore down the maypole at Merry Mount"; and that in *Confidence* James showed, as Hawthorne had shown before him, how foolhardy it is to try to experiment with the emotional life of other people. However, Poirier believes that since the disparagement of "systematic intellectual experimentation" was part of the intellectual heritage which was available to many other writers, James was not directly influeced by

Hawthorne in his handling of this subject. Furthermore, neither in his other works nor in those of Hawthorne is this theme a subject, as it is in *Confidence,* for "a sportive and trivial comedy of errors." Nevertheless, just as there is something "thoroughly villainous" about Hawthorne's scientists, so is there something "unattractive" about James's. For James, "the deeper psychology" which Hawthorne cared for "includes a perception of human vampirism as James himself reveals in *The Sacred Fount*." Poirier believes that *The Europeans* represents "that moment in James where he himself became engaged, if not in the 'deeper psychology,' then at least in the effort to make unconscious motivation a more consistently effective part of the actions he dramatizes." Poirier also notes that long before Hawthorne and James complained that America lacked the high civilization necessary to the writing of novels, Cooper had already done so in the preface to *Home as Found.*

In chapter 1 of *A World Elsewhere: The Place of Style in American Literature* (New York: Oxford University Press, 1966), Poirier argues that the works which constitute a distinctive American tradition "resist within their pages the forces of environment that otherwise dominate the world," and that such writers as Cooper, Melville, Hawthorne and James try through style temporarily to free their heroes "from the social forces which are ultimately the undoing of American heroes and quite often their creators." These novelists promote eccentricity both in their fictional heroes and in the imaginative environments they create for them, although they are reluctant to admit this fact. Instead, they try

> to hide their true intentions under disingenuous complaints that they are victims of historical necessity. They ask us to believe that the strange environments they create . . . are a consequence not of their distaste for social, economic, and biological realities but of the fact that these aren't abundant enough in American life. Cooper, Hawthorne, James . . . all suggest that they would be happier if the social "texture" of American life were "thicker" even while they make every sort of literary effort to escape even the supposedly thin "texture" which American society does provide. In the passage from Hawthorne [preface to *The Seven Gables*] , in similar passages froom Cooper and James, the talk about "romance" is always connected with the supposition that America could not provide an environment which sustained American novelists. (9-10)

However, the greater American authors do try, "even when they are sure of failing, as Hawthorne was," to create an environment that might allow, despite "the perpetually greater power of reality," "some longer existence to the hero's momentary expansion of consciousness." But when they succeed, as James sometimes does, they are "accused of neglecting the 'realities' of sex, economics, or social history." In the same chapter, Poirier writes also on the obsession of American writers "with plans and efforts to build houses": the houses in Cooper's fiction, Hawthorne's *House of the Seven Gables,* James's Fawns in *The Golden Bowl,* Faulkner's Sutpen's Hundred in *Absalom, Absalom!* "The building of a house," he writes, "is an extension and an expansion of the self, an act by which the self possesses environment otherwise possessed by nature," and thus joins "forces with the powers of nature itself."

In chapter 3, "Visionary to Voyeur: Hawthorne and James," pp. 93-143, Poirier admits that he is dealing with "very familiar materials." He states, for example, that it is "more accurate to say that James uses rather than studies Hawthorne"; that the earlier novelist "is an 'example,' a point of reference by which James defines himself"; and that *Hawthorne* is essentially "James's effort to discover his own relation to New England and to the American past." If Hawthorne "was a 'valuable example' of the earlier type of American genius," he writes, "James's study of him is in part an announcement that James is himself an example of a later type." Poirier finds James's statement in chapter 5 of *Hawthorne,* that "the good American of which Hawthorne was so admirable a specimen was not critical," equally "a description of James, the spectator and the observer, and of those characters, like Ralph Touchett and Strether, for whom he shows a conspicuous affection." Of James's passage about the items of high civilization unavailable in America, Poirier remarks that "the peculiarity of this passage is that it equivocates by exaggeration, by mimicry of a shallow . . . [English] view of what constitutes society." But surely James meant this passage to be taken more seriously than Poirier seems to, as the novelist's reply to Howells's review clearly shows (Lubbock, *Letters,* I, 71-74). Poirier admits, however, that some of James's characterizations of Hawthorne are undeniable, and that these characterizations indicate the "essential differences between the two writers and between the worlds to which each belonged." For illustration, he contrasts "The Maypole of Merrymount" with *The Europeans.* "Thematically," he writes:

> "The Maypole of Merrymount" and *The Europeans* are much alike. Each is about a contest between . . . "jollity and gloom" for dominion in New England; each is enacted in a New England dominated either by Puritanism or, in James's novel, by some later modified form of it. But the *way* in which the contending forces are defined and in which the narrator sounds in each work is radically different. The characters and James himself as narrator of *The Europeans* are wholly defined by their tones of voice, by their conduct in dialogue and in social relations, and by the extent to which they can deal with the phenomenon of the Baroness Eugenia, confronting her American relatives with her "large element of

> costume." Everyone in the novel is revealed through verbal, social, and sexual manners, and the differentiations are extremely delicate and exacting. By contrast, nothing can be inferred from the way the characters sound in Hawthorne's story: they have no existence in the social and sexual world where James's characters come to life. As a narrator, Hawthorne . . . projects no social or class type; he never observes social conduct, but only the degree to which his characters are submissive to allegorical definition. James is accurate enough when he complains that Hawthorne "had certainly not proposed to himself to give an account of the social idiosyncrasies of his fellow citizens." (Poirier, pp. 104-105)

However, although James does "locate symptoms of social deprivation in Hawthorne, he is not very successful in his diagnosis of them." According to James, Hawthorne is "thin" because America is "thin." In *The Europeans,* he

> wrote a novel about Hawthorne's own time and place which Hawthorne himself presumably could not have written. He literally brings into that "thin" environment an element of contrast–the Europeans–without which the sweet but essentially silent American could have no novelistic existence.
>
> Missing from James's account is the ample evidence from Hawthorne's fiction and especially from his prefaces that, far from feeling deprived by what James thinks is lacking in his society, Hawthorne was usually anxious to escape from what it did offer. Nearly every novel and story is about his own and his characters' entrapment in . . . "artificial system," the control exerted over consciousness not only by social organization but by literary conventions. (105-106)

Poirier's overall argument is that Hawthorne's fiction "is in the American literary tradition of stylistic struggle." It is a struggle to reveal the limitations of Puritan allegory and "to cast off the restraints of literary and social artificiality." His greatest achievement in this respect is *Blithedale,* "a novel that clarifies the degree to which James was unable to see either the genius of Hawthorne or the extent to which Hawthorne's concern for the self and its environment resembled what were to be his own later preoccupations." Poirier's comments on *Blithedale* and *The Ambassadors* are evaluated in the fourth essay in this test.

Terrence Martin in chapter 2 of *Nathaniel Hawthorne* (New Haven, Connecticut: College and University Press, 1965), also discusses the concern both Hawthorne and James had for the romance. He comments on Hawthorne's distinction, in the preface to *The Seven Gables,* between the romance and the novel, and James's own distinction in the preface to *The American*; James's enumeration, in *Hawthorne,* of the items of high civilization which were absent from Hawthorne's society, and Hawthorne's own listing in the preface to *The Marble Faun.* He notes, however, that "whereas Hawthorne writes of the absence of shadow in American life, James writes of the absence of a texture of life that belongs to a mature society." A typical situation in a James story would be "related" to society to a much greater degree than a typical situation in a Hawthorne story. "Thus, when James speaks of related or encumbered experience, he is not referring precisely to what Hawthorne would consider an insistence on actualities." James's definition of the romance considers technique and execution; he looks for a unique "*general* attribute" of romance to fit all cases. His "analysis of the romance assumes and takes critical advantage of the fact that romances had been created" before. Hawthorne's statements, however:

> suggest that the romance was for him a working, formulative concept out of which a writer might seek to create fiction and not a retrospective elucidation of the general attributes of whatever romance he might know. Whereas James theorizes after the fact of creation, Hawthorne theorized as a prerequisite of creation. . . . As Hawthorne saw it, his essential problem was to create not simply fiction but the conditions of fiction; and it led him to confront, on a neutral ground, a kind of experience that James identifies in retrospect . . . as liberated or disencumbered. (45-46)

Martin next interprets "The Haunted Mind," and observes that Hawthorne's analysis of the haunted mind "bears an interesting relation to James's notion of 'disengaged, disembroiled, disencumbered' experience." James's discussion of the romance concerns execution; it assumes, and is subsequent to, the creation of romance. Hawthorne, however:

> focuses on the *conditions* of imaginative creation, on an aspect of the creative process prior to that of execution. The difficulty of creating fiction in the "broad and simple daylight" of his native land . . . encouraged Hawthorne to cultivate the resources of the haunted mind which gave him access to a frightening world of disengaged experience. To employ such resources, one risked the danger of . . . finding the night of the haunted mind and the day of actuality to be mutually exclusive. The initial problem in making fiction became one of blending the imaginative and the actual . . . so that the creation of romance would be possible. To say that disengaged experience came from the haunted mind is . . . to employ James's term to describe the exigencies of the creative situation as Hawthorne saw them. (47)

But, of course, Hawthorne's and James's attitudes toward the romance were different. It is more precise to define the "haunted" experience which Hawthorne shaped into fiction as "*pre*-encumbered, *pre*-engaged"; it was "genetically liberated, of its nature presocial." James, on the other hand, spoke of "*dis*encumbered or *dis*engaged experience—experience liberated from its social relatedness into the unrelated state of romance by the 'insidious' craft of the artist."

Martin's comments, in chapter 3, on "The Threefold Destiny" and "The Beast in the Jungle" are evaluated in the sixth essay in this text. His comments in chapter 6, on James's comparison of *The Scarlet Letter* to Lockhart's *Adam Blair* were previously published in his article, "Adam Blair and Arthur Dimmesdale: A Lesson from the Master," *American Literature,* 34 (1962-63), 274-79, and are reviewed in the third essay. (Martin does not mention this previous publication.) In chapter 10, "A Significant Legacy," pp. 177-80, Martin indicates that Hawthorne's exploration of the meaning of an ancestral past, his sense of community, his concern over the danger of abstraction, and his treatment of the artist and society "have constituted a significant legacy for Americn fiction." The work of such writers as James, Faulkner, and Robert Penn Warren "explores the meaning of the human condition in a manner familiar to readers of Hawthorne." In James's work one finds "a deep implied sense of community, which sustains the various judgements he makes on his Americans who confront European experience": Christopher Newman in *The American,* Lambert Strether in *The Ambassadors,* the many Americans estranged from a sense of community in *The Portrait of a Lady,* especially Gilbert Osmond, "a consummate egoist, whose self-devotion is worthy of any Hawthorne villain." Many of James's American characters, "like those of Hawthorne, are equipped with Puritan consciences, which have become portable, more refined, but not attenuated with the passage of time." James also shares Hawthorne's interest in the relation of the artist to society. Although the "problems of his artists are not precisely those of Hawthorne's," the theme of the artist is in his work second in importance only to that of American innocence confronting European experience. "Hawthorne came early and did much," Martin concludes; the fact that "significant later writers have found it important and even necessary to do similar things is the fullest tribute to the enduring quality of his achievement."

Partial Treatments of the Relationship

Most of the foregoing observations were made in studies which were either entirely or in part addressed directly to the James-Hawthorne question. Many other writers who have discussed James or Hawthorne separately have also commented in some degree on the James-Hawthorne relation. For the most part, these are reviewed below chronologically.

The three essays which touch on the James-Hawthorne relation in Philip Rahv's *Image and Idea* (Norfolk, Connecticut: New Directions, 1949), were all previously published. "The Dark Lady of Salem," pp. 22-41, "The Heiress of all the Ages," pp. 42-62, and "Attitudes Toward Henry James," pp. 63-70, first appeared in the *Partisan Review,* 8 (September-October, 1941), 362-81; 10 (May-June, 1943), 227-47; and the *New Republic,* 108 (February 15, 1943), 220-24, respectively. In "The Dark Lady of Salem," Rahv contrasts Dimmesdale's need for repentance with Hester's readiness to put the past behind her and escape to some place where she can fulfill her love without shame or fear. In chapters 17 and 18 of *The Scarlet Letter,* she does persuade the minister to flee to England, but in the end he "cheats her of her triumph by publicly confessing his sin on the scaffold; and that, of course, is *his* triumph":

> This thin-skinned clergyman is the ancestor of all those characters in Henry James who invent excruciatingly subtle reasons for renouncing their heart's desire once they are on the verge of attaining it. But in James there are also other characters, who, while preserving Dimmesdale's complex qualities of conscience and sensibility, finally do succeed in overcoming this tendency to renunciation. Lambert Strether of *The Ambassadors* and Milly Theale of *The Wings of the Dove,* whose ideal aim is "to achieve a sense of having lived," are plainly cases of reaction against Hawthorne's plaint: "I have not lived but only dreamed of living!" (*Image and Idea,* p. 35)

In "The Heiress of all the Ages," Rahv considers the stages of development in their transatlantic relations through which James's American heroines go. His discussion of *Roderick Hudson* includes comments on the nightscene in chapter 22 where Mary Garland confesses to Rowland Mallet that her stay in Italy has changed her conception of life. In America, she says, "things don't speak to us of enjoyment as they do here," where beauty is intermixed with everything, and penetrates one's soul "saying that man wasn't made, as we think at home, to struggle so much and to miss so much, but to ask of life . . . some beauty and some charm." This passage, says Rahv, recalls the relation of the early James to Hawthorne:

> For Mary is essentially a figure from a novel such as *The Blithedale Romance* or *The Marble Faun* brought forward into a later age; and because of the shift of values that has occurred in the meantime, she is able to express in a mundane fashion those feelings and sentiments that in Hawthorne are still somewhat hidden and only spoken of with a semi-circular quaver, as if from under a veil. (49)

The Portrait of a Lady points to another area of similarity. As Isabel Archer's marriage to Gilbert Osmond illustrates, many of James's characters who entrap others are frequently driven by mercenary motives, and, like Osmond, they accomplish their aim "by stimulating a sympathy and understanding that fascinate the victim and render her (or him) powerless." This kind of evil is similar to "the 'unpardonable sin' by which Hawthorne was haunted—the sin of *using* other people, of 'violating the sanctity of a human heart.'" Chillingworth in *The Scarlet Letter* and Miriam's model in *The Marble Faun* are sinners of this type. James's evil characters, however, "have none of the Gothic *mystique* which is to be found in Hawthorne. Their motives are transparent."

In "Attitudes Toward Henry James," as in "The Dark Lady of Salem," Rahv once again observes that the chief contradiction in James's fiction is that it "represents a positive and ardent search for 'experience' and simultaneously a withdrawal from it," and here again James is related to Hawthorne, "whose characters, likewise tempted by 'experience,' are held back by the fear of sin. And Hawthorne's ancestral idea of sin survives in James, though in a secularized form. It has entered the sensibility and been translated into a revulsion . . . against any conceivable crudity of scene or crudity of conduct." For James any failure of discrimination was sin. James also replaced Hawthorne's fanciful concern with the religious mythology of New England by a fanciful concern with history.

Very few studies have been addressed directly to Hawthorne's *and* James's morality, or to the ethical implications of their works. Yvor Winters' "Maule's Curse: Hawthorne and the Problem of Allegory," and his "Henry James and the Relation of Morals to Manners," *American Review*, 9 (September-October, 1937), 339-61, 482-503, are two separate articles with virtually no direct comparison drawn between the two authors. In "Maule's Curse," the only reference to James is when Winters remarks that Hawthorne could hardly create "human beings," and that "even the figures in *The Scarlet Letter* are profoundly unsatisfactory . . . for they draw their life not from specific and familiar human characteristics, as do the figures of Henry James, but from the precision and intensity with which they render their respective ideas" (355). In the second article, Hawthorne is referred to only at the very end, where Winters writes that James's "work partakes in a considerable measure of the allegorical character of the work of Hawthorne" (503). When this article was reprinted as "Maule's Well, or Henry James and the Relation of Morals to Manners," in *In Defense of Reason* (Denver: Allan Swallow, 1937), 300-16, the two sections which were added on (pp. 316-43) contained only two references to Hawthorne. While considering "the excessive subtlety" with which the characters in *The Awkward Age* scrutinize each other, Winters found that these characters "remind one—and James, since his plight for the moment is their own, likewise reminds one—of Hawthorne scrutinizing Dr. Grimshaw's spiders with insanse [sic] intensity, but with no illumination" (321). Winters also found it "difficult if not impossible" to grasp the differences between the Pendrels and the Midmores in *The Sense of the Past.* "James, like the characters in *The Awkward Age,* becomes so watchful for symptoms that he appears to become self-hypnotized; in this again he resembles the later Hawthorne" (324).

Quentin Anderson, in "Henry James and the New Jerusalem," *Kenyon Review,* 8 (Autumn, 1946), 515-66, sees James's moral commitment as influenced by his father's theology and psychology. In the last pages of his article (564-66), he turns to the "far greater moralist Hawthorne, for an illustration of . . . the consequences of James's morality." But his observations here are too constricted to be widely applicable. He examines the plot of "The Snow Image," a story which, "like the works of Henry James, is an account of the nature of human consciousness." The mother, Mrs. Lindsey, is conscious of man's inescapable limitations, but "she also knows that love cannot safely be denied." In James's morality, however, "the limitations are transcended." James hypostatized them as selfish materialism and spiritual love and made them characters, aspects of the apocalyptic union of God and human society. "To do this destroys the tragic ambivalence of the mother's awareness . . . of the human dilemma in which James had not the strength to rest." Ultimately, therefore, James was not a tragic novelist but a novelist of his father's theodicy.

Anderson further compares "My Kinsman, Major Molineux" with James's "moral physics." Robin, like James's heroes, moves "from a region of primal innocence to the city to seek his fortune." But he almost retreats, like James's characters, from the image of his self invoked by his commitment to life. Finally, however, he does stay in the earthly city. Anderson concludes that those "who hold fast to Hawthorne's sense of our limitations will not be tempted to take part in Henry James's 'marriage' of appearance and reality—a shotgun wedding in which the parties are constrained to love."

In *The American Henry James* (New Brunswick, New Jersey: Rutgers University Press, 1957), Anderson makes more observations on James's relation to Hawthorne. Some of these are reviewed in the fourth section of this essay, and others in the third essay. In chapter 5, "The Portrait Theme," Anderson considers the character of Sam Scrope in "Adina," the intaglio of incalculable worth he obtains from Angelo, and how the narrator's feeling that Sam's motive in cheating Angelo was a kind of jealousy of Italy prompts his subsequent actions. "His innocence blasted by Scrope's action," he writes, "Angelo comes, like Hawthorne's faun, to a knowledge of evil and a desire for revenge." But a more vivid issue in "Adina" is "the relation between those who can love, and therefore are proper begetters and possessors of art, and those who, like Sam Scrope or Gilbert Osmond, have no fount of life in them, and attempt to grasp what others have made." This in turn illustrates James's sense of the past, which "is far removed from Hawthorne's feeling that the evil men do lives after them," a view which implies "that we are not fully responsible, and denies the possibility of a great community of those who are conscious." The question in James is how to discover the evil in us and recognize it for what it is. The past cannot be feared of itself, for it is merely an index of our possibilities.

Adeline Tintner's "The Spoils of Henry James," *PLMA,* 61 (March, 1946), 239-51, is better retitled "The Museum World" in Leon Edel, ed., *Henry James: A Collection of Critical Essays* (Englewood Cliffs, New Jersey: Prentice-Hall, 1963), pp. 139-55. Tintner's subject, of course, is similar to Matthiessen's in "James and the Plastic Arts," *Kenyon Review,* Autumn 1943, pp. 533-50. Tintner explains that although *The Marble Faun* was the first American novel set in an environment of art, Hawthorne continually restricted "the action of the setting on his personal conflicts." Art was useful to him only when it allegorized the struggle of man's conscience. James, however, believed that works of art "give out a meaning proper to themselves." In his fiction "art is no longer symbolic of the fate of Christian man; it has become a collection of idols in a religion satisfying all human needs." Whereas Hilda realized that art "cannot comfort the heart of affliction," the hero of "Travelling Companions" believes that "in moments of doubt and depression I find it of excellent use to recall the great picture (Leonardo's *Last Supper*) with all possible distinctness." James's early characters give themselves to art with complete trust.

Alexander Cowie squeezes into two pages of *The Rise of the American Novel* (New York: American Book, 1948) many of the observations which have already been made on James's relation to Hawthorne. In chapter 8, "Nathaniel Hawthorne," he finds *The Marble Faun* very valuable as an interpretation of "the grandeur and enchantment of Rome." Although Howells and James later used Rome and Florence as settings for their narrratives, neither "ever wrote a single book which was so indissolubly linked with the Eternal City." Cowie also notes that by the time Hawthorne went to Europe, his native proclivities were so set that he remained a New Englander, and this was both an asset and a liability. At times he agreed with James "that New England's lack of certain types of tradition was a real handicap." But this enabled him to concentrate instead on "the ruins of human passion" and "the antiquity of the soul."

Cowie's enumeration of the aspects common in both Hawthorne and James is in chapter 16, "Henry James." "James had neither forerunners nor authentic imitators," he states, rather echoing T. S. Eliot. Other writers might stimulate him, but he was pupil to none. However, he had "a precursor, Hawthorne," whom he always found "a source of technical inspiration and even of ideas." But their relationship was not that of master and pupil; it was rather that of colleagues. Their themes, materials, and even modes of development were similar. They were both interested in "appearances," and James's prolonged emphasis on one phase of action also sometimes "suggests the 'tableaux' of Hawthorne." The perfect focus and economical use of slight substance in *The Scarlet Letter,* for example, "appealed to James's sense of form." Furthermore, both writers were attracted by "the spiritual domination of one character by another": in Hawthorne, Zenobia and Priscilla in *Blithedale*; in James, Kate Croy and Milly Theale in *The Wings of the Dove,* and Olive Chancellor and Verena Tarrant in *The Bostonians.* Their villains too, like Lionel Croy in *The Wings of the Dove* and Hollingsworth in *Blithedale,* resemble each other: "sinister men whose actions are all the more horrible for being set against an evil background never fully explored." "Hawthorne would have been fascinated by the vague but fearful grip of evil in 'The Turn of the Screw.'" Above all else, both writers subordinated the merely physical facts of their stories to the implications and inferences that could be drawn from those facts.

Later in the chapter, Cowie repeats that in *The Bostonians* the theme of the spiritual subjection of a malleable character (Verena) to the uses of a more aggressive one (Olive) would have endeared the work to Hawthorne. But he notes that whereas the ideas for James's stories usually came to him through reading or conversation, with Hawthorne this was rare; Hawthorne usually "started with an abstraction and sought an embodiment for it," a method which James also occasionally used. And both writers were not concerned with "gratifying a popular appetite for the crude facts of experience." In *What Maisie Knew,* for example, Beale and Ida Farange are divorced before the story opens. (Cowie might have added that in *The Scarlet Letter,* the adultery likewise occurs before the action of the story.) Lastly, Cowie finds that although James "was fundamentally a religious person," theology "interested him little, and those religio-philosophical questions that so absorbed Hawthorne . . . seem not to have agitated" him in the least.

Austin Warren's *Rage for Order* (Ann Arbor: University of Michigan Press, 1948), contains two rather odd observations. In chapter 6 on Hawthorne, he finds that the main weakness in *The Seven Gables* "is in its plot and in its narrative method," which "is almost that of a succession of tableaux. The characters do not really develop or change." Neither do they act on each other as James's do in *The Golden Bowl.* In most of his works, Hawthorne presents scenes of conversation—usually between two people—which are merely expository and do not advance the action. In chapter 9, "Henry James: Symbolic Imagery in the Later Novels," a revised version of "Myth and Dialect in the Later Novels," *Kenyon Review,* 5 (Autumn, 1943), 551-68, Warren praises the structure in James's later novels, and the relationship between his characters. James was very attentive to "defining" relationships, he writes. He specialized in "the relation between two. Hawthorne was

James's great predecessor in this study, especially in those masterly chapters of *The Scarlet Letter* describing Chillingworth's sadistic operations on Dimmesdale." But this contradicts Warren's earlier assertion that Hawthorne's characters do not act on each other. It seems more accurate to say that relationships in *both* Hawthorne and James are never static, although it is more widely true of James that a change in each one of his relationships "affects a corresponding change in another."

What is more appalling, even for 1943, is Warren's remark that unlike Hawthorne's, James's "people are not tempted by pride to isolate themselves from their fellows; even the shy protagonists are free from pride or inferiority: they reach out their hands to association." It is difficult to imagine Dr. Sloper (*Washington Square,* 1880), or John Marcher ("The Beast in the Jungle," 1903)–to mention only two–as characters who "reach out their hands to association." On the contrary; just as Dr. Rappaccini "cares infinitely more for science than for mankind," so does Dr. Sloper frequently refer to his "thirty years' medical practice," and the fine perceptions and great wisdom he possesses as "a distinguished physician."

In *The Great Tradition* (1948; reprinted Garden City, New York: Doubleday, 1954), F. R. Leavis notes that James's earliest work was influenced mainly by Hawthorne, as is apparent in his use of symbolism, which developed "into something that characterized his later work as a whole." In chapter 3 on James, he quotes the novelist's observation in chapter 5 of *Hawthorne* that "Hawthorne is perpetually looking for images which shall place themselves in picturesque correspondence with the spiritual facts with which he is concerned." Likewise, Leavis observes, James's own "concern with spiritual facts expresses itself not only in what obviously demands to be called symbolism, but in the handling of character, episode, dialogue, and in the totality of the plot." "The Jolly Corner," "The Figure in the Carpet," and "The Great Good Place" are all examples of his remarkable use of symbolism. "The more we consider James's early work (and his early work in relation to the later), the more important does Hawthorne's influence appear." Although not as interested in manners as James, Hawthorne devoted himself to "exploring profoundly moral and psychological interests in a poetic art of fiction." His approach to morals was psychological, and his influence on James must have countered Jane Austen's, "for whom moral interests [were] bound up with manners."

For James, writes F. W. Dupee in *Henry James* (1951; reprinted New York: William Morrow, 1974), Hawthorne was "the contemplative, retiring and only occasionally successful artist." Hawthorne remained for James "a benign paternal figure, very suggestive in all that he had accomplished, very challenging in all that he had left unaccomplished." Like Hawthorne, James "had a fervid sense of the past," appreciated "the changeless element in 'the human heart,'" and "experienced mingled feelings of pride and shame at being a man of imagination in a relentlessly practical society." He imitated Hawthorne's very subjects and tone, as is seen in "The Romance of Certain Old Clothes." Although he termed Hawthorne's disgust with nudity in sculpture a mark of provinciality, he himself had a "distaste for a literature of servants, prostitutes, and adventurers." It is also clear—as evidenced, for instance, by Isabel's fleeing from Goodwood's kiss in *The Portrait*—that with all his wider experience, he was "more Puritan—if not simply less human—than Hawthorne, for whom, in *The Scarlet Letter,* the color of adultery is also the color of life-blood and of roses." In most of James's novels "the process of becoming one's self excludes physical intimacy with others." Gilbert Osmond, however, shows by his independent richness of being how far James went beyond Hawthorne in portraying evil. Osmond makes Hawthorne's Judge Pyncheons and Chillingworths look "somewhat waxy."

In his "Introduction" to *The Ghostly Tales of Henry James* (New Brunswick, New Jersey: Rutgers University Press, 1948), pp. x-xii, Leon Edel tries to put in better perspective the views of those critics who have emphasized James's "saturation with Hawthorne's fantasies and allegories, [and] his admiration for such tales as *Rappacini's Daughter* [sic] and *Young Goodman Brown*." He points out that if James read Hawthorne closely, he also read Poe, translated Mérimée's *La Venus d'Ille,* was acquainted with Balzac's supernatural tales, knew Charles Dickens' ghost stories, was devoted to *Blackwood's* magazine, invoked E. T. A. Hoffmann, and his imagination was stirred by ancient houses "with their family histories, their muniment rooms."

Earl Roy Miner takes up the same topic in "Henry James's Metaphysical Romances," *Nineteenth Century Fiction,* 9 (June, 1954), 1-21. Miner terms many of James's stories not "ghostly tales" but "*metaphysical* romances," fruits of "a vast and varied tradition of supernatural literature" which goes as far back as Chaucer's time. He traces the development of this genre from the "ghostly thrillers" of the "sensation school," through Poe's use of supernatural elements to reveal character, to Hawthorne's moral romances which integrate even the ethical elements into supernatural fiction. As such, Miner observes, works like "Rappaccini's Daughter," "The Birthmark," and *The Scarlet Letter* all point forward to James, "because they deal with one of his great themes, the integrity and sanctity of human individuality and personality."

Miner's argument is that James was directly indebted to both Poe and Hawthorne. For James, fiction did not exist without thematic elements and ethical considerations. And although Hawthorne called himself a romancer and James a realist, the preface to *The Turn of the Screw* proves that in many stories James was concerned not with realism but with sustaining the illusion of romance. His distinction between "the real" and "the romantic" in the preface to *The American* also uses terms similar to Hawthorne's in the preface to *The Seven Gables.* Like Hawthorne, James believed that the "romancer must be true without being real," and one way he did this was through the use of the supernatural.

In his interpretation of *The Turn of the Screw,* Miner indicates that "the horror of the story lies not in the mere presence of the ghosts . . . nor in the governess' corrupting the children . . . but in the horror which we are made to feel with the governess as she finds out that the children who are apparently so . . . innocent, are corruption and depravity itself." In this "James owed a still larger debt to Hawthorne," for it was from Hawthorne that "he learned also that abnormal characters are satisfying in literature only when psychological and moral depravity go hand in hand . . . when moral values are expressed through motivation, in a suitable plot."

The various observations on Hawthorne and James in Randall Stewart's *American Literature and Christian Doctrine* (Baton Rouge: Louisiana State University Press, 1958) could be expanded into a separate essay. Stewart agrees with Matthiessen that Hawthorne, James, and T. S. Eliot form one tradition. They were all Puritans, and their life and work was heavily influenced by Puritanism. There is in all three "a vein of asceticism, of restraint, of discipline." They assume human imperfection and the long discipline necessary to human improvement, and they are all concerned with the nature and purpose of the human experience. In *The Scarlet Letter* and *The Ambassadors,* for example, the "authors believe that the grand aim of human experience is . . . 'thy dross to consume, thy gold to refine.'" Their works are, among other things, a criticism of the Puritan spirit, which they show sometimes as bigoted, narrow and repressive, as in "The Maypole of Merrymount." Lambert Strether too in *The Ambassadors* "is a product of a Puritan culture, and his limitations . . . reflect a Puritan asceticism" (17). But these authors are not anti-Puritan. "Their moral earnestness stamps them indelibly . . . with the Puritan stamp," and when their Puritan-Christian discipline merges with the classic, they may be called Christian humanists.

James, like Hawthorne and Melville, was furthermore concerned with "the loss of innocence, and the snares of a refined egotism." Many of his characters travel from America ("innocence") to Europe ("knowledge"). However, unlike Hawthorne's Goodman Brown, whose traumatic experience proves utterly blighting, Strether in *The Ambassadors* thrives and grows in grace and knowledge, in character and understanding, and becomes more humane. As for egotism, although Osmond in *The Portrait* does nothing as melodramatic as Elliston's cry in "Egotism; or, The Bosom Serpent": "It gnaws me! It gnaws me!", James, probably remembering Hawthorne's tale, "says of him, 'His egotism lay hidden like a serpent in a bank of flowers.' Osmond (like Aylmer in 'The Birthmark') tries to remake his young wife, Isabel, after his own notion of excellence." In "The Beast in the Jungle," James, again like Hawthorne, emphasizes the necessity of suffering.[8] James, Hawthorne, and Melville are all "'counter-romantics' because they recognize

Original Sin . . . show the conflict between good and evil . . . show man's struggle toward redemption . . . [and] dramatize the necessary role of suffering in the purification of the self. They do not apotheosize the self . . . but warn against its perversities. . . . They side with the orthodox, traditional Christian view of man and the world" (106). They were all dissatisfied with nineteenth-century romanticism, which inflated the individual. Hawthorne's stories illustrated the periods of "self-trust"; James's "dramatized the miseries of the overcultivated Ego."

Christof Wegelin's *The Image of Europe in Henry James* (Dallas: Southern Methodist University Press, 1958) is extremely well documented. Wegelin notes that even before James listed the items of high civilization absent from America, many other Americans had complained about the plain and scanty diet for the imagination in the New World (6). Cooper had done so in *Notions of the Americans;* so had Hawthorne in the preface to *The Marble Faun.* James had further incorporated something like a travesty of his list in "The Point of View." Like many Americans before him, James also had a strong sense of the past. But in him "the lingering past became part of a stream of time extending into the present and accounting for it," and only Hawthorne before him approached this kind of vision. Wegelin feels also that Bewley in *The Complex Fate* "mixes highly perceptive comment with rash generalizations," for although Hawthorne told James much about America, his influence was not exclusive; "James learned of the tradition of his native land through many channels besides the work of Hawthorne."

Wegelin next discusses Hawthorne's frequent use of "the fable of the American claim to an English estate": in *Our Old Home,* for instance, and in *Dr. Grimshawe's Secret.* But Hawthorne's deep and compulsive attachment to Europe was often checked by a morally charged aversion to hereditary aristocracy. His argument against England rested on "the contrast between the vitality which America derives from her freedom from the weight and ruin of tradition, and . . . the torpor of England's bondage to a dying past." In this, of course, he foreshadowed "James's similar contrast between the moral spontaneity of Americans and the carefully cultivated manners of Europeans." In *The Marble Faun,* it was partly through the American characters that Hawthorne expressed his sense of "the contrast between the bleak but morally unencumbered prosperity of America and the aesthetically rich but morally heavy atmosphere of a Rome haunted by the 'majestic and guilty shadows' of the past." However, Hawthorne's attitude toward Rome remained deeply ambivalent. If "James finally ceased to draw a clear line between aesthetic and moral values, Hawthorne's failure to integrate the aesthetic background with the moral story of his Italian novel suggests at least" that he was aware of the tension between them. Later in the text, Wegelin notes that the figure of the American claimant to an English estate in "A Passionate Pilgrim" symbolizes the same traditional home-feeling for

England which Hawthorne expressed in *Our Old Home* and in *Dr. Grimshawe's Secret.* He also comments on Hawthorne's and James's Puritan moral concern, and notes that James's romantic appreciation of the "historical color" of Europe reveals an awareness of "the dead hand of the past" which is similar to the moral overtones in Hawthorne's work. Like Hawthorne, James for many years felt that the spell of Italy was both an opportunity and a nuisance,[9] and in his early Italianate stories "the links between the scenic and the human aspects" permitted him "little more psychological realism than Hawthorne achieved in *The Marble Faun.*" The generic description of Conte Valerio in "The Last of the Valerii," for example, "indicates not so much what the Italian is like as how the American narrator first sees him—very much as Hawthorne had seen Donatello of his *Marble Faun.*" Lastly, Wegelin observes that James's later novels, "outgrowing the strict limits of realism," took on "the form, if not of 'romances' in the sense in which Hawthorne had used the term, yet of fables of the inner life which depend less on the multiplicity of external detail than the young aspirant to realism had felt desirable" (47).

In "The Rise of the International Novel," *PMLA,* 77 (June, 1962), 305-10, Wegelin suggests that the term *international fiction* should be reserved for those works which *dramatize* the contrasts between different social customs, political institutions, and the like. Hence, Cooper's historical romances of Europe, for example, or Melville's *Redburn* or *Israel Potter,* are not really "international." None of these or other such works reveal an awareness of what James called "the complex fate of being an American." Even in Hawthorne,

> the international element remains essentially apart from the action. In *The Marble Faun* (1860) Donatello's origins may go back to an arcadian Tuscany; Miriam's fate may be vaguely tied to her cosmopolitan background; Rome's dust may be blood-soaked; yet—as Hawthorne was the first to know—the novel has small concern with 'Italian manners and character.' Nor does the contrast between the American and the Italian or European way of judging conduct function dramatically. (306)

In *Dr. Grimshawe's Secret,* however, "the international plays a more essential role;" the story is "really *about* the American relation to Europe." But even here "the relation between the international element and the action is somewhat tenuous." In the international fiction of W. D. Howells, Edith Wharton, and especially James, however, "the contrast between Americans and Europeans is central, the action in their novels deals with social involvement." Thus, Wegelin concludes, one may agree with Oscar Cargill that *The American* is the first international novel ("The First International Novel," *PMLA,* September 1958, pp. 418-25), or, with some adjustment of one's definition, one may claim the title "for almost any of the novels which deal with Americans in Europe, even for *The Marble Faun*."

J. A. Ward's conclusion in "Henry James and the Nature of Evil," *Twentieth Century Literature,* 6 (July, 1960), 65-69, is that "James's fiction reflects, if not the synthesis, certainly the co-existence of a Puritan concern with evil and a Transcendental concern with experience." Ward finds that evil in James "is present at the basis of every human situation, and it is at least latent in the soul of every man." It is "manifest in its effects, not in its causes." A frequent motif in James's fiction is the pattern of the person who at first seems the victim emerging as the victimizer, the very source of evil. "It is this obscure and irrational quality in his sense of evil that links James . . . to the diarists of the Puritan theocracy . . . and to Hawthorne, many of whose characters were obsessed by their own guilt." Thus, the resemblance which James in chapter 1 of *Hawthorne* noted between his predecessor and the Puritans is equally true of his own fiction: "To him as to them, the consciousness of *sin* was the most important fact of life."

But Ward finds some important differences between the two writers. James tends to concentrate on the good man's reaction to evil, rather than on the guilty man's obsession with his own sin. His vision of evil more often resembles that of Hilda in *The Marble Faun,* "the innocent made aware of evil, than it resembles the concern of Miriam with her own guilt." Unlike Hawthorne, James has little interest in "the sinner's sense of morality or in his feeling of guilt after the sin." In *The Golden Bowl,* for example, Charlotte Stant and Prince Amerigo seem unconscious of their guilt; "the perpetrators of the evil cease their disruptive affair not because, like Arthur Dimmesdale . . . they are too burdened by conscience to continue, but simply because they are defeated by the strategy of Maggie Verver." Furthermore, evil in James is always a negation. His characters are never devoted to evil for its own sake; those who injure others do so through the pursuit of good. Neither does he "characterize pure egotism, as does Hawthorne; rather he delineates characters whose perception is limited." Occasionally he invests "a particular family or civilization with a pervasive miasma, suggestive of ineradicable evil." But unlike Hawthorne, who in *The Seven Gables* uses the house of Pyncheon to symbolize hereditary evil destroying each member of the family, James does not treat evil beyond the level of psychology. Even in *The American,* "hereditary evil operates merely as an inclination, not a compulsion, which can be rejected" by each of the Bellegardes. Ward also notes that the harmful domination of one person over another, which James called "omnivorous egotism," is his version of Hawthorne's "Unpardonable Sin." His conclusion, of course, is that although James altered "the traditional Puritan consideration of evil by focusing on the sinned-against rather than the sinner," he perhaps even more than Hawthorne reflected a Puritan disposition in his view of life as a kind of pilgrimage. His innocents are sent into the world "not simply to resist temptation but to encounter experience, to face evil, to suffer," and ultimately to achieve salvation.

In "Images of Value and the Sense of the Past," *New England Quarterly,* 35 (March, 1962), 3-26, Allen Guttmann indicates that the house was one of the dominant images of value in nineteenth-century America: "the house is the visible symbol of tradition, of permanence, of man's mastery of the primary environment, of civilization"; it contains, in James's phrase, "the sense of the past." James, of course, was distressed by America being a houseless land; thus, he "returned to England in search of a sense of the past."

Guttmann argues that the image of the house is used by both the writers who affirm and those who reject the values of society. In *The Seven Gables,* Hawthorne consciously manipulates the symbolism of the house to stand as a token of the Pyncheons' evil past. Holgrave wants to tear down the rotten past and have each generation build its own houses. But Hawthorne disagrees; Clifford realizes at the end of his train ride that he cannot flee from society or from the past, and he returns home. Holgrave too, surprisingly, suddenly converts, accepts the past, and suggests that houses should be built of stone, so as to give that impression of permanence essential to all happiness. But "Hawthorne was true to himself when he turned Holgrave from his radicalism. It was Hawthorne's conviction . . . that the human heart itself is the root of all evil. The past is wicked because men are wicked."

Guttmann observes next that James shared many of Hawthorne's concerns; in his work "we find the correlation of the house and the sense of the past." In *The Sense of the Past,* the old house in England which Ralph Pendrel inherits and returns to is "a piece of suggestive concrete antiquity." In *The Portrait,* Isabel Archer moves from an old house in Albany to Gardencourt and finally to Palazzo Roccanero. But, like the house in Albany, Osmond's villa is shut off from the world. Isabel "had ventured from the house in Albany only to return . . . to another house more restrictive"; she "moves in the end from nature to civilization, from a dreadful freedom to an endurable thralldom." "James agreed with Hawthorne. The plans for the Perfect House are . . . visionary." From the standpoint of the image of the house, Guttmann observes, "Hawthorne and James are conservatives in that they sought a sense of the past." Phoebe Pyncheon and Isabel Archer and Ralph Pendrel all *find* houses, and both the House of the Seven Gables and Gardencourt "affirm the possibility of permanence and the values of society." Guttmann's conclusion is that in the image of the house "the American writer seeks a reconciliation. The house is an artifact, but it is set . . . in the native landscape." Clifford "returned to his 'dreary' home because he remembered its garden and because he loved Phoebe. . . . Gardencourt, like the mansion in 'The Great Good Place,' is a country house. . . . Nature and Civilization *can* be reconciled."

"Images of Value and the Sense of the Past" is less disappointing if read as a general rather than a specialized or rigorously thought out critical essay. Guttmann also tends to wander from literature into sociology. Richard Gill's achievement is much higher in *Happy Rural Seat* (1972), which is reviewed later in this essay.

The observations on the James-Hawthorne relationship in Earl Rovit's "James and Emerson: The Lesson of the Master," *American Scholar,* 33 (1964), 434-40, are not different from those made earlier by Buitenhuis (1959) and Quentin Anderson (1962). Rovit argues that James's greatest spiritual indebtedness was to Emerson, "the master whom he failed to acknowledge until very late in his career." James's criticism of Emerson was just as ambivalent as his criticism of Hawthorne. Although in *Hawthorne* he approved certain aspects of Hawthorne's work, he withheld the praise of total artistic success. The "writing on Hawthorne exhibits the same curious evasiveness as the writing on Emerson. The words 'charming' and 'fancy' recur monotonously, especially in places where one would want a specific, unambiguous statement." Obviously James greatly admired and respected both men, but he patronized and disparaged them as artists.

In the 1890's, however, James revised many of his judgements. The later James is much less arrogant and much more *aware,* and he "has the confidence to pursue precisely those deficienceies in form for which he criticized Hawthorne. The characters of the later fictions–the John Marchers, Milly Theales, Maggie Ververs, Spencer Brydons–are clearly *figures* rather than persons. And the thematic constructs of these fictions . . . move inexorably into allegorical range"; allegory is no longer "one of the lighter exercises of the imagination." This new direction leads both to a new concept of art and to "a willing acceptance of Hawthorne's and Emerson's as well." The main point James expounds in his letter to the Hawthorne Centenary (*see* the first essay) is Hawthorne's ability to develop *as a human being.* Hawthorne, James writes, "*had* developed from within–as to feeling, as to form, as to sincerity and character." This, says Rovit, is James's new understanding of the function of art. "*Form* is achieved when the artist comes to 'free possession of himself.'" Paradoxically, it is during these years that James found "Hawthorne and Emerson deficient as artists because they seemed so successful as human beings." He was caught once again "in the prison of his American dilemma": he believed that "Americans are inferior artists if they are successful human beings."[10]

The writers Joel Porte considers in *The Romance in America* (Middletown, Connecticut: Wesleyan University Press, 1969) are Cooper, Poe, Hawthorne, Melville, and James. Most of his few comments on the James-Hawthorne relation are not new. He calls Coverdale's statement in chapter 5 of *Blithedale,* that Hollingsworth glared at his companions "from the thick shrubbery of his meditations, like a tiger out of a jungle," "a startling figure that clearly looks forward to Henry James" (Porte, p. 128). As indicated in the fourth essay, this observation was previously made by Lucke (1953) and Monteiro (1962). On James's comment in chapter 3 of *Hawthorne,* that the "fine thing in Hawthorne is that he cared for the deeper psychology," Porte says that in a sense this can be seen as Hawthorne's Jamesian concern with form—all one has to do is substitute "art" for "psychology." He also notes that the preface to *The American* parallels that to *The Marble Faun.* His conclusion is that if "the great lesson James learned was that his true subject lay in the geographically unlocatable realm between society (or nature) and the responding consciousness . . . he had as much to learn from Melville or Hawthorne as from George Eliot" (229). Porte's comments on *The Marble Faun* and *The Golden Bowl* are considered in the fifth essay.

John Tytell in "Henry James and the Romance," *Markham Review,* 5 (May, 1969), 1-2, first discusses Poe's and Hawthorne's "two different conceptions of the romance." These two writers, he says, "proved formative literary influences on [James's] idea of romance." Tytell uses "De Grey: A Romance" to define "James's own conception of romance as a form," and to point out "the effect of his realistic tendencies on the romance form." He finds that James's "method is not as symbolic as Hawthorne's." But the main problem with the story is that the author "waits for the final part of his story to establish his mood," whereas in Poe's and Hawthorne's stories romance "succeeded as the mood was sustained, filtered and woven throughout the tale. James, instead, melodramatically exaggerates certain moments in the late stages of the story, and the result is a gothic departure from romance as Hawthorne had envisaged it." And the "signs of the confusion in the disjointed ending of 'De Grey' recur in the melodramatic moments of *Roderick Hudson, The American,* and *Washington Square.*" In many ways, James's "understanding of the potential of romance was in advance of his actual practice," as several comments in his early criticism show. Hawthorne would undoubtedly have subscribed to many of these comments. In his own development of the romance form, James progressively substituted action for mood, and this became a crucial step in his progress towards realism. "James deserves special recognition as an exponent of realism," Tytell concludes, and "De Grey" is an important example of how he assimilated the lessons of Poe and Hawthorne and then veered off in his own direction.

For one who insists so frequently on the French influence on James, Leon Edel finds "a touch of Hawthorne" in surprisingly many of James's works. Edel's comments in *Henry James,* 5 volumes (New York: J. B. Lippincott Co., 1953-72) are all reviewed below. In volume I, *The Untried Years, 1843-1870* (1953), Edel observes that those "critics who suggest that Henry's feelings for things American . . . were derived from Hawthorne have . . . assumed that books played a greater role in his life than the use of his eyes and ears and imagination." And if he "submitted to the *Atlantic* two rather

Hawthorne-like tales . . . it was to meet Howells's preferences at this time for the romance and not necessarily because he had himself fallen under" Hawthorne's influence.[11] In volume II, *The Conquest of London, 1870-1881* (1962), Edel notes that in "The Last of the Valerii," "a Roman count, a kind of sleepy, well-fed Donatello, marries a young American girl. In the ground of Valerio Villa, a statue is disinterred, much in the manner in which Hawthorne describes the digging up of a Venus, or as Merimee recounts a similar occurrence" in "La Venus d'Ille" (II, 102). However, if "the tale is thus an amalgam of Hawthorne and Merimee, its denouement is pure James."[12] According to Edel, "Benvolio" was James's "sole venture" into the allegorical form,

> since he considered allegorical writing unworthy of the realist in Fiction. . . . The tale was frankly like one of Hawthorne's allegories, and the old philosopher and his daughter in it might have been Rappaccini and Beatrice; only there was no evil in the Jamesian garden and there is none in the tale. Perhaps Henry James, finding himself plying his trade on American soil, felt that he had to fire some salute to his predecessor. "Benvolio" was a modest salute indeed, and its allegory has in it less of the universal than of the autobiographical. (II, 190)

Edel also notes that in enumerating the items of high civilization absent from Hawthorne's America, James in chapter 2 of *Hawthorne* "had taken his cue from Hawthorne himself" (preface to *The Marble Faun*). Actually, "James was also echoing the very cadences of still another" predecessor, Cooper in *Notes of the Americans.*

In volume III, *The Middle Years, 1882-1895* (1962), Edel comments on the accusations by various people that James in *The Bostonians* had lampooned Elizabeth Peabody, Hawthorne's sister-in-law. Although James "pleaded not guilty," Edel says, there is a "close relationship" between the names Peabody and Birdseye. "A 'bird's eye' is indeed a 'pea-body.' Henry James had perhaps imitated life more than he himself allowed." Edel suggests also that in the title character of *The Aspern Papers,* "James evokes himself as he was, and as he would have liked to be—a kind of Hawthorne figure liberated from the parochial and from all Puritan constriction." In volume IV, *The Treacherous Years, 1895-1901* (1969), Edel observes, while discussing "The Great Good Place," that the great good place was a very old fantasy of Henry James's. In *Roderick Hudson*

> he had depicted a similar place, near Fiesole, where Rowland Mallet finds peace within a cool cloister, and lays his hand on the arm of a Brother to whom he speaks of the temptations of the devil. James had always been fascinated by the moment in Hawthorne's *Marble Faun* when Hilda . . . filled with the horror of the crime she has

> accidentally witnessed, goes to confession—though a Protestant—to ease herself of her burden. In a monastery the world's burdens drop away; this had indeed been the theme of . . . *Guy Domville*. . . . The craving for a great good place and the touch of a Brother's hand had existed for years. (IV, 241)

Edel's other comments on *The Marble Faun* and *Roderick Hudson* are discussed in the fifth essay.

In volume V, *The Master, 1901-1916* (1972), Edel points out that James "had been saturated with Shakespeare from his earliest days." He had treated the subject of Shakespeare's home in "The Birthplace," and written an introduction to *The Tempest.* He knew Shakespeare's grave well, "and he knew by heart the cryptic doggerel he invoked bespeaking the curse on anyone who would disturb Shakespeare's bones." Hawthorne too "had visited the Birthplace and described it in a touching essay." The unidentified essay by Hawthorne which Edel refers to and quotes from is "Recollections of a Gifted Woman," *Atlantic Monthly,* 11 (January, 1863), 43-58; reprinted in *Our Old Home* (1863; reprinted 1970), pp. 90-119. Part of the essay is quoted below:

> I should consider it unfair to quit Shakspere's house without the frank acknowledgement that I was conscious of not the slightest emotion while viewing it, nor any quickening of the imagination. This has often happened to me in my visits to memorable places. . . . It is pleasant, nevertheless, to think that I have seen the place; and I believe that I can form a more sensible and vivid idea of Shakspere as a flesh-and-blood individual now that I have stood on the kitchen-hearth and in the birth-chamber; but I am not quite certain that this power of realization is altogether desirable in reference to a great poet. The Shakspere whom I met there took various guises, but had not his laurel on. . . . But I draw a moral from these unworthy reminiscences and this embodiment of the poet, as suggested by some of the grimy actualities of his life. It is for the high interests of the world not to insist upon finding out that its greatest men are . . . very much the same kind of men as the rest of us . . . because a common mind cannot properly digest such a discovery, nor ever know . . . how small a part of him it was that touched our muddy or dusty earth. . . . When Shakspere invoked a curse on the man who should stir his bones, he perhaps meant the larger share of it for him or them who should pry into his perishing earthliness, the defects or even the merits of the character that he wore in Stratford, when he had left mankind so much to muse upon that was imperishable and divine. (*Our Old Home,* pp. 99-100)

One "suspects that Henry James," Edel continues, "knowing this essay, must have very early accepted Hawthorne's view, so close was it to his own" (Edel, V, 147). As Edel later points out, James also went in quest of Hawthorne's birthplace; James's comments on Salem, the Old Manse, and the House of the Seven Gables (*The American Scene,* 1907) were given in the first essay.

Mention has already been made of Allen Guttmann's "Images of Value and the Sense of the Past" (*New England Quarterly,* March 1962, pp. 3-26). In "The Houses that James Built," *Texas Quarterly,* 1 (Winter, 1958), 176-96, R. W. Stallman writes on how James's reading of *The Marble Faun* affected the composition of *The American* and *The Portrait*; in "Life in a Picture Gallery," *Texas Studies in Literature and Language,* 11 (1969), 761-77, Jay Bochner writes on "things" in *The Portrait* and *The Marble Faun.* Stallman's and Bochner's articles are both reviewed in the fifth essay.

In *Happy Rural Seat: The English Country House and the Literary Imagination* (New Haven, Connecticut: Yale University Press, 1972), Richard Gill does not focus on any specific works by the two authors; his remarks on Hawthorne's influence on James are general in nature. In chapter 1, pp. 19-93, and in appendix B, pp. 253-59, he indicates that James's numerous country houses—Gardencourt, Medley, Poynton, Mellows, Fawns, and many others—"have an unmistakable symbolic resonance": they are all "a symbol . . . of the 'great good place.'" The country house allowed James's imagination to fuse "the historical and the personal, the traditional and the visionary," and he used it to dramatize his recurring themes of withdrawal from society and return to it, "retreat and counterattack," isolation and community. In this he was influenced by such writers as Richardson, Fielding, Jane Austen, George Eliot, Dickens, and, of course, Hawthorne, who was undoubtedly the "primary influence." It "seems but a short step from the ancestral dwelling" in *The Seven Gables* "to the symbolic residences of James." In reading Hawthorne, James discovered "a general notion of symbolism that he could adopt to his own fictional purposes." When analyzing the symbolism in *The Scarlet Letter,* he noted that "Hawthorne is perpetually looking for images which shall place themselves in picturesque correspondence with the spiritual facts with which he is concerned" (*Hawthorne,* chapter 5). Such terms as "image" and "correspondence" show that James had discovered in *The Scarlet Letter* "a symbolic method he would practice in the future. . . . Finding in Hawthorne's symbolism the rationale for his own treatment of the country house as an image that 'corresponded' with the spiritual and social facts that engaged him, James must also have taken the old mansion in *The House of the Seven Gables* as one of his models." Furthermore, "some of the motifs that attend the house symbol in James might also be traced to Hawthorne's influence. The garden imagery . . . may have its source in the Pyncheon garden, whose Edenic attributes Hawthorne elaborately describes in chapter 10 of *The House of the Seven Gables.*" The device of the portrait in *The Sense of the Past* may also have been suggested by Colonel Pyncheon's portrait.[13] However, one must remember that "mysterious portraits play their part in the Gothic fiction with which James was also highly familiar." Hawthorne too, of course, exploited such Gothic devices as haunted castles and lugubrious mansions, and James might as readily have been influenced by Hawthorne in the use of these props and motifs as by Walpole, Poe, and the whole "school of horrors."

The last part of John McElroy's "The Hawthorne Style of American Fiction," *Emerson Society Quarterly,* NS 19 (2nd quarter, 1973), 117-23, contrasts the Hawthorne school of American fiction with that of Poe:

> In Hawthorne and Poe, two schools of American writing originate. Poe was seemingly more original than Hawthorne because Hawthorne's fiction has obvious American connections with Irving and Cooper and because Poe made such a point of his originality in some of his essays. The followers of Poe–Clemens and Hemingway–were also fond of presenting themselves as "originals." James and Faulkner–Hawthorne's followers–were less chary of acknowledging their master. . . .
>
> Writers of the Hawthorne school are strongly conscious of native place and strongly ambivalent toward it; they are deeply conscious of a native social tradition of "history"; and they repeatedly invoke the past, which they consider more heroic . . . than the present though not necessarily better than the future can be. For Hawthorne, James, and Faulkner, geography is a vital part of history, but James, like Cooper, conceived of an historical continuum entirely in physical terms. The past for James is, generally, "Europe," or rather an idea of Europe that can be traced to his twin assumptions that America had no culture . . . and that culture is inexorably a function of a great deal of time. Hawthorne too felt this lack of history in the New World and bemoaned the unsettled condition of America. He compensated for the lack of a past by frequent evocations of "Eden," a most ancient, human time-place which could have certain applications to America.
>
> The chief bequest of Hawthorne to James and Faulkner was the invention of retroaction, or the style of fiction which progresses by discovering what has gone before. . . . It was rather a necessity for Hawthorne . . . to conceive some sort of special rhetorical strategy to compensate for the thinness of subject in America. The rhetoric of retrospection magnifies the importance of trivial historical and social subject-matter, and for Hawthorne's disciples trivia continued to be quite usable subject-matter. (121-22)

Thus James evolved *The Ambassadors* from a platitude reported to him by Jonathan Sturges (*Notebooks,* pp. 225-28). McElroy is amused to find in chapter 2 of *Hawthorne* James wondering why Hawthorne recorded in his notebook "such a tiny affair as a dog chasing his own tail, when page after page of James' own writing contains nothing so lively as that."

"In the fiction of Hawthorne, James, and Faulkner alike," McElroy continues, there is more "explanation" than "action," whereas Poe, Clemens, and Hemingway "have little to say about the past and write stories that brim with action." The theme of *A Connecticut Yankee,* for example, "is the meaninglessness of human history, a statement quite antithetical to the imagination revealed in *The House of the Seven Gables, The Ambassadors,* or *Absalom, Absalom*!" Furthermore, "Hawthorne's romances typically start from a description of a place," its history, and its people, whereas Poe "typically writes in the first person about some private experience that is not contained in history or society nor locatable geographically." And Poe makes the individual supreme and self-sufficient. It is in his school that the theme of the individual against society, or, better stated, "freedom from society for the individual," flourishes. "In the Hawthorne school, one finds the quite different theme of the 'individual in society.' . . . In this view, self-sufficiency has no virtue. The unbreakable force of history and society must be acknowledged and tragically experienced."[14]

General Dissertations

Of the twenty-three Ph.D. dissertations reviewed in this study, ten have discussed some general aspect of the relation between James and Hawthorne. One of the most original of these is Frederick J. Masback's "The Child Character in Hawthorne and James" (Syracuse, 1960). Masback suggests that Hawthorne's and James's use of the child character—that is, a boy or girl before puberty—is the one fictional device which furnishes a key to their entire relationship. Hawthorne was the first major American author to make the child an important plot and thematic element, and James inherited this serious conception of the child character. Their interest was in the child's situation in the adult world rather than in the child's world as a separate realm. Hawthorne often presents a confrontation between adult materialism and other kinds of illusions—a result of "knowledge" and "experience"—and childhood idealism. In James, however, the confrontation results in something more complicated than "a simple choice between unquestioned innocence and unmistakable evil." His innocent children are usually morally neutral rather than positively good, and they are often subject to the pressures of adults of opposing views who try to possess them. Hawthorne, who was forever concerned with the unpardonable sin of violating another's personality, surprisngly neglected this theme of the adult's drive to possess the child. Furthermore, whereas Hawthorne's children often seem to be independent of society, James attaches his children to some adult, usually for economic support. And although both authors portray children who die as a result of their contact with the world, Hawthorne also tries to suggest that the child is both a victim and a savior. In most of James's works, however, the adults are unaffected by the child's death. (Masback, pp. 2-8)

According to Masback, Hawthorne created only one corrupt child, Ilbrahim's fiend-friend in "The Gentle Boy," and he did not indicate how the child became corrupt. James, however, does specify: in "Grenville Fane," for example, or in "Master Eustace." James also provided a more convincing case of a child's corruption in *The Turn of the Screw* (Flora). Masback terms Pearl and Maisie Hawthorne's and James's main examples of "the painful progress from innocence to virtue," and Nora Lambert in *Watch and Ward* James's only other child to make a successful although unconvincing "transition." Many of James's children, he observes, are destroyed by "knowledge," while Hawthorne's are made "stronger and wiser, more able to cope with the world" (10).

Both Hawthorne and James, Masback continues, presented the child's moral world as "a microcosm of the adult's moral world." Furthermore, both authors discovered in the child character a symbol which could unite "their deepest personal concern, the alienation of the artist, with their most urgent artistic theme, the growth of moral consciousness." Both the child and the artist become alienated because of their moral consciousness and society's inability to understand or accept them. For both the child and the artist, "the gift of vision must be accompanied by isolation from society" (15).

Masback next considers the statue of the child with the dove and the snake in *The Marble Faun,* a statue which symbolizes the struggle between God and the devil for the integrity of man's soul. Hawthorne started early to dramatize "the reaction which occurs when pure innocence is suddenly thrown into an evil world." There are many children in his works, and such "child-like" men as Dimmesdale, Coverdale, Clifford, Owen Warland, Donatello, and Septimus Felton. There are also "child-like women" like Phoebe, Priscilla, and Hilda. Hawthorne always yearned for the comfort and security of childhood, and he always admired child-like innocence. (16-30)

The rest of the section on Hawthorne is taken up mainly by an elaboration of the above observations. Masbeck details the situation of Ilbrahim's fiend-friend and notes how, in comparing Catherine's and Dorothy's fitness to bring up Ilbrahim, Hawthorne skirted a situation which James frequently treated: "that of two persons representing opposite moralities . . . attempting to gain control over a child." And while James often allowed the child to choose between the alternatives, Hawthorne always let the adults do the deciding. Hawthorne never recognized the connection between this situation and his favorite theme of the violation of personality. The closest he came to it was in the relationship between Dr. Grimshawe and Ned. Hawthorne held the child's personality as sacred, and "considered the parent-child relationship . . . as almost devine" (45).

As for the symbolic relationship between the child and the artist, Masback indicates that "The Snow Image" is Hawthorne's "only important use of the child as an artist in his work." Masback further notes that in his last years Hawthorne tried some new techniques such as "using the child as a point-of-view character," a possibility which enthralled James in *What Maisie Knew*. But even in *Dr. Grimshawe's Secret* this technique is not fully developed. And in *The Dolliver Romance*, Pansie shows how Hawthorne "treasured the idea of the superior moral insight of the child from the beginning to the end of his career." Masback's comments on *The Scarlet Letter* and *What Maisie Knew* and on *The Marble Faun* and *Roderick Hudson* are considered in the third and fifth essays respectively.

In the section on James, pp. 151-280, Masback indicates that James's child characters seem "less realistically observed than Hawthorne's." For various reasons, James always found it difficult to communicate with or understand children, and this sharply contrasts with "the close rapport and understanding which always existed between Hawthorne and most children." But James's children are probably "psychologically more valid and fictionally more dramatic" than Hawthorne's, since they are rarely faced with an abstract choice between good and evil, but have to choose between "adults who represent varying moral positions." And while evil in Hawthorne is usually an obvious outside threat, which his children easily reject or overcome, in James the "evil" person usually has as much claim upon the child as the "good" person. James also found death a satisfactory way of culminating his children's history. Most of his children are destroyed by their inability to withstand the pressures of the adult world, whereas Hawthorne's children usually emerge from their "encounters" with a "tough shell of virtue over the original soft core of innocence." Hawthorne abandoned early the motif of death.

Masback discovers "some typical Hawthornean elements" in many of James's early works. He finds "My Friend Bingham" slightly resembling "The Gentle Boy" and "Roger Malvin's Burial," and calls Nora in *Watch and Ward* "a typical Hawthorne sunshine girl." James's description of her as "a vague spot of light on a dark background" recalls Hawthorne's description of Pearl. But James advanced beyond Hawthorne's idea of the "spirit-child." Whereas Pearl, for example, is presented as partially human and partially spirit-child, James's children are always "created of, by, and for this earth." But the final achievement of these earthly children is usually gauged in spiritual terms, whereas the spiritual mission of Hawthorne's children is often measured in human terms. Masback points out also that the fates of Morgan Moreen in "The Pupil" and Dulcino Ambient in "The Author of Beltraffio" parallel Ilbrahim's fate in "The Gentle Boy," and that in *The Other House* Jean Martle commits the worst crime for both Hawthorne and James: she tries to destroy Effie Bream's personality. The governess in *The Turn of the Screw* too commits Hawthorne's "Unpardonable Sin" when she tries to "possess" Miles and Flora. In the section on Hawthorne, Masback had noted that except for *The Scarlet Letter* and "The Great Stone Face," the mother-figure in most of Hawthorne's fiction is overshadowed or eliminated by the father-figure (pp. 97-106). James, Masback now finds, progressively eliminated *both* parents as a factor in the child's development (226). In "The Author of Beltraffio" (1884), both parents are alive; in *The Other House* (1896), only one parent is alive; in *The Turn of the Screw* (1898), both parents are dead.

Masback's last chapter, "Two Roads Diverge," pp. 281-87, restates many of the above observations. Masback explains that whereas Hawthorne provides most of his children with "a kind of intuitive knowledge and spiritual insight as part of their birthright," James's children develop these qualitites through observation and experience. Masback suggests a biographical explanation as to why Hawthorne's children seem created to show the triumph of innocence over iniquity, while James's seem to show the very opposite. Although both men were essentially introverted, Hawthorne succeeded more than James in overcoming this impulse. He raised a family and even had a political career. James's interests, on the other hand, were mostly literary. Thus, his lack of external commitment is reflected in his child characters, just as Hawthorne's own achievements as a man and artist parallel his child characters' successful "transition from the secluded innocence of childhood to the practical demands of the adult world."

Except for the direct connections between the child character and the artist, Masback's remarks on the relation of the artist to society add nothing new to Baxter's (1955) and Fussell's (1958) findings which are reviewed in the section on "The Artist and Society." Both Hawthorne and James, Masback explains, recognized that some alienation from society was necessary for the artist. But Hawthorne realized that this tendency could become the artist's greatest vice, while for James it was always the artist's greatest virtue. Hawthorne's artists and child characters start with a vision of the beautiful so superior to society's that they are tempted to isolate themselves from other people. Many of his artists do exactly this, perhaps because he felt the artist could not maintain his vision if he remained in contact with the masses. His dilemma was resolved by the child character, who does not need to give up his vision in order to establish contact with the world. James's artists and child characters, on the other hand, gain their vision gradually. As they get more deeply involved in life, they slowly realize that such an involvement destroys the freedom they need to maintain their insight. They thus adopt a pattern of renunciation, preferring spiritual independence to material rewards. His children usually give up their lives in order to maintain their integrity. This is the ultimate distinction between the two authors' child characters: Hawthorne's "wage and win their battle to join and strengthen the chain of humanity"; James's, "very much entangled in the chains of humanity, seek a spiritual release even if it means death."

One should mention an earlier observation by Matthiessen which contradicts Masback's general thesis, and which could modify the development of some of his arguments. After considering the case of Ilbrahim in "The Gentle Boy" and how the baby-fiends, including his invalid friend, pelted him with stones, Matthiessen concluded that Hawthorne was "far removed . . . from any of the transcendental variants of the romantic belief in the unspoiled innocence of children. His discernment may have opened a door for James, leading to *The Turn of the Screw;* for Hawthorne did not draw back from depicting the extremes of natural depravity" (*American Renaissance,* 1941, p. 217).

James Robert Bashore, Jr., divides his 709-page dissertation, "The Villains in the Major Works of Nathaniel Hawthorne and Henry James," 2 volumes (University of Wisconsin, 1959), into three parts. The first part (247 pp.) is mostly on Hawthorne; the second part (413 pp.) is on James; the last part (28 pp.) is on both authors.

What Bashore lacks is selectivity. Like Raymond A. Miller, Jr., who proposes to consider "Representative Tragic Heroines" in the works of five American authors, and then devotes considerable space to various women characters only to conclude that they are *not* tragic heroines (*see* the section on "Feminist Perspectives"), Bashore discusses virtually all the fiction of Hawthorne and James, so that the word "major" in his title becomes an anomaly. His basic assumption is that the villains of both writers are particularized ethical and aesthetic formulations of the struggle between "good" and "evil" forces. He also suggests that if these writers are representative of their times, their villains should be "reflections of changing cultural attitudes toward the problem of evil."

Both Hawthorne and James, Bashore observes, were influenced by Christian ideology. Although Hawthorne criticized Puritanism, the solidarity of its system appealed to him. For him the world was dual, both good and evil. One of his major notions of sin involved the isolation of man from man, and his fiction often works toward a solution wherein the individual expiates his sin by coming to terms with society. However, his villains in general seem much stronger than his good characters. Bashore's long list of Hawthorne's villains includes Butler in *Fanshawe,* who is "a failure" as a villain "because he is not sufficiently motivated"; Wakefield, who "is *not* a major villain"; the Rev. Mr. Hooper, Aylmer, Rappaccini, Giovanni, Dimmesdale, and Hollingsworth.

He also notes that although Hawthorne seems to believe that scientific knowledge encourages "prideful tendencies," he "does not insist that pride develops *because* of science." Bashore indicates further that in *The Marble Faun,* Hawthorne's contrasting themes of "innocence and evil, the new and the old, the temporal and the timeless, life and death, will and emotion, art and actuality, America and Europe," all suggest James. However, the villains of Hawthorne's "last phase" "tend to be criminals rather than sinners": one might say that the later Hawthorne "shifted from *sin* to *crime,* from inner evil to outer guilt." Bashore's conclusion is that "Hawthorne rapidly moved from the conventional gothic villain to one placed in the contexture of New England legend and history"; "from the villain of convention toward the 'psychological' villain who is 'sinful,' introspective, and yet conscious of his social responsibility."

Most of the direct connections between Hawthorne and James are in volume II. Bashore suggests that James is best approached "from the 'artistic' path" first, just as Hawthorne is best approached from the "moral" first. Like Hawthorne, James sought "a 'counterpoise' of mind and heart in his characters"; like Hawthorne, he created many innocent men, women, and children: Maisie, for example, "is a lineal descendant of Pearl." However, although several "good" people die in both Hawthorne and James, there is little indication in Hawthorne "that in such deaths those left alive will benefit." Beatrice Rappaccini dies needlessly, whereas Daisy Miller's and Milly Theale's deaths bring about some good.[15] And whereas in Hawthorne it is usually the villains who isolate themselves, in James it is the good people who live in isolation. The dilemma a Jamesian hero faces is "how to become detached [in order to know himself] and still gain knowledge which must be acquired through social experience." It is thus not surprising that Hawthorne's themes of egotism and selfishness were James's too.

Bashore finds many parallels between Hawthorne's and James's works and attitudes. But his string of isolated observations produces no unified impression; rather, it seems that whenever he finds a theme shared by both novelists, or an aspect which James handles like Hawthorne, or differently from Hawthorne, he mentions the fact, often without trying to suggest why such is the case. Even part 3 of his dissertation, which specifically compares and contrasts the two authors, does not add up to a coherent whole. Rarely are the various observations used to reveal something beyond themselves.

Hawthorne and James, Bashore explains, "hold similar attitudes toward a God and toward Catholicism."[16] Unlike Hawthorne, however, James does not employ Biblical images or refer to writers of religious significance such as Bunyan. Neither does he handle evil in the same way Hawthorne does. Bashore pairs many of James's early stories with Hawthorne's works: "Poor Richard" with *Fanshawe* (Richard Clare and Butler, "Crawford's Consistency" with "Lady Eleanore's Mantle" (Elizabeth Ingram and Lady Eleanore),

"Professor Fargo" with *Blithedale* (Miss Gifford and Priscilla, Prof. Fargo and Prof. Westervelt; hypnotism),[17] "A Problem" with "Roger Malvin's Burial" (David and Reuben), "The Ghostly Rental" with "Roger Malvin's Burial" (religious attitudes in general, confession scenes in particular), "The Story of a Masterpiece" with "The Prophetic Pictures" and *The Seven Gables* (use of the portrait), "A Passionate Pilgrim" with *Septimus Felton* and *Dr. Grimshaw's Secret* (British-American relations), "Master Eustace" with "The Bridal Knell," and "De Grey: A Romance" with "The Threefold Destiny." He points out also that "Osborne's Revenge" presents the Hawthornesque theme of initiation.

One of James's few stories whose Hawthornesque elements he considers at some length is "Adina" (II, 115-19), which he says was influenced by *The Marble Faun.* He finds parallels between Sam Scrope and the Spectre of the Catacombs, and between Angelo and Donatello. Both works also share "the innocence-fall theme," and James's story too has frequent "references to 'the Capuchin convent at the edge of the Alban Lake.'" However, the denouement of "Adina" is different from that of *The Marble Faun.* The relatively easy deposition of evil in "Adina" "suggests the general weakness of James's stories which use the 'charm' device." The evil in these stories does not reside in character but in *things.* James's sense of evil, while it partook of Hawthorne's sense, was modified and sometimes almost negated "by an aesthetic sense of *things* as reflectors of personalitites." Sam Scrope's "illgotten intaglio reflects the worst part of his nature and thereby becomes, itself, a kind of curse; when the curse is broken, Scrope's personality returns . . . to its more usual equilibrium." James is here tempted "to let the symbol of evil become *per se* the only evil, thus neutralizing the central responsibility of character which Hawthorne felt so strongly."

One wishes Bashore had analyzed those of James's novels he sees as Hawthornesque in the same way as he analyzes "Adina." He has not done so. Most of the correspondences he draws between James's longer works and Hawthorne's fiction are cluttered with minute, insignificant details. For example, he notes that when Isabel Archer in *The Portrait* becomes acquainted with evil, she undergoes a Hawthornesque change similar to that undergone by Goodman Brown and Hester Prynne. "As Young Goodman Brown dashed through the forest in a frenzy of grief and exultation at seeing the evil in the world," he writes, so Isabel develops some violent impulses, and moves and speaks faster after her marriage. And,

> as knowledge of sin leads Hester to flaunt the Scarlet Letter, so Isabel affects "a kind of amplitude and brilliance in her personal arrangements which gave a touch of insolence to her beauty." And as Hawthorne remarks that the arch-fiend is not more terrible than

> a human being so frenzied as Goodman Brown, so Ralph . . . sees that "The free, keen girl has become quite another person."

Bashore goes on to note, in the same vein, the traits Osmond shares with Chillingworth and with Aylmer in "The Birthmark." Very little illumination, it seems, is added to these works by correlating them so. Bashore also explains that *Roderick Hudson* is "generically related to Hawthorne by virtue of its innocence-experience motif," and that in *The Bostonians* the "[Selah] Tarrant-Verena-Olive-Basil combination automatically suggests Hawthorne's Westervelt-Priscilla-Zenobia-Hollingsworth." He further compares Verena and Milly Theale (*The Wings of the Dove*) with Hilda in *The Marble Faun;* characterization and villainy in *The American* with the same in *The Seven Gables,* "The Grey Champion," and "Rappaccini's Daughter"; *The Turn of the Screw* with *The Marble Faun,* "Rappaccini's Daughter," and *The Scarlet Letter;* and *The Golden Bowl* with "Lady Eleanore's Mantle."[18]

Bashore discusses also a number of general topics. He finds that Hawthorne's and James's use of "eye" imagery is similar (in *The Scarlet Letter* and in "Four Meetings"; "eye" and "teeth" imagery in *Blithedale* and in "Daisy Miller"). But in *Hawthorne* James had objected to the romancer's fortuitous symbols; thus he tried to integrate his own with characterization. James also used Hawthorne's "leftness" motif–which represents aloofness, coldness, and disdain–to describe Osmond's and Madame Merle's characters. Other topics Bashore discusses in Hawthorne and James include motivation, "natural depravity," and ethics. He indicates that whereas in Hawthorne essence, motive, and deposition of villainy are generally interdependent, James insists that all characters be judged only by their motives. His conclusion is that in those stories where James "suggested villainy by 'parts' rather than by full description, by 'eyes,' 'left,' hands, etc., " he was probably unconsciously "trying to avoid Hawthorne's trap of allegory." But in his shift of emphasis "almost entirely to the *motives* of his characters," regardless of the consequences, he created, ethically, "a world of inversion which would be completely foreign to Hawthorne."

In part 3, "General Summary" (II, 414-29), Bashore compares and contrasts Hawthorne's and James's villains. Here again, short, barely related observations–many of them previous made–predominate. He notes, among other things, that both authors had a repugnance toward zealots, but evinced varying degrees of idealism; that for Hawthorne egotism usually led to isolation, for James it often led to "immoral aestheticism"; that Hawthorne usually presented his "dream" scenes through the device of "alternate possibilities," but James presented his through the "complex point-of-view method"; that James sometimes viewed the relationship between men and women as parasitical, but Hawthorne did not; that Hawthorne dealt with the scientist as villain, but James did not; that the physical ugliness of Hawthorne's villains "is generally an outward . . . sign of an inward and spiritual corruption," whereas in James's early stories, there are hints that the actions of his villains "are *caused* by their physical make-up"; that the development of Hawthorne's villains, more than that of James's, closely reflects the circumstances of his biography; and, finally, that whereas "James's characters often try to resolve the values within society," Hawthorne's aim simply at "reconciliation."

Two other people have discussed Hawthorne's and James's villains. Eleven years after Bashore, Milton Herbert Kornfeld wrote "A Darker Freedom: The Villains in the Novels of Hawthorne, James, and Faulkner" (Brandeis, 1970). In American fiction, Kornfeld explains, the villain is the archetype of a dark freedom, the "freedom of unrepressed, uncivilized desire and untrammeled appetite." Gilbert Osmond, Chad Newsome, and Goodman Brown are all free men, and in order to safeguard their freedom, they must keep their consciousness "closed to the possibilities of experience." Hawthorne, James, and Faulkner all deny the villain any moment of recognition, and thus his suffering never becomes fully meaningful to himself. However, all the three authors suggest that although villainy "cannot be conclusively defeated," it can at least be "temporarily vanquished."

In the chapter on Hawthorne, pp. 14-50, Kornfeld indicates that Hawthorne's fiction "is concerned with original sin, the inevitability of evil, or whatever constitutes human frailty." The characters he concentrates on are Ethan Brand, Dimmesdale—who is not a villain because he seeks pardon—Chillingworth, Giovanni in "Rappaccini's Daughter," and the Rev. Mr. Hooper in "The Ministrer's Black Veil." In the chapter on James, pp. 51-104, Kornfeld explains that James's evil, unlike Hawthorne's, is "domesticated"; in James's novels the horrible is incorporated into everyday life. Whereas Hawthorne's villains and his victims are aware of all the evil in the world, James's lack this cosmic awareness; evil in James works "at the most private levels of consciousness." His villains "are not driven by archetypal urgings"; they "are motivated by intensely private and pragmatic considerations," and compared to Hawthorne's, they "fall short of the tragic potential" found in such characters as Chillingworth or Ethan Brand. Whereas Hawthorne could use characterization to explain an abstraction, to give "some concrete embodiment to a sense of extrapersonal activity, like original sin, in the Universe," James's characters "are entirely themselves . . . and evil is wholly an inter-personal, private transaction." Osmond in *The Portrait* is not an "arch fiend in the manner of Chillingworth." His evil exists only for Isabel, just as in *The Ambassadors* Chad Newsome's evil exists only for Lambert Strether. James's "characterization of villainy as an experience ultimately perceived in privacy," Kornfeld observes, "suggests that . . . moral reality is primarily solipsistic."

The characters by James whom Kornfeld considers include Winterbourne in "Daisy Miller"; Dr. Sloper in *Washington Square;* Gilbert Osmond, whose cold intellectual nature is similar to Chillingworth's; Chad Newsome; Lambert Strether, whose role is analogous to Robin's in "My Kinsman, Major Molineux"; the narrator of *The Aspern Papers;* and Merton Densher, Milly Theale, and the Croy family in *The Wings of the Dove.* At the end of the chapter on Faulkner, he notes that the

> majority of villains in Hawthorne and James, and those of Faulkner, have lost the power to discriminate in ethical situations, partly through inherent inadequacy, partly through deliberate choice . . . and partly through indifference. The cause . . . [and] the effect of this disappearance of conscience has been the withering of consciousness . . .
>
> For Chillingworth and Ethan Brand insight and feeling were still possible. . . . In Henry James the villains . . . hovered on the verge of a conscious appreciation of their cruelty, but . . . [most] were able to triumph over the deliberating effects of insight and conscience. Here at last, in Faulkner, the battle has been totally lost. . . . The finality and closure which Hawthorne could achieve at the end of *The Scarlet Letter* or "Ethan Brand" is a resource not available to . . . James or Faulkner, not because they see the world more complexly . . . but because they are more ambivalent about the possibilities of justice and the capacities of men to deal meaningfully with experience and the problem of evil. (141-43)

Kornfeld's conclusion is that the "characterization of villainy in American literature underwent a transformation in the hundred-year period beginning with Hawthorne and ending with Faulkner." Whereas Hawthorne's villains "do suffer because of a conscious recognition of their behavior and struggle to suppress that knowledge," the Jamesian villain "is no longer the guilt-ridden outsider but has managed to successfully disguise and domesticate himself and become a more conventional member of his society." The language and imagery used to define and explore evil have also changed. "Theological language was still available to Hawthorne, it still carried meaning for his readers, and the demonic could be effectively invoked through Satanic allusions and religious conceptions like the fortunate fall." In James, however, the villain has undergone a "demythologization" and evil has become "part of the fabric of the ordinary."

Gaillard FitzSimmons Waterfall's "The Manipulation Theme in the Works of Nathaniel Hawthorne and Henry James" (University of South Carolina, 1973) adds nothing significant to what has already been written on Hawthorne's and James's villains. Waterfall explains that the manipulation theme deals with the attempts by a character to control both his life and the lives of others, and that the two Americans "whose works particularly reflect a fear of this danger" are Hawthorne and James. The moral concerns of both these writers, the characters they created, and the problems they faced as American artists were all similar. In the five chapters on Hawthorne (pp. 6–52), the characters Waterfall examines include the "Religious Manipulators" (the Puritans and the Quakers in "The Gentle Boy"), the "Dangerous Idealists" (Septimus Felton, Aylmer, Hollingsworth, Zenobia), and the "Godlike Scientists" (Dr. Cacaphodel, Matthew Maule, Westervelt, Dr. Rappaccini, Chillingworth, Ethan Brand). In chapter 6, "A Kinship," pp. 53-58, Waterfall observes that, "unlike many of Hawthorne's manipulators, James's are seldom clear-cut, satanic villains . . . committed to the pursuit of evil for its own sake"; rather, they "are usually motivated by physical passion or material desires." But neither author emphasizes "man's natural depravity." They are both "concerned with sin rather than with any natural evil outside of human control."

In the four chapters on James (pp. 59-112), Waterfall finds that James's manipulators, "though Hawthornesque in appearance, became progressively Jamesian" as the novelist developed his own techniques. He compares James's "prohibitive moralists" to Hawthorne's New England Puritans: in "Daisy Miller," for example, the transplanted, self-righteous American society in Europe "proves as cruel, unrelenting, and harmful as that which inflicted wounds upon Edith and Edgar, Hester and Ilbrahim." And in *Washington Square* Dr. Sloper's "arrogant assertion of morality . . . [reminds] one of Endicott, Richard Digby, or Goodman Brown." Waterfall compares also "The Author of Beltraffio" and *The Turn of the Screw* with "The Gentle Boy," and *The Princess Casamassima* and *The Bostonians* with *Blithedale.* Where James went beyond Hawthorne, he explains, is in his depiction of "harmful characters" who "need not be possessed, depraved . . . in order to commit great wrongs." Evil in James's fiction is often increased by "benevolent puppeteers": Ralph Touchett in *The Portrait,* Miss Pynsent in *The Princess Casamassima,* Lambert Strether in *The Ambassadors,* and many others. Waterfall further compares "Madame de Mauves" and *The American* with *The Seven Gables* (family curse), *The Princess Casamassima* with *The Seven Gables* (Paul Muniment and Judge Pyncheon), *Washington Square* with *Blithedale* (Townsend and Hollingsworth), and *The Wings of the Dove* with *The Marble Faun* (Milly Theale and Hilda). He also notes, as Bashore had noted earlier, that James, unlike Hawthorne, had little interest in the prideful scientist. His closest equivalent to Hawthorne's "scientific models" are the dehumanized aesthetes whom he endowed "with the scientific traits of cold objectivity and prying analysis." Waterfall compares, in this respect, the narrators of "The Aspern Papers" and *The Sacred Fount,* and Oliver Lyon in "The Liar," with the unnamed artist in "The Prophetic Pictures," and Robert Acton in *The Europeans* with Chillingworth and Ethan Brand.

In his "Conclusion," pp. 113-18, Waterfall restates many of the above observations. He notes that Hawthorne's villains "are sometimes dark and misshapen," whereas James's "show few physical indications of their depravity"; that James's characters are less symbolic, and their motives more credible, than Hawthorne's; and that perhaps "the greatest difference between the manipulators of the two authors is the absence [in James's fiction] of any great Promethean characters." Selah Tarrant and Professor Fargo "seem pitifully insignificant when compared with Rappaccini, Roger Chillingworth, Ethan Brand, or even young Matthew Maule." Waterfall's comments on *Blithedale* and *Roderick Hudson* are discussed in the fourth essay.

Two people have written on the mysterious in Hawthorne and James. In "The Uncanny in the Supernatural Short Fiction of Poe, Hawthorne and James" (University of Los Angelos, 1967), Paul Arthur Newlin finds that two obvious similarities between Hawthorne and James are their senses of the past and their uses of ambiguity. These writers, as well as Poe, used the uncanny in many of their tales "because the uncanny was the quality which best linked illusion and reality." Hawthorne's tales, Newlin indicates, "rely strongly upon American folk tradition for their effect." His use of European Gothic devices was directed less at the senses and more at the conscious. After quoting from the preface to *The Seven Gables,* Newlin notes that

> For Henry James, the choice of a method which would best express the truth of the human heart led from Hawthorne's example of the romance to the technique James defined as realism; but before James came either to his definition or to his perfection of his technique, he tried to represent the truth of the human heart in tales and romances highly reminiscent of Poe's and Hawthorne's efforts to heighten sensibilities into a perception of the real through the uncanny. (238)

Although James abandoned the romance for realism in his novels, he retained "the romance idiom for his supernatural short fiction." Newlin further discusses how Hawthorne's definition of the romance in the preface to *The Seven Gables* served James early in his career, and how "Hawthorne's concept of the romance as a literary type provided a framework in which the past and multiple interpretations of the fancy could be manipulated to provide the kind of short fiction James sought to write."

Many critics, Newlin continues, have noted the similarities in structure and content between *The Seven Gables* and "The Romance of Certain Old Clothes." However, in James's story "the setting in the past is not fully exploited," and the unseen ghost " is an inartistic and unbelievable creation." "De Grey: A Romance" utilizes two Hawthornesque themes: the curse theme and the theme of inherited sin, but here "the pattern of Hawthornean romance begins to take on distinct Jamesian qualities." Whereas Hawthorne "frequently dealt with a historical-religious setting in which colonial American history and Puritan doctrines combined or played against each other," often with a thin line or none at all "between humane morality and superstitious evil," James improvises "upon such historical-religious settings in 'De Grey' by introducing a medieval European curse to be played against a seemingly intellectual theology of a Catholic priest." As a result, he produces a more realistic and more credible story. Newlin also compares Margaret Aldis in "De Grey" with Beatrice Rappaccini (carriers of "organic evil"), and he finds in "A Passionate Pilgrim" and "The Ghostly Rental" "tangible evidence" of Hawthorne's and Poe's influence on James's use of the past. "The Third Person" too, he says, "could have had its basis in Hawthorne's 'Legends of the Province House.'" After commenting on how in "The Jolly Corner" "the imagined . . . becomes real as a result of a clearly expressed and well-planned attempt by Spencer Brydon to bring it about," and how in *The Sense of the Past* Ralph Pendrel, to quote Matthiessen, "has the consciousness of exchanging places with the figure of his . . . ancestor," Newlin explains that this does not mean "that James at the end of his career was merely imitating Hawthorne's device of showing omnipotence of thought through paintings that came to life;" it merely shows "how James has advanced Hawthorne's device." Newlin's conclusion is that James profited from Poe's and Hawthorne's earlier efforts "by writing with a greater pscyhological emphasis that was freed from European Gothic and allegorical conventions." And whereas Hawthorne "manipulated psychological insights in an effort to show life as it *should* be lived," James "chose psychological insights in an effort to show how life *is* lived" (357).

In "American Gothicism: The Evolution of a Mode" (Kent State, 1972), Pamela Jacobs Shelden concentrates on Brown, Poe, Hawthorne, and James. She does not, however, delineate explicitly any direct link between Hawthorne's and James's works. She defines Gothicism as "that literary tradition of terror which places man in a situation which is inexplicable in nature, circumstances that lead him on to the confrontation of evil and to a maze of ambiguities for which there is often no explanation" (34-35). In the chapter on Hawthorne, pp. 210-68, she analyzes *The Scarlet Letter;* she also notes the similarlity between Hawthorne's description, in his prefaces, of the romanticist's task and James's distinction, in the preface to *The American,* between the real and the romantic. In the chapter on James, pp. 269-370, she points out that although James admired Hawthorne's tales of fancy, he criticized him "as too much 'a man of fantasy' and not enough the realist." Thus James in his own fiction "insisted on the solidity of specification demanded in realism." Shelden analyzes "The Ghostly Rental," and compares the relationship between Captain Diamond and his daughter with that between Dimmesdale and Chillingworth; "The Friends of the Friends," in which James, like Hawthorne in *The Scarlet Letter,* "employs the gothic manuscript convention," a prop he uses again in *The Turn of the Screw;* and "The Jolly Corner." She notes also that in *The Portrait,* the ghosts of Gardencourt don't appear to Isabel until the last chapter of the novel, "when she, like Dimmesdale and Goodman Brown who return from the forest, is no longer an initiate into experience and evil." But most of all, James shares with Brown, Poe, and Hawthorne the belief "that terror is a concomitant of man's fear of the measureless region within" (361).

Each of the other four dissertations is on a different subject, and none contains any very original or significant observations on the James-Hawthorne relation. Charles George Hoffman's "The Development of the Short Novel in Hawthorne, Melville, and James" (University of Wisconsin, 1952) is not primarily a study of "influence," although Hoffmann does point out some specific parallels between Hawthorne's and James's works, and does at times even consider the question of influence. Hoffmann explains that in America, the short novel as a genre began with James, who was influenced by the French tradition of the *nouvelle.* Hawthorne, on the other hand, was more influenced by the German tradition of prose fiction, especially the German Gothic tale. He turned to the short-novel form after writing many short stories, and *The Scarlet Letter* is his only short novel. James, by contrast, wrote short novels throughout his creative years.

In the section on Hawthorne, pp. 21-108, Hoffmann finds that Hawthorne's short stories before 1850 contain all the techniques, themes, style, and characterization which are found in *The Scarlet Letter.* This work itself, like James's *The Spoils of Poynton,* started as a short story, and both works retain "the compactness of the narrative action" associated with the short story form. However, Hawthorne's literary development ended rather than began with *The Scarlet Letter;* he did not develop artistically after that. Where he developed was in the probing of the theme of evil and sin, and if James is a psychological realist, so was Hawthorne, for it was his concern for the "truth of the human heart" which James called "the deeper psychology."

Hoffmann considers numerous stories which Hawthorne wrote before 1850: "The Gentle Boy," "Young Goodman Brown," "The Antique Ring," "Alice Doanne's Appeal," and many others. The "idea" of these and Hawthorne's other stories, he explains, after commenting on Hawthorne's *American Notebooks,* "is in most cases an abstract, moral statement; it is the central idea or theme that is only later given fictional reality." James too used this method of the "idea," but differed "from Hawthorne in that for him it was only a starting-point for creation rather than the 'moral' to be particularized in fiction." In the chapter entitled "*The Scarlet Letter* as a Short Novel," Hoffmann observes that Hawthorne was not consciously following the model of the form when he wrote it. Unfortunately, Hoffmann's definition of the short novel is not exclusive or rigorous enough to explain convincingly why he considers *The Scarlet Letter* a short novel. *Fanshawe,* "Hawthorne's shortest novel," he declares "not a short novel in form," but rather "a complete novel" whose "shortness is the result of a lack of development . . . not the result of compactness and economy of structure through techniques." *The Seven Gables,* like *The Scarlet Letter,* is a "Romance" in terms of "approach or method," but it does not achieve "a successful balance between content and form, idea and technique, structure and narrative action. *The Scarlet Letter* has this balance." But this is true of many long novels too, which integrate just as well form and content, technique and theme. Unless the characteristics which distinguish the short novel from the short story and the long novel are more restrictive, and are more specifically identified and rigorously applied, the decision as to which works are short stories, which short novels, and which long novels may appear arbitrary.[19] Even more irritating are the frequent unnecessary repetitions throughout Hoffmann's dissertation. Nowhere is this more annoying than in the section on Hawthorne. With more discipline, the 405 pages of this text could have been reduced, to its advantage, by as many as fifty pages.

Hoffman defines *The Scarlet Letter* as a short novel almost entirely in terms of what it shares, in an "extended" form, with Hawthorne's short stories: the themes, the symbolism, the allegory, the device of "multiple choice," etc. He observes that in this novel, Hawthorne is, like James, concerned with the consequences of adultery; "he focusses his attention on the psychological effects of sin and guilt." A "typical example" of James's "treatment of adultery" is his *nouvelle* "Madame de Mauves," in which "the emphasis is on the attitudes and manners of the characters involved after the revelation of adultery rather than on the adulterous relation itself." In contrast to Hawthorne, however, James's heroines—Madame de Mauves, Isabel Archer, Maggie Verver, and others—"are betrayed by their adulterous husbands."

In the section on James, pp. 203-366, Hoffmann indicates that James, unlike Hawthorne, "was seldom able to confine his 'little ideas' within the limits" of the short-story form. But he too served his apprenticeship by writing short stories, and these contain "the elements of technique, theme, and style" which are found in his major novels. However, although such early stories as "A Problem" and "The Romance of Certain Old Clothes" can be called Hawthornesque, they are "isolated cases of direct influence." The most significant affinity between them is that they both cared for "the deeper pscyhology," were interested in "appearances," and "were acutely aware of . . . evil in the world and in human nature." But each saw evil differently.

Hoffman examines many of James's *nouvelles,* and makes numerous minor references to Hawthorne throughout this section. He likens the final chapter of "Madame de Mauves" to that of *The Scarlet Letter,* and notes that the "germ" for *Washington Square* is "an anecdote based on a real life situation" (*Notebooks,* pp. 12-13), a method which James used frequently, and which "is similar to the method used by Hawthorne in the notebooks, except that whereas with Hawthorne the idea was often an abstract or allegorical statement, with James it was often a situation or an incident." Hoffmann's comparison of *The Scarlet Letter* with *The Spoils of Poynton* and *The Turn of the Screw* will be considered in the third essay, and that of *The Seven Gables* with *The Europeans,* and "Ethan Brand" with "The Beast in the Jungle" in the sixth essay. In his "Conclusion," pp. 367-83, he observes again that the three nineteenth-century writers who illustrate the development of the short novel in America are Hawthorne, Melville, and James, and that their short novels, and their literary development as a whole, are closely related. Hawthorne's approach to the short novel was "accidental"; he was not a conscious writer of such novels. James, however, "brought to the American short novel a conscious awareness of it as a literary form."[20]

Arnold P. Hinchliffe's "Symbolism in the American Novel, 1850-1950; An Examination of the Findings of Recent Literary Critics in Respect of the Novels of Hawthorne, Melville, James, Hemingway and Faulkner" (Manchester University, England, 1963) is very disappointing. Had Hinchliffe limited his authors to three, or concentrated only on specific works by these authors, or even examined only a number of recurrent images in these authors' works, his dissertation might have gained more depth and cohesion. As it is, "Symbolism in the American Novel" is little more than a fragmented collection of annotated quotations from a host of books and articles on symbolism in the various works of these authors. Hinchliffe's subject is too wide, the authors he considers too many, the time they span too long, and too many critics have written on symbolism in *The Scarlet Letter,* in *Moby Dick,* in *The Golden Bowl,* in *A Farewell To Arms,* in *Absalom, Absalom!*—to mention only a single work by each author—to be accommodated in a dissertation that would be both comprehensive and cohesive. Hinchliffe examines the critical responses not only to the novels of these five authors, as his title suggests, but to their shorter works as well.

His work might have achieved more perspective had he examined at greater length, within each of his six sections, the interrelations—if any—between the uses of symbolism by these authors; if he had attempted more frequently something similar to what he does in the last section of his dissertation, where he notes, for example, that it is only in his "final phase" that James used objects directly as symbols. In *The Golden Bowl,* for instance, the bowl acts as a central organizing symbol, and the whole novel is full of concrete images (673). Hinchliffe feels that in many ways the bowl is a nuisance. "It is mechanical, but as symbol it most clearly shows the difference between Hawthorne and Melville and James when each writer uses a symbol. James does not contemplate the bowl and explain it in terms of a narrative about people—he has the narrative into which he introduces the bowl, almost as a decorative appendage." Similarly, in *The Sense of the Past* "James uses a Hawthornesque portrait as a device intended . . . to hold past and present, Europe and America together; but again the portrait is nothing more than a crucial device in a symbolic situation." "Symbols were in fact part of James's manner," he concludes; "when he has one central symbol he uses it as explicator where Hawthorne and Melville challenge letter and whale, making them produce meaning; where they at their best explore, he explinas." One would have liked to see more such comparisons. In general, however, the references from one author to another in the main body of the text are rare, and often they are undeveloped. Hinchliffe tends also to rely too heavily on British critics. The emphasis below is mainly on those of his observations which relate directly to the James-Hawthorne question.

Hawthorne, Hinchliffe argues, combined three themes which have occupied American writers for a long time: "the place of an artist in a society which did not recognize his usefulness, traditional classicism versus natural man, and the international theme." Among Hawthorne's short stories, he finds "The Prophetic Pictures" "a curiously Jamesian tale." He divides Hawthorne's women into two groups: "dark oriental ladies with intellectual freedom and frail daughters of light who win in the end." Compared with James, he says, Hawthorne could not handle women—except for Hester Prynne. But this should "not blind us to James's inabilities":

> He chose the Hawthornean type of blonde to portray and turn into a princess (the Dove only better in treatment than Hawthorne's) and rejected the kind of American girl Catherine Sloper represented; a rejection he seems to have regretted only in the final sketches of Rosanna Graw where solidity of flesh anchors her down; Maggie Verver, in spite of her affectionate ugly ordinary little name, is too ethereal by far; the tower motif from *The Marble Faun* returns with Rosanna as a rude and confident gesture indeed. (36n.)

Later, he agrees with F. I. Carpenter (*American Literature and the Dream*) that "Hawthorne is afraid of Hester. He was never able to do as much as James with transcendental women, hence the pairs of women who fall" (Hinchliffe, p. 62).

In the chapter on *The Scarlet Letter,* Hinchliffe contends that "Hawthorne's concern with human relationships [in this novel] is only metaphorically theological; it is ultimately as secular in nature as Henry James's." In the chapter on *The Seven Gables,* he notes that the way Hawthorne uses plastic objects in this novel anticipates James's "emblematic use of artistic objects" in his own novels, and that in Phoebe's relationship with Hepzibah and Clifford "Hawthorne touches lightly on the vampire theme which James explores more completely." In the chapter on *Blithedale,* he finds that

Zenobia "looks forward . . . as a symbolic figure to Mme. de Vionnet" in *The Ambassadors,* and that in the figure of Coverdale Hawthorne is "tragically involved in the morality of observation," an issue which James too explored. Lastly, in the chapter on *Transformation,* he notes that James admired Hilda so immensely that her influence can be felt even in such a late work as *The Wings of the Dove.* Donatello too, as an orphan expelled by his sin "from the sunshine of Eden . . . looks forward to the list of orphans in James." Hinchliffe indicates further that with Hawthorne, as with James, "it was the image . . . which always came first; the idea of a woman wearing a letter, followed the letter" (131). Later, in the section on James, he remarks again that the starting point for both novelists "was a 'germ' which in Hawthorne's case was often an abstract or allegorical statement, and for James a situation or incident" (297).

The emphasis in the James section is on the novelist's "major phase." Hinchliffe warns that although Hawthorne is undoubtedly "the starting point, and the only one," for a discussion of James's symbolism, one must distinguish between "what Hawthorne meant to James and what that inferred meaning means to us." After all, James was very critical of Hawthorne's allegory and symbolism; hence, in James's own "symbolic" novels, the symbols never exist outside the text.[21] Hinchliffe contends that it was not "Hawthorne the curious allegorist and the symbolist romancer that attracted" James; it was rather the Hawthorne who "combined in a singular degree the spontaneity of the imagination with a haunting care for moral problems" (*Hawthorne,* chapter 7). "This was an American writer James could understand," Hinchliffe writes; and Hawthorne's example was both an inspiration and "encouragement to attempt a similar career."

As one would expect, most of Hinchliffe's comments on the James-Hawthorne relation are restatements of what various critics have said about the relation. Thus he notes the echoes of *Transformation* in *Roderick Hudson,* but deplores the fact that in *The Wings of the Dove,* the echoes of Hilda and the doves from *Transformation* have "tended to make the Dove image central and obscure the princess image which is peculiarly James's own." He further connects the "I" of *The Sense of the Past* to Coverdale in *Blithedale,* relates Mr. Touchett and Isabel Archer in *The Portrait* to Holgrave and Hepzibah in *The Seven Gables,* and shows that James's use of portraits as symbol and theme in several of his works is similar to Hawthorne's use of mirror emblems. In response to those critics who "worry about the moral loss" in James's later novels, he contends that although "James's values are ambiguous . . . they are not mixed." James preserves, "through the rich ironies of his later style and imagery"–which are "much more rewarding than Hawthorne's clumsy avowed alternatives"–"the ethical neutrality which is his total value."

Most of Hinchliffe's references to Hawthorne in the James section are to *Transformation* and *The Seven Gables.* He calls *The Ivory Tower* "very much

The House of the Seven Gables in modern dress." *The Sense of the Past* too is a "Hawthornesque story." The symbol of the picture in this story joins the past and the present, just as it does in Hawthorne. Both *The Ivory Tower* and *The Sense of the Past,* Hinchliffe continues,

> are very much in the spirit of *The House of the Seven Gables*—two families, old curses, greed, the symbol of a house, symbol of a portrait and miniature. And it is not accidentally that Ralph remembers the confession scene in *Transformation* . . . when he comes to visit the Ambassador, confessing that he knows nine out of ten compatriots approach the Ambassador with a story. This recalls Hawthorne's own reflections as Consul at Liverpool. It is significant that only in close association with Hawthorne does he use the symbol as Hawthorne has done as a means of forcing significance; in these last two novels it seems clear that the symbol was to explore meaning, not simply express it. (399)

Furthermore, the theme of *The Sense of the Past,* like that of *The Seven Gables,* "is precisely that the present, even the future, is the proper environment for man. . . . As in *Transformation* the thickness, the history of Europe was to be rejected for the country of the cowboy."

In the last section of his dissertation, Hinchliffe observes that the lack of concrete artistic materials forced Hawthorne to withdraw occasionally from society, "and withdrawal led to guilt." It is this "expatriation," in time or in space, which binds all the five writers together. However, since "Hawthorne, Melville and James use symbolism in a highly individual way . . . only the most tentative 'tradition'"can be suggested by their works, although a literary relationship between them can be demonstrated. "What holds these five writers together," he concludes, "is probably less symbolism and more their collective pessimism" (680).

In "Opposition and Balance: A Characteristic of Structure in Hawthorne, Melville, and James" (Columbia, 1967), Stephen Francis Martineau tries to define one particular type of open-endedness in the nineteenth-century American novel. He argues that the structure of Hawthorne's *The Scarlet Letter,* Melville's *The Confidence-Man,* and James's *The Sacred Fount* and *The Golden Bowl* "is based on an immediate statement of opposition" which establishes "two worlds of contrasting qualities" with "no possibility of resolution, no final unity of vision . . . ever entertained." All the three authors "are concerned with the proximity and fusion of opposition on three levels—within each created character, within each individual world, and within the conflict of two opposing worlds." And these opposites are both irreconcilable and inseparable. In *The Scarlet Letter,* for example, the embroidered letter emphasizes both Hester's "punishment and her individuality that rebels against that punishment; equally Adam Verver . . . has a quality innocence that indicates both helplessness and cruelty." But in neither work is there a "desperate search for unity"; rather, there is "an acceptance of and resignation to an essentially [sic] discordance of existence," and a desire to create through structure "an artistic unity from the experience of this double vision."

Chapters 1 and 2 are on Hawthorne and *The Scarlet Letter* respectively. Martineau finds *The Scarlet Letter* Hawthorne's "only fully extended example" of the oppositional structural framework. He discusses the polarity "set up through the juxtaposition . . . of the wild-rose and the prison," and the contrast thus "set up between man and nature, restriction and freedom." All these opposing elements are inseparable, and the richness of the novel "stems both from the conflict of these opposites within the central characters and from the individual's efforts to reconcile that conflict within his own consciousness." The images of the scarlet letter too "work in opposite directions"; even Pearl is characterized in "opposites."

In chapters 5, 6, and 7, Martineau argues that most of James's novels too show "a conflict of two opposing worlds or individuals," and that James's aim is to balance "the values of these two worlds. . . . The result is opposition without resolution." Although both Hawthorne and James are thus related, their methods are different. Hawthorne uses "a strong element of external technique to define the internal struggle." Although Hester's conflict is internally presented, "this internal conflict is mirrored by a supporting external opposition." The rose and the prison, the scarlet letter, Pearl, all "act as external supporting evidence of her internal struggle." James, on the other hand, "works altogether without the external representation; he presents his opposition" purely within the individual. When Hester first emerges from the prison, her identity has already "been anticipated by the imagery of the rose and the prison," and she is "accompanied by the outward complexity of the scarlet letter." In Charlotte Stant's case in *The Golden Bowl,* however, the opposition is conveyed at first "purely through the imagery of the Prince's viewpoint," and "is then extended and expanded within her gradual development throughout the novel." Martineau continues:

> With James the technique is all gradual development through the expanding consciousness; no accoutrement are needed outside the reality of the human world, for this technique of opposition works entirely within the sphere of human relationships. In . . . Hawthorne there is always the sense of a very formal structure, which often conveys . . . an almost too conscious awareness of the need for restraint. In James this formal structure remains concealed behind his human creations, behind the intensity of felt life. (122-23)

In *The Golden Bowl,* innocence and guilt, freshness and staleness are all related and balanced in the development of each character. These two pairs of opposites "exist rooted together, in the same way as the wild-rose and the prison in *The Scarlet Letter*," and Maggie "attempts to do what Hester Prynne strives for in *The Scarlet Letter,* to bridge two opposing worlds." But, like Hester, she "too is caught between the two, and cannot find a resolution." What is presented in *The Golden Bowl,* Martineau argues, is

> the division between the moral and the aesthetic . . . between freedom and restriction, revealing thus an interesting parallel with the two worlds of *The Scarlet Letter* and the two halves of Hester and Dimmesdale's identities. But while in *The Scarlet Letter* the opposition is expressed primarily through the unresolved conflict within the individual, in *The Golden Bowl* it is stated through a juxtaposition of two codes of existence, and a revelation of the limitations of both; the worlds are also shown as irreconcilable. (170)

Martineau discusses also "the balance in the structure of *The Sacred Fount*," and concludes that the opposition in all these novels

> is developed on two levels–within the larger framework of structure and within the presentation of each central character, and the external statement complements the inner conflict. In *The Scarlet Letter,* the initial opposition of rose and prison supports the inner conflicts of Hester and Dimmesdale . . . in *The Sacred Fount* the relationship of vampire to victim projects its conflict onto the Narrator's identity; and in *The Golden Bowl,* the contradictions within the individual identities of Adam, Maggie, the Prince and Charlotte foreshadow Maggie's failure to close the gap between the moral and aesthetic worlds. . . . And while the complexity of the novels stems from the double emphasis at every level, the clarity emanates from the patterned design. (183-84)

Martineau's comparison of *Blithedale* with *The Sacred Fount* is evaluated in the fourth essay.

The writers David Joseph Thompson concentrates on in his "Societal Definitions of Individualism and the Critique of Egotism as a Major Theme in American Fiction" (Brown, 1972) are Hawthorne, James, Faulkner, and R. P. Warren. Thompson finds that each generation of Americans–"Puritans, colonials, republicans, early, mid, and late nineteenth century Americans"–displays two conflicting tendencies: an emphasis on individualism, and a concern for the welfare of others. "The richest and most articulate expression of the American critique of egotism," he claims, is in the works of the above four authors. In the chapter on Hawthorne, pp. 152-85, he examines "Egotism; or, The Bosom Serpent" and *Blithedale.* Hawthorne's concern with isolation, he explains, arose largely "from his personal experience with the problem." Hawthorne believed that an individual isolates himself from God, man, and even nature largely because of pride in his self, and that the end result of this pride is egotism. His approach to the problem of egotism was moral, and it was shaped by a Christian perspective. "Egotism," which could "stand as a paradigm for the fate of many Hawthornean egotists," "traces a complete cycle wherein Roderick Elliston falls prey to sin, condemns himself to withering isolation, but returns finally to moral health and abandons his isolation." In this tale and others like it, "the focus is on an individual psyche." In *Blithedale,* however, the subject is "the composition and failure of human communities," and once again "egotism plays a central role." Thompson's discussion of *Blithedale* is reviewed together with his discussion of *The Portrait* in the fourth essay.

In the chapter on James, pp. 186-227, Thompson observes that James's fiction, in the main, demonstrates a moral sense that has "a strong element of individualism." Yet, the propositions which this moral sense nurtures derive ultimately from the Christian emphasis on "otherness" or charity. According to Thompson, the roots of this paradox can be traced to James's "incomplete" American identity. Although he recognized that being an American involved an unprecedented emphasis on "the importance of the individual" (*Hawthorne,* chapter 2), and although "his fiction constitutes a refusal to sacrifice the individual to society," he nevertheless harbored grave reservations about the ultimate effects of this individualistic ethos on the community. He was also conscious of "the failure of Americans to honor in their relationships with one another the sacred integrity of the human being." Both in his own mind and in his fiction, he sought to reconcile the conflicting tendencies resulting from this situation. The only work by James which Thompson discusses is *The Portrait.* His conclusion is that Hawthorne, James, Faulkner, and Warren succeeded in merging the individual ego with the social, and thus showed the way in which egotism could be transcended and community achieved (Thompson, pp. 279-80).

The Artist and Society

Two general aspects of the James-Hawthorne relationship have received much critical attention: the relation of the artist to society as revealed in the two authors' works; and the heroines the two writers created, as well as the attitudes of these writers towards their women characters. One of the finest studies of the relation of the artist to society in both novelists' works is Annette K. Baxter's "Independence vs. Isolation: Hawthorne and James on the Problem of the Artist," *Nineteenth Century Fiction,* 10 (1955), 225-31. After Henry St. George in chapter 5 of "The Lesson of the Master" relates the limitations which set apart the life of the artist, Paul Overt asks whether the artist isn't "a man all the same?" "I mostly think not," replies St. George; "You know as well as I what he has to do: the concentration, the finish, the independence he must strive for from the moment he begins to wish his work really decent." Baxter finds that the implications of this statement—"that ultimately the artist's achievement depends on the degree to which he is not 'a man all the same'"—lies at the heart of what Hawthorne and James considered to be the artist's problem. Because James was acutely aware of the need for concentration and finish, the predominant theme of his stories of artists is "the struggle against the second-rate." He was so obsessed with technique that he tended to overlook the risk which for Hawthorne was inherent in the artist's need for independence. To James independence meant "a multitude of sweet discomforts" which promised "higher compensations":

> Independence never threatened to resemble that isolation which transformed Hawthorne's painter in "The Prophetic Pictures" into a being as coldly unsympathetic with the frailties of humanity as he was subtly exact in the rendering of them. Indeed, if James himself became the ideal artist of Hawthorne, possessing "a force of character that seems hardly compatible with its delicacy" ["The Artist of the Beautiful"], the phenomenon may find its explanation in a temperamental stolidity which kept his independence from becoming either an estrangement or an embitterment. (226)

Hawthorne, on the other hand, felt that a dedicated artist was especially "threatened by the specter of isolation." To be totally absorbed in the creative process meant a loosening of the ties which bind one to the mass of humanity, and a final alienation like Owen Warland's, the Prophetic Painter's, Clifford's in *The Seven Gables,* and the romantic poet's in "The Canterbury Pilgrims."

But the sin of isolation was not confined to the artists. "Hawthorne's seeker after the Unpardonable Sin, the scientist in search of the secret of existence, the deliberate desecrator of the human soul, Ethan Brand, and Aylmer, and Rappaccini, are all denied the experience of human sympathy." However, these people are willing agents of their fates. The artists, on the other hand, "are engaged in the uplifting, not the desecration, of the human soul," and their isolation is "often borne with difficulty, not in the calm and knowledgeable spirit" of the scholar-demons. For the artist, isolation is "as necessary for his creative, as it is unhealthy for his human, development." This is the paradox from which Hawthorne always tried to free himself.

All of James's artists, Baxter explains, are acutely aware of the gulf between themselves and the "others." But they are not abruptly separated from them as Hawthorne's artists are; in fact, they are "brought closer by their intermittent yearning for identification with the 'others'" than their situation would warrant. Neither do they have the Prophetic Painter's cold heart nor Owen Warland's elevated spirit to explain their predicament. James viewed "isolation as the exercise of a continuously rigorous independence of taste, a jealous retention of private standards of aesthetic valuation." His solution to his artists's problem—"Our doubt is our passion and our passion is our task. The rest is the madness of art" ("The Middle Years")—is less of a solution than an exhortation to the artist to believe only in his talent and plunge deeper into its abyss. But many artists cannot find strength in the act of isolation. Like Theobald in "The Madonna of the Future," and Clement Searle in *A Passionate Pilgrim,* they become incapable of functioning even within partial isolation and descend from the status of the misunderstood to that of the outcast. James, however, "identified himself with the misunderstood artist rather than the outcast; his Hugh Verekers ["The Figure in the Carpet"] outnumber his Theobalds. Consequently, his vision of the artist . . . relates to an individual rather than to a type" (228).

Since to Hawthorne the artist "represented but another instance of humanity in isolation," James's solution "would have appeared too restrictive to be satisfying." Hawthorne was acutely aware of how isolation could culminate not only in the obscurity he recalled in the preface to *The Snow Image,* "but in a deadening of interest in the common concerns of man." "Thus James's prime virtue for his artist—unqualified dedication to his craft—is transmuted into a vice" in the Prophetic Painter's case. "Singleminded loyalty to a concept beyond self becomes in the end a corrosive operation of the ego deadlier than the outcome of a more conventional selfishness."

But neither for Hawthorne nor for James was the creative life *of itself* the answer to the artist's problem. Both novelists assumed that the ideal artist would avoid a number of pitfalls. Hawthorne's Prophetic Painter, for instance, loses "his humanity in the impersonality of his concern with that of others," and the poet in "The Canterbury Pilgrims" loses "his interest in others through an excessive concern with his own personality." James's pitfalls were commonly those of the too sanctified, like Theobald, or the too secular, like Henry St. George and Neil Paraday ("The Death of the Lion"). The contrasts in the pitfalls of these artists, Baxter indicates, crystallize the major "difference in Hawthorne's and James's views of their problem":

> James located the satisfactory equilibrium of the artist somewhere between the demands of art and the need for human relationships. Society could not be a compulsive force for his ideal artist while he had the strength to maintain his artistic independence; it was not therefore a force to be dismissed or ignored. Individuals organized into groups, individuals pitted against the group, these composed the realities of the human isolation which it was the artist's function to explore. (230)

The artist's problem was how "to use society without being used by it." But even in their partial isolation, James's artists frequently violate the equilibrium. For Hawthorne, on the other hand, any satisfactory equilibrium had to be "consonant with the strictures of art and the overwhelming requisite of the artist's humanity." Hawthorne saw the dangers of dehumanization in the artist's situation "as an internal, rather than an external, threat." Since the ideal artist's function was to express perfection, or "the more-than-human," he had to be, of necessity, detached "from imperfection, from humanity." His recurring problem was how "to rise above humanity without losing his humaneness." As in James's case, however, Hawthorne's artists, even in their total isolation, fail to sustain their particular equilibrium. "If James asked his artist to be but partially a man, and Hawthorne that he be more than a man," neither granted him "the accessibility of other alternatives." It is only by the example of their careers that they may have taught, contrary to their works, "that the artist in the long run need not surrender claim to being 'a man all the same'" (231).

Another fine essay on the relation of the artist to society in James's and Hawthorne's works is Edwin Fussell's "Hawthorne, James and 'The Common Doom,'" *American Quarterly*, 10 (1958), 438-53. Fussell notes that one of Hawthorne's commonest subjects was "the antithesis of isolation and communion," but that it was not until *Septimus Felton* that he realized "that the hankering for earthly immortality may represent the extreme form of man's constant temptation to withdraw from human communion." James too was preoccupied with a similar problem: the theme of what Hawthorne called "the common bond and destiny" (*Septimus Felton*), and James "the common doom." This shared interest, Fussell says, "springs in part from roughly analogous conditions in the lives" of both novelists, as well as their similar temperaments. Septimus Felton, one reads, "shunned the glances of his fellow men," whom he considered "not as fellows, because he was seeking to withdraw himself from the common bond and destiny." This is the story Hawthorne often told; most of his best fiction "concerns people who do or do not achieve relation to 'the common bond and destiny.'" And he wrote well about them because their problems were his too. "Both as man and writer he spent his life trying . . . 'to open an intercourse with the world.'" And he felt he had succeeded. But he always feared that his need for privacy might lead him back to the kind of isolation which he had succumbed to for twelve years as a youth. He was always nervous about the kind of "vast intellectual development" which transformed Ethan Brand from a "brother-man" to "a cold observer." He believed that by concentrating on "our common nature" the artist could avoid the charge of "aesthetic egotism." However, the artist's necessary detachment could easily lead to a "withdrawal from the human communion." It is to this conflict, Fussell indicates, that we owe Hawthorne's "gallery of isolated creatures" who try "to put themselves into relation with other people and thus with some world of reality" (441).

James too was concerned with the "common bond and destiny": in *The Bostonians* (Olive Chancellor), *The Wings of the Dove* (Milly Theale), "The Beast in the Jungle" (John Marcher), "The Altar of the Dead" (George Stransom), and *The Sacred Fount.* In all these works, James emphasizes the sin of isolating oneself from the common life, and "the blessedness of establishing communion with others." What is most moving in his works "is what people have in common rather than their differences," and this perception that people are ultimately alike frequently arises from "vastating" experiences. James viewed "mankind as a passionate suffering body, in which love, sorrow, and death are all tangled together, and in which individual men are reduced to the equality in which, paradoxically, they find their highest distinction." It was a sad vision, but also "a deeply emotional affirmation of life."

The finiest section in Fussell's essay is that which considers the theme of the "common doom" in James's work in the context of his life. Fussell suggests that the apparently unrelated experiences of James's "'obscure hut' [sic], his personal relation to the Civil War, his youthful encounter with Hawthorne's writing, his emancipation from 'the James family' and his dedication to the career" of artist all converge in the "pattern underlying the theme of 'the common doom': isolation, 'vastation' and communion" (446-47). Hawthorne especially affected him when he himself was beginning "to open an intercourse with the world," and "Hawthorne's theme became his partly through his personal enaction of it." As a youth, James too experienced "feelings of alienation": his family was different from other families, and he himself was different from the rest of the family. Yet, his father emphasized the need for social harmony—a reminder to James that disconnectedness was not a virtue. All these elements, Fussell explains, are "related to one of his most powerful themes: being different, he must become like." Hence the psychological significance of his "injury": he welcomed it precisely because it enabled him "to enter the communion of the wounded. The half-expressed idea seems to be that James, wounded, was proven susceptible to death and thus capable of sharing the common experience (the Civil War). In his own mind it followed that he could now become a native writer like Hawthorne." This is the "tragic fellowship" he writes about in *Notes of a Son and Brother.*[22] Although after his "pilgrimage" to some American troops he compares himself to Whitman,[23] Hawthorne is more to the point. And since it was during these months that he took in "the full sweet sense" of Hawthorne's work, it is not surprising that his observations on Hawthorne in *Notes of a Son and Brother* turn up together with those on the end of the war:

> The end of the war is associated in James's mind with the sense of the mysteriously fused deaths of Lincoln and Hawthorne. The end of the war and Hawthorne's death coincided with the publication of his first signed stories, as the beginning of the war and his reading of Hawthorne coincided with his dedication to fiction; *that* consecration in turn somehow sprang from his "vastation" and the sense of sharing in the common doom (Hawthorne's theme) that he managed to make of it. The small boy became the adult writer, and the way in which he became a writer, as with Hawthorne (though James mastered the experience as Hawthorne perhaps never did), colored much of his production. James always retained something of the influence of Hawthorne because his starting-point had been the same and . . . because when his own fate had been precarious the elder writer had helped see him through. (Fussell, p. 449)

Fussell's comments on *Hawthorne* were indicated in the first essay. He suggests that what is important in James's list of the items of high civilization unavailable to Hawthorne is the implication that when all these things are left out, what remains to the American is the opportunity "to open an intercourse with the world." This emphasis by Hawthorne "continued to work in James long after he had solved the personal problems that permitted the influence originally to operate so powerfully," and part of the reason for this is because James's long residence abroad kept the idea of alienation fresh in his mind.

In *Ivory Towers and Sacred Founts: The Artist as Hero in Fiction from Goethe to Joyce* (New York: New York University Press, 1964), Maurice Beebe claims that most artist-novels are self-portraits of their creators. To study them is to discover, among other things, a great deal about the relationship of the artist to society. The artist-novel, Beebe explains, assumes that creative man is a divided being, man *and* artist. The "man" has normal appetites and desires, and seeks personal fulfillment in experience, while the artist-self desires freedom from the demands of life and is concerned mainly with "the transcendence of life through creative effort." Thus the Sacred Fount tradition equates art with experience; here art is essentially the re-creating of experience. The Ivory Tower tradition, on the other hand, exalts art above life and insists that the artist can make use of life only if he is detached from it. "In one of its many forms, the Ivory Tower is a lofty perch from which Hawthorne, in 'Sights from a Steeple,' visualized himself a 'spiritualized Paul Pry'" witnessing man's deeds and searching into his heart, but "retaining no emotion peculiar to himself." The Ivory Tower is always the artist's private retreat; it is the Great Good Place of Henry James. There are, Beebe points out, many variations of these basic themes, but the situation of the typical artist-hero is essentially that of the Divided Self of the artist-man wavering between the Ivory Tower and the Sacred Fount, between the aesthetic demands of his mission as artist "and his natural desire as a human being to participate in the life around him" (18).

In the Sacred Fount tradition, the artist finds the source of his art in observation or inspiration. But he can also be destroyed by his art, as is shown in James's *The Sacred Fount.* Beebe notes further that the idea of proportionate shrinkage and intensity is behind most of the "magic portrait" stories like Hawthorne's "The Prophetic Pictures," stories in which the model seems to fade away as the portrait takes on life. The inference here is that since "there is only so much life to be lived, that which is turned into art is made unavailable for living." Later, Beebe notes that Hawthorne was aware "that the artist may commit the sin of appropriating people from the world of observable reality for the sake of his controlling vision," and thus violate the souls of others (189). Likewise, although James believed that observation leads to imaginative insight, he too was convinced that "there is danger in observation, for the artist who observes too closely may appropriate life for a selfish purpose":

> Like Nathaniel Hawthorne, from whom many of his ideas about art seem to derive, James made of the detached observer not only an aesthetic ideal, but also an ethical one. Both Hawthorne and James insisted that the true artist must be detached in order to see clearly, and the really good observer . . . is sympathetically aware of the life about him without trying to appropriate it. Nothing is worse than the exploitation of a human soul: Nathaniel Hawthorne called it the "unforgivable sin," and in Jame's [sic] fiction it appears frequently as "emotional cannibalism," the worst of sins because it is the one most likely to blunt the freedom of the individual consciousness. Both novelists recognized that the very purity and objectivity of the artist's vision makes him susceptible to the crime, for the intensity of his insight may "expose" reality and with it the sanctity of the soul. The painters in James's "The Story of a Masterpiece" and "The Liar" are akin to the artist in Hawthorne's "The Prophetic Pictures" in that they commit for the sake of art a sin as reprehensible as that of Roger Chillingworth, who would read the secrets of the human heart for personal revenge, or Gilbert Osmond, who would appropriate Isabel Archer for his collection of treasures. (206)

Beebe find the idea of the Sacred Fount, or the vampire theme, in many of James's works: "De Grey: A Romance," "The Last of the Valerii," "Longstaff's Marriage," *The Sacred Fount,* and even *The Ambassadors* (the relationship between Chad Newsome and Madame de Vionnet). He notes also that whenever love is depicted in James's fiction, it seems tainted with vampirism, especially in the stories of writers and artists: in *Roderick Hudson,* for example, and in *The Princess Casamassima.* In his discussion of Hawthorne, he indicates that when *The Scarlet Letter* is placed in the context of the works that preceded and followed it, it reveals some of the reasons for Hawthorne's decline as an artist. Hawthorne "seems to have moved from Ivory Tower to Sacred Fount and only seldom to have maintained a balance along the way." At first he obviously held himself aloof from the normal claims of life, but some of his early stories show a growing sense of guilt at setting himself apart from "the great chain of human sympathy." Because as a novelist he was committed to observation of his fellowmen, "he came to feel that the artist's power to expose the human soul could lead him to the 'unforgivable sin.'" Hester in *The Scarlet Letter* "represents the type of the alienated artist"; "she is obviously an outcast from the community." In *The Seven Gables* and *Blithedale,* Hawthorne, like Coverdale, was overwhelmed by life and ceased to be a real artist. His case "shows how art may be defeated by life." The parallels Beebe draws between *Blithedale* and *The Sacred Fount* are discussed in the fourth essay.

Six other people have written at some length on the relation of the artist to society in Hawthorne's and James's works. In *The American Adam* (Chicago: University of Chicago Press, 1955), pp. 191-93, R. W. B. Lewis notes that many American writers have known "that individual men in America were isolated and lonely," and have suggested that the cure for this isolation is "communion": something in the line of Hawthorne's remark about opening "an intercourse with the world," symbolized, in *The Seven Gables,* by Clifford's impulse to throw himself from the window of the old mansion into the midst of the crowd below. However, both Hawthorne and James had different notions about "the location and the character of the community" they belonged to. "For Hawthorne, there were the moral influences and artistic prototypes pressing down through the past, sources at once of repression and freedom." For James, experience "was nothing else than the awareness of an achieved communion: man's apprehension of himself . . . in his social being." Nevertheless, both men "sympathized with that sense of things which made communion difficult and even, as it seemed, altogether unnecessary." One almost wishes Lewis had elaborated on these contrasts and similarities. But that, of course, is not the principal subject of *The American Adam.*[24]

Chapter 2 of Quentin Anderson's *The American Henry James* (1957) has several undeveloped references to Hawthorne. Anderson notes that one group of James's prentice work reflects an influence by Hawthorne, but only in superficial matters: "The Romance of Certain Old Clothes" sounds like an addition to "Legends of the Province House," and "Professor Fargo" is reminiscent of *Blithedale.* The atmosphere and moral conclusions of these stories "suggest second-rate Hawthorne." Another group of early stories reflects "an attempt to come to terms with the Hawthorne vision," but these too "employ Hawthorne's themes only to vary their significnace." Both "Adina" and "The Last of the Valerii," for example, "have a figure reminiscent of Hawthorne's character in *The Marble Faun*," but the latter story "effectually subordinates its 'faun' . . . to his American wife, who has a moral authority Hilda never gains."

More relevant to the present topic are Anderson's comments on "Benvolio," which he sees as "an attempt to throw a bridge between Hawthorne's chief concerns" and James's earliest problems in using European experience. As Benvolio says, art for art's sake, or anything that does not multiply one's relations with life, produces nothing but ennui. And to multiply one's relations one must be involved with the world. However, the *source* of "variety and spontaneity" is not society but the artist's imagination. Hawthorne, who feared "the awful impersonality of intelligence," nevertheless had a "deep and abiding trust in the power of society as a great *existing* brotherhood." In "Benvolio" "James turns on Hawthorne, saying in effect, 'There is no need to fear the impersonality of intelligence—your awful scientists and reformers are just spectres; intelligence is manifest only in *persons,* in style, whereas the "great warm human heart" [*The Scarlet Letter*] . . . with which you figure brotherhood cannot really be trusted.'" Thus he takes "Rappaccini's Daughter" and turns it "topsy-turvy: Scholastica and the father who had trained her are wholly benign; they have separated themselves from the world on the world's behalf." The artist, in other words, sees the world "under the aegis of the imagination."

Anderson's conclusion is that Hawthorne, who trusted the world "to arrive in its slow, bumbling, and incomplete fashion at a sense of moral reality, was largely unintelligible to James," whose moral vision "was at once more completely unified and more diverse," and who found in social fact "not the hard floor of inescapable circumstance, but an array of symbols useful to depict social flux." James was incapable of seeing an alternative to Hawthorne's "bootstrap myth." "For Hawthorne the world was largely intractable to our purposes, offering conditions both foreign and fatal to us; while in James nothing is discernible save the triumphs and defeats of the imagination" (40).

As was indicated in the first section of this essay, one aspect Bewley considers in the essay entitled "The American Problem" in *The Complex Fate* (1952), pp. 55-78, is Hawthorne's concern with solitude as a "crime." His principal observation is that because Hawthorne could not function effectively as an artist in his society, he frequently withdrew from it. But this created a sense of guilt, for in solitude one incurred the danger of becoming socially alienated. This was the impossible dilemma which eventually ruined his art. There was an irreconcilable conflict between the demands of his genius and those he deemed the American society to make on the citizen. The three stories Bewley selects as revealing most about Hawthorne's concept of solitude are "The Devil in Manuscript," "Ethan Brand," and "Wakefield."

In *The Eccentric Design* (1959), pp. 221-23, Bewley notes that James frequently considers the "conflict between the artist and social morality," the same conflict which "proved a stumbling block to Hawthorne." Bewley feels that Dolcino Ambient's danger in "The Author of Beltraffio" is more real than Esther's or Joe Bartram's in "Ethan Brand." The pattern in James's story "has nothing of that irresolution that characterizes Hawthorne's fear of the artist as a danger to society and the individual." According to Bewley, one of James's finest commentaries on "the danger to the artist in withdrawing from the intimacy of personal relationships" is presented in "The Lesson of the Master." Ultimately for the artist security lies, in James's world, where Hawthorne would sense danger: "in sophisticated detachment from the world and from personal relationships capable of imposing obligations on the artist strong enough to encourage him to betray his own genius." Hawthorne's sense of his Puritan ancestors "was too strong to permit him ever, on such a subject as art, to rise to the magnificence of Dencombe's dying speech in 'The Middle Years.'" (As indicated above, Annette Baxter finds Dencombe's affirmation not a "solution, but rather an exhortation to the artist to plunge deeper into the abyss of his talent"–*Nineteenth Century Fiction,* 1955, p. 228.)

Three dissertations have included sections on the artist and society in Hawthorne and James. Barrie Stewart Hayne's "The Divided Self: The Alter Ego as Theme and Device in Brockden Brown, Hawthorne, and James" (Harvard, 1964) is more on the artist *as* artist than on the artist *in* society. Hayne includes also a section on Poe, pp. 152-200, and another on Melville, pp. 335-84. He explains that the nineteenth-century American artist is a divided self: divided between himself and his "surrogate in the work of art," whom he uses either "for self-exorcism or self-aggrandizement"; sometimes the surrogate unites those tendencies which in the artist are not one. Brown, Hawthorne, and James were all part idealist and part realist, and were thus "faced with the necessity of binding within [themselves] diverse and warring concepts." It is this need, and the fear of failure, which directed these writers to the literary device of the divided self. Hayne analyzes the various devices which these authors used to dramatize the theme of the double: mesmerism, occultism, somnambulism, vampirism, metempsychosis, portraiture, and the affinity between close relatives, dead or alive. The "master-mastered" theme too, he points out, is an extension of the double theme.

In chapter 3, "The Magnetic Chain: Hawthorne and Ahab," pp. 201-334, Hayne notes that Hawthorne was always concerned about the function of the artist, and that he feared that, since the artist "pries into private areas which ought properly not to be his concern," he may be himself a violater of the human heart. Hawthorne presented two kinds of artists: "the poet-seer," who finds the real in the ideal, and "the analytic prober of the psyche." He himself was of the first kind. The second kind includes all those manipulators and moral dissectors who are unsympathetic to their characters, and this is the type of artist Hawthorne feared he might become. Holgrave, according to Hayne, is Hawthorne's most flattering portrait of the artist, and "the kind of artist he might have sought to be." In Holgrave the head and the heart are in proper balance; he is at once speculative and active. During Hawthorne's most creative period, he succeeded in reconciling the ideal with the real. When, beginning with *The Marble Faun,* he departed from his usual method, and proceeded not from idea but from actuality, he was "unable to translate the reality into symbol and idea." "That reconciliation breaking down, it was left to Henry James to insist upon that 'solidity of specification' which realism comprehends." "To see Hawthorne's aim as an artist in this light," Hayne observes:

> is to see so many of his characters as surrogates of that artist. Not only the prying artists like Coverdale . . . or those who refuse to pry, like Holgrave, and so represent a true surrogate, a representation of Hawthorne's aims achieved, but also those like Hollingsworth, whose failure to balance in the proper proportion the head and the heart, the ideal and the real, destroys them. . . . [The] important point is that Hawthorne, with these two polarities in his mind, one thematic, one philosophic, was himself constantly split by opposing forces, and his characters, depending upon whether they fail to join up their cleft personalities or whether they succeed, represent respectively his pessimistic and optimistic prognosis . . . of the artist, and himself. (323-25)

Hayne also relates the "master-mastered" theme in *The Scarlet Letter* (Chillingworth and Dimmesdale) to that in *The Bostonians* (Olive Chancellor and Verena Tarrant), and the theme of "the metempsychotic return through time" in *The Seven Gables* with that in "The Jolly Corner" and *The Sense of the Past.*

In chapter 4, on James, pp. 385-500, Hayne indicates that James too was torn between the ideal and the real, and that he dramatized the tension thus produced "in the pairs of artists . . . [who are] both in a measure his surrogates." There is the artist whose commercial success destroys his talent, and the talented artist who is unrecognized. James was often "torn between the yearning for popular acclaim and the impulse towards artistic perfection regardless of that popular acclaim." But the two types of artists are actually complementary, and the kind of artist James approved of was one in whom the realist and idealist are in proper balance. Hayne finds the central themes of "The Madonna of the Future" carrying "all the doubts and some of the defiance of the closing lines of 'The Artist of the Beautiful.'" "Benvolio" too "has suggestions of 'Rappaccini's Daughter,' though somewhat in reverse." Over and again Hayne emphasizes that "James restored the balance between the Actual and the Imaginary which had failed Hawthorne in his last period," although the balance which was restored was of a different order. "James, then," he writes:

> takes Hawthorne a step further, and it is as an advance that James's use of Hawthorne is to be seen, rather than a *volte-face* . . . Hawthorne's romances and tales passed early into James's consciousness. James claimed for some of his earliest stories . . . the same kind of latitude that Hawthorne had claimed for his. . . . Some of his works of the 'seventies . . . show the author of *The Marble Faun* in their background. And at the end of the same decade he paid his fullest and most explicit tribute to his American master, at the same time . . . reaching towards the explicit formulation of his own principles of fiction. . . . Finally, at the very end of his career, James returned to Hawthorne with *The Sense of the Past*. . . . Hawthorne in his final unfinished work was groping . . . towards a formulation of the international theme. . . . "The Madonna of the Future" . . . looks both forward to *Roderick Hudson* and back to *The Marble Faun*. Hawthorne, then, helped James to formulate the international theme, and encouraged him to connect it with a transfer of power between the representatives of Europe and America. . . . In another way, too, James borrowed from Hawthorne, taking over that pair of characters . . . who by usurpation of the personality of one by the other became inextricably linked. (398-400)

Hayne's comments on the indebtedness of *The Bostonians* and *The Sacred Fount* to *Blithedale* are discussed in the fourth essay. He also notes that in both "The Liar" and "Owen Wingrave," James uses the portrait as Hawthorne had earlier used it; that the unnamed girl in *In the Cage* "looks back to . . . Coverdale"; and that, contrary to what some critics have said, James's failure to finish *The Sense of the Past* was not due to "a failure to resolve the split in himself comparable to Hawthorne's final disintegration. . . . [It] was due to death rather than to disinclination." The American *Zerrissenheit* had neither the searing nor the finally destructive effect on James that it had on Hawthorne. "James dramatized, again and again, the doubleness of consciousness, the ambiguities of existence . . . by means of various versions of the double theme. But in him, however near at times the split may have been, the fusion was maintained" (500).

John Michael Kaman's "The Lonely Hero in Hawthorne, Melville, Twain and James" (Stanford, 1973) is not exactly on the artist's relation to society, but his analysis of *Blithedale* and *The Ambassadors* has some general relevance to the topic. And since Kaman does not explicitly compare the works of the above authors, his chapter on Miles Coverdale and that on Lambert Strether are reviewed below rather than in the fourth essay. Kaman explains that the American hero separates himself from his community by repudiating its values, and that the test he faces is whether to remain true to his inner sense of values or to re-enter and accept the mediocrity of his community. His "loneliness is produced by a pair of related contradictions": being and consciousness on the one hand, and freedom on the other. In *Blithedale,* "Coverdale wants to join the community of labor and the realm of human activity but finds he can do so only at the cost of both his freedom and his vision. He finishes his narrative as a bachelor comfortably undisturbed by human contact." In *The Ambassadors,* Strether "hangs on precariously to his sense of everpresent possibility. To choose and thus to act become the only impossibility for to do so is to narrow infinite potentialities to a single existent actuality."

In chapter 1, "Miles Coverdale's Dilemma," pp. 14-45, Kaman argues that *Blithedale* is in part "a self-examination of the role of artist-observer," and that the basic contradiction in the novel is between vision and reality. Coverdale's greatest fear at Blithedale is that he will lose his vision; he represents "the artist as voyeur." "He first seeks to escape human society in general and later the society of Blithedale." In thus removing himself from society, he alienates himself from the substance of his art, and "in each instance he is forced by impulses he seems not to understand to return to that which he sought liberty from." His "inability to commit himself either to his vision or to the material world" mirrors Hawthorne's own self-doubts. Furthermore, as artist, Coverdale invests "reality with a meaning or spiritual significance that it does not apparently possess," by either consciously inflating reality, or consciously suppressing information. "For Coverdale, being, in its gross materiality, has to be transformed into a purely visionary realm of consciousness to be at all significant." Kaman's verdict is that in *Blithedale* Hawthorne "was attempting a resolution of the most basic contradiction the novelist faces as an artisan: the contradiction between experience and perception, being and consciousness." His use of Coverdale as his investigator is a reflection of his unending investigation of his own role in a material society. Coverdale's inadequacy and ineffectuality mirror "the fear Hawthorne harbors about the necessity and functionality of his own vision." (In the chapter on Melville, p. 47, Kaman points out that whereas "Coverdale feels that individuality is realized in solitariness . . . [Hawthorne] feels somewhat differently. . . . The idea that man is a solitary rather than a social being is developed more as the aberration of a minor poet than as a description of human existence.")

In chapter 4, "The Privacy of Lambert Strether," pp. 113–45, Kaman observes that for Strether, loneliness is the medium of all experience, and thus any "alliance becomes a compromise of individual integrity." In James's world, the basis of vision and intelligence lies "in the observation of observation." Since participation blurs intelligence, the highest refinements of consciousness can be achieved only by outsiders like Strether, "voyeurs to the experience of others." In Paris, Strether develops "a purely subjective awareness of the possible" in its infinite sense, but he is at last isolated and alone in the full enjoyment of his powers. It is his sense of the possible that isolates him from full participation in human affairs. He refuses to choose "because any choice . . . must always exclude some possibilities and thus impoverish human experience." Thus his liberation, his "enlarged sense of possibility," becomes more confining than his previous conformity. *The Ambassadors,* then, illustrates the full "consequences of that vision of the solitary and lonely hero which inform" all the novels Kaman has examined (the other two are Melville's *Pierre* and Twain's *Huckleberry Finn*). *Blithedale* "ends in an isolated but comfortable physical existence for its bachelor observer." At the end of *The Ambassadors,* what awaits Strether in America is nothing but isolation. "He is a man wholly without human connection who affirms his own subjectivity in the absence of any real means of acting upon his environment" (145).

Harriet Rose's "The First-Person as Artist in the Works of Charles Brockden Brown, Nathaniel Hawthorne, and Henry James" (Indiana University, 1973) includes a chapter on Jack London, pp. 134–40, and another on F. Scott Fitzgerald, pp. 141–44. Rose observes that nineteenth-century American fiction is full of artists who "often display criminal overtones, become guilty of aesthetic fraudulence, and . . . end as creative failures." Such characters are often found "in fiction narrated by the first person, where the 'I' is an artist . . . close to the writer's own psyche." In Brown's *Arthur Mervyn,* Hawthorne's *Blithedale,* and many of James's stories of writers and artists, the narrator has "to choose between a figure of true art, who offers a future of aesthetic fertility . . . and a corrupt artist." The narrator repeatedly makes the wrong choice; lured "by the dark figure away from aesthetic fulfillment, he moves rather toward . . . creative impotence." Often he himself displays negative characteristics. Coverdale, for example, "is a poet whom his peers look upon as 'not in earnest,'" and Westervelt is a false artist who wears a "strange philosophical guise in terms of art." Similarly, James's stories are full of counterfeit writers, impostors, and windbags. "Opposed to the shadow is . . . a divine muse" who offers the artist "the gift of inspiration": Priscilla in *Blithedale,* for instance, or Miss Churm in James's "The Real Thing."

In chapter 2, on *Blithedale*, pp. 36-75, Rose examines Hawthorne's romance "in terms of its elaborate fairy tale motif": Zenobia and Priscilla are the muse figures who "promise to inspire Coverdale with true art," while Westervelt and Hollingsworth, both frauds, beckon him "to join them on the easy road to . . . false art." Coverdale himself, a detached observer, is as much a figure of false art as these two villains. At the end of the story he leaves his shelf of half finished poems incomplete "and ultimately abandons his literary profession."

In chapter 3, pp. 76-114, Rose analyzes James's "The Real Thing," "The Madonna of the Future," "The Coxon Fund," and "The Death of the Lion"; in chapter 4, pp. 115-33, she concentrates on *The Aspern Papers*. In James's later works, she shows, the muse has lost "even her limited ability to offer the artist the promise of aesthetic fulfillment." This is the case of Serafina in "The Madonna of the Future" and Juliana in *The Aspern Papers*. Whereas in *Blithedale* "lifting the veil was an optimistic possibility for the hero," in *The Aspern Papers* "the veil has become far more pessimistically a token of corruption and fraud."

Feminist Perspectives

Many studies, especially during the seventies, have been addressed to Hawthorne's and James's—as well as other American novelists'—heroines, and the attitude of these novelists toward women characters in general. The two most worthy are Pratt's and Montgomery's essays reviewed below. But before that, a foil for them should be provided: Wendy Martin's "Seduced and Abandoned in the New World: The Image of Women in American Fiction," in *Woman in Sexist Society*, edited by V. Gornick and B. K. Moran (New York: Basic Books, 1971), pp. 226-39. Martin's essay includes a rather simplistic evaluation of three of Hawthorne's and three of James's women characters.[25] American fictional heroines, Martin observes, "have reenacted Eve's fall from grace and thereby inherited the legacy of Eden." As daughters of Eve they are destined to dependency and servitude because, "like their predecessor, they have dared to disregard authority or tradition in the search for wisdom or happiness; like Eve, they are fallen women, eternally cursed for eating the apple of experience." Many of the major American novels "perpetuate the archetype of the fallen woman, thereby conditioning women to accept their inferior status." An example of an heiress of Eve's legacy is Hester Prynne in *The Scarlet Letter*. She is doomed to wear the scarlet A, "and her fall from grace is underscored by her apparent loss of beauty." Added to this is the burden of her cruel public punishment. Although, while in the woods, she tried to free herself, her efforts "were useless and she was forced to forfeit her sexuality." Hawthorne reminds us that "independent thought and emotion, that is, self-reliance, can be dangerous for women," which is ironic, "since self-reliance is an American virtue, and male protagonists . . . are praised for their courage in breaking out of the confines of traditional society." Although Hester does harsh penance by spending the rest of her days counseling women in similar predicaments, Hawthorne undermines her position by concluding that no "mission of divine and mysterious truth should be confined to a woman stained with sin. . . . The angel and apostle of the coming revelation must be a woman, indeed, but loft, pure, and beautiful; and wise, moreover, not through dusky grief, but the ethereal medium of joy" (*The Scarlet Letter,* chapter 24).

Blithedale, according to Martin, "is Hawthorne's secular version of *The Scarlet Letter.*" Priscilla, passive and pristine, represents piety; Zenobia, stately and commanding, represents passion. Like Hester, Zenobia is warm, generous, and passionate. Ironically, although she is a champion of women's rights, she "submits to Hollingsworth's egotism and capitulates to his very traditional definition of woman as man's subordinate." And, in a moment of self-abasement, she drowns herself. Coverdale too "reveals his own chauvinism" at the end of the novel: he too loved Priscilla, "whom he had described earlier as a 'gentle parasite, the soft reflection of a more powerful existence.'" In revealing his own preference for the "gentle parasite," "Coverdale was perhaps echoing Hawthorne himself, who had strong antifeminist predilections" (230).

The characters Martin examines in James's *The Bostonians* are Verena Tarrant, "an articulate and passionate public speaker for woman's rights"; Olive Chancellor, politically more sophisticated than Verena; and Basil Ransom, who despises feminists and tries "to convince Verena to give herself to a man rather than a movement." Although Verena despises his philosophy, she is irresistibly drawn to him. However, James too expresses his own misgivings about her fate by confiding that Ransom cannot redeem her. But while the conclusion of the novel reveals James's essential sympathy for Verena, he nevertheless places her in "an either/or situation no man would really face": she has to choose between a husband and her ideas, and she "is damned if she does and damned if she doesn't." Isabel Archer in *The Portrait* is a much stronger person than Verena. Attractive, articulate, and intelligent, she wants to actively shape her own life. James tells us that Isabel is really "frightened of herself," but it is difficult "to imagine the cause of this fear unless she has internalized the conventional definition of wife and worries that her ego is too assertive to permit her to be pious, passive, and supportive." On the one hand, she wishes to choose her fate; on the other, "she is afraid of not being able to meet social expectations." Although her life as Mrs. Osmond is one of active suffering, she remains committed to her marriage vow. Ironically, she too is imprisoned by her own sense of duty. After considering works by five other authors, Martin concludes by suggesting that fiction "can contribute to changing female consciousness and man's concept of woman by providing a vision of a new Eve, of a woman who is self-actualizing, strong, risk-taking, but also capable of loving and being loved" (238).

In "The American Galatea," *College English,* 32 (May, 1971), 890-99, Judith H. Montgomery discusses the myth of Pygmalion and Galatea, and how the nineteenth-century American woman became Galatea. She argues that this myth fuses two basic impulses in man: creation and possession. "At the instant of life," she writes, "Galatea thus incorporates woman's archetypal dilemma: she is both inferior and superior, but never equal to Pygmalion." The three works Montgomery analyzes at length are *Blithedale, The Portrait,* and Edith Wharton's *The House of Mirth.* Her analysis of Hawthorne's and James's novels is reviewed in the fourth essay.

In fiction, as in life–Montgomery observes–"man struggled to realize the perfect woman and to portray the consequences of failure to conform to that image." Hawthorne's interest, she finds, does not lie "with the successful Galatea, but with the failed one. He does not serve Pygmalion's vision, but he does portray the consequences of the American heroine's failure to achieve or to maintain herself within the narrow distinctions of perfection which had come to define her. He is the delineator of 'the woman who swerves one hair's breadth out of the beaten track.'" James, however, is not so objective, perhaps because he wrote "during the period in which the confinement of the American woman by the Galatean myth was most stringent." At the end of her discussion of *The Portrait,* Montgomery examines Isabel's decision to return to Osmond from England after Ralph's funeral. "Once in England," she writes, the shock of the various events and revelations

> leave Isabel in a moral suspension. If she returns to Osmond, it will be entirely on his terms. . . . If she does not return, she tarnishes . . . her marriage vows. The choice is between fulfillment of the self and fulfillment of the image. By introducing as her only remaining future a life of lust with Caspar Goodwood, James forces Isabel consistently into a role as object, as the reflector of men's desires. As such a woman, Isabel must choose only the fulfillment of the image. (895-96)

It is therefore incorrect to assume that by her actions she surpasses the limitations of her life, and to applaud her choice as moral and vital. For it is neither. In returning to Osmond she denies herself. "It is a choice spiritually immoral; yet, given her evolution," she is afforded no real alternative. Montgomery's conclusion is that although James "does not permit Pygmalion's impulse literally to kill this heroine . . . such slow, internal death may well surpass that grosser end."

The most judicious of the feminist studies in this section is Linda Ray Pratt's "The Abuse of Eve by the New World Adam," in *Images of Women in Fiction,* revised edition, edited by S. K. Cornillion (Bowling Green, Ohio: Bowling Green University Popular Press, 1973), pp. 155-74. Pratt examines a number of women characters in *Blithedale, The Marble Faun, The Portrait,* and Cooper's *The Deerslayer* "in terms of the ubiquitous Edenic myth." Her thesis is that these novels reveal the "superior humanity" of the heroines. Many critics, she observes, have shown that "characterization in the American novel has often denied women the . . . complexity of full defined human beings, and that the role women have played in the American novel as a whole has been overshadowed by the male heroes." However, it is a fact that the male characters in these novels often "suffer the same lack of fully human delineation. This condition is especially true in the nineteenth-century novel where, with the exception of those of Henry James, characters are often more abstractly symbolic than humanly detailed." Where recent feminist criticism goes astray, Pratt points out, "is in analyses and interpretations which depart widely from the context of . . . the controlling worlds of the novels themselves." Such criticism illustrates "certain societal attitudes toward women rather than the function of women characters within the context of a specific novel." What Pratt attempts is "a critical feminist approach . . . that will [both] reveal more accurately the nature of female characters within the world of the novels," and suggest "the attitudes of the authors toward women in nineteenth-century America."

Many critics, Pratt observes, have suggested that Hawthorne and James "are not narrow Edenic ideologues preaching the inviolable innocence of the American Adam." It would be unsafe, therefore, to "assume that their light-dark women characters represent a rigid dualism of good and evil." In *The Scarlet Letter,* for example, Hester is far more attractively human than any of the men surrounding her; in *Blithedale,* it is Zenobia who controls our interest at the end of the novel; and in *The Marble Faun* "Miriam is singularly more real than any of her companions." James too "reserves the greatest moral triumphs for women and leaves to men such roles as the naively egotistical Christopher Newman, or the bumbling Lambert Strether." Pratt's argument is that Hawthorne uses the pure and impure women to represent the pre- and post-lapsarian Eve. "The pre-lapsarian Eve can never enter the world of experience and be humanized by worldly contact." She is necessarily "a static and abstract companion to the unfallen Adam." The post-lapsarian Eve, on the other hand, "has been humanized by the experience of evil, but she is rejected by the Adamic hero who must protect his innocence. She is further ostracised by a society absorbed in its own Edenic illusions." The women characters who are post-lapsarian Eves often "emerge as the most human figures of all." Furthermore:

> The role of women in Cooper, Hawthorne, and James appears to be inextricably bound by the degree to which the novelist is imprisoned by Edenic myth. Thus, the freer the novelist is from the attractions of Edenic innocence, the greater the measure of human status afforded the women characters. James, who most completely rejects the appeal of an Adamic American, creates the kind of fully defined woman who most nearly approaches the level of Eliot's Dorothea Brook. The escape from the Garden into the fallen world means woman's release from symbolic abstraction into the condition of humanity. (Pratt, pp. 157-58)

Pratt's comparison of *Blithedale* and *The Marble Faun* with *The Portrait* is reviewed in the fourth and fifth essays. Her observation is that perhaps because Hawthorne was attracted by naive innocence, it is his Priscillas, the pre-lapsarian Eves, who find happiness in life, although his Zenobias, the post-lapsarian figures, earn the "higher innocence." And it is his men who are morally timid and intellectually shallow, and all the beauty, wisdom, and vitality of the women "are finally inadequate to shake the men from their fearful dependence on the male illusion." James, she finds, is the major nineteenth-century American author who denied most the validity of American innocence; in the figure of Isabel Archer he rejected "the limits imposed on women by such Americans as Cooper and Hawthorne." Pratt's interpretation of Isabel's refusal of Caspar Goodwood in order to return to Osmond is very different from Montgomery's. Isabel's character, she argues, is a combination of both pre- and post-lapsarian Eve figures. "If viewed in the perspective of the dual nature of Eve," her choice is certainly wiser than that by "the undisciplined Zenobia. As the post-lapsarian Eve, Isabel's rejection of Caspar, the 'American Adam,' frees her to grow while it incapacitates him in a static illusion. Her qualified acceptance of the role of wife to Osmond . . . imposes on the fallen world the knowledge of sin and redemptive wisdom which is the essential function of Eve." In returning to Rome, Isabel moves "out of the garden (literally Gardencourt) into the world of experience." What Caspar offers her is a return to a pre-lapsarian state, an escape from life. If "she is to make any meaning out of her life, her fall from innocence to wisdom must move her back into the world of experience," and that means the world of Osmond. Although social freedom from Osmond is as impossible for her as Caspar's naive promise of a new beginning, "her understanding of Osmond's nature . . . frees her from Osmond's moral and spiritual influence." Thus, in her final choice she rejects both the role of pre-lapsarian Eve which the Adamic Caspar wishes her to play, and the restrictions of obedient effacement which Osmond demands. Pratt's conclusion is that, contrary to some critical opinion, neither Hawthorne nor James was truly "callous to the plight of women in American society"; neither were they consistent advocates of the Adamic innocence. If their words are re-evaluated in the light of social and sexual realities, one discovers that their "women characters often surpass the so-called heroes in moral complexity and human veracity."

One other published work includes a discussion of Hawthorne's and James's women characters: Leslie A. Fiedler's *Love and Death in the American Novel,* revised edition (New York: Stein and Day, 1966), pp. 302-305. Fiedler indicates that although *The Marble Faun* was the first international romance in which the Fair Maiden and the Dark Lady clearly stood for American innocence and European experience, Hawthorne only tentatively approached the theme; the dark-haired Miriam remains just another tourist attraction for Hilda, the snow maiden, and Kenyon, the genteel artist. It was not until James that the Dark Lady-Fair Girl archetype, and the myth of the American in Europe, were fused into a rich and unified subject.[26] It is in his use of the pattern of dark worldly lady and light innocent maiden that James is most deeply indebted to Hawthorne. The Nice American Girl appears variously in *The Portrait, The Wings of the Dove,* and *The Golden Bowl.* She is derived partly from Minny Temple, James's cousin, and partly from Hilda, "Hawthorne's prototypical sketch of the American Girl abroad." Just as Hawthorne portrayed Hilda as the Lady of the Doves, so did James characterize Milly Theale in dove imagery. Maggie Verver is even more profoundly linked to Hilda. Just as Hawthorne, making a spiritual portrait of his wife, said that Hilda's womanhood is "incompatible with any shadow of darkness or evil," and that she "would die of her first wrong-doing–supposing for a moment that she could be capable of doing wrong," James too said that Maggie Verver "'wasn't born to know evil,' 'must never know it,' thus joining her to the strange breed of human [sic] whom Hawthorne had first imagined as blond and snow-white enough to be exempt from original sin."[27] This shows that both novelists "confused the symbolic figure of innocence, projected by Sentimentalists as a blond Maiden, with certain fair girls whom they actually knew."

Fiedler observes further that James often provided his dove girls foils like Madame Merle in *The Portrait,* Kate Croy in *The Wings of the Dove,* or Charlotte Stant in *The Golden Bowl.* These dark-haired, dark-eyed counter-virgins circle nervously about their more passive opposites, their destined prey, "drawn by an ambivalent love, much like the passion that joined and divided Hawthorne's Zenobia and Priscilla." Lastly, James augmented the charm of his blond virgins' chastity with the magic of money, and here again he may have taken a cue from Hawthorne, who in chapter 24 of *The Scarlet Letter* tells us that "Pearl–the elf-child–the demon offspring . . . became the richest heiress of her day, in the New World." Like Pearl before them, James's heroines aspire not only to be American aristocrats, ennobled by wealth, but real princesses too.[28]

Of the five dissertations that have discussed women characters in Hawthorne and James, Sharon Welch Dean's "Lost Ladies: The Isolated Heroine in the Fiction of Hawthorne, James, Fitzgerald, Hemingway, and Faulkner" (University of New Hampshire, 1973) is the strongest. "Lost Ladies" is essentially an extension of Montgomery's "The American Galatea" (1971), which Dean lists in her bibliography. "In much of the best American fiction," Dean indicates, women are essentially domestic objects. But for the lost woman, "even the domestic role is denied her. Because she is a sexual threat or because love is impossible in a wasteland society, she is exiled by women who conform more than she, by men, and by the world as a whole." She thus seeks an impossible escape from isolation, usually through an illicit love relationship, and when this fails, she "practices some form of martyrdom as the only role left her." Such women appear frequently in the fiction of the above novelists, and these portraits reveal the author's vision of womanhood, and his vision of life. For Hawthorne and James, the social order must survive, and the woman who threatens to destroy it must atone for her sin. "The Hawthorne and James lost woman, therefore, accepts isolation *for* society rather than continuing to seek isolation *from* society." According to Dean, all the above authors fail to provide the lost woman with "a viable alternative to isolation." Furthermore, Hawthorne's and James's "lost woman is seen as a 'dark lady' of experience in contrast to a light girl who is variously portrayed as shallow because she lives in a 'cloistered virtue,' or devastating because she pretends perfection" and uses her power to manipulate others.

In the chapter on Hawthorne, pp. 11-40, Dean argues that Hester, Zenobia, and Miriam either are never loved at all, or find only temporary love. Both *The Scarlet Letter* and *Blithedale* focus on "the error a woman falls into because she can find no legitimate outlet for her feelings or talents." But in neither work does Hawthorne provide the mature woman in America with any alternative to her frustrating situation. Hester, Zenobia, and even Miriam all finally renounce, for the sake of the law and the community, what happiness they might have had through their illicit sexual involvements.

In the chapter on James, pp. 41-95, Dean claims that the reason James, in *Hawthorne,* stressed his predecessor's preference for solitude over sociability is because at that time "James was pledging celibacy as a way of maintaining the peace he needed as a writer, and his emphasis on Hawthorne's success in relative solitude is part of this pledge." Few of James's heroines, Dean explains, love and are loved in return. In most of his works, "reciprocated and passionate love is not involved." It is not until his last three novels that he committed himself to portraying heroines similar to Hester, Zenobia, and Miriam. However, unlike Hawthorne's heroines, James's "do not try to ignore society." Instead, they manipulate it, and this too leads to isolation. And more than Hawthorne, James recognized from the earliest that love always involves the issue of power. In both *The Wings of the Dove* and *The Golden Bowl,* love cannot be separated from James's two symbols of power, money and sex:

> Where Hawthorne sees love as essential in marriage, James sees money as essential. To Hawthorne's insight that a woman like Hester . . . too often marries without love because society dictates she must marry, James adds the need of a woman to push for a marriage which will make her financially comfortable. The power of money usurps the power of love. And to Hawthorne's view of sex as an expression of unity even when the partners are forced to separate, James adds the dimension of sex itself as a disunity. In both *The Wings of the Dove* and *The Golden Bowl* . . . money and sex undermine love. (44)

Although James's other heroines too recall Hawthorne's, Dean observes, "they do not carry on Hawthorne's conception of the lost woman." The lost woman is innocent in the sense that she is ignorant, not guiltless. And she "always suggests overt sexuality. On the bases of innocence and sexuality," therefore, many of James's heroines are not clear examples of the lost woman.

Earlier, Dean had remarked that "Hawthorne preferred brunettes" (40). James too, she indicates, "intended the dark women to be the more admirable heroines" of *The Wings of the Dove* and *The Golden Bowl.* Milly Theale is a major heroine because Kate Croy makes her so, just as Miriam makes Hilda important. And, of course, "in real life [James] admired women who were more Kate Croys than Milly Theales." In *The Wings of the Dove* and *The Golden Bowl,* James deals

> sympathetically with the plight of a fully sexual woman in the nineteenth century. In this sense these are the novels that most resemble *The Blithedale Romance.* And in these, not in *The Bostonians,* the heroines want the fulfillment of love and marriage that Zenobia seeks in Hollingsworth. But in *The Wings of the Dove* the question of fulfillment through love is largely an aside, for unable to marry, Kate Croy can remain loyal to her blood ties and thus retain some meaning in her life. Losing Densher, as Zenobia loses Hollingsworth, she need not resort to suicide. Unlike both Zenobia and Kate, Charlotte attaches an importance to marriage so great that it can be sought without love. She does so because she is alone in the world. (79-80)

But James, like Hawthorne, cannot endorse adultery. Where in Hawthorne illicit sex is doomed, in James it is perverted as well as doomed. And James is very close to Hawthorne in the belief that illicit sexuality isolates the two people from the larger community and its laws. Hence the absence of any "really private scene between intimates" in all of Hawthorne and James: behind Hester and Dimmesdale in the woods is Pearl; behind Charlotte and the Prince is the butler they must deceive. The point here is that society, in some form, is always near enough to have to be contended with. "What James wants . . . even more than Hawthorne, is isolation for some purpose beyond the self." Kate's and Charlotte's attempts to escape isolation, like those of Hawthorne's lost women, "are doomed to fail because these attempts go against the laws of the community and, therefore, still involve isolation."

In her last chapter, pp. 186-201, Dean emphasizes that all her five authors use their heroines "as a vehicle to explore the conflict between isolation and community." For Hawthorne, "if the community imposes isolation upon a woman, the woman herself is no less sinful when she welcomes it because of selfish pride instead of enduring it for the sake of another." Thus in all his novels "the value of the social order is reasserted." Like Hawthorne, James in *The Wings of the Dove* and *The Golden Bowl* stresses that "though the community isolates, the community must survive." Once the heroines of these five novelists "learn about the futility of creating an isolation of two," "they in some way renounce for the sake of the community or the individual." This idea of renunciation, according to Dean, constitutes both the triumph and failure of these novelists. Because of their tendency to idealize their lost heroines, they often create "a type of woman whose [passionate] response to life is unrealistic or even perverse." But they never create for these women any meaningful outlet for this response. Furthermore, these writers make passionate love "somehow unAmerican." With the exception of Faulkner, all the lost women of the other four novelists are in some way foreign: Hester is clearly British; Charlotte is an expatriate American. The more negative heroines, on the other hand—the Hildas and the Maggie Ververs—are all Americans. Although each of the five authors "bemoans the fact that the mature woman has no place in society, the only place he can create for her, even in his fiction, is an isolated martyrdom." And this "may be the greatest failure on the part of each of these authors."

Another readable dissertation is Judith Joy Fryer's "The Faces of Eve: A Study of Women in American Life and Literature in the Nineteenth Century" (University of Minnesota, 1973). Fryer indicates that the myth of America as the New World Garden of Eden attained its first fictional ripeness in the works of Hawthorne, and that it culminated in those of James. The women by these authors, as well as those by Melville, Holmes, and Howells "are not women at all" but mere reflections of nineteenth-century attitudes toward women. Fryer identifies four different faces of the American Eve. The temptress "is Hawthorne's 'dark lady'—Beatrice Rappaccini, Hester Prynne,

Miriam"; often she is condemned by the novelist as a deviant from society. The American princess is Eve before the Fall; "she is the 'pale maiden' of Hawthorne and Melville—Priscilla, Hilda, and Lucy—and Henry James' Daisy Miller, Milly Theale, Maggie Verver and, ultimately, Isabel Archer." The great mother, a manipulating and possessive figure, appears primarily in James; and The new woman, the "free" and "equal" woman of the utopian novels, is ironically "not a person at all, but a caricature": Zenobia, Olive Chancellor, and others like them.

In chapter 2, "The Temptress," pp. 41-127, Fryer argues that Hawthorne created "the most complex version of the temptress archetype." Beatrice, Hester, and Miriam are all temptresses. Zenobia, of course, is "the 'new woman'"; she is not so much a deviant from society as "a shaper of a new set of mores in a new community." In chapter 3, "The American Princess," pp. 128-205, Fryer explains that the American Eve before the Fall is characterized by a "combination of innocence *and* self-reliance." Priscilla and Hilda are Hawthorne's American princesses; James's include Isabel Archer, Daisy Miller, Milly Theale, and Maggie Verver. Unlike the American Adam, however, "Eve as American Princess is never given a chance . . . to be really self-reliant." She is always attracted to a prince: Priscilla is seen in relation to Hollingsworth and Coverdale, Daisy Miller in relation to Giovanelli and Winterbourne. Hilda, of course, was the first American girl to go to Europe—except for Pearl, who went there at the end of *The Scarlet Letter.* And Hilda "kept her innocence by acting like an angel. Daisy Miller goes to Europe to demonstrate that Hilda's kind of innocence is a myth":

> It is Daisy's audacity that makes her a new and important type in American fiction. Where innocence had been associated in Hawthorne with goodness and boldness with badness, James gives us here a type of American girl who is both bold and good. In *The Wings of the Dove* James will return to the Hawthorne formula and separate his innocent and bold heroine into good and bad, pale maiden and dark lady; and this American Princess, too, will die—clearly of a broken heart. (151)

It is not until *The Golden Bowl* that the American princess lives happily ever after, and even then, it is only after "she has learned to compromise with the imperfect Old World." Fryer's comments on *Blithedale* and *The Bostonians,* and on *The Marble Faun* and *The Wings of the Dove,* are evaluated in the fourth and fifth essays respectively.

In chapter 4, "The Great Mother," pp. 206-85, Fryer indicates that the "key to the mother-figure in James' fiction" is *possession*: this is the case with the governess in *The Turn of the Screw,* and Madame Merle and Mrs. Touchett in *The Portrait.* In chapter 5, "The New Woman," pp. 286-364, she notes that for a long time James failed "to get inside a woman's consciousness," and presented her merely in terms of her environment. Later—perhaps because he had come to terms with his own sexuality—he succeeded in creating "a woman of real vitality—Madame de Vionnet in *The Ambassadors*." But Madame de Vionnet is not an American. "It would take a woman to get inside the consciousness of a woman, to portray her as a *person*," Fryer declares. One should point out here that when Montgomery (1971) considered the question of "whether female authors have been able to create heroines more successfully human and independent," she found that Lily Bart in Edith Wharton's *The House of Mirth* "is, if anything, still more the essence of the American Galatea than Isabel Archer." Furthermore, nineteenth-century authors of the "domestic" novel "were often women; yet they subjected their heroines to the same strictures as those imposed by male novelists." (Montgomery, pp. 896-97) Pratt (1973) explained that perhaps "the American devotion to Adamism suggests some reasons why nineteenth century America did not produce great women writers . . . . The cultural pursuit of innocence demanded of American women precluded knowledge of the ways of the world," and the "'damned scribblers' who did write generally used their fiction as an extension of woman's accepted role" (Pratt, p. 170).

Maude Cardwell Ross's "Moral Values of the American Woman as Presented in Three Major American Authors" (University of Texas, 1964) describes "the patterns of moral values in the conduct" of Hester Prynne, Maggie Verver, and Faulkner's Eula Varner. Ross does not consider the question of influence at all, although in her conclusion she does mention some similarities between the three heroines. Her first chapter is on Hester, pp. 11-43. She argues that Hester "follows first the code of nature and then the code of mastery." But neither goal enables her to gratify her spontaneous desires. At the end of the novel she adopts the code of altruism, but even this "is incapable of fully satisfying anyone. There is, in fact, no ideal code of moral values" in the novel. We are shown that a new moral code must be found, but we are "given only hints as to what this new code may be."

The second chapter is on Maggie Verver, pp. 44-103. Ross explains that the Jamesian standard requires his men to follow the code of power, and his women the code of love. Adam Verver adheres wholeheartedly to the code of power, but because Maggie has no mother to guide her in the following of the code of love, at first she obeys the principles of the code of power. Later she discovers and follows the code of love. After considering Faulkner's *The Hamlet, The Town,* and *The Mansion,* Ross concludes that "Hester Prynne, Maggie Verver and Eula Varner follow three different codes of moral values . . . but are remarkably similar in the relationships they have with others." They all

> seek value in the eyes of others, and a gratification of their spontaneous desires. A follower of the code of altruism, Hester Prynne

> counts on reaching this goal in heaven. To do so, she . . . partially identifies herself with other people, and submits to . . . God. Hester looks forward, however, to a happier time, when a woman will be able to achieve her goal on earth, by adhering to a different code. . . . A follower of the code of love, Maggie Verver hopes to reach her goal in heaven, but is more interested in reaching it on earth. . . . In addition, she values a state of rapture that arises from her complete identification with others. (188)

Hester, Maggie, and Eula all identify themselves with others, "and they do so in a way that their heroes can do only with difficulty": Arthur dies immediately after his initial identification with his townspeople, and "Adam and Amerigo make no attempt to identify themselves with anyone but Maggie." Clearly, all the three heroines are "morally and spiritually superior to [the] men."

William John Krier's "A Pattern of Limitations: The Heroine's Novel of the Mind" (Indiana University, 1973) has no discussion of the James-Hawthorne relationship. However, chapter 3 includes an interpretation of *The Scarlet Letter* (pp. 70-79); chapter 4, pp. 80-98, is on "Daisy Miller" and "Madame de Mauves"; and the last chapter, pp. 99-129, is exclusively on *The Portrait.*

Of the twenty-three dissertations reviewed in the various essays in this text, the most embarrassing is "Representative Tragic Heroines in the Work of Brown, Hawthorne, Howells, James, and Dreiser" (University of Wisconsin, 1957), by Raymond Andrew Miller, Jr. With the possible exception of the dissertation by John E. Pyron, Jr., [29] Miller's is the one which adds least to our understanding of its subject. Furthermore, Miller disregards, apparently without any qualms, the basic practices of scholarly research. Instead of a bibliography, for example, he writes:

> Bibliography data on the authors covered will be found in *The Literary History of the United States* . . . in Lewis Leary's *Articles on American Literature, 1900–1950* . . . and in James Woodress' . . . *Dissertations in American Literature, 1891–1955.* . . . Therefore it has been deemed inadvisable merely to repeat this data here.
>
> An attempt has been made to base the present thesis as far as possible on the writings of the authors themselves, rather than to rely on secondary opinions. The footnotes to the individual chapters indicate clearly what items have been especially useful. (466)

The endnotes to chapter 5 on James, pp. 420–21, do not include a single reference to secondary material. Those to chapter 3 on Hawthorne, pp. 275–81, include only four references to secondary material: James's *Hawthorne,* an essay by Jane Lundblad, N. H. Pearson's Introduction to Hawthorne's *Complete Novels and Selected Tales,* and Mark Van Doren's—spelled "Doran" twice—*Nathaniel Hawthorne.* Although it might be commendable to advise a freshman to base his "thesis as far as possible on the writings of the authors themselves," beyond the freshman stage to ignore or disregard previous work on one's subject is an irresponsibility which incurs, at best, the danger of duplicating scholarship.

Much of Miller's work is a paraphrasing of the plots of the various novels he writes about. From another angle, one wishes he had retitled his dissertation: "Are there any Tragic Heroines" in the works of these authors? In many instances he narrates the actions of a woman character, only to conclude that she is not a tragic heroine. His subject is not, of course, a comparison of the tragic heroines of these authors. He does, however, make one minor reference to the James-Hawthorne relationship. In the chapter on James, he notes that although Christina Light in *Roderick Hudson* is illegitimate, James presents her "as something of great price." When she is introduced to the bidders at her mother's ball, James describes her "as glowing with 'the white light of a splendid pearl.'" In *The Scarlet Letter,* Hawthorne too "names the child of such a union Pearl" (393). But Miller does not refer to Pearl again in his subsequent discussion of Christina's "innocence."

In the chapter on Hawthorne, Miller finds that Ellen Langton (*Fanshawe*), Priscilla, Miriam, Phoebe, and Hepzibah are all *not* tragic heroines; only Zenobia and Hester are. As for James's women characters, he finds that Isabel Archer, Milly Theale, and Marie de Vionnet are all tragic heroines. Christina Light is not a tragic heroine in *Roderick Hudson,* but she is in *The Princess Casamassima.* In general, the chapter on James is better handled than that on Hawthorne; it contains less paraphrasing of plots and more interpretations of the texts.

Chapter 3

The Scarlet Letter

Of Hawthorne's four completed long romances, Henry James was most fascinated by *The Scarlet Letter,* the work which influenced the greatest number of his works. *The Scarlet Letter* has been paired with, alphabetically, *The Ambassadors,* "The Beast in the Jungle," *The Bostonians, The Golden Bowl,* "The Jolly Corner," "The Liar," "Madame de Mauves," *The Portrait of a Lady, Roderick Hudson, The Spoils of Poynton,* "The Third Person," *The Turn of the Screw, What Maisie Knew,* and *The Wings of the Dove.* Of these fourteen works, *The Portrait,* followed by *The Bostonians* and *Roderick Hudson,* has been compared in greatest detail with *The Scarlet Letter;* the last on the scale is *The Ambassadors,* whose possible link with Hawthorne's romance has been suggested but not developed. This review considers first the pairings which have received the most detailed critical attention, then those whose suggested links need more scrutiny.

James's evaluation of *The Scarlet Letter* in chapter 5 of *Hawthorne* (1879) is well known. He called the book not only Hawthorne's masterpiece, but "the finest piece of imaginative writing" America had as yet produced. Of its age-old theme of the wife, the lover, and the husband, he noted that what interested Hawthorne was not Hester's and Dimmesdale's love story, but "their moral situation in the long years that were to follow." And here, Hawthorne's emphasis is on Dimmesdale's guilt; after the first scene Hester becomes "an accessory figure; it is . . . upon her guilty lover that the author projects most frequently the cold, thin rays of his fitfully-moving lantern."

James found the main faults of the book to be "a want of reality" and an "over-ingenuity," both of which come out vividly when *The Scarlet Letter* is compared with Lockhart's *Adam Blair.* Lockhart's novel is "the history of the passion," Hawthorne's "the history of its sequel;" Lockhart was struck with the warmth of his subject, "Hawthorne with its coldness; the one with its glow . . . the other with its shadow, its moral interest." Furthermore, James found Lockhart's sense of incident "more vivid," and his lovers "more actual and personal." In short, Lockhart was subtle, refined, "substantial"; Hawthorne was simple, ordinary, "thin."

James was also disturbed by the symbolism in *The Scarlet Letter,* which he felt "is overdone at times, and becomes mechanical." The mystic A which eats into Dimmesdale's flesh is a case in point. But these defects, he declared, "are of the slenderest and most venial kind. . . . they are mere light flaws and inequalities of surface."

Reading through these comments, one feels that James is "perpetually" contradicting himself. After enumerating what he considers the "weaker spots" in the novel, he admits that "these things do not precisely constitute a weakness in *The Scarlet Letter;* indeed, in a certain way they constitute a great strength." And, whatever he gives with one hand, he seems to want to take away with the other. More exactly, his criticisms are *specific:* the novel's "historical coloring is rather weak," with "little elaboration of detail"; its symbolism is "superficial," and its people are not characters but "representatives, very picturesquely arranged, of a single state of mind." His praises, on the other hand, are *vague:* the book is "beautiful, admirable, extraordinary;" its purity is "indefinable," its conception light, its "charm, very hard to express." This is true of his comments, not just on *The Scarlet Letter,* but on Hawthorne's other works as well. In the chapter on Hawthorne's "Early Writings," for example, although he praises the originality and the "infinite grace and charm" of such "masterpieces" as "Roger Malvin's Burial," "Rappaccini's Daughter," and "Young Goodman Brown," and terms them "glimpses of a great field, of the whole deep mystery of man's soul and conscience," he nevertheless belittles them as "small things," "little sketches," "such trifles," which it "would be a mistake to insist too much upon." Julian Hawthorne spoke of a "shyness"—rather than an "arrogance"—that pervades the biography, and quoted James allegedly admitting: "But how can a barely known scribbler like me offer criticism on [Hawthorne]?"[1] What is more to the point, however, is Quentin Anderson's observation that it is "in his choice of episodes and themes for praise and dispraise that James gives himself away."[2] Just as he praised as "highly original" and ingenious Hawthorne's use of Chillingworth (that is, his making Chillingworth live with and upon Dimmesdale), so did he create similar characters himself. And his criticism of Hawthorne's "people" as mere representatives of a single state of mind applies as well to the characters in such works as "The Beast in the Jungle" and *The Golden Bowl.*[3]

Before considering those critics who have found specific parallels between *The Scarlet Letter* and various works by James, one should mention Terence Martin's "Adam Blair and Arthur Dimmesdale: A Lesson from the Master," *American Literature,* 34 (1962-63), 274-79. Martin examines the grounds on which James based his analogies between Hawthorne's novel and Lockhart's *Adam Blair.* He notes that although Hawthorne knew three of Lockhart's works, "there is no record of his having read *Adam Blair.*" Martin discusses the differences in plot, characterization, and structure of the two works, and suggests that part of the reason why James saw so many similarities between the two works is that *The Scarlet Letter* contains

> such a definitive portrait of a fallen minister that any novel with a similar character is likely to be brought in for comparison. More specifically, however, James perceives so great an analogy because of the way in which he reads *The Scarlet Letter.* As James sees it, Dimmesdale is to *The Scarlet Letter* what the title characters is to *Adam Blair.* The crucial point is that he reads *The Scarlet Letter* as if it were a novel entitled *Arthur Dimmesdale.* (277-78)

What James fails to see, according to Martin, is the central position of the scarlet letter itself in Hawthorne's romance.

The Portrait of a Lady

The Portrait of a Lady is the work by James which has been most frequently compared with *The Scarlet Letter,* and the most perceptive analysis of their similarities is in the chapter on *The Portrait* in Laurence Bedwell Holland's *The Expense of Vision: Essays on the Craft of Henry James* (Princeton, New Jersey: Princeton University Press, 1964). Holland finds *The Scarlet Letter,* Lockhart's *Adam Blair,* and James's comments on both all underscoring and illuminating the plot of *The Portrait.* He also notes that the names of *Adam Blair*'s two main characters—"the wife and the widower who commit the adultery"—"are Charlotte and Adam, the names decades later of the adulterous wife and the widower she marries in James's *The Golden Bowl.*" Furthermore, "the name of Adam Blair's young wife, who dies in the first chapter, is Isabel." To Holland, the most important similarity between *Adam Blair* and *The Scarlet Letter* is "the ambivalent splicing in each of the roles of lover and parent, and the dominance finally of the institution of the family and the role of the parent." Both novels define and dramatize patterns of marital and familial responsibility, and these are some of the very pressures that impel the plot of *The Portrait.* In *The Scarlet Letter,* the final emphasis is on Pearl's subsequent destiny: Dimmesdale confesses and embraces her; Chillingworth bequeaths to her a considerable amount of property, thus making her the richest heiress in the New World; and Hawthorne hints at a mature Pearl enjoying an adult life of comfort, independence, financial and emotional security, and high status. In *The Portrait,* what Hawthorne treated by way of suggestion James treats more emphatically, although his novel conceives the future "as an urgent and unresolved crisis rather than as the hoped-for resolution of one." *The Portrait,* Holland feels, is

> a response to Hawthorne's novel so profound as to constitute a reworking of the earlier work's materials. . . . The reworking entailed, however, one basic transformation of its materials: to bring the institution of marriage into the center of focus, to treat the "great undertaking of matrimony" as a vital and problematic form, and to mold the action around and within it, rather than to leave that institution remote in the background and dim in the future and to found the present action on alternatives to it. (25-26)

Thus in *The Portrait* James brought back the Isabel who existed in name only in *Adam Blair* "and assigned to her as wife the burdens of tutelage, rescue, and experience which she shares with Charlotte Campbell [and] Hester Prynne." Furthermore:

> The two views of marriage that are polarized in *The Scarlet Letter* are presented also in *The Portrait:* the sheerly conventional marriage figured in the failure of Hester and Chillingworth . . . and the marriage posited for Pearl, marriage as a form of fruition and aspiration. But in James's work they are manifest in many and complex versions which render their extremes less patently antagonistic. Marriage as a hollow factitious form . . . and marriage as a form of fulfillment and creative possibilities . . . are more intimately and problematically related. Indeed, one of the creative functions of the plot is to constitute this close relation between the two by splicing together the immediate plan for Isabel's marriage and the more long-range provisions, still unsettled at the novel's end, for Pansy's. . . .
>
> James's plot accordingly enabled him to solve a technical problem that Hawthorne handled less satisfactorily (the structural relation between the bulk of the work and its conclusion, between the destiny of Hester, Dimmesdale, and Chillingworth and that of Pearl) and to mediate more successfully the shift from the older generation's opportunities to the younger's that his novel helps to make a burden and a mission for American culture. (26-27)

Holland also points out two specific echoes of Hawthorne in *The Portrait.* The first is the art which Madame Merle shares with Hester Prynne. In chapter 19 of *The Portrait,* one reads that when Madame Merle was not writing or painting or playing the piano, "she was usually employed upon wonderful tasks of rich embroidery . . . an art in which her bold, free invention was as noted as the agility of her needle." The second echo is sounded in chapter 22, where Osmond and Pansy are first introduced and Madame Merle broaches her plan for Osmond's and Isabel's marriage. At the end of that chapter, Osmond remarks that Pansy is "as pure as a pearl." Later, as Holland notes, "it seems to Isabel that Pansy indeed might 'make a perfect little pearl of a peeress.'" And, of course, the Little Pearl in *The Scarlet Letter* is herself transformed in the denouement into a peeress.

In *The Battle and the Books: Some Aspects of Henry James* (Athens Ohio: Ohio University Press, 1964), some of the correspondences Edward Stone draws between *The Scarlet Letter* and "The Liar," and those between "The Custom-House" sketch and "The Third Person," seem rather forced or drawn out (his style, too, is very sloppy in many places). But those he draws between *The Blithedale Romance* and "The Beast in the Jungle" are a possible exception; so are those between *The Scarlet Letter* and *The Portrait* in "Appendix A. Hawthorne's and James's 'Deeper Psychology,'" pp. 207-10.

Stone agrees with previous critics that Hawthorne was acutely sensitive to situation, and that he preferred character to action. James too, in "The Art of Fiction," emphasized that character is "the determination of incident," and that incident is "the illustration of character." After Dimmesdale's meeting with Hester Prynne in the forest and his learning the true identity and nature of Chillingworth, he returns to his study. Immediately after this Chillingworth seeks him out, but Dimmesdale refuses the physician's ministrations. Hawthorne writes:

> All this time, Roger Chillingworth was looking at the minister with the grave and intent regard of a physician towards his patient. But, in spite of his outward show, the latter was almost convinced of the old man's knowledge, or, at least, his confident suspicion, with respect to his own interview with Hester Prynne. The physician knew, then, that, in the minister's regard, he was no longer a trusted friend, but his bitterest enemy. So much being known, it would appear natural that a part of it should be expressed.

"They do indeed 'perceive by antennae,'" Stone observes. "These are the antennae which Isabel Archer would perceive by," as James points out in *The Art of the Novel: Critical Prefaces* (New York: Charles Scribner's Sons, 1934), p. 56:

> Isabel, coming into the drawing-room at Gardencourt, coming in from a wet walk or whatever, that rainy afternoon, finds Madame Merle in possession of the place, Madame Merle seated, all absorbed but all serene, at the piano, and deeply recognizes, in the striking of such an hour, in the presence there, among the gathering shades, of this personage, of whom a moment before she had never so much as heard, a turning-point in her life.

Stone's conclusion is that if James was one of the founders of the new novel of psychological realism, he owed as much to Hawthorne as he did to Daudet.

In the passage Stone quotes from James's *Critical Prefaces,* the novelist is of course commenting on the first meeting between Isabel Archer and Madame Merle in chapter 18 of *The Portrait.* Although this too is a good "incident" to illustrate how James's characters "perceive by antennae," a better one—and one which more closely parallels the incident in chapter 20 of *The Scarlet Letter*—occurs in chapter 52 of *The Portrait.* In chapter 51 Isabel learns from the Countess Gemini Madame Merle's true identity, just as in chapter 17 of *The Scarlet Letter* Arthur learns from Hester Roger's true identity. The recognition scene in chapter 20 of Hawthorne's novel is thus more accurately paralleled by that in chapter 52 of *The Portrait,* the moment when Madame Merle perceives that Isabel knows the true relation between Madame Merle and Gilbert Osmond. Madame Merle, James writes:

> had not proceeded far before Isabel noted a sudden break in her voice, a lapse in her continuity, which was in itself a complete drama. This subtle modulation marked a momentous discovery—the perception of an entirely new attitude on the part of her listener. Madame Merle had guessed in the space of an instant that everything was at an end between them, and in the space of another instant she had guessed the reason why. The person who stood there was not the same one she had seen hitherto, but was a very different person—a person who knew her secret. This discovery was tremendous, and from the moment she made it the most accomplished of women faltered and lost her courage. But only for that moment. Then the conscious stream of her perfect manner gathered itself again and flowed on as smoothly as might be to the end.

Even the openings of both scenes are quite similar. In *The Scarlet Letter,* Hawthorne writes:

> While occupied with these reflections, a knock came at the door of the study, and the minister said, "Come in!"—not wholly devoid of an idea that he might behold an evil spirit. And so he did! It was old Roger Chillingworth that entered. The minister stood, white and speechless, with one hand on the Hebrew Scriptures, and the other spread upon his breast.

In *The Portrait,* James writes:

> The portress returned at the end of some five minutes, ushering in another person. Isabel got up, expecting to see one of the ladies

> of the sisterhood, but to her extreme surprise found herself confronted with Madame Merle. The effect was strange, for Madame Merle was already so present to her vision that her appearance in the flesh was like suddenly, and rather awfully, seeing a painted picture move. . . . Her being there at all . . . made Isabel feel faint.

The chapter entitled "The Mighty Individual" in Edwin T. Bowden's *The Dungeon of the Heart: Human Isolation and the American Novel* (New York: Macmillan, 1961), pp. 66–102, includes an examination of *The Scarlet Letter* and *The Portrait.* However, the few parallels he draws between Hester Prynne and Isabel Archer are too imprecise to be of much significance, and many of his observations are so general that they apply to the two heroines just as easily as they do to numerous other characters.

Bowden calls both Hester and Isabel "a great symbol of American isolation"; they both are isolated against their will, but in the end "regain a meaningful relationship with others." Isabel's final decision, like Hester's, is not to surrender to her isolation, but rather to rejoin her lot to that of mankind. "Like Hester Prynne," Bowden writes,

> Isabel Archer discovers that the relationship with her own soul is the answer to the problem raised by her external isolation from others. By forgetting self in the dedication to a larger life the self is no longer isolated. In *The Scarlet Letter* the answer is made in religious terms: humility before God, the loss of selfish pride, is not to lose life but to find it. In *The Portrait of a Lady* the answer is made in moral terms: to forget one's self for the satisfaction of moral responsibility . . . is not to deny life but to affirm it. (101–102)

Thus in the end both heroines defeat the isolation of the spirit and reach out "from the dungeon of the heart to a larger life."

There are, of course, other parallels Bowden draws: Hester's self-sufficiency and Isabel's self-esteem, Osmond's and Chillingworth's preying on their wives' hearts, the novels' contrasting settings. But his greatest thrust is on the heroines' final decision.

One critic before Bowden had also likened Isabel's return to Osmond to Hester's return to New England. In "James's *Madame de Mauves* and Hawthorne's *The Scarlet Letter*," *Modern Language Notes,* 73 (December, 1958), 580-86, Robert F. Gleckner notes that when Longmore in chapter 3 of *Madame de Mauves* asks Euphemia why she remains in France, she replies that "one may be very American and yet arrange it with one's conscience to live in Europe. My imagination perhaps . . . helped me think I should find happiness here. . . . This isn't America . . . but it's quite as little France. France is out there beyond the garden . . . but here . . . in my mind, it's a nameless . . . little country of my own. It's not her country . . . that makes a woman happy or unhappy." Hester too, observes Gleckner, "lives in her country of the mind and the edge of the forest." He further believes that when writing of Euphemia's insistence of remaining with her husband, as well as Isabel's return to Osmond, James must surely have recalled the passage in chapter 5 of *The Scarlet Letter* where Hawthorne writes:

> It may seem marvellous, that, with the world before her . . . free to return to her birthplace . . . and there hide her character and identity under a new exterior . . . and having also the passes of the . . . forest open to her . . . this woman should still call that place her home, where . . . she must needs be the type of shame. But there is a fatality . . . which almost invariably compels human beings to linger around . . . the spot where some great and marked event has given the color to their lifetime. . . . Her sin, her ignominy, were the roots which she had struck into the soil. . . . All other scenes of earth . . . were foreign to her, in comparison. The chain that bound her here was of iron links, and galling to her inmost soul, but never could be broken.

Peter Buitenhuis too, in his introduction to *Twentieth Century Interpretations of "The Portrait of a Lady"* (Englewood Cliffs, New Jersey: Prentice-Hall, 1968), p. 9, notes that the "most obvious predecessor of Isabel Archer in American fiction is Hester Prynne. . . . At the end of the novel she, like Isabel Archer, refuses the easy way out and chooses to return to the town where she had made her original decision and live out its consequences."

Charles R. Anderson, in "Person, Place, and Thing in James's *The Portrait of a Lady*," *Essays on American Literature in Honor of Jay B. Hubbell,* edited by Clarence Gohdes (Durham, North Carolina: Duke University Press, 1967), pp. 164-82, writes at length on Isabel Archer's meditative midnight vigil in chapter 42 of *The Portrait.* It is during this vigil, of course, that Isabel reviews the high hopes of her life and its tragic outcome. In the first paragraph of the chapter, James writes:

> After he [Gilbert Osmond] had gone she leaned back in her chair and closed her eyes; and for a long time, far into the night and still further, she sat in the still drawing-room, given to her meditation.

After she has explored the meaning of her life, at the end of the chapter James writes:

> When the clock struck four she got up; she was going to bed at last, for the lamp had long since gone out and the candles burned down to their sockets.

Although Isabel remains in the house of darkness, Anderson notes, "she has seen the light," and the device James uses to render her new understanding is the retrospective meditation. Before James, many novelists had used this device to speed up the narration or to comment on the story through the mouth of a character. Thus in chapter 20 of *The Scarlet Letter* Hawthorne has Dimmesdale meditating as he returns alone from his rendezvous with Hester in the forest. The second paragraph of that chapter begins thus:

> In order to free his mind from this indistinctness and duplicity of impression . . . he [Dimmesdale] recalled and more thoroughly defined the plans which Hester and himself had sketched for their departure. . . .

In a brief expository flashback Hawthorne summarizes an episode that would have filled a chapter or more if rendered in dramatic dialogue. In *The Portrait,* however, the retrospective meditation is not a summary of merely a past episode; "it refers to the entire novel–retrospectively to all that has gone before, prospectively to all that follows." Anderson does not imply, of course, that James was here consciously improving on Hawthorne.

The Bostonians

There has been only one extended evaluation of the relation between *The Scarlet Letter* and *The Bostonians:* R. W. B. Lewis's "The Tactics of Sanctity: Hawthorne and James," *Hawthorne Centenary Essays,* edited by R. H. Pearce (Columbus, Ohio: Ohio State University Press, 1964), pp. 271-95.[4] Lewis draws correspondences between *The Bostonians* and *The House of the Seven Gables* as well. He finds the Hawthorne aspect of *The Bostonians* so pervasive that "James's novel seems at times to be composed largely of cunning rearrangements and inversions . . . of ingredients taken over from Hawthorne." In addition to its similarities with *The Blithedale Romance,* which critics have frequently pointed out, *The Bostonians* carries forward and downward from *The Scarlet Letter* and perverts elements derived from *The Seven Gables.* In both *The Scarlet Letter* and *The Bostonians,* Lewis finds, "the theme of the heart's sanctity is closely associated with a question about the condition of women." In chapter 3 of *The Scarlet Letter* Dimmesdale argues, with respect to Hester's case, that "it were wronging the very nature of woman to force her to lay open her heart's secrets . . . in the presence of so great a multitude"; in chapter 2 Hawthorne himself says there "can be no outrage . . . against our common nature . . . more flagrant than to forbid the culpirt to hide his face for shame;" and, in chapter 17, Hester is able to say to Dimmesdale during their forest meeting that what the two did had a consecration of its own precisely because neither had violated the sanctity of the other's heart.

In *The Bostonians,* the "new truths" to which Olive Chancellor passionately appeals in chapter 3 are, "like those of *The Scarlet Letter,* ideas bearing chiefly upon the unhappy condition and possible future status of women. There are times," Lewis writes, "when Olive Chancellor . . . markedly resembles Hester Prynne." In chapter 24 of *The Scarlet Letter* Hawthorne had written of Hester:

> Women, more especially,—in the continually recurring trials of wounded, wasted, wronged, misplaced, or erring and sinful passion . . . came to Hester's cottage demanding why they were so wretched, and what the remedy!

In chapter 5 of *The Bostonians,* James says of Olive:

> The unhappiness of women! The voice of their silent suffering was always in her ears, the ocean of tears that they had shed from the beginning of time seemed to pour through her own eyes.

And just as Hester had once "imagined that she herself might be the destined prophetess," so does it seem to Olive at times that "she had been born to lead a crusade." Her crusade, like Hester's, is to be a religious one. In chapter 13 of *The Scarlet Letter,* after reflecting upon "the whole race of womanhood," Hester arrives at her vision of social and sexual revolution:

> As a first step, the whole system of society is to be torn down, and built up anew. Then, the very nature of the opposite sex . . . is to be essentially modified, before woman can be allowed to assume what seems a fair and suitable position. Finally, all other difficulties being obviated, woman cannot take advantage of these preliminary reforms, until she herself shall have undergone a still mightier change.

In chapter 5 of *The Bostonians,* James observes that Olive's "sacred cause," her "just revolution,"

> must sweep everything before it; it must exact from the other, the brutal, blood-stained, ravening race, the last particle of expiation! It would be . . . a new era for the human family, and the names of those who had helped to show the way . . . would be names of women weak, insulted, persecuted, but devoted in every pulse of their being to the cause, and asking no better fate than to die for it.

The above passage, of course, is more hysterical in its tone, and its attitude toward the male race is more savage, than Hawthorne's.

The Scarlet Letter is set among the Bostonians of the 1640's, a people for whom, Hawthorne tells us, "religion and law were almost identical." *The Bostonians* is set among the Bostonians of the 1870's, a people for whom, Lewis points out, "*religion and ideology* were becoming almost identical." And both Hawthorne's and James's pairings "are portrayed as the absolute enemy of . . . the sanctity of the individual human heart." Both Basil Ransom and Olive Chancellor are violated by ideas, and they use these ideas to violate the individuality of others, particularly of Verena Tarrant. And this is where James carefully revises Hawthorne, for "the social revolution proposed by Olive Chancellor would, in its consequences, reverse those of the movement that Hester Prynne might have led. Hester's new sect would bring with it a relationship between man and woman grounded on mutual reverence; Olive apparently would like to see that relationship destroyed once for all." The relationship she establishes in the novel is a paradigm of falsehood; it is sexually, morally, religiously, and politically wrong. With the possible exception of Miss Birdseye, Lewis observes, there "is no one in *The Bostonians,* like Hester or Dimmesdale (for his moment of insight) . . . who has or acts upon a clear sense of the heart's sanctity." Lewis's conclusion is that

> James, in *The Bostonians,* is exploiting Hawthorne to suggest a view opposite to Hawthorne's about the fundamental *course* of human affairs. . . . James saw the American character moving away from, not toward, a belief in the sanctity of the human heart; away from, not toward, relationships consecrated by that belief. Where Hawthorne, in *The Scarlet Letter,* made tragic drama out of the possibility of religious legalism yielding to individual reverence, James, in *The Bostonians,* in an equally impressive display of prophetic power describes individual reverence yielding to a religion of ideology. (294)

Thus in *The Bostonians* James has "made his comment upon the American scene by . . . reassembling themes and motives and devices and language from Hawthorne and then by twisting and reversing them" (295).

Roderick Hudson

Quentin G. Kraft's "The Central Problem of James's Fictional Thought: From *The Scarlet Letter* to *Roderick Hudson*," *ELH,* 36 (1969), 416-39, is to date the only extended evaluation of the relation between the two works, and Kraft quickly warns that his concern is not with the type of influence that accounts for an apparent likeness between one novel and another.

Kraft finds *Roderick Hudson* setting up the problems which always preoccupied James, and doing so in a way which links it with *The Scarlet Letter.* The central problem in both novels is the opposition between freedom and morality. In *The Scarlet Letter* Hawthorne could not resolve the problem in any satisfactory way; his novel reveals the freedom-morality opposition as absolute and therefore irresolvable. This is especially clear during Hester's and Dimmesdale's forest meeting, a meeting which crystallizes their essential difference. To Hester, their adultery was not a sin; it was, rather, something holy or sacred. And this, to Dimmesdale, is sacrilege. What separates Hester from the Puritan community and makes her free is her conviction that whatever emerges from the deepest reaches of human nature is sacred; what binds Dimmesdale to the Puritan society is his radical distrust of the very nature of the human being. And Hawthorne seems to suggest that "Dimmesdale would be wrong to violate his moral convictions to satisfy his human desires," a solution Kraft finds unsatisfactory, since Hawthorne has also suggested that the conflict "between freedom and morality involves a further opposition between life and death. Since the choice of morality seems to entail death"–Dimmesdale dies just after he confesses his guilt and re-affirms his commitment to Puritan morality–"it provides no adequate alternative to the choice of freedom even if that means an amoral or immoral life." Kraft's explanation is that Hawthorne could not unite morality and freedom because that would have meant "an evasion of some hard facts of human nature." And, since he placed primary value in human relationships, and "doubted the existence of a distinctly *human* nature in the isolated human creature," the tension of *The Scarlet Letter* may be redefined as "an opposition between man's isolated being and his human being." Hawthorne valued morality highly because he felt that "the human is realized only within the context of personal relationships and that genuine relationships require something more than the desires of the isolated self." Ultimately, therefore, *The Scarlet Letter* defines "the pre-requisites for human relationships and therefore human being":

> it shows that the either-freedom-or-morality choice is unsatisfactory because genuine human relationships require not only that freedom be qualified by moral concern but also that morality exists within a context of freedom. What the novel fails to show is how the conditions can be created or where they can be found. In his uncompromising concern for achieving distinctly human being . . . [Hawthorne] deprived himself of a place to live. He could return Dimmesdale to town and to death–not because he simply valued morality more than freedom but because neither town nor forest provided the conditions for living in terms authentically human. (422-23)

The Scarlet Letter, Kraft finds, shares with *Roderick Hudson* not only its theme but its structure as well. Structurally, both novels are characterized by a "thwarted dialectic." Although *Roderick Hudson* seems to invite "either-or" judgements, it supports, like *The Scarlet Letter,* only a "both-and" view. The issues enjoined in James's novel "are not simply freedom vs. destiny but one variety of freedom vs. another." Kraft shows that Rowland, who believes in free will, seems the most bound, whereas Roderick, who believes in destiny, seems the most free. But the opposition between these two characters is not merely a polarity between selflessness and selfishness. Roderick is selfish partly because "he so freely abandons him*self* to whatever evokes a response in his sensibility," and Rowland is selfless partly because "he exercises such control over his self." Thus, one may more accurately say that in Roderick we have "a self-forgetful selfishness" and in Rowland "a self-conscious selflessness."

After considering, among other things, Roderick's relation to Christina Light, and Rowland's to Mary Garland, Kraft concludes that although the opposition in James's novel is essentially one of characters–Roderick and Rowland, Christina and Mary–"the characters become opposed because their approaches to life are different. And when these differences produce conflict, they reveal a complex of value tensions: respose vs. restlessness, reason vs. imagination and feeling, society vs. the individual, morality vs. freedom, form vs. vitality." And it is James's handling of these value tensions, Kraft feels, "that relates *Roderick Hudson* back to the problem of *The Scarlet Letter*"; for, taken at its most general level:

> *Roderick Hudson* seems to question the . . . relation between . . . life as potential, and the forms it may take. And part of its power as a novel results from the two uncompromising answers it suggests: (1) that life needs some form if it is to be realized in living and (2) that forms, at least the already available forms, tend to inhibit or confine or even destroy life. . . . Thus the question [James] asks here . . . is in effect the same as Hawthorne's: is life to serve morality or morality to serve life. . . . What we may conclude is that in *Roderick Hudson* James, like Hawthorne in *The Scarlet Letter,* could not be satisfied with the simple choice of either freedom or morality; he . . . sensed that life achieves its full human potential only in a synthesis combining . . . both the one and the other. But at this point he could show no more than that the synthesis is humanly needed; like Hawthorne, he could not show how the need is to be satisfied. (439)

Two other links between *The Scarlet Letter* and *Roderick Hudson* have been suggested. In his dissertation entitled "Representative Tragic Heroines in the Work of Brown, Hawthorne, Howells, James, and Dreiser" (University of Wisconsin, 1957), Raymond A. Miller, Jr., observes that although Christina Light is illegitimate, James presents her as something of great price. When she is introduced to the bidders at her mother's ball, the novelist describes her as glowing with "the white light of a splendid pearl." In *The Scarlet Letter,* Miller notes, Hawthorne too "names the child of such a union Pearl" (393). To Sanford E. Morovitz in "*Roderick Hudson:* James's *Marble Faun,*" *Texas Studies in Literature and Language,* 11 (1970), 1427–43, Mary Garland as a personality "can be vaguely linked to Hester Prynne" (1440n.). Neither of these suggestions, however, was developed.

"Madame de Mauves"

Robert F. Gleckner's "James's *Madame de Mauves* and Hawthorne's *The Scarlet Letter,*" *Modern Language Notes,* 73 (December, 1958), 580-86, has already been mentioned. Starting from F. O. Matthiessen's observation in *American Renaissance* (New York: Oxford University Press, 1941), p. 298, that "James' technical development was a direct response to his sense of Hawthorne's limitations," particularly Hawthorne's use of allegory and what James called "a certain superficial symbolism," Gleckner sets out to show how James's story profited in three main areas from both the greatness of Hawthorne's novel and the flaws he detected in it. He finds in "Madame de Mauves" an "implicit criticism of Hawthorne's allegorical method," an "unusual use of that method in Longmore's dream in the forest," and a direct response to the explicit criticism in *Hawthorne* of certain scenes in *The Scarlet Letter.* The three elements he concentrates on are characterization, theme, and structure. He finds in Hester Prynne and Euphemia de Mauves a "basic, if odd, kinship": Hester, from a small English village, comes to American and sins; Euphemia, from New York, comes to Auvergne and Saint-Germain and remains "innocent." Dimmesdale and Hester have an opportunity to escape the scene of their sin, "ironically the core of militant Puritan morality; Longmore and Euphemia, both 'innocent,' can escape from a corrupt world *to* the world of Puritan morality." But both women choose finally to live with their new worlds. Ultimately they both come to live in isolation, and ultimately they both triumph over their worlds of sordid experience. And, as already indicated, Gleckner feels that James must have recalled the second paragraph of chapter 5 of *The Scarlet Letter* when writing of Isabel Archer's return to Osmond as well as Euphemia's insistence on remaining with her husband.

In both novels, Gleckner further points out, the husbands are insidious: "Chillingworth the diabolic torturer of Dimmesdale, M. de Mauves the devil's advocate who offers his wife to Longmore." Their roles too are somehow similar, and the effects of their villainy are identical. "Longmore refuses to capitulate to the Baron's standards of morality and leaves Euphemia, while Hester and Dimmesdale cheat Chillingworth's revenge by exposing themselves on the scaffold. Deprived of their triumphs both antagonists waste away": chapter 24 of *The Scarlet Letter,* chapter 9 of "Madame de Mauves."

Thematically, Gleckner finds that both works consider the "dichotomy between appearance and reality, hypocrisy and truth, essential and apparent character." In chapter 2 of "Madame de Mauves," for example, the Baron's mother advises Euphemia to be her "own sincere little self only"; in chapter 24 of *The Scarlet Letter,* after Dimmesdale has uncovered his own stigma, Hawthorne advises: "Be true! Be true! Be true!" Gleckner next discusses the structural relation between the two works. The formal, symmetrical structure of *The Scarlet Letter,* he argues, rests on three main scenes; that of "Madame de Mauves" on four. In James's story, the first scene, in which Longmore first tries to probe the causes of Euphemia's sorrow, parallels Hawthorne's scene in which Pearl questions Hester about the significance of the scarlet letter; the second scene, where Longmore, just returned from Paris, tries to tempt Euphemia with a vision of a better life, parallels Dimmesdale's and Hester's meeting in the forest, where they envision a new life abroad and contemplate their escape. In the third scene, Longmore, escaping from M. de Mauves' offer of his wife, "moves alone through the forest to the world beyond, a world of pastoral simplicity, idyllic, romantic, natural . . . the same world of escape . . . which the forest and sea represent for Dimmesdale and Hester." The fourth scene is Longmore's dream of Euphemia. This scene is presented "in precisely the same terms as the brookside scene in *The Scarlet Letter*," and both scenes "foreshadow allegorically the final destruction of the illusory freedom . . . which Nature seems to offer."

Lastly, Gleckner selects from "Madame de Mauves" a few examples which show James's implicit awareness of what he considered the limitations of Hawthorne's method. Of *The Scarlet Letter,* James had complained that Hawthorne's imagination "plays with his theme so incessantly . . . that the thing cools off." Thus in "Madame de Mauves" James "builds his effects, instead, in terms of dynamic human relationships. . . ." James had further called allegory "quite one of the lighter exercises of the imagination," and singled out the brookside scene in chapter 9 of *The Scarlet Letter* as an illustration of how Hawthorne heaps heavy allegorical meaning on an already eloquent scene. When he himself uses Hawthorne's dividing stream in chapter 7 of "Madame de Mauves," Gleckner observes, "its context is a dream." This provides him a kind of protection from his own criticism, and also helps to make allegory seem "spontaneous." Unlike Hawthorne, who tries to make the real allegorical, James tries to make the allegorical real. And Longmore's very comment on his dream at the beginning of chapter 8—"No great arrangement was needed to make it seem a striking allegory"—is, in effect, "James's own comment on the Hawthornesque quality of the whole conception." His point, like Hawthorne's, is that the forest world of freedom is an illusion. "Hence, in both novels, the renunciation, the sacrifice is a necessary condition to the preservation of good, of reality, of truthfulness, of the dignity and inviolability of the human soul." To arrive at this, "James makes unusual use of Hawthorne's method . . . and then, by means of Longmore's comment, he rescues himself from the limitations of that method."

Before Gleckner, Charles G. Hoffman had mentioned, in his dissertation on "The Development of the Short Novel in Hawthorne, Melville, and James" (University of Wisconsin, 1952), one general similarity between *The Scarlet Letter* and "Madame de Mauves": in both novels the authors are concerned with the consequences of adultery rather than with the adulterous relationship itself; they both focus their attention on the psychological effects of sin and guilt (pp. 84, 107n.). Unlike Hawthorne's heroines, however, James's heroines–Madame de Mauves, Isabel Archer, Maggie Verver–are betrayed by their adulterous husbands. Hoffman calls the final chapter in both works anti-climactic (225)–he makes the same observation in his book, *The Short Novels of Henry James* (New York: Bookman Associates, 1957), p. 15.

"The Liar"

In Chapter 3 of *The Battle and the Books,* Edward Stone erroneously alleges that in *The Complex Fate,* Marius Bewley invited us to compare *The Scarlet Letter* and "The Liar."[5] Stone finds Oliver Lyon very different from Roger Chillingworth, and sees no correspondence between James's lovers and Hawthorne's. He also finds the final effects of the two stories extremely different. The "surface features" of both stories, however, he finds comparable. In both *The Scarlet Letter* and "The Liar," he writes, we see

> the progressive degeneration and self-corruption of a rejected and malicious leech as he goes about perpetrating his revenge on a victim whose own wrongdoing seems more and more condoned by contrast. Accordingly, we have the eventual defeat of hatred by its very triumph. Just as Arthur had been an adulterer without . . . lessening his value as spiritual leader of the community (in fact, his preaching increases in effectiveness as a *result* of his sin), so Clement's captivating person endears him to all despite the harmless failing of his telling outlandish lies. (83–84)

After noting another similarity between Clement and Arthur, Stone advises that "to equate the situation of these two men in this quantitative way alone is silly." He believes there are stronger correspondences between Oliver and Everina Brant. In its "duel between Oliver and Everina," he writes, "'The Liar' presents a situation exactly the counterpart of this of Hawthorne's. If for Arther we substitute Everina, what we have is no less than a retelling of Hawthorne's story." Both novelists focus on the man plotting revenge, and on "the effect on the secret sinner of the act of concealment." And, in terms of function, Oliver is even more closely analogous to Roger than Everina is to Arthur.

Stone next considers the differences between the two stories. In *The Scarlet Letter,* Arthur eventually confronts his conscience, tells the truth and thus destroys Roger. In "The Liar," until Oliver springs his trap on her, Everina is guilty of nothing. "It is in this divergence," Stone argues, "that we begin to understand what was wrong with James's idea":

> To the extent that Everina steadfastly refuses to reveal her "secret" to Oliver, she is a fit counterpart to Arthur . . . but in resorting to a lie at last instead of confronting her pursuer, she is in no way to be thought of in terms of . . . Arthur. Her lie is a most believable one, yet it demonstrates how the very success of James's story from one point of view turns out to be a failure from another. For in replacing with a novelistic plausibility the melodramatic apotheosis of Hawthorne's romance, James forfeited this last effect without a compensatory gain. (86)

The Scarlet Letter may show "a want of reality and an abuse of the fanciful element," but Roger's sense of grief and of violation of his honor is very real. Oliver's, on the other hand, is "thoroughly implausible and contrived." There is very little correlation between offense and revenge in "The Liar." Oliver is a "bloodless animation of mere curiosity," and incapable of true passion; Roger is a proud and awe-inspiring figure.

One might repeat that no one but Stone ever suggested that "The Liar" be equated with *The Scarlet Letter,* or that Oliver is closely analogous to Roger, or that Everina is a fit counterpart to Arthur. One might choose to compare and contrast the two stories–if that adds in any way to our understanding of both works. One might argue that "The Liar" is an inferior, shallow story, or that there was something wrong with James's idea, or that Oliver is unbelievable as a character. But to do this one does not have to refer to *The Scarlet Letter* and assume that James's intentions in "The Liar" were similar to Hawthorne's in *The Scarlet Letter.*

"The Beast in the Jungle"

Jane Gottschalk's "The Continuity of American Letters in *The Scarlet Letter* and *The Beast in the Jungle*," *Wisconsin Studies in Literature,* 4 (1967), 39–45, should never have been published. Not only are there virtually no new insights in her entire article, she does not even look at previous opinions and judgements from a different perspective. Instead of developing her own argument, in many instances she merely quotes the views of other critics. Even more irritating, instead of reading the preface to *The House of the Seven Gables,* or James's *Hawthorne,* she chooses to rely on other people's summaries of these works.

Both *The Scarlet Letter* and "The Beast in the Jungle," Gottschalk finds, have a common underlying perception of man, both consider motives and psychological tensions essential to human action, and both illustrate essentially moral and spiritual values. In general, Hawthorne and James belong to the same tradition in American letters. They are both concerned with ideas and values; they differ only in execution. In the preface to *The Seven Gables,* Hawthorne distinguishes between a novel and a romance; in "The Art of Fiction," James distinguishes only between a good novel and a bad one. "Thus in their theories," Gottschalk writes, "Hawthorne and James agree on values in life and literature . . . but disagree on the execution of the work of art." In *The Scarlet Letter* and "The Beast in the Jungle," the differences she discusses include setting—the Boston of 1647-54 *vs.* the London of James's era—and point of view: Hawthorne is an omniscient narrator who frequently intrudes with his own opinions; James tells his story only from Marcher's point of view, although in the process he too reveals his own ideas. The similarities, however, she finds to be quite many. The themes of both stories "dramatize the effects of erring but free-willed action"; the "instigating action" in each story—the adultery in *The Scarlet Letter,* the presentiment Marcher expressed to May Bartram in James's story—"happened before the effect is revealed in the characters"; each work has a scene "in which the fading heroine glows for a moment"; chapter 17 of *The Scarlet Letter,*[6] chapter 4 of "The Beast": the ending of both stories is in a cemetery; and both authors use names suggestively and functionally: Marcher and Chillingworth suggest "the bleakness of early spring," May and Dimmesdale "the vitality and bloom of late spring." Furthermore, in both works

> the heroines are strong characters, hinting at a common head and heart theme in their relationships to the men in the fictions. Both Marcher and Chillingworth illustrate the futility of the head alone. It is Chillingworth's intellectuality which is ultimately responsible for the tragedy, and it is the tragedy of Marcher that his inability to feel is what sets him apart from other men . . .
>
> Psychological tensions give to each fiction the quality they have in common, and old-as-men pride is the basis. (41)

Gottschalk finds, however, that Marcher's kind of pride is different from Chillingworth's or Dimmesdale's. She accounts for the differences in the psychology of the characters by the fact that Hawthorne belonged "with the early psychologists who were primarily religious and ethical," whereas James wrote during the middle period "before the post-Freudians." After commenting on the "sense of isolation" in both works; Hawthorne's symbolism which tends toward moral allegory and James's which tends toward ironic imagery; the "jungle" in Marcher's life and the moral wilderness of the forest in *The Scarlet Letter;* and the "common doom" referred to by Marcher and the "common bond and destiny" frequently mentioned by Hawthorne, Gottschalk concludes by observing that despite the necessity for human relationships so frequently emphasized by both Hawthorne and James, man "is essentially alone":

> But he can further isolate himself through sin, as in *The Scarlet Letter,* or he can do so by self-absorption, as in "The Beast in the Jungle." Both works depend on a perception of values that are not material, both subordinate action and dialogue to an analysis of conduct, and both works have universal application despite their differences in approach and execution. They show a continuing tradition in American letters. (43–44)

Midway through her essay Gottschalk admits that "these are surface similarities." Had she added he word "superficial," she might have persuaded herself not to submit the essay for publication.

The Golden Bowl

Most of the remaining eight works by James which have been compared with *The Scarlet Letter* have not been examined in the same detail as the preceding six. L. B. Holland's comments on *The Scarlet Letter* and *The Golden Bowl,* however, are quite specific and microscopic. In *The Expense of Vision,* Holland begins the chapter on *The Golden Bowl* by discussing the scene in chapter 28 where Adam and Maggie Verver, in doorways at opposite ends of the long picture gallery at Fawns, "stand mute in a confrontation which becomes an unexpected 'communion.'" He calls this scene "the epitome of James's artistry in *The Golden Bowl* and . . . an image at once of the crisis it brings to life and of the process which resolves it." After relating what happens in the scene, he observes that by the end of the chapter, "Charlotte's cry has produced for Maggie a shared communion over even vaster distances, not with her father but with her husband . . . in London. There in an empty house . . . he paces the floor or sits restlessly smoking 'ceaseless cigarettes,' trying to escape the sound of Charlotte's 'high coerced quaver' but determined to face the consequences of his marriage and waiting . . . for nothing more or less than to be at his wife's side." "What Maggie calls at one point the '"funny form"' of her life with her husband, father, and stepmother and their interlocking marriage," Holland continues:

> is matched by the funny form of James's novel, and the scene in the gallery at Fawns, with Charlotte's speech releasing her shriek of pain, illuminates the form of *The Golden Bowl* and the perilous marriage it achieves with its materials. The speech, though brief, is distinctly set off from the narrative, and the haunting relevance of prose which verges on the irrelevant, suggesting an immanence of meaning beyond what is, word for word, quite lucidly clear, recalls the scene in *The Scarlet Letter* on which it seems to draw for resources of formal effect. In [chapter 22] of Hawthorne's work, Hester Prynne listens to Dimmesdale's sermon, standing "statue-like" at the foot of the scaffold outside because she cannot find room inside the crowded church. Hester's "intentness," the resonant power of Dimmesdale's voice, and the fact that the church walls filter out the "grosser medium" of words and leave only the "murmur and flow" of Dimmesdale's voice, enable Hester to hear only the "undertone" and "solemn grandeur" and to catch in the sermon "a meaning for her, entirely apart from its indistinguishable words." What her ear discerns beyond the words–across the interval of social space and through the walls which separate her, as in Maggie's case, from the rest of the audience and from the speaker himself–is "the shriek, as it might be conceived," the "cry of pain" of a "human heart . . . telling its secret" and asking "sympathy" for sorrow or "forgiveness" for sin. (333-34)

There is in James's prose, as in Hawthorne's, a "tension between words and their more compressed or intimate meanings," and his prose, again like Hawthorne's, seeks a "communion across intervals of social space and the barriers of verbal medium." In *Hawthorne* James had warned against the limitations of allegory, which "is apt to spoil . . . a story and a moral, a meaning and a form." In *The Golden Bowl,* Holland observes, "James avoided the severance between surface and substance, between instrument and import, on which Hawthorne's allegorical mode rests and made the interaction of medium and substance more intimate and more compressed."

Later in the chapter, Holland notes that the drama in *The Golden Bowl* takes place in a world of pressures and forms which James, in *Hawthorne,* had defined only in terms of their absence. But these "absent things" are present in *The Golden Bowl* "only as ghosts of their former embodiments or projected versions of their future forms, and the ostensible England of its setting is a world in decay which is still continuous with a world . . . which James's imagination had recognized in the America of Hawthorne.' (377).

In *The Golden Bowl,* as in Hawthorne's America, there is no state, no sovereign, no aristocracy: "only their dim remnants appear at times"; no church and no clergy: "only their remnants and effigies"; and no Epsom or Ascot "in the accessible environs of Matcham and Fawns." What looms large, instead, "is not a void but the forms . . . which remained for the provincial American of Hawthorne's later generation: the strained institutions of the family, commerce, marriage, and the arts which James challenges but also celebrates."

"The Third Person"

Another relation Edward Stone discusses in *The Battle and the Books* is that between "The Custom-House" sketch and "The Third Person." In "Appendix B. Hawthorne's and James's 'Third Person,'" pp. 211-19, Stone says that the circumstances of the writing of James's story, as well as the curious relationship between the three persons that it develops, show that this story owes part of its flavor to certain passages in "The Custom-House" preface to *The Scarlet Letter.* Both Hawthorne and James were concerned with ghosts, and Hawthorne's relationship to some of the ghosts in his *American Notebooks* is similar to James's: it is casual, even social. These ghosts are different from those Hawthorne invokes so objectively in his tales; these are personal, ghosts of people "whose blood he had in his own veins." Some passages in "The Custom-House" sketch, Stone finds, "remind us of details and effects of James's story": "Like the Misses Frush's Marr, Hawthorne's Salem was at one time a busy port but now is in discard. Hawthorne speaks of its once 'bustling wharf' as being now 'dilapidated' and 'burdened with decayed wooden warehouses'"; in "The Third Person," James describes Marr as "a little old . . . historic south-coast town which had once been . . . mistress . . . of the 'channel.'" And just as Hawthorne has ties of blood and affinity with this relic of a town, Stone observes, so do the Misses Frush have their origin in Marr.

Stone's next comments are a feat befitting a contortionist. In "The Custom-House" sketch, he writes, Hawthorne summons up his two ancestors, Major Hathorne and his son Colonel Hathorne, and imagines them talking about him in his presence—he being the third person. In "The Third Person" the two ladies "accidentally invoke their third person by their own curiousness about the family's history." In order to put these ghosts to rest, Hawthorne and Miss Susan first try to acquiesce in their guilt. But "atonement by deputy" fails in both cases, and Hawthorne's ancestors consider themselves absolved of their guilt only after they discover Hawthorne's occupation. In "The Third Person," after Miss Susan's act of atonement fails, it is Miss Amy who succeeds in appeasing their ghost, and her approach succeeds because, like Hawthorne—who admitted in the sketch that strong traits of his ancestors' nature had intertwined themselves with his— "'strong traits' of Cuthbert's nature 'have intertwined themselves' with hers."

Stone lastly points out the differences between the two works. In James's story, the family's ancient transgressions are matched; in Hawthorne's sketch they are counteracted. More significantly, "The Third Person" reveals "a complexity of relationships . . . not attempted in the Custom House sketch. [James's] two Misses Frush are as finely characterized as the two Hathornes are vague." Despite all this, however, "in the light, amused touch of his story, James does not depart very noticeably from Hawthorne's passages," and if "The Third Person" is the lightest and sunniest of his ghost tales, "The Custom-House" sketch displays most memorably what he called Hawthorne's "duskily-sportive imagination."

Roger B. Stein's verdict in his review of *The Battle and the Books* is most appropriate here: Stone "makes the study of the influences on James and the impact of his work a game of critical ingenuity rather than a deeper study of the still ambiguous impact of one of our major artists"—*New England Quarterly,* 38 (December, 1965), 558.

What Maisie Knew

Four people have connected Pearl in *The Scarlet Letter* with Maisie in *What Maisie Knew.* After commenting on how, during Hester's and Dimmesdale's meeting in the forest—as well as during the preceding chapters—one increasingly wonders exactly "how much of the situation this strange child understands," F. O. Matthiessen observed, in *American Renaissance,* pp. 278-79, that except for "the stiff layers of allegory," Pearl's conception is based on "exact psychological notation." Furthermore, he found her suggesting directly James's *What Maisie Knew,* although James intentionally complicated the problem by "having both parents divorced and married again," "making the child the innocent meeting ground for a liaison between the step-parents," and "confining his report on the situation entirely to what could be glimpsed through the child's inscrutable eyes." Alexander Cowie too, in *The Rise of the American Novel* (New York: American Book, 1948), p. 853n., felt that the life of little Pearl must have been "in the back of James's mind when he undertook to show the effect of evil on a little girl in *What Maisie Knew*." And James R. Bashore, Jr., in his dissertation on "The Villains in the Major Works of Nathaniel Hawthorne and Henry James," 2 volumes (University of Wisconsin, 1959), noted that Maisie "is a lineal descendant of Pearl," except that she achieves salvation through her own moral growth, whereas Pearl "is saved through the confession and repentance of other parties to the situation" (II, 39).

The most extended discussion of the relation between Pearl and Maisie is in Frederick J. Masback's dissertation, "The Child Character in Hawthorne and James" (Syracuse University, 1960). Like Matthiessen, Masback finds Pearl's conception "psychologically valid." Maisie, however, whom he calls James's least convincing child character, he finds functioning merely as a point of view. One senses "a real child under all the symbolic trappings of Pearl," he writes, "but only Henry James behind Maisie's consciousness."

Masback discusses many similarities and differences between Pearl and Maisie. Both girls have a moral influence on others and thus save them, and they both save themselves. And the terms James uses in speculating about Maisie's ability to save herself "suggest the kind of knowledge which might be available to Pearl."[7] However, whereas Pearl participates in shaping the drama of her existence—except after the novel's climax, when her fate depends on what Dimmesdale does—Maisie is mostly passive, *until* the climax of her moral life, when she becomes the agent of her own fate. At the end of the two novels both Pearl and Maisie die as children and begin to live as mature adults.

Masback draws a few other parallels between Pearl and Maisie: Pearl has intuition from the first, but it is not until the lat scaffold scene that she rationally understands what she has always known intuitively. Maisie, by contrast, is mostly engaged in acquiring knowledge, but her final decision is based on intuitive perception. After Pearl's moral climax, she seems a worldly success; Maisie's chances of material success, on the other hand, are rather uncertain. In his last chapter, Masback somewhat reverses an earlier observation and says that while Pearl helps bring about Dimmesdale's confession, which in turn changes his life as well as Hester's and Chillingworth's, Maisie has very little effect on the lives of others. His conclusion is that what Maisie finally acknowledges is the same as what Pearl recognizes on the final scaffold scene: "the weakness of the human heart and the nature of the human condition."[8]

"The Jolly Corner"

Gordon Duncan Reynolds does not exactly compare *The Scarlet Letter* with "The Jolly Corner"; he clearly states that his aim in his dissertation, "Psychological Rebirth in Selected Works by Nathaniel Hawthorne, Stephen Crane, Henry James, William Faulkner, and Ralph Ellison" (University of California at Irvine, 1973), is not to prove influences or relationships among the works he analyzes, but merely to point out certain "recurring patterns" and "the particular uses of those patterns in the works themselves." He divides the psychological rebirth process into six stages. First, the character's "immature, inadequate mental identity" is broken down; second, he experiences mental aberrations; third, guides help him find his way, or they may hinder his progress; fourth, he enters a death-like state. On awakening, he sees everything in a new way, and, at the end of the process, he feels an increase in confidence, energy and insight. Reynolds shows that both Arthur Dimmesdale and Spencer Brydon—as well as the other characters he analyzes—go through all these stages (Hester and Chillingworth are the "guides" in *The Scarlet Letter,* Alice Staverton in "The Jolly Corner").

The Turn of the Screw

Charles G. Hoffmann compares *The Scarlet Letter* with *The Turn of the Screw.* In his dissertation on "The Short Novels in Hawthorne, Melville, and James," (University of Wisconsin, 1952) he notes, first, that James's introduction to his story and Hawthorne's "Custom-House" introduction are similar: they both contrast by implication the everyday world with the extraordinary events about to be narrated, and they both have a "discovered" manuscript in which are recorded past events. This gives each narrative a historical air and removes the author from any immediate involvement in it. One should point out, however, that Hawthorne and James are here using the literary convention of the frame device; this "similarity" is not necessarily an aspect of direct "influence."

Hoffmann finds further that the recurrent imagery in both works is used in a similar way. In both, light imagery suggests innocence and beauty, while darkness suggests evil and ugliness. However, neither author limits the use of light imagery to a two-valued contrast. To show that each author's intention is to illustrate the existence of evil in goodness, Hoffmann analyzes the first paragraph of chapter 6 of *The Scarlet Letter,* and the dialogue between the governess and Miles in chapter 11 of *The Turn of the Screw.* What Hawthorne is saying here, according to Hoffmann, is that "innocence and beauty can be corrupted or tainted," and what James presents is the "ambiguity between outward action and inward intention," "the discrepancy between appearance and reality." The above observations by Hoffmann are on pp. 189, 286-87, and 315-17 of his dissertation, and on pp. 72, 83-84, and 91-93 of his *Short Novels of Henry James.*

The Spoils of Poynton

The third work by James Hoffmann compares with *The Scarlet Letter* is *The Spoils of Poynton.* After remarking that the epilogue to James's story, like the last chapter of *The Scarlet Letter,* "is dramatically unnecessary and unsatisfying," he enumerates a few other similarities between the two works. None of these similarities, however—even the "three-part principle of structure" he says both works share—is unique to this pair. The main difference between the two novels, he finds, is that in *The Scarlet Letter* the problem of evil is presented in all its aspects, whereas in *The Spoils of Poynton* it is surprisingly missing. In James's novel good and bad are defined aesthetically, not morally. Whereas Hawthorne empahsizes the *sin* of pride, Mrs. Gereth's pride in material possessions is not based on immoral greediness but rather on "an appreciation of their aesthetic worth." ("The Short Novel in Hawthorne, Melville, and James," pp. 282-85; *The Short Novels of Henry James,* pp. 67-70.)

The Wings of the Dove

Quentin Anderson's analysis of *The Wings of the Dove* is one of the finest illustrations of how James, in his last three novels, fell victim to what he considered a fault in *The Scarlet Letter.* In chapter 9 of *The American Henry James* (New Brunswick, New Jersey: Rutgers University Press, 1957), Anderson observes that except for Chad Newsome in *The Ambassadors,* Merton Densher in *The Wings of the Dove,* and Prince Amerigo in *The Golden Bowl,* almost all the characters in James's last three novels have a dual function: each "appears as an individual in the world of the novel," and also "functions as one of the impulses determining human behavior, or as one of the ideal limits of human action" (236). In *The Wings of the Dove,* this is true of Milly Theale, Sir Luke Strett, Susan Shepherd, Kate Croy, Maud Lowder, Lord Mark, Mrs. Condrip, and Lionel Croy. James wrote this novel, as well as the other two, "out of a completely unified and consistent sense of the meaning of human action," and this is the very thing he had accused Hawthorne of doing when he wrote that the people in *The Scarlet Letter* are not characters but "representatives, very picturesquely arranged, of a single state of mind." *The Wings of the Dove* too, Anderson indicates, "treats 'representatives' of a *single* complex abstraction—human nature as James conceived it" (239). Although James went to Europe because he needed the complexity of surfaces offered by an old society, he never came to feel its actual variety. It was not persons that interested him but the differentiated instances of the operation of the components of human nature as he conceived it. And this is not unlike Hawthorne's practice, in which "society is neither loved nor understood. What is prized is a mode of relating isolated figures to one another which depends on some abstract thesis about the nature of their common humanity."

The Ambassadors

There has not been any comparison of *The Scarlet Letter* and *The Ambassadors.* However, Robert Emmet Long suggests, in "'The Ambassadors' and the Genteel Tradition: James's Correction of Hawthorne and Howells," *New England Quarterly,* 42 (March, 1969), 50n., that there is "an interesting similarity between Hawthorne's scaffold scenes in *The Scarlet Letter,* denoting stages of conscience, and James's balcony scenes in *The Ambassadors,* representing progressive stages of consciousness." Nobody has as yet taken up this suggestion.

Chapter 4

The Blithedale Romance

Next to *The Scarlet Letter,* the work by Hawthorne which influenced the greatest number of James's works is *The Blithedale Romance.* This romance has been paired with, alphabetically, *The Ambassadors,* "The Beast in the Jungle," *The Bostonians, The Europeans, The Portrait of a Lady,* "Professor Fargo," *Roderick Hudson,* and *The Sacred Fount.* Of all the Hawthorne-James pairs, *The Blithedale Romance* and *The Bostonians* has been most frequently analyzed. The review below considers this pair first, and concludes with the pair least discussed: *Blithedale* and *The Europeans.*

In his lifetime, James made three extended evaluations of *Blithedale.* In chapters 4 and 5 of *Hawthorne* (1879), he called *Blithedale* Hawthorne's lightest, brightest, and liveliest novel. He commended especially its point of view, and noted a basic resemblance between Miles Coverdale, the narrator, and Hawthorne–especially the Hawthorne of Brook Farm. Coverdale, he wrote, "is a picture of the contemplative, observant, analytic nature . . . a portrait of a man . . . whose passions are slender, whose imagination is active, and whose happiness lies, not in doing, but in perceiving–half a poet, half a critic, and all a spectator." And this, precisely, was the part that Hawthorne played socially at Brook Farm, so that some of his companions "accused him of coming to the place as a sort of intellectual vampire, for purely psychological purposes." James regretted, however, that at Brook Farm Hawthorne let off his fellow-communists too easily. Had he been a satirist, they would have fared far worse. "There is no satire whatever in the *Romance*," he declared. In *The Bostonians,* of course, James compensated for this omission.

James found Zenobia Hawthorne's "only very definite attempt at the representation of a character," his "nearest approach . . . to the complete creation of a *person*." He dismissed the speculation that she was modeled on

Margaret Fuller, and warned that, although Miss Fuller was, in Hawthorne's imagination, "the starting-point of the figure of Zenobia," one should not too closely connect the characters of both women. Once a novelist gets a hint for a story, he explained, the inevitable tendency of the imagination "is to divergence, to following what may be called new scents." Although the two women resemble each other in some ways, there are strong divergences too: Miss Fuller was "plain and strenuous"; Zenobia is "beautiful and sumptuous . . . a woman in all the force of the term." Of the other two main characters, James was especially fascinated by the grasp that Hollingsworth, "the heavily treading reformer," lays upon Zenobia, drawing her into "the gulf of his omnivorous egotism." However, he found "this barbarous fanatic" more successful as a type than as a person. Priscilla too, "with her mysterious relation to Zenobia . . . her mesmeric gifts . . . her identity with the Veiled Lady, her divided subjection to Hollingsworth and Westervelt," he found not well developed as a character. "As the action advances," he concluded, "we get too much out of reality," and the latter portions of the novel show "a certain want of substance and cohesion." Nevertheless, *Blithedale* "is still a delightful and beautiful" book, full of deep and delicate touches.

In 1897 James wrote an introduction to the selections from Hawthorne in the *Library of the World's Best Literature,* edited by Charles Dudley Warner (New York: R. S. Peale and J. A. Hill, 1897), XII, 7053-61. Although Warner included no selections from *Blithedale,*[1] James devoted over a page to this romance. He pointed out its "value as a picture of manners," and praised Hawthorne's "appetite that could often find a feast in meagre materials." Once again he expressed his disappointment that Coverdale let off the radicals and reformers and philanthropists at Blithedale too easily; he should have ground them in the mill of his satire. And, once again, he praised the characterization of Zenobia and Hollingsworth.

As Peter Buitenhuis has correctly observed in "Henry James on Hawthorne," *New England Quarterly,* 32 (June, 1959), 216-20, by 1897 James's appreciation of Hawthorne had grown considerably. Whereas in 1879 he had pictured Hawthorne as an artist starved for fictional material, in 1897 he praised his ability to reap a bushel from arid ground. This larger sympathy with Hawthorne enabled him to discover in the novels many things that he had missed in 1879. Thus in 1897 he was able to write on values in *Blithedale* which he had not admitted in the earlier study.

In his 1904 letter to the Hawthorne centennial, published a year later in the *Essex Institute Historical Collections,* 41 (January, 1905), 55-62, James once again praised *Blithedale* as one of Hawthorne's classics. He commended especially its "artistic economy which understands *values* and uses them." As he had remarked in 1897—that Hawthorne turned the bare necessities of America into artistic virtues—he once again indicated that *Blithedale* is one example of how Hawthorne "read the romantic effect into the most usual and contemporary things," and how, through the use of an appropriate tone, he took up the angular New England "reforming Real" and transformed it into something "rich and strange."

The Bostonians

The Bostonians is, of course, the work most frequently compared with *Blithedale.* With respect to both these novels, it is interesting to note that just as Hawthorne was accused of having modeled Zenobia after Margaret Fuller, so was James accused of having modeled Miss Birdseye after Elizabeth Peabody, Hawthorne's sister-in-law. And James defended himself in terms similar to those he had used in defending Hawthorne. In his reply to William James, he denied that Miss Peabody was his starting-point or example.[2] "Miss Birdseye was evolved entirely from my moral consciousness," he wrote. The only definite connection between the two women was their spectacles, which "were always in the wrong place." But this was true of many other old people. He apologized, nevertheless, for any unintended resemblances, and promised to write to Miss Peabody, if necessary, explaining that Miss Birdseye was a creation, not a portrait of her.

The most extended analysis of *Blithedale* and *The Bostonians* is Marius Bewley's "*The Blithedale Romance* and *The Bostonians,*" which first appeared in *Scrutiny,* 16 (Winter, 1949), 178-95, and was later reprinted in *The Complex Fate: Hawthorne, Henry James and Some Other American Writers* (New York: Chatto and Windus, 1952), pp. 11-30. On the Peabody-Birdseye question, Bewley believes that James defended himself so earnestly—and yet so unconvincingly—against the charge that he had modeled Miss Birdseye on Miss Peabody precisely because he felt guilty about it.

Bewley argues that although James said that the idea for *The Bostonians* came from Daudet's *L'Évangéliste,*[3] this "serves only as a distraction." If *Evangéliste* helped to focus James's question, Hawthorne had already provided the answer, and possibly James just "failed to note the rate at which he was taking hints from . . . Hawthorne." *Blithedale,* according to Bewley, provided James "a background scene which he wished . . . to improve upon." From Hawthorne's novel he used, first, the theme of women's rights. Verena's speech at Miss Birdseye's in chapter 8, for instance, is quite similar to the dialogue in chapter 14 of *Blithedale.* And the idea for Selah Tarrant's mesmerism, which "calms" Verena before her talks, also came "from the somewhat similar performance of Westervelt over the Veiled Lady."

Bewley writes at length about the similarities between Westervelt and Selah Tarrant. Both men are mesmerists, and both have highly questionable personal histories. Just as the gold band around Westervelt's teeth reveals him as a moral and physical humbug, so does Selah Tarrant's terrible smile illuminate his lack of moral quality. Selah is the father of a girl prodigy, whom he literally sells to Olive Chancellor; Westervelt is the brother-in-law of Priscilla, also a girl prodigy, and he exploits her in the same way that Selah exploits Verena. James, however, strips Selah of all Gothicism, and thus shows his evil more vividly, whereas the evil in *Blithedale* is not concretely presented.

Blithedale's "chief suggestiveness," Bewley finds, was in the way Hawthorne described Zenobia's strange domination over Priscilla. Although in *Blithedale* this theme of dominance is ultimately incoherent, in the Chancellor-Tarrant relation James developed it clearly and comprehensively. Zenobia, of course, "except in her dominating quality, does not equate with Olive Chancellor." Neither is she as aggressive as Chancellor. Priscilla too is merely a victim we can hardly feel sympathy for. In the end, she turns out to be Zenobia's half-sister, and the two fall in love with the same man. But neither of these situations adequately explains the psychological attraction between them. In describing their friendship, Bewley argues, Hawthorne was not consciously attempting anything similar to James. James's intention, as he explains in *Notebooks,* p. 47, was to "study one of those friendships between women which are so common in New England," a theme whose psychological aspects Hawthorne had accidentally blundered into and was incapable of evaluating.

In chapter 5 of *Hawthorne,* James expressed his dissatisfaction with the relationship between Zenobia and Priscilla. In *The Bostonians,* Bewley writes, James avenged Zenobia "by showing in Olive Chancellor what, in such a relation, Zenobia would have been." During her first private interview with Verena, for example, Olive shows the same morbid shyness, nervous manner, and flood of emotion as Priscilla does during her first meeting with Zenobia. On the other hand, it is Verena who is as "highly coloured" as Zenobia, and both women are almost defined in the purity and innocence of their theatricality. Thus, in *The Bostonians,* James gave Verena both Priscilla's role and, more appropriately, Zenobia's beauty, charm, and eloquence.

In *Blithedale,* Bewley continues, Zenobia's motives for victimizing Priscilla are obscure; in *The Bostonians,* Olive Chancellor's are in her own character. In *Blithedale,* again, the theme of dominance is parcelled out: Westervelt and Hollingsworth dominate Zenobia, and Zenobia dominates Priscilla. In *The Bostonians,* all these dominances are compressed into Olive Chancellor's dominance over Verena, and the theme is more fully developed, and is treated with more understanding, than in *Blithedale.* James relates his characters to each other, defines their respective functions, and turns the shadows and confusion of *Blithedale* into the brightest clarity.

In the end, both Zenobia and Olive Chancellor court martyrdom–Zenobia literally, in chapter 27, and Olive figuratively, in chapter 42. Although

Priscilla and Verena are "saved" at last, it is a questionable salvation. In a glimpse, years later, of Priscilla with Hollingsworth (chapter 28), it appears she has suffered equally with the culprit in the expiation of his "crime." The prospect for Verena is better. James, less explicit than Hawthorne, ends his novel by noting that Verena's tears, as she was about to be united with Ransom, "were not the last she was destined to shed."

There are several other observations Bewley makes in his essay. He finds that Hollingsworth and Basil Ransom have affinities too. They both, as indicated above, "save" their heroines by marrying them at the last minute: in chapter 42 of *The Bostonians* James is largely improving upon hints from chapter 23 of *Blithedale.* Of characterization in general, Bewley notes that James found *Blithedale*'s "failure" to concern itself more with the Utopians at the community very useful in writing his own book. Whereas *Blithedale*'s characters fade away from time to time "into unrealized shadows," those in *The Bostonians* are "sharply defined and clearly lighted." Bewley finds also that *The Bostonians* is satirical in a way that *Blithedale* failed to be. His conclusion is that the relationship between *Blithedale* and *The Bostonians* is, "point by point, nearer than between any other of Hawthorne's and James's novels." In *The Bostonians* James improved upon suggestions from *Blithedale* such as women's rights, mesmerism, and the neurotic friendship between two women; Hawthorne's novel also offered him a suggestive set of characters. But the relationship between these two novels is more than merely a case of simple parallelism; for, as both novels show, James was not only indebted to Hawthorne, both men worked in, and made, a tradition. *The Bostonians* succeeds so well because it had before it a tradition trained in handling moral quantities in the American scene. It is thus unimportant whether or not James was conscious of "using" *Blithedale* for his novel; he "had known Hawthorne too long and too intimately to be much concerned with him at that level of awareness."

In the "Correspondence" section of *Scrutiny,* 17 (Spring, 1950), 53-55, Leon Edel took Bewley to task for having discarded "the 'hard' fact of James's notation of the Daudet source" and thus substituted "the speculative for the concrete." Edel takes James's words in *Notebooks* too much at face value. He finds *The Bostonians* "drawn from personal experience first," for Hawthorne's material "belonged also to James's 'visitable past.'" The sources of the novel, he argues, are "deeper than any one book," and they include "the combined effect of James's return to America in 1881 . . . and his re-reading of *L'Évangéliste.*" In his desire to write an American story, "it is Daudet who furnishes the real clue and shows us the direction: and this leads us not to Hawthorne but to Calvin," for this was the experience "James had had in the daily life of his father, and his Swedenborgian passion." Edel further argues that James's interest in the situation of women also leads back to his father's "many writings on marriage and divorce and on the role of women in the Fourierist phalanx." What Bewley describes as a "distraction," he concludes, is only a distraction to Bewley himself.

In Bewley's reply in the same issue, pp. 56-60, he first quoted James's letter to his brother about *The Bostonians:* "I had the sense of knowing terribly little about the kind of life I had attempted to describe . . . I was afraid of the reproach (having *seen* so little of the whole business treated of), of being superficial and cheap . . ." He then re-emphasized that *Blithedale,* which James had known for years, gave him "the kind of reassurances he was looking for," whereas *L'Évangéliste* did not. It is not that Hawthorne "revealed to James for the first time the facts of New England life, but that he was the first to have shown him those facts used *in art* with any effectiveness." With Edel, everybody flows into everybody else: Daudet into Calvin, Calvin into Swedenborg, Swedenborg into Fourier, and Fourier into James and *The Bostonians;* only "poor Hawthorne" is "excluded from the mystic circle." Bewley is sure without James's specific reference to Daudet Edel would not have been aware of *L'Evangeliste*'s "resemblances" to *The Bostonians.*

Randall Stewart, in his review article on Bewley's *Complex Fate* in *American Literature,* 26 (January, 1955), 580-83, noted that "James is much more critical of Olive Chancellor and Verena Tarrant than Hawthorne is of Zenobia and Priscilla," and that, although "the more strenuous satire of James's novel makes it superior to Hawthorne's," *Blithedale* excels in other qualities, like "emotional depth, and wisdom of the heart."

The second extended analysis of *Blithedale* and *The Bostonians* is Robert Emmet Long's "The Society and the Masks: *The Blithedale Romance* and *The Bostonians,*" *Nineteenth Century Fiction,* 19 (September, 1964), 105-22. Like R. W. B. Lewis's comparison of *The Scarlet Letter* and *The Bostonians* in "The Tactics of Sanctity: Hawthorne and James," *Hawthorne Centenary Essays,* edited by Roy Harvey Pearce (Columbus, Ohio: Ohio State University Press, 1964), pp. 271-95,[4] Long's essay concerns itself with Hawthorne's and James's "mutual interest in the individual." Without suggesting that this "mutual interest" is better illustrated by comparison of *The Scarlet Letter* and *The Bostonians,* rather than of *Blithedale* and *The Bostonians,* Long's essay, meticulously documented and extremely fine in its own right, never quite attains the depth of vision which emerges out of Lewis's. One might suggest, therefore, that Long's "The Society and the Masks" be read in conjunction with Lewis's "The Tactics of Sanctity."

Long observes that although *Blithedale* and *The Bostonians* both describe the age of reform in nineteenth-century New England, the traditon which they form has been "little written about and hardly understood at all." He further feels that criticism has not made clear the degree to which Hawthorne influenced James in writing *The Bostonians.* He finds that Bewley's conclusion, while justified, "turns away from further examination of Hawthorne's influence prematurely." For example, Bewley never asks why James, "who might have created excellent characters entirely independent of" *Blithedale,* was "at such pains to model his characters after Hawthorne's." Long promises to concentrate not only on characterization, but also on the novel's milieu, its themes, and James's desire to write "a very *American* tale."

In chapter 4 of *Hawthorne,* James had complained that in *Blithedale* "there is no sketching of odd figures—no reproduction of strange types of radicalism." In *The Bostonians,* Long finds, James "deliberately created characters which he regretted not finding sufficiently in" Hawthorne's novel. Selah Tarrant, for one, "is the sum of all the radical tendencies of the time and of the odd figures dwelling in the humanitary Bohemia of Boston." But the meaning of the novel is not concentrated in one single character; rather, it belongs "to a whole order of unrest." Ultimately all the questions about James's characters refer back to the social conditions of American life which he was writing about. Thus, in James's analysis of democracy in the novel, Olive Chancellor and the feminists represent just "one of the instances of the breakdown of established standards." As "the traditional distinctions between the sexes waver and become unclear, individuals are produced who are really neither male nor female," such as the feminized Mr. Pardon, or the masculine Mrs. Farrinder. James is here using the "situation of women" "as part of, and as a symbol for, the confusion of standards which democracy encourages." *Blithedale*'s theme, "like that of *The Bostonians,* is that an entire community had committed a self-deception in the name of new truths." In *Blithedale* James found a "casebook of movements and reforms which were exposed to be forms of humbug." The cults and political manias which Hawthorne had described were "taken by James to exemplify democratic unrest."

Long also discusses the similarities between Westervelt and Selah Tarrant, and a number of details in *Blithedale* which are echoed in *The Bostonians.* In chapter 23 of *Blithedale,* for example, Hawthorne writes about the "epoch of rapping spirits" and "tables upset by invisible agencies"; in chapter 10 of *The Bostonians,* James writes about "those exciting days of [Selah Tarrant's] mediumship, when the table, sometimes, wouldn't rise from the ground, the sofa wouldn't float through the air." In *Blithedale,* again, although it is Zenobia who originally speaks of "new truths," in chapter 26 she tells Coverdale: "There are no new truths, much as we have prided ourselves on finding some." Similarly, in chapter 3 of *The Bostonians,* when Olive asks Ransom whether he does not believe in the new truths, he replies: "I have never yet encountered in the world any but old truths." "The 'one true system' which the colonists hope to found at Blithedale is ridiculed in *The Bostonians,*" and Zenobia's "new truths'. "become a shibboleth in James's novel." These and other interpolations from *Blithedale* recommended themselves to James, Long feels, "because the conservatism of Hawthorne, his skepticism about progress and reform, gave James a standard against which he might judge and criticize the manners of his characters."

Long next discusses Coverdale's and Ransom's practical attitudes, and the implications of Zenobia's and Olive Chancellor's balked personal fulfillments. But the most formative influence of *Blithedale,* he finds, is its theme that the characters at the Experiment "have all disguised their own identities by embodying themselves in public purposes." Blithedale itself is a public cause, but the project "collapses under the . . . egos of its members." In chapter 25 of *Blithedale,* during the masquerade that begins in chapter 24, Zenobia tells Hollingsworth: "You are a better masquerader than the witches and gypsies yonder; for your disguise is a self-deception." Long calls this scene the epiphany of both *Blithedale* and *The Bostonians,* for the characters in James's novel too "live for external purposes and public projects, and thereby disguise their own identities." Although Olive is described in chapter 1 as "very honest" and "full of rectitude," by the end of the novel her rectitude, like Hollingsworth's, is revealed as a self-deception. Even her "concentration of purpose" (chapter 11) recalls Hollingsworth's "tremendous concentrativeness" (chapter 15). Both of them are obsessed with one subject: reform. And all the other characters in *The Bostonians* wear masks too: Mrs. Farrinder, Miss Birdseye, the Tarrants . . .

In both novels, Long further finds, sexual attraction and domination underlie most of the action. In *Blithedale,* the collapse of the Experiment shows, in part, that sexual compulsion has a deeper place in human desires than moral earnestness. And the various dominations in the novel also have a sexual suggestion: they "imply, somewhat like the sexual urge, the demands of the individual ego which separate men, the psychic drive to assert oneself over others."

Whereas in *Blithedale* the dominations are many—Zenobia and Hollingsworth dominate Priscilla; Westervelt dominates Priscilla and Zenobia; Coverdale is drawn to Zenobia, to Hollingsworth, and to Priscilla—in *The Bostonians* the forces center about Verena. She is dominated by her parents, by Olive Chancellor, and by a series of suitors. Domination and sex in this novel merge "into the single primary motive of sex." Although James undoubtedly derived the "idea of a false claim made upon the heroine by a member of her own sex, and in the name of political ideas," from Daudet's *L'Evangeliste,*

> the broader implications of a whole aberrant society which lived for artificial causes and reforms leads back to *The Blithedale Romance,* where these attitudes are understood as an estrangement from life. Here public solicitude is revealed to be less fundamental than the drives of the individual ego, expressed in domination and sex. In *The Bostonians* James has used sex as a reality principle that is allied with life and creative energy; in expressing what is personal

> and individual, it asserts the primary importance of the self . . . .
>
> The selfless, democratic society, whose vast solicitude is with "others," has been made equivalent to feminization and sexlessness. The ideal of Ransom, by contrast to James's Boston, is a masculine one; the virile society he implies protects the primacy of the individual, permits him to develop in his own way, encourages his right to his own discriminations. (121-22)

It is this "mutual interest in the individual" in both novels, Long concludes, that "is perhaps their real affinity." To recognize this is at the same time to realize that Hawthorne's influence "goes much further than similarity in subject or even in characterization." In these two novels both writers

> addressed themselves to truth and hypocrisy in American life, and attempted to say what seemed to them to be the essential truth of the society they described. They did so as moralists, as novelists whose primary interest was the illusive nature of appearance and reality. In both novels there is a similar form, which pivots about the idea of a society that is a form of "mock-life," and in both the description of their characters is embodied in the wearing of masks. (122)

The Bostonians is thus James's interpretation of *Blithedale,* and "interpreting it as he did James both brought Hawthorne into his own criticism of New England manners, and at the same time illuminated *The Blithedale Romance* by finding in Hawthorne's novel about the disguise of the self an unconscious allegory of democracy."

Essentially, most of Martha Banta's observations on *Blithedale* and *The Bostonians* in *Henry James and the Occult* (Bloomington: Indiana University Press, 1972) are similar to Long's. "The possession by the self of what is not the self," Banta writes in chapter 4 ("The Vampire Breed," pp. 81-104), "was a major sin in the tradition James inherited, whether from Nathaniel Hawthorne's abhorrence of the desecration of the sanctity of the human heart or his father's denunciation of 'spiritual snatching.'" Like other nineteenth-century writers, James was obsessed with the vampire theme, which he frequently used to dramatize male-female relationships. Banta finds that in "Professor Fargo" and *The Bostonians,* in *Blithedale,* and in William Dean Howells's *The Undiscovered Country,* physical vampirism is used as a "metaphor for the excess of *doing* as well as *being*." Furthermore, she finds that all these works are closely "related in theme and matched in many details of character and plot."

Blithedale was published in 1852, *The Bostonians* in 1886, and in 1901 James published *The Sacred Fount.* "This fifty-year span," Banta writes, "marks the path from Blithedale to Newmarch taken by James's awareness of what he might make of a merger of an old literary tradition, a new psychology attentive to psychic powers, and his own continued, and heightened, concern over human relationships." Banta notes that a scene in chapter 23 of *Blithedale* adumbrates a scene in chapter 8 of *The Bostonians;* it mirrors

> Miss Birdseye's social gathering in Boston (at which Verena Tarrant appears to speak "inspirationally" in response to her father's mesmerizing hands). In Hawthorne's version Miles Coverdale describes the odd-lot of Bostonians filled with "mystic sensuality" who gather to witness the marvels performed by the Veiled Lady. On questioning " a pale man in blue spectacles," Coverdale is told "stranger stories than ever were written in a romance." He is told of "instances of the miraculous power of one human being over the will and passions of another," and of the ways in which a wizard may take human character—"but soft wax in his hands"—and "mould it" into "guilt, or virtue" as "he should see fit." With "horror and disgust" Coverdale listens to these statements, which intimate "the individual soul was virtually annihilated." (90)

Banta, like Long, discusses Coverdale's and Zenobia's prying, Zenobia's influence over Priscilla, her sexual desire for Hollingsworth, and the contest of wills "waged among Zenobia, Westervelt, and Hollingsworth to see who can win Priscilla." In her analysis of *The Bostonians,* she discusses the merger of Olive's and Verena's souls into one, the battle of wills between Olive and Basil Ransom, Selah Tarrant's cheap mesmerism, and James's "adroit use of the nomenclature of vampirism." She further notes that "James even picks up that bit of strange business used between Zenobia and Priscilla in *The Blithedale Romance;* on leaving a party, Olive 'prepared to throw a fold of her mantle, as she had once before, over her young friend. . . . This gesture of symbolic enfolding will occur yet again before the struggle over Verena comes to its heated climax."[5] In *The Bostonians,* she concludes, James concentrated on "psychic assault" and thus grounded the plot of his novel "upon a massive metaphor for will."

Howard Kerr's basic observations on *Blithedale* and *The Bostonians* in *Mediums, and Spirit-Rappers, and Roaring Radicals: Spiritualism in American Literature, 1850–1900* (Urbana: University of Illinois Press, 1972) are similar to Banta's in *Henry James and the Occult* (1972), and hence to Long's in "The Society and the Masks" (1964). Kerr refers frequently to Banta's dissertation, "The Two Worlds of Henry James: A Study in the Fiction of the Supernatural" (Indiana University, 1964), but his observation that Banta "pointed out similarities among *The Blithedale Romance,* 'Professor Fargo,' *The Undiscovered Country,* and *The Bostonians,* without explicitly suggesting any general relationship among the latter three"

(146–47n.) must not be applied to her book as well. Banta's tracing of the path from "Professor Fargo" through *The Undiscovered Country* to *The Bostonians*—see, for example, her long passage quoted at the end of the section on *Blithedale* and *The Sacred Fount* in this essay—is actually superior to Kerr's, and the general line of her argument is more plausible. One of Kerr's main emphases is indicated by his comment on Bewley's *Complex Fate.* By "mistakenly placing *The Undiscovered Country* (1880) after *The Bostonians* (1886) in time," he writes, "Bewley overlooked a very important point on 'the line of influence' stretching from Hawthorne to James" (212). What Kerr emphasizes is the intermediate position of Howells between Hawthorne and James; thus his remarks that in "rediscovering Boston . . . James [in *The Bostonians*] seems to have glanced at Howells's map of New England, *The Undiscovered Country"* (215); or that "Verena Tarrant and Basil Ransom may have profited in particular from James's reading of Howells" (213–14); or that "Ransom himself was perhaps a more deliberate attempt to improve on Howells" (214). Many other critics, including Banta, have written on the similarities between *Blithedale, The Undiscovered Country,* and *The Bostonians,* but Kerr places more emphasis on Howells's novel than they do. Kerr further argues that "James's satiric attitude toward reform in *The Bostonians* was more reminiscent of such writers as Orestes Brownson and Bayard Taylor than of Hawthorne or Howells" (216). But he does, of course, see similarities between *Blithedale* and *The Bostonians.*

In chapter 3, "Ghosts and Ghost-Seeing," pp. 55–81, Kerr observes that although Hawthorne disliked mesmerism—which he accepted "as physiological fact" but "denied that it was in any way supernatural"—he used it profitably in *The House of the Seven Gables* and *Blithedale* "as one version of the unpardonable sin." But he was always skeptical of the spirits, and *Blithedale* shows that by the 1850's he "had grown disgusted with spiritualism and mesmerism alike." Nevertheless, his treatment of spiritualism in his works "was at least indicative of its serious literary potential":

> "Rappaccini's Daughter," *The House of the Seven Gables,* and *The Blithedale Romance* have properly been identified among the literary prototypes for William Dean Howells and Henry James's explorations of the wizard-medium relationship in terms of spiritualism in *The Undiscovered Country* (1880) and *The Bostonians* (1886). In these two novels Howells and James, more objectively critical of the spiritualistic movement than Hawthorne was ever to be, were successfully to translate the occult ambience of magnetic wizard and trance maiden into thoroughgoing studies of prophetic and mediumistic personality. But even here Hawthorne had preceded them with his own faltering attempts to explore the same relationship. (65)

Kerr's analysis of *The Bostonians* appears in the first part of chapter 8, "The Young Prophetess." He examines the struggle between Basil Ransom and Olive Chancellor for the control of Verena, Verena's mediumistic personality, and James's criticism of the American spiritualistic experience. He finds that *The Bostonians* "resembles both the anti-reform satires and the magnetic romances of the 1850's, while also anticipating the studies of psychical consciousness which lay ahead in James's supernatural fiction." In satiric tone and atmosphere, James's novel "harked back to an earlier time. In its attitude toward reform it differed from the satires of mid-century chiefly in being more ironic and less fearfully melodramatic; its use of the language of reform would have made sense to readers of [*Blithedale*]." Kerr's conclusion is that in *The Bostonians* "James supplemented Hawthorne's mesmeric materials with his own observations of spiritualism and reform"; his novel, in many ways, "reworked the feminist, utopian, and magnetic materials which Hawthorne had dealt with in *The Blithedale Romance* (1852) at the very time spiritualism was replacing mesmerism as a subject of occult interest."

Chapter 7 of Irving Howe's *Politics and the Novel* (New York: Avon Books, 1957) includes a section on *Blithedale,* "Hawthorne: Pastoral and Politics," pp. 167-78, and another on *The Bostonians,* "Henry James: Politics and Character," pp. 186-203. Howe observes that the few American writers who have seen the *idea* of politics as a fruitful subject for the novel, including Hawthorne and James, "could not find enough supporting material in their experience or their environment with which to give this theme a full embodiment." Thus in those nineteenth-century American novels which deal with politics, ideology is sometimes treated "as if it were merely a form of private experience." *Blithedale* was the first novel to treat the theme of "how social and individual experience melt into one another," a theme which reached its fulfillment in *The Bostonians.*

At the end of his interpretation of *Blithedale,* Howe concludes that Hawthorne's novel is "abundant in potentialities" but "limited in realization." However, James saw enough possibilities in its subject to base *The Bostonians* upon it, a novel Howe calls "the masterpiece that Hawthorne's book might have been." As he explains in the preface to *Politics and the Novel,* Howe's section on *The Bostonians* forms part of his introduction to the Modern Library edition (1956) of that novel, pp. v-xxviii. In that introduction he relates more directly to *The Bostonians* some of the comments on *Blithedale* which he makes separately in *Politics and the Novel.* He finds that Hawthorne's influence on James was extensive. Because Hawthorne's moral sense, which was largely detached from orthodox faith, had no "buoying social vision" to thrive in, he turned to allegory, in which he could "sustain the moral sense as an independent force." James's moral sense too was acute and troublesome, but he managed "to embody and test it through portrayals of social manners and relations." But both novelists treated similar themes. They were obsessed by the problem of integrity; that is, now an individual, "involved as he must be in limiting and treacherous social relationships," can maintain his personal uniqueness. Hawthorne's Unpardonable Sin of taking into one's hand another person's destiny was also James's.

Howe finds *Blithedale* "in many ways a forerunner of *The Bostonians*," but considers James's complaint about the lack of satire in *Blithedale* "hardly to the point, for James failed to see that no matter what Hawthorne said about his fellow-colonists at Brook Farm they held for him the attraction of abundant and savored experience." What tempted him at the Experiment was not the ideas of the reformers but rather "their implicit faith in the possibility of human communication." As such, they could hardly serve as objects of satire. In *The Bostonians,* however, James's reformers "no longer have the capacity for a large irregular experience, they have declined into eccentric chatter." Thus his complaint about the lack of satire in *Blithedale* is not really a criticism but an anticipation of "the assumptions from which *The Bostonians* would later be written."

Howe finds more accurate James's criticism that the action of *Blithedale* gets progressively "too much out of reality," and that the story should have concerned "itself more with the little community in which its earlier scenes are laid" (*Hawthorne,* chapter 5). As Howe correctly points out, the same criticism could be made of *The Bostonians,* whose "first 150 pages treat brilliantly of the world of Boston reform and the remainder narrows down to a personal struggle between Olive Chancellor . . . and Basil Ransom." However, Howe defends James against this charge, and shows that in *The Bostonians* James avoided the weakness of many American writers, including Hawthorne, who treat an American political theme. James had fewer hopes and illusions, and he avoided "that surrender to the 'evasive tendency' . . . which occurs about midway through so many American novels dealing with the life of politics."

Of the relationship between Verena and Basil Ransom, Howe notes that through Verena's constant though indirect taunts at Ransom's failure, James shows his awareness that even the most apparently feminine character can have "an aggressiveness that is almost as great a threat to male assurance as the open assaults of the feminists." And this idea, that passive femininity can subdue male energy as aggressive feminism cannot, further links *The Bostonians* to *Blithedale.* In *Blithedale* the saturnine Hollingsworth "is finally captured and tamed by Priscilla, a pale New England maiden."[6] However, Hawthorne betrays a deeper, although more cautious, hostility toward Priscilla and all that she stands for than James does toward Verena.

Through Olive Chancellor, Howe concludes, "James registers the full and terrible price that is paid by a first-rate intelligence as it is ravaged by social disorder and psychological obsession." From one point of view, therefore, she is a descendant of Hawthorne's villains, except that she commits the Unpardonable Sin of manipulating human beings "not from some sourceless malignity but from her own clearly specified sickness and vulnerability."

The real pioneers of the *Blithedale-Bostonians* studies are Stephen Spender and F. O. Matthiessen, although neither of them analyzed at length the relation between these two works. In the chapter on James's early novels in *The Destructive Element* (Boston: Houghton Mifflin, 1936), Spender observed that although James absorbed the tradition of European literature, his work never lost "the virile influence of Hawthorne." Spender connected the death theme in such novels as *Roderick Hudson* and *The American* to "a tradition derived from Hawthorne." Of Zenobia's suicide, he believed that if James had written the novel, "he could not have accepted the sanguine view of a providence that killed Zenobia and spared Priscilla." He noted further that in "a typical Hawthorne novel such as *The Blythedale Romance* [sic], there are all the typical properties of an early James story or novel. There is Priscilla," who is easily imposed on by Zenobia; Coverdale, who is constitutionally incapable of participating in the lives of his companions; and Hollingsworth, "the grandfather of characters like Caspar Goodwood" in *The Portrait of a Lady* or Waymarsh in *The Ambassadors.* Lastly, Spender noted that "James differed from Hawthorne in being a puritan who did not believe in the puritan morality."

Unlike Spender, who did not directly connect *The Bostonians* to *Blithedale,* F. O. Matthiessen did relate James's novel, through *The House of the Seven Gables,* to *Blithedale.* In *The Seven Gables,* after Hepzibah takes in Holgrave as a lodger, she discovers in chapter 5 that he has "the strangest companions imaginable;—men with long beards, and dressed in linen blouses . . . reformers, temperance-lecturers, and all manner of cross-looking philanthropists." He had even made "a speech, full of wild and disorganizing matter, at a meeting of his banditti-like associates." In chapter 12, Phoebe learns that before his present phase as a daguerreotypist, Holgrave had been a schoolmaster, a salesman, a newspaper editor, a peddler, a student and practitioner of dentistry, a public lecturer on mesmerism. He had also visited Europe, and traveled across much of the United States. But, "amid all these personal vicissitudes, he had never lost his identity. . . . He had never violated the innermost man, but had carried his conscience along with him." In Holgrave, Matthiessen observes in *American Renaissance* (New York: Oxford University Press, 1941), p. 331, "Hawthorne has presented a detailed portrait of one of Emerson's promising young Americans." James's own formulation of the New England character in his review of Guérin's *Letters* was similar to Hawthorne's. In "The Letters of Eugénie de Guérin," *Nation,* 3 (September 13, 1866), 206-207, James wrote:

> A very good man or a very good woman in New England is an extremely complex being. They are as innocent as you please, but they are anything but ignorant. They travel; they hold political opinions; they are accomplished Abolitionists; they read magazines and newspapers, and write for them; they read novels and police reports; they subscribe to lyceum lectures and to great libraries; in a word, they are enlightened. The result of this freedom of enquiry is that they become profoundly self-conscious. (206)

This, Matthiesen indicates, was "the kind of world James tried to project in *The Bostonians* (1886), where the mixture of reformers and blue-stockings is a late aftershine of Brook Farm and *Blithedale*." In chapter 1 of *The Bostonians,* for example, Mrs. Luna talks of "those weird meetings" of "witches and wizards, mediums, and spirit-rappers, and roaring radicals" of Boston. In chapter 4 we read that Miss Birdseye "belonged to the Short-Skirts League . . . [and] to any and every league that had been founded for almost any purpose whatever." Mrs. Farrinder too "lectured on temperance and the rights of women," and labored "to give the ballot to every woman in the country." *Blithedale* is similarly dotted with references to illustrious prophets and progressive people, reformers and philanthropists, lecturers on the rights of women and epochs of rapping spirits—chapters 8, 14, 16, 23, 24, etc.

Oscar Cargill, Peter Buitenhuis, and Susan Kuhlmann have also discussed *Blithedale* and *The Bostonians.* In his interpretation of *The Bostonains* in *The Novels of Henry James* (New York: Hafner Publishing, 1961), Cargill refers to the parallels Matthiessen, Bewley, and Howe have drawn between James's novel and *Blithedale,* but finds the resemblance Bewley notes between Priscilla's throwing herself into the arms of Hollingsworth in chapter 23 of *Blithedale* and Verena's similar collapse into the arms of Ransom in chapter 42 of *The Bostonians* (*Complex Fate,* pp. 23-25) "too common to romantic fiction to be of consequence" (Cargill, p. 127). He further notes, as is obvious, that James's use of *Blithedale* "does not preclude his use of other books" (139n.).

Leon Edel would probably concur with most of Buitenhuis's observations on *Blithedale* and *The Bostonians* in *The Grasping Imagination: The American Writings of Henry James* (Toronto: University of Toronto Press, 1970). Buitenhuis argues that *The Bostonians* "derives directly from French naturalism and signifies a radical . . . shift in [James's] fictional method and style" (141). He admits that Hawthorne's influence on this novel is important; in *The Bostonians* James was obviously recalling the reformers of *Blithedale.* But "the romance elements that dominate Hawthorne's fiction and that James himself had drawn on for some early tales . . . were almost totally abandoned in *The Bostonians* in favor of a sharp realism." Buitenhuis finds Bewley's claim that James's novel is almost completely indebted to *Blithedale* very "misguided":

> Some of the elements that Bewley claims that James drew directly from *The Blithedale Romance* for *The Bostonians* he used earlier in *Professor Fargo.* Verena is as much like [Colonel Gifford's] daughter as she is like Priscilla . . . and Selah Tarrant is more like Professor Fargo than he is like the magician Westervelt. . . . By the time that James wrote *The Bostonians* he had assimilated and turned to different use characters and events that had their origins in Hawthorne's fiction. (141-42)

This, of course, does not negate Bewley's claim. On the contrary; it reemphasizes James's indebtedness to Hawthorne. The fact that there are similarities between *The Bostonians* and "Professor Fargo" may merely suggest that James was indebted to *Blithedale* for both works. Earlier in his book, Buitenhuis himself considers this very suggestion (pp. 72-74). "Most of the characters in *The Bostonians,*" he now states, "had predecessors in James's own fiction. Basil Ransom is evolved from a long series of conservatives, generally European in origin." Echoing Edel, he too asserts that the "primary soucre for *The Bostonians* is named by James himself": Daudet's *L'Evangeliste.*

Chapter 4 of Susan Kuhlmann's *Knave, Fool, and Genius: The Confidence Man as He Appears in Nineteenth-Century American Fiction* (Chapel Hill: University of North Carolina Press, 1973), pp. 75-90, includes a discussion of *Blithedale, The Undiscovered Country,* and *The Bostonians,* but virtually none of her observations on Hawthorne's and James's novels is new. She discusses Hawthorne's fascination with the sin of manipulation, especially the manipulation by a "spiritualist" who uses and displays another person as a "medium." In both *Blithedale* and *The Bostonians,* "a character claiming supernatural authority utterly dispossesses and claims for his own use the soul of a helpless girl": Westervelt and Priscilla in Hawthorne's novel, and Selah Tarrant and his daughter Verena in James's. In *The Bostonians,* of course, Olive Chancellor quickly buys Selah off and becomes herself Verena's mentor. Like Bewley before her, Kuhlmann observes that Verena has the qualities of both Priscilla and Zenobia. She writes also on Westervelt's "contamination" of Zenobia's life, Coverdale's "use" of life as material for his imagination, and Hawthorne's exploration of "the theme of artistic creation as . . . a travesty of life." But no really new insights emerge about *Blithedale* and

The Bostonians; a manipulator is always a manipulator, even when renamed a "Confidence Man."

Two dissertations include comparisons of *Blithedale* and *The Bostonians.* In "The Divided Self: The Alter Ego as Theme and Device in Brockden Brown, Hawthorne, and James" (Harvard, 1964), Barrie S. Hayne terms *The Bostonians* "the chief evidence in the case for James's indebtedness to Hawthorne." But Hayne discusses the differences between James's novel and Hawthorne's more than their similarities. And he is heavily indebted to Bewley, whom he refers to frequently.

Hayne finds that in *The Bostonians* James took the counters he found in *Blithedale* "and moved them into a series of different patterns." Whereas in *Blithedale* it is Priscilla who seeks Zenobia's friendship, in *The Bostonians* it is Olive who comes to Verena, and, although Verena is less deliberately the victim than Priscilla, from the first she "is more ready to be Olive's victim than Bewley seems willing to admit." Hayne too, like Bewley before him, notes that Olive's nervousness links her with Priscilla just as Verena's red hair and magnetic qualities ally her with Zenobia. Nevertheless, he finds that Olive is Zenobia's "clearest reincarnation." Verena too, he explains, "has more in her of Priscilla than of Zenobia," and Mrs. Farrinder, the prophetess of Roxbury, the site of Brook Farm, is the one most like Zenobia. These observations are on pp. 408-24 of "The Divided Self."

Hayne draws other parallels between *Blithedale* and *The Bostonians,* but none of them is new. He calls Selah Tarrant the Westervelt of *The Bostonians,* but finds him a more realistic character. He notes further that Olive and Verena are more psychologically real than Zenobia and Priscilla; that *The Bostonians* "ends with an explicit parallel to Hollingsworth's rescue of the Veiled Lady"; that James's final hint about the tears Verena's and Ransom's marriage may bring "is only less startling" than the ending of *Blithedale;* and that Ransom's views about his generation being womanized are more distinctly James's than Hollingsworth's are Hawthorne's.

Judith J. Fryer's dissertation, "The Faces of Eve: A Study of Women in American Life and Literature in the Nineteenth Century" (University of Minnesota, 1973), also includes an analysis of *Blithedale* and *The Bostonians.*[7] In her last chapter, "The New Woman," pp. 286-364, she explains that although the "woman question" was a burning issue to the novelists of the nineteenth century, those who devoted themselves to it created not women but caricatures. "Hawthorne's Zenobia is a leader of the women's movement; yet she commits suicide because of her unrequited love." And Olive Chancellor is at best a lesbian, at worst "a terrible devouring mother figure." But, of course, Hawthorne and James are both male novelists; only "a woman, it seems, can write realistically about the awakening of a woman to her own identity."[8] Later in her chapter, Fryer observes:

> James admired Zenobia as Hawthorne's most complete person; yet when he came to create his own lady-reformer, he could hardly have created less of a *person.* Zenobia and Olive Chancellor could not be more different: where Zenobia is almost defined by her sexuality, Olive has "absolutely no figure" and is "unmarried by every implication of her being" (19, 18); where Zenobia's laugh is mellow, delectable, "not in the least an ordinary woman's laugh," Olive is "a woman without laughter," her smile is one of exceeding faintness, like "a thin ray of moonlight resting upon the wall of a prison" (19, 18); where Zenobia is characterized by warmth associated with hearth-fires, summer sun and hothouse flowers, Olive's eyes have "the glitter of green ice" and she gives "a certain appearance of feeling cold" (19). James had felt that the least felicitous part of *The Blithedale Romance* was the domination of Priscilla by Zenobia; when he came to write his novel about the "new woman," he made the domination of Verena the central issue. Both Hawthorne and James were concerned . . . [with] "the relations of the sexes." But where Hawthorne equated strength and independence . . . with sexuality and made his lady-reformer the most passionate of his women, James made Olive Chancellor his most perverted woman. [Fryer, pp. 310-11. Fryer's parenthetical references are to the 1956 Modern Library edition of *The Bostonians*.]

Unlike Zenobia, Fryer continues, Olive hates her sexuality. "Her focus in the women's movement is not the achievement of sexual equality . . . but hatred of men." She is a portrait of James's own hatred of both women and reformers. "If Hawthorne was threatened by the powerful and independent new woman, he was also attracted to her; he made her beautiful, compelling, heroic and tragic. But for James she was only dry, strenuous, perverted and ridiculous." Fryer also finds James's disclaimer of having modeled Miss Birdseye after Elizabeth Peabody as unconvincing as Hawthorne's argument with respect to Zenobia and Margaret Fuller.

"The Beast in the Jungle"

Four people have written on the relation between *Blithedale* and "The Beast in the Jungle." In "The Inception of 'The Beast in the Jungle,'" *New England Quarterly,* 26 (1953), 529-32, Jessie Ryon Lucke suggests that in spite of James's explanation in *Prefaces,* p. 246, the original inspiration of "The Beast" was, "all unconsciously perhaps," the passage in chapter 5 of *Blithedale* which James quoted in chapter 5 of *Hawthorne.* This description of

Hollingsworth glaring upon people "like a tiger out of a jungle" "was the 'accidental determinant,' so elusive to the author, which ultimately resulted in James's story of the man who was obsessed by his own peculiar destiny so that life passed him by." James's use of *Beast* instead of *tiger* "is mere substitution," for in chapter 2 of the story the beast is explicitly called a tiger: "a man of feeling didn't cause himself to be accompanied by a lady on a tiger-hunt." Furthermore, John Marcher and Hollingsworth are rather similar. In chapter 2 of "The Beast," for instance, one reads that Marcher "wore a mask painted with the social simper, out of the eyeholes of which there looked eyes of an expression not in the least matching the other features"; and, again: "Marcher softly groaned with a gasp, half-spent, at the face . . . [which] had always had its incalculable moments of glaring out, quite as with the very eyes of the very Beast." In chapter 5 of *Hawthorne,* James had expressed his fascination with the grasp that Hollingsworth, "this barbarous fanatic," had laid upon Zenobia, drawing her "into the gulf of his omnivorous egotism." Marcher, Lucke points out, is not as barbarous, but he is certainly as fanatic and perverted, and May Bartram "is drawn into the gulf of his omnivorous egotism" just as Zenobia is into Hollingsworth's. And both egotists are responsible for the deaths of the two women.

Lucke further indicates that Hawthorne's sentence about Hollingsworth's "intensity with which he contemplated his own ideas, and the infrequent sympathy which they met with from his auditors"—the sentence which James omitted from his quotation—is perhaps the most indicative of his debt to Hawthorne, for in chapter 2 of "The Beast" we read that it wasn't in Marcher either to tell any one his obsession, "for nothing but the amusement of a cold world would have waited on it." And, just as Hawthorne thinks that Hollingsworth's only salvation would be the experience of "committing some huge sin in his proper person," so does James analyze Marcher's malady as complete rejection of experience of any sort. Lucke's conclusion is that Hawthorne's passage which James quoted in *Hawthorne,* together with its omitted sentence, was responsible "not only for the title of the story, for the underlying symbolic idea of the springing tiger, for the character of the hero as the egoist deranged by prolonged concentration of his own ideas, but for the philosophy pervading all of James's later work—experience, *living,* is all that matters, a theme developed in detail in *The Ambassadors*."[9]

In "Hawthorne, James and the Destructive Self," *Texas Studies in Literature and Language,* 4 (1962), 58-71, George Monteiro considers, in addition to *Blithedale* and "The Beast," Hawthorne's "Wakefield" and James's *The Ambassadors.* Although he agrees that James probably got the central image for his story from *Blithedale,* he finds Lucke's full claim "extravagant and misleading." Monteiro argues that from what James said in *Hawthorne* about Hollingsworth's characterization, he possibly saw that Hawthorne's image of the tiger, "was somewhat out of proportion for Hollingsworth in that it was too much of a psychological image for his relative insensitivity." Furthermore, in *Blithedale* this image is given as the narrator's; in "The Beast," Marcher himself conceives his fate in terms of the stalking-beast image. And, although Marcher's existence, like Hollingsworth's, is controlled by one idea, "his *idée fixe* differs from Hollingsworth's in quality. Hollingsworth is a vehement social reformer who fails either to analyze or to question the . . . social vision that warps his life." Marcher, on the other hand, doesn't want to do anything; rather, he desires and expects something exclusive and personal to be *done* to him. "It is misleading, then," Monteiro observes, "to say that his actions are expressive of his will in conjunction with his persistent idea in the way that we can say that Hollingsworth's decisions are made to accord with his controlling social principles, for the very possibility of Marcher's making any meaningful decision is precluded by his immobilizing sense of personal fate."

It is not Hollingsworth, therefore, Monteiro continues, but rather Miles Coverdale "who is directly and meaningfully related to Marcher." Sensitive, very self-conscious, and somewhat intellectual, Coverdale is emotionally detached from all the life around him. Because he is unable to engage himself emotionally, all he can do is passively watch others live. He thus insulates himself against all passions and all adventures.

The rest of Monteiro's essay is mostly an analysis of the theme of the *unlived* life in "Wakefield," and how Hawthorne's focus here prefigures James's concerns in "The Beast." After comparing Marcher's "perverse domination over May Bartram" with Wakefield's desire for similar domination over his wife,[10] Wakefield's "negative" action with Marcher's inaction, and May's ultimate freeing of herself from Marcher's power with Mrs. Wakefield's gradual shedding of all traces of her husband's domination, Monteiro observes:

> Wakefield's and Marcher's necessary divorcement from the center of their lives through their secret conceptions of self occurs, in a sense, because, no less than Strether and Coverdale, they want genuine experience. Consequently, each attempts at the outset of his *adventure* to apprehend and then to shape the meaning of his life through an act of will. Yet even though it is the *lived* life above all that he seeks, each is unaware that the kind of experience he eventually calls forth results necessarily from his having made a cult of personality. In Marcher's case, because his compulsive receptivity to the quality of experience he desires . . . precludes the possibility of his being quick to any other kind of experience, his ideal conception of self is, in its consequences, as morally destructive

> as Wakefield's attempt to measure and evaluate his social and personal self through calculated experiment. (69)

In *Notebooks,* p. 312, Matthiessen and Murdock had noted that in such a work as "The Beast," James "progressed beyond Hawthorne's method of presenting, as in *Ethan Brand,* an allegory of the Unpardonable Sin." Monteiro's observation is that:

> Considering the current taste for realistic rather than allegorical symbolism . . . *qua* method James had gone beyond "Ethan Brand" (so had Hawthorne, for that matter). But in conception and achievement James was never able to equal Hawthorne's Wakefield, whose physical withdrawal was . . . the final decadent flowering of the kind of life that had always been his . . . whose absurd absence should have revealed to him the emptiness and meaninglessness of his life, but whose confusion at the last far surpassed his understanding. (70)

Hawthorne clearly prefigured "one of the major aspects of the modern image of man," Monteiro continues. In their treatment of this type, both Hawthorne and James showed that "a secret conception of self, by its very nature, tends to destroy the possibility for genuine moral experience." Marcher's complaint that "it was failure not to be anything" suggests that the valid test of any conception of self requires action. But it was Hawthorne who discovered that "such a conception could . . . destroy the possibility that the individual might have for meaningful actions of any efficacy." And it was Hawthorne who first perceived the necessity for modern man to recognize that total blame for his failure to realize his full capacity for moral growth "lay in the destructive egocentricity of his personality. The account of Wakefield's experiment," Monteiro concludes, "marks the beginning in America of the enduring literary concern with the nexus of the critical failure of personality and the destruction of the individual capacity for moral growth."

In chapter 4 of *The Battle of the Books: Some Aspects of Henry James* (Athens, Ohio: Ohio University Press, 1964), Edward Stone analyzes James's use of names in "The Beast," and the complex "imagery of the months and seasons" which is imbedded in these names. He finds the name Marcher suggesting the hero's "monotonously methodical progress toward his unwitting doom" (122). In addition to being a marcher, the hero is also a *March-er;* and, significantly, the heroine's name is *May.* And the month which comes between them is April. Furthermore, both James's "story and the year begin in autumn, rise steadily to a zenith in spring, then slope sharply to a conclusion in autumn." This position of months, Stone concludes, cannot be coincidental; it is a deliberate attempt by James "to provide an underscoring to the already fairly legible lettering of his little parable. In short . . . the calendar in James's tale was designed as a backdrop to his play." As such, Hawthorne's *Blithedale* provided James with a useful precedent:

> In *Blithedale* Hawthorne had superimposed a symmetry of the seasons . . . on the symmetry of his plot, so that we can see the reformers proceeding from spring (growth and hope) to summer (fruition and growing disenchantment) to fall (decay and disaster). And not the least fascinating of James's comments on *Blithedale* is that it "leaves in the memory an impression analogous to that of an April day—an alternation of brightness and shadow, of broken sun-patches and sprinkling clouds." For in James's own story, is not the most important of all the month of April—it being required to serve as two mediums, one exact and the other approximate? Can it not be seen to bear this weight in the story? (123)

Stone goes on to consider the functions of April in James's story, but he draws no further correspondences between *Blithedale* and "The Beast."

Except for a slightly different phraseology, David J. Thompson's comments on Hollingsworth and Marcher in particular, and on the tiger image in *Blithedale* and "The Beast" in general, are mostly an expansion and synthesis of Lucke's and Monteiro's observations. In his dissertation, "Societal Definitions of Individualism and the Critique of Egotism as a Major Theme in American Fiction" (Brown, 1972), pp. 186-89, Thompson indicates that what the tiger metaphor expresses in both *Blithedale* and "The Beast" is Hollingsworth's and Marcher's egotism. He argues that Hollingsworth's idea of reform is merely a "surrogate" for his own self; he is unconsciously obsessed with himself. Marcher too is obsessed with his conception of the personal destiny that awaits him, and his obsession, like Hollingsworth's, results in "the sacrifice of the woman who loved him," and "a tragic warping of his own humanity." Hollingsworth's egotism too destroys both Zenobia and himself. "Thus, the obsession of Marcher and Hollingsworth, an obsession with self, has a double effect, harming both self and others."

The Ambassadors

The most extended analysis of *Blithedale* and *The Ambassadors* is Robert Emmet Long's "'The Ambassadors' and the Genteel Tradition: James's Correction of Hawthorne and Howells," *New England Quarterly,* 42 (March, 1969), 44-64. Long discusses mainly the relation between Miles Coverdale, Theodore Colville in Howells's *Indian Summer,* and Lambert Strether; the emphasis below is on his analysis of Coverdale and Strether.

Long had previously compared *Blithedale* with *The Bostonians;* his comparison of *Blithedale* with *The Ambassadors* seems in some places informed by a bent not unlike that which informed his earlier essay. He argues that *The Ambassadors* is a correction of Hawthorne's and Howells's "understanding of the American mind." He finds in Coverdale's "timidness and lack of force," and in his simultaneous attraction to the richly sensuous and worldly Zenobia and the spiritual Priscilla, "the clue to the hesitating and indecisive" Lambert Strether. In both *The Ambassadors* and *The Bostonians,* he observes, James "uses sexuality to describe and define cultural attitudes." Initially, the America of *The Ambassadors* finds expression "in two incompatible forms: a vestigial Puritanism in the manners and fine scruples of Lambert Strether; and a new, materialistic, commercial New England of Mrs. Newsome and the Pococks." However, the two forms are in the end not that different. The Newsomes are merely a later product of the Puritan past, and their instinctive response to experience as moral abstraction, their identification with mind against imagination, has its origins in New England Protestantism. The main issue of *The Ambassadors,* therefore, is that of "mind vs. imagination," with New England, which stands for mind, law, and moral order, on one side, and Europe, which represents imagination and freedom, on the other. And these are the same distinctions James had seen Hawthorne dramatize in such works as "The Maypole of Merrymount" and *The Scarlet Letter.* Long notes also that the stages of Strether's experience abroad are highlighted by a series of scenes in gardens which have Hawthornean overtones, and that Waymarsh, in his severity of attitude, resembles "one of Hawthorne's men of 'iron.'" He also discusses Strether's realization, in England, of the limitations of his former life in New England; the brilliant, dazzling, sensuous world of the imagination represented by Gloriani; "James's intimation that great art and a 'high civilization are both connected . . . to forbidden knowledge"; the fact that a high civilization may develop the aesthetic imagination at the expense of the moral; and Strether's final discovery that beneath the art and romance of Europe is "something as sinisterly old as the first evil." Although in the end Strether does return to New England, Long observes, he has also been able to step outside of his consciousness and "experience an opposing kind of consciousness that is equally 'valid.'"

The incident which furnished the germ of *The Ambassadors,* of course, is Howells's belated recognition in Paris of his having missed life (*Notebooks,* pp. 225-28). In *The Ambassadors,* Long suggests, James develops this sense "so as to explain the deep origins of such a phenomenon." In *Indian Summer,* Howells

> represented youth and romance as follies to be avoided; Colville returns to America fundamentally unchanged, and the threat of Europe remains blurred and unclear. Similarly, Hawthorne's Cover-

> dale, the father of the Colville-Strether type, is not defined as culturally symptomatic; he is drawn as a peculiar psychological type, but not as a social type characteristic of his environment. Yet . . . Coverdale—in his indecisiveness, his yearnings toward art and his withdrawal—has a social explanation which Hawthorne has not drawn out. Of the three heroes . . . only Strether had been defined clearly as a *social* manifestation of the Puritan inheritance. In James alone, this hero type's hesitations, his fainthearted yearnings for the artist life, are defined in their relation to sex. Art and sex are equivalent terms in *The Ambassadors,* as they are not clearly in Hawthorne and Howells; and James . . . makes Europe stand for these things. . . . Strether's discovery near the end creates a dilemma—for he learns that art (which is the glory of life) has its vital source in the same fierce play of energies as sexuality (the irrational principle of life). To deny one is to deny both. Given this analysis, and Strether's moralistic New England background, Strether's conflict in sensibility has a solidity and cultural relatedness. (Long, pp. 62-63)

Long thus agrees with Bewley (*Complex Fate,* pp. 21-27) that James was able to relate his characters to their cultures in a way Hawthorne failed to do. He also points out that James gives different values to the experience of Europe from those apparent in Hawthorne's fiction:

> James suggests Hawthorne at many points in *The Ambassadors* by casting Strether's drama in the form of a conflict between the senses and the moral law, using even Hawthornian gardens and the theme of temptation and a fall. A curiously shrinking gentility in Howells kept him from probing very far into the life of the senses; in Hawthorne such a temptation is very vivid, yet even more authoritative is the moral grip of the past—the stern, austere vision of the Puritans. Hawthorne's sinners are not gay for long. In *The Marble Faun* . . . the dark and sensuous Miriam (with her mysterious European past) is contrasted with the virginal and saintly Hilda, a product of New England, who . . . is ensnared unwillingly in European corruption. Hawthorne implies the gravest doubt that these two cultures should mingle. Fascinated by the sensuous Miriam, Hawthorne yet gives his authority to the pallid Hilda, daughter of the Puritans. (63-64)

In *The Ambassadors* James's values are not theologically oriented; "the debate is rather on a level of cultural attitudes implying modes of consciousness. James enjoins the mingling of these cultures, the crossing of these forms of consciousness, invites entrance into the 'destructive element.'" *The Ambassadors* is thus "an implicit correction of Hawthorne's moral dramas of renunciation of the world." In his late period James was not, as is sometimes suggested, isolated in his own art; he was "involved in problems common to the nineteenth century America and its imaginative writers." His interpretation of Hawthorne's themes "indicates his historical sense, his sense of the 'usable' past, and how it may give depth and relevance to his own work."

Before Long, Richard Poirier too had compared Coverdale with Strether. In chapter 3, "Visionary to Voyeur: Hawthorne and James," of *A World Elsewhere: The Place of Style in American Literature* (New York: Oxford University Press, 1966), pp. 93-143, Poirier observes that James "brings extravagantly to life tendencies which Hawthorne had earlier located" in *Blithedale,* and that to "a surprising degree, Coverdale is an anticipation of" Lambert Strether. Hawthorne recognized that "one consequence of idealism gone sour can be the self-absorbed fastidiousness of a character like Coverdale—or [Gilbert] Osmond." Thus, "Coverdale might be thought of as Hawthorne's reply for such patronizing as he was to receive from James":

> He is a parody of a figure common in James's fiction—of the man who finds in Style, in the "picturesque," in observing manners and customs, in extorting secrets from social interchange, the kind of exhilaration that earlier American heroes found in a communion with natural surroundings or in the violent activity that could take place between the hero and elements of his natural environment. (123)

In *Blithedale* Hawthorne "shows how the romantic dream of creating an environment for the self rather than submitting to the environment authorized by 'artificial systems' becomes a form of aestheticism." Coverdale is thus "a prediction of the kind of hero, justifying himself by appeals to superior sensibility," that appears so frequently in the works of Joyce, Lawrence, Faulkner, and James. In all these writers "the expressed contempt for the way the world organizes itself is accompanied by aggressive efforts in the hero's imagination to give it an alternative order," and American writers often define such efforts in metaphors of artistic creation.

Poirier finds that as a creator, Strether is a much more lovable character than Coverdale. Strether tries "to transform the things he sees into visions," to give them the composition of *objects d'art.* And James's attempts "to make Strether's vision-of-reality-as-art into something like reality for the reader" are similar to the manipulations by Coverdale, for Coverdale's retrospective narration gives him also the attributes of someone who "shapes events as if they belonged not in real time but in the patterned time of art." And Coverdale, like Strether, discovers that life, "notably the life of others, will not be shaped by the often conflicting pressures of his aestheticism and his morality." Poirier finds the second paragraph of chapter 19 of *Blithedale* to be Jamesian in a number of ways, notably in Coverdale's "pretension that he is the guardian of other people's experience." Except for the melodrama and the offensive character it exhibits, the roles of Coverdale, Hollingsworth, and Zenobia in this passage "might be occupied by Strether, Chad, and Madame de Vionnet"; and, like Hollingsworth and Zenobia, Chad and Madame de Vionnet too fail to live up to the imagination of the man observing them.[11]

In Coverdale, Poirier continues, Hawthorne objectifies and criticizes certain tendencies in himself which sometimes victimized him: "the distortions of reality by art or by style." And here he is closest to James, who was always "fascinated by . . . situations in which people are treated as *objects d'art*." In these instances there is in James, as in Hawthorne in *Blithedale*, "a marked degree of personal projection into the central characters and with it a degree of self-criticism." In *The Ambassadors*, for instance, there is an aspect of James enacted by Strether when he sees reality "in images that remove it from time and nature . . . . In James, as in Hawthorne's creation of Coverdale, there is both a criticism of characters who perhaps care too much about merely 'seeing into' things," and "a fascination . . . in the moments thus produced." Poirier's conclusion is that *The Ambassadors* is superior to *Blithedale* "mostly because it is a loving book in which Strether's limitations burst forth in the directions opened by James's excitement and compassion." What James says in *The Ambassadors* is that "the creative imagination is finally responsible not for what it receives from reality but for the reality it creates." Hawthorne, on the other hand, never admits "in his characterization of Coverdale that perhaps self-enchantment isn't the only result of living imaginatively off the lives of others. The result can also be a gift to the general human consciousness, represented by the reader, of what life *might* be." James today is intensely more exciting and contemporary than Hawthorne because he manages "to protect the imagination of pleasure from almost all moral and social categories." Today, more than ever before, art is conceived as an activity rather than as a product, and it is remarkable that "Hawthorne should be even tangentially connected with this development." "The connection between Strether and Coverdale," Poirier observes,

> is of a significance greater than anything it tells us about the relationship of Hawthorne and James. Coverdale the poet, Strether the man who is busy "converting" life into artistic still lifes, illustrate the fact that an indifference to social reality, even a solipsistic one, is not to be taken as a sign that such characters or their creators are socially deprived. Quite the reverse. They retreat from society into a sort of aesthetic dandyism. (142-43)

Two other people have commented on the relation between *Blithedale* and *The Ambassadors.* Years before Long and Poirier, F. O. Matthiessen had noted, in *American Renaissance* (1941), pp. 297-98, that although a long distance separates Coverdale, who contributed unwittingly "something of his own self-conscious coolness to the story he was reporting, and Lambert Strether, whose rich sense of all that was unfolding enabled James" to center his composition so perfectly, the stages of development between the two characters "are precisely those of James' experiments," and his "natural starting point was provided by Coverdale's own recognition of his role"–at the end of chapter 11 of *Blithedale*–as resembling "that of the Chorus in a classic play, which seems to be set aloof from the possibility of personal concernment, and bestows the whole measure of its hope or fear . . . on the fortunes of others, between whom and itself this sympathy is the only bond." Hawthorne, of course, was aware by the end of *Blithedale* that his device had not entirely succeeded, for he had Coverdale admit at the beginning of chapter 29: "I have made but a poor and dim figure in my own narrative, establishing no separate interest, and suffering my colorless life to take its hue from other lives." "That very danger was what James," Matthiessen pointed out, was eager in his later period to circumvent, "for he had grown determined to give 'not my own personal account of the affair in hand, but my account of somebody's impression of it . . . some more or less detached . . . though thoroughly interested . . . witness or reporter.'" Matthiessen does not pursue the relation between *Blithedale* and *The Ambassadors* beyond this point.[12]

No more does Albert E. Stone, Jr., claim that James's portrayal of Strether as a "solitary innocent" is exclusively indebted to Hawthorne's portrayal of Coverdale. In his introduction to *Twentieth Century Interpretations of "The Ambassadors"* (Englewood Cliffs, New Jersey: Prentice-Hall, 1969), p. 19, Stone observes that despite obvious "differences in characterization, narrative method, and setting, *The Ambassadors* shares with other American novels certain conceptions of the hero, his career in society, his fate." He indicates that Strether, Coverdale, and Cooper's Natty Bumppo are just a few of the many American solitary innocents "whose 'Adamic' actions often assume unreal or symbolic or melodramatic form," whose minds play games with ordinary experience, and whose moral imagination finally impels them to take visual but not actual possession of their world. Many of James's other characters–Christopher Newman, Isabel Archer, Milly Theale–"are all romantics set down in a real world which they . . . try to transform." These observations, as should be evident, are similar to those Poirier detailed in *A World Elsewhere* (1966).

The Portrait of a Lady

Two of the three people who have compared *Blithedale* with *The Portrait of a Lady* have done so within the feminist context, rather than in terms of "influence." In "The American Galatea," *College English,* 32 (May, 1971), 890-99, Judith H. Montgomery discusses the myth of Pygmalion and Galatea, and how the nineteenth-century American woman became Galatea. She argues that this myth fuses two basic impulses in man: creation and possession. "At the instant of life," she writes, "Galatea thus incorporates woman's archetypal dilemma: she is both inferior and superior, but never equal to Pygmalion." The three works Montgomery analyzes at length are *Blithedale, The Portrait,* and Edith Wharton's *The House of Mirth.*

In fiction, as in life—Montgomery observes—"man struggled to realize the perfect woman and to portray the consequences of failure to conform to that image." In *Blithedale* there is Zenobia, "the dark, brilliant and independent daughter of a first marriage," and Priscilla, "the pale, charmingly weak and dependent daughter of the father's second marriage"; and, of course, "it is the fair, helpless and adoring girl who marries, and the dark independent who must die without love." Zenobia is also a feminist, "a woman who aspires to the condition of a human being, regardless of her sex." Denied the opportunity to exercise her intellect and talents by public speaking, and comparing her enforced silence with Hollingsworth's earnest oratory, she exclaims against these limitations, only to be reprimanded by the men characters. Even Coverdale, who says he is willing to "grant" women intellectual, social, and political liberties, always sees her only in physical terms. And his secret love for Priscilla, revealed at the end of the novel, also explains his increasing reservations about Zenobia. Although struck by her exotic beauty, he finds her lacking in certain "feminine" qualities, and Hawthorne reinforces this by hinting "darkly and repeatedly at [her] passionate, unhappy, earlier marriage." By contrast, Coverdale admires Priscilla because she is pale, and delicate, inept, adoring, prone to falling down when she runs . . . (*Blithedale,* chapter 9). However, Hawthorne's "severest vision of Pygmalion" is not Coverdale but Hollingsworth, who reprimands Zenobia for her views about women's rights and utterly crushes her hopes, while at the same time "comforting Priscilla's fears and firmly establishing the accepted role of women as dependent servitors of men." Although Zenobia's love for him makes her falter once, she cannot live by denying herself in order to fit Pygmalion's image of what she should be; so she drowns herself, naming Hollingsworth as her murderer for having refused to allow her both independence and love.

Montgomery's verdict is that, when one considers Hawthorne's other works such as *The Scarlet Letter,* "Rappaccini's Daughter," and "The Birthmark," it becomes evident that "his interest lies not with the successful Galatea, but with the failed one. He does not serve Pygmalion's vision, but he does portray the consequences of the American heroine's failure to . . . maintain herself within the narrow distinctions of perfection which had come to define her. He is the delineator of 'the woman who swerves one hair's breadth out of the beaten track.'" Such objectivity, Montgomery finds, cannot be so easily ascribed to James, perhaps because he wrote "during the period in which the confinement of the American woman by the Galatean myth was most stringent." According to Montgomery, Isabel Archer in *The Portrait* is James's best protrayal of the American Galatea. It is Isabel's large inheritance, of course, that liberates her, and, naturally, that inheritance comes through the intercessions of a male cousin, Ralph Touchett. But Ralph has to share Pygmalion's role with Gilbert Osmond, who marries Isabel hoping to mold her into the choicest of his art objects. But Osmond later discovers that Isabel is too full of ideas. She too discovers that he is the diametric opposite to what she had expected; he is utterly conventional, and the bright future she had expected becomes "the dark alley, dead-end."

Montgomery next examines Isabel's decision to return to Osmond from England after Ralph's funeral. "Once in England," she writes, the shock of the various events and revelations leave her in a moral suspension. If she returns to Osmond, she will remain a mere doll, a shell of his ambitions. "If she does not return, she tarnishes the last free choice she has made, her marriage vows. The choice is between fulfillment of the self and fulfillment of the marriage. By introducing as her only remaining future a life of lust with Caspar Goodwood, James forces Isabel consistently into a role as object, as the reflector of men's desires. As such a woman, Isabel must choose only the fulfillment of the image." It is therefore incorrect to assume that by her actions she surpasses the limitations of her life, and to applaud her choice as moral and vital. For it is neither. "She returns herself to a lifetime of servitude," where she will continue to be denied the exercise of her intellect and her freedom. In returning to Osmond she denies herself. "It is a choice spiritually immoral; yet, given her evolution," she is offered no real alternative. Montgomery's verdict here is that although James "does not permit Pygmalion's impulse literally to kill this heroine . . . such slow, internal death may well surpass that grosser end."

In "The Abuse of Eve by the New World Adam," *Images of Women in Fiction,* revised edition, edited by Susan K. Cornillon (Bowling Green, Ohio: Bowling Green University Popular Press, 1973), pp. 155-74, Linda Ray Pratt examines a number of women characters in *Blithedale, The Marble Faun, The Portrait,* and Cooper's *The Deerslayer* "in terms of the . . . Edenic myth." Her thesis is that, contrary to what some feminist critics have indicated, what these novels reveal is the "superior humanity" of the heroines. The emphasis below is on her comments on *Blithedale* and *The Portrait.*

Many critics, Pratt observes, have suggested that Hawthorne and James "are not narrow Edenic ideologues preaching the inviolable innocence of the

American Adam." It would be unsafe, therefore, to "assume that their light-dark women characters represent a rigid dualism of good and evil." In *Blithedale,* for example, it is Zenobia who controls our interest at the end of the novel, and James too reserves the greatest moral triumphs for his women characters. Pratt's argument is that Hawthorne uses the pure and impure women to represent pre- and post-lapsarian Eve. "The pre-lapsarian Eve can never enter the world of experience and be humanized by worldly contact," while the post-lapsarian Eve is "humanized by the experience of evil," but is as a result "rejected by the Adamic hero who must protect his innocence." Perhaps because Hawthorne was attracted by naive innocence, it is his Priscillas, the pre-lapsarian Eves, who find happiness in life, although his Zenobias, the post-lapsarian figures, earn the "higher innocence." In *Blithedale,* "Hawthorne's subject is the fate of the pre-lapsarian Eve whose Adam refuses the saving embrace. The judgement against Zenobia is that she is a woman"; she is "evil" because she has had sexual experience. Her "suspected 'knowledge'" is what Coverdale is afraid of; hence his later claim that he secretly loved the pale and sickly Priscilla. For him as well as for Hillingsworth, the escape from the post-lapsarian Eve is through devotion to Priscilla, the pre-lapsarian Eve. And, after Zenobia's accusations against Hollingsworth, it is Priscilla's "unworldly love" that saves his "self-image and restores his sense of Adamic innocence." But Priscilla does in a sense fail him, for, as the last chapters show, his concept of Adamic identity becomes totally dependent on her reassurance, "and that dependency 'casts out his own vitality' and his integrity."

Pratt next discusses Zenobia's suicide. She finds Coverdale only half-right when he says, in chapter 28, that it is "a miserable wrong . . . that the success or failure of woman's existence should be made to depend wholly on . . . one species of affection; while man has such a multitude of other chances, that this seems but an incident." It is true, Pratt notes, that

> the very existence of a fallen Eve depends "on one species of affection," but Hawthorne's novels repeatedly suggest that man's existence is equally dependent on his ability to offer that affection. Coverdale is wrong when he claims that men have a multitude of other chances, as the cases of Hollingsworth, Coverdale, Kenyon, Donatello, and Dimmesdale must illustrate. None of the Adamic figures were ever truly innocent . . . all they accomplish in rejecting such post-lapsarian Eves as Zenobia, Miriam, and Hester is their own damnation.
>
> In refusing the reality of women who are touched by the world, these false Adams condemn themselves to a life of self-deception and moral infancy. Their lives become a series of repeated refusals of

> the truth, for though dead, the truth of Zenobia is "still hovering about the spot and haunting it." (165)

It is Hawthorne's men, Pratt asserts, who are morally timid and intellectually shallow, and the women's "beauty, wisdom, and vitality are finally inadequate to shake the men from their fearful dependence on the male illusion."

Of the major nineteenth-century American authors, Pratt finds James the one who most completely rejected the validity of an Adamic American, and thus created women characters who are fully human. For illustration, she analyzes in detail the last chapter of *The Portrait;* her interpretation of Isabel's refusal of Caspar Goodwood in order to return to Osmond is very different form Montgomery's. Isabel's character, she argues, is a combination of both pre- and post-lapsarian Eve figures. "If viewed in the perspective of the dual nature of Eve," her choice is certainly wiser than that by "the undisciplined Zenobia. As the post-lapsarian Eve, Isabel's rejection of Caspar, the 'American Adam,' frees her to grow while it incapacitates him in a static illusion. Her qualified acceptance of the role of wife to Osmond . . . imposes on the fallen world the knowledge of sin and redemptive wisdom which is the essential function of Eve." In returning to Rome, Isabel moves "out of the garden (literally Gardencourt) into the world of experience." What Caspar offers her is a return to a pre-lapsarian state, an escape from life; he wants to obliterate her life and purpose in an act of total possession. If "she is to make any meaning out of her life, her fall from innocence to wisdom must move her back into the world of experience," and that means the world of Osmond. Although social freedom from Osmond is as impossible for her as Caspar's naive promise of a new beginning, "her understanding of Osmond's nature . . . frees her from Osmond's moral and spiritual influence." Thus, in her final choice she rejects both the role of pre-lapsarian Eve which the Adamic Caspar wishes her to play, and the restrictions of obedient effacement which Osmond demands. "With wisdom as unappreciated as that of Zenobia," Pratt observes,

> Isabel nevertheless insists on pursuing her post-lapsarian purpose in a world of confounded Adams.
>
> In the figure of Isabel Archer James rejects the limits imposed on women by such Americans as Cooper and Hawthorne. More than any other major nineteenth-century American author, James denied the validity of American innocence. Uncommitted to the preservation of innocence and unambiguous as to the educational value of sin, James has no necessity to force women into pre- and post-lapsarian dichotomies. His women characters are more fully human because they are less abstract and less symbolic. (169)

Pratt's conclusion is that, contrary to some critial opinion, neither Hawthorne nor James was truly callous to the plight of women in America. And, if their works are re-evaluated in the light of social and sexual realities, one discovers that their "women characters often surpass the so-called heroes in moral complexity and human veracity."

The third person to relate *Blithedale* to *The Portrait* is David J. Thompson. The chapter on Hawthorne in his dissertation, "Societal Definitions of Individualism . . ." (Brown, 1972), includes an analysis of "Egotism" and *Blithedale,* pp. 169-82. "Egotism," he argues, presents the thesis that society becomes impossible when men come together only under the guise of their self-interest; it also shows the corrosive effect egotisms have on human relationships. But Hawthorne's focus in this story is on an individual psyche; in *Blithedale,* his concern is "the composition and failure of human communities," and here, once again, egotism plays a central role. Hawthorne believes that "the mainspring of action in society is self-interest," and that human communities fail precisely because people fail to contain their egotisms. *Blithedale* "offers multiple examples of the destructive effects which . . . [egotism] works upon the community of man": Hollingsworth exploits Zenobia's passions and Priscilla's affections so that their wealth can enable him to realize his project of prison reform; Old Moodie wastes a fortune and his wife to satisfy his appetite; Westervelt exploits Priscilla's occult powers for his own gain; even Coverdale uses other people to further his own ends. But Hawthorne does not merely depict egotism; he also suggests "the means of remedying this serious flaw." In both "Egotism" and *Blithedale,* repentance and love provide the means of retribution. At the end of *Blithedale,* we learn that Hollingsworth has given up his plan of prison reform; instead, he has "been busy with a single murderer." With Priscilla's love ever beside him, "he has regained a measure of humanity from which he had been cut off by his egotism." In these two works, therefore, Hawthorne addressed himself to "a central problem of American society: How should the individual's relationship to society be constituted?" His preference was "a relationship which honors the needs and welfare of the community."

In the chapter on James, pp. 195-221, Thompson notes that James, like Hawthorne, rejected self-centered individualism as a pattern of social conduct. In *The Portrait* he provided an answer to the opposition between the claims of the individual and those of society. Isabel Archer is independent and idealistic, but also detached, proud, and manipulative. When she rejects Lord Warburton, for instance, she fears that maybe her action is due to *pride,* that her inflated self-image is holding out for someone better. And her pleasure in her power over Lord Warburton and Caspar Goodwood reveals her apparent awareness that in order to remain independent and control her own fate, she must manipulate the lives of those close to her, lest they manipulate her instead. And this amounts to "an unconscious violation of the humanity of those sacrificed." Although her manipulation never results in the kind of destruction that Hollingsworth's egotism visits upon Zenobia, in James's fictional world her "egocentric delight in her power over others constitutes a grave fault." And it is this flaw which makes her marry Osmond. Precisely because Osmond represents so little, he becomes a possessed object which her romantic artistry hopes to transform into a work of art. She is devoted not to him but to her idealistic conception of what her husband should be. And this is not unlike Hollingsworth, who also "embodied himself in his idealistic scheme of reform to such an extent that he . . . made an idol of himself out of his project." Osmond becomes an instrument of Isabel's will much the same way as Zenobia became a mere tool to provide money for Hollingsworth's plan of reform. For James as for Hawthorne, Isabel commits the unpardonable sin: she fails to reverence the inviolable sanctity of another human being. And, in possessing Osmond, she finds herself possessed irrevocably. Thus handicapped, she comes to realize that her sole means of salvation lies in her making the limitations of her marriage an occasion of service to others. By accepting responsibility toward Pansy, whom James endows with a "virginal spirituality" similar to that possessed by Hawthorne's "light" heroines, Isabel "exorcises the serpent of egotism much as Roderick Elliston exorcises his bosom serpent by forgetting himself in the thought of another."[13]

The Portrait, Thompson concludes, is "James's major treatment of . . . the opposition of the imperatives of the individual versus those of society"; and his response to the problem of egotism is similar to Hawthorne's. As did Hawthorne, James showed that "idealism, innocence, and the rescuing impulse can all serve . . . to disguise the selfish motivation of the individual who wears these masks." He further indicated that the cure Hawthorne prescribed for Elliston's egotism is also "the restorative nonpareil for an all too common malaise."

The Sacred Fount

Six people have paired *Blithedale* with *The Sacred Fount.* In *Ivory Towers and Sacred Founts: The Artist as Hero in Fiction from Goethe to Joyce* (New York: New York University Press, 1964), pp. 206-14, Maurice Beebe observes that although both "Hawthorne and James insisted that the true artist must be detached in order to see clearly," they also recognized that the very purity and objectivity of his vision makes him susceptible to the crime of violating the sanctity of the human heart. *Blithedale* and *The Sacred Fount,* Beebe indicates, have a strong thematic affinity; they both show how "the esthetic ideal of detachment can lead to the ethical crime of exposure." And many of their details are very similar:

> Both are told from the point of view of detached observers who are usually considered self-portraits of their creators. Hawthorne's Miles Coverdale and James's unnamed narrator both retire to an isolated gathering of intellectuals. . . . There they become interested in the mysterious relationships which seem to exist between their fellow guests; in both cases, what is observed is a situation of entangled dominances, the possession of one human soul by another. Both narrators attempt to solve the riddle of these relationships by observation and investigation, and their attempt . . . is resented by the objects of their curiosity. Both begin by feeling intellectually superior to the people whom they scrutinize, and both ironically are defeated by a failure of detachment. By studying emotional cannibalism, they find themselves taking parasitical nourishment from the human puzzle upon which they have come to rely emotionally. (206-207)

Furthermore, both Coverdale and James's narrator are disturbed by the nature of their inquiry. When, in chapter 19 of *Blithedale,* the puzzled Coverdale tells Zenobia, who resents his curiosity, that *he* would be happy to be followed everywhere by an "indefatigable human sympathy," she replies: "We must trust for intelligent sympathy to our guardian angels, if any there be." In chapter 9 of *The Sacred Fount,* Lady John replies to a similar defense by James's narrator in similar terms: "You can't be a providence and not be a bore. A real providence *knows;* whereas you . . . have to find out." Both narrators treat other people as pawns. As James's narrator admits in the last paragraph of chapter 13:

> That I had done it all and had only myself to thank for it was what . . . was more and more for me the inner essence of Mrs. Briss's attitude. I know not what heavy admonition of my responsibility had thus descended on me; but . . . it paralyzed me. And . . . this was the price . . . of the secret success, the lonely liberty and the intellectual joy. . . . The special torment of my case was that . . . the satisfaction of curiosity and the attestation of triumph, was in this direct way the sacrifice of feeling. . . . I wasn't there to save *them.* I was there to save my priceless pearl of an inquiry and to harden, to that end, my heart.

In chapter 18 of *Blithedale,* Coverdale too says:

> That cold tendency, between instinct and intellect, which made me pry with a speculative interest into people's passions and impulses, appeared to have gone far towards unhumanizing my heart.

The irony of *The Sacred Fount,* Beebe observes, is that the narrator's theory "is weakened by his compulsion to view Mrs. Server more emotionally than intellectually. His attraction to her, like Coverdale's romantic interest in Priscilla, represents the way in which the detached observer may succumb to life."

Beebe mentions two differences between *Blithedale* and *The Sacred Fount.* He finds the intricate plot of James's novel more complex than Hawthorne's; he also notes that whereas Hawthorne sympathizes with Coverdale and finds himself at the end equally stalemated between art and life, "James treats his narrator with subtle irony throughout," and intends him to be seen "as deluded, if not villainous."

As already indicated in the section on *Blithedale* and *The Bostonians,* Martha Banta notes, in chapter 4 of *Henry James and the Occult* (1972), that the fifty-year period between the publication of *Blithedale* (1852) and *The Sacred Fount* (1901) marks "the path from Blithedale to Newmarch taken by James's awareness of what he might make of a merger of an old literary tradition, a new psychology attentive to psychic powers, and his own continued, and heightened, concern over human relationships" (90). After discussing, among other things, the narrator of James's story, his theory about the soul-suckers at loose on the grounds of Newmarch, and the question of whether the narrator does not sin more than he saves, Banta explains:

> Fifty years had passed since Miles Coverdale . . . found it as dangerous to peer as to be peered upon. In Hawthorne's time the old folk-theme of vampirism was no longer crudely represented as physical depletion alone. But from the years of Hawthorne's maturity to the first years of the twentieth century further sophistications continued to change the writer's approach to matters of psychic vampirism. This change is marked by the implied metaphors and the phrases used to describe that part of a man's being he most fears to have taken from him by human powers stronger than his own.
>
> *The Blithedale Romance:* theft of *souls* in a secularized version of the age-old combat between the forces of damnation and salvation, of Devil and God. "Professor Fargo": irrational personal magnetism winning over scientific *mind,* fraud triumphant over truth, sexual mastery and the corruption of innocence by Yankee shrewdness. . . . *The Bostonians:* desire to annihilate *personality* in order to turn the victim into a mechanized puppet. *The Sacred Fount:* the destruction of the previous equilibrium between unconsciousness and *self-consciousness,* with all secrets dragged forth into the fierce light of knowing.

> Soul, mind . . . personality, and self-consciousness: these are different words for what is essentially that intangible, unnameable quality which gives man his unique existence. The words implied differ because the . . . men who dramatized the struggles involving that contrast wrote out of an increasingly secular vision. Where vampires once were said to endanger men's bodies by sucking away blood, the source of physical life, they were then shown as stealing what is even more essential–that inner, non-material substance called "soul" as a hold-over from more religious times, subsequently named "mind," "personality," "self-consciousness"–words more expressive of the secularized psychology of the age. (103-104)

Banta's conclusion is that James did so much with the vampire theme because it "got at the core of his unfaltering concern with human consciousness, knowledge, power, and will."

The earliest people to relate *Blithedale* to *The Sacred Fount* were Philip Rahv and Frederick C. Crews. In "The Dark Lady of Salem" *Partisan Review,* 8 (September-October, 1941), 362-81, reprinted in *Image and Idea* (1949), pp. 22-41, Rahv called Coverdale the ancestor of many Jamesian characters, including "the spying, eavesdropping protagonist of *The Sacred Fount,* whose neurotic fear and envy of life find an outlet in a mania of snooping and prying into the lives of his neighbors. In this nameless Jamesian snooper," Rahv noted, "the 'peephole' motif reaches its culmination" (*Image and Idea,* p. 38).

As indicated above, Maurice Beebe found the intricate plot of *The Sacred Fount* more complex than *Blithedale*'s. Seven years earlier, Frederick C. Crews had reached a different verdict. In "A New Reading of *The Blithedale Romance*," *American Literature,* 29 (May, 1957), 147-70, Crews praised *Blithedale* for "the complexity and consistency of its structure," which is composed of "a surface plot, an imaginative reconstruction of that plot by a narrator, and a symbolic commentary of both" (169). In no other book, Crews declared, "does the narrator's changing attitude toward his narrative constitute a rival plot which overtakes and is eventually matched against the other." The nearest approach to this is *The Sacred Fount,* "and James's failure is the measure of Hawthorne's success." James eliminates everything from his book except the tedious, falsifying mind of his narrator, whereas Hawthorne gives us "glimpses of the truth *within* the false narrative . . . so that we can see the two plots separating and then converging." The greatness of *Blithedale,* Crews reasserted, lies in its author's "ability to express his deepest judgements through a narrator who is himself a subject of judgement" (169).

Most of the comments on *Blithedale* and *The Sacred Fount* in Barrie S. Hayne's dissertation, "The Divided Self" (1964), pp. 470-80, are similar to

Beebe's. Hayne calls the narrator of James's story "a Miles Coverdale who lives in the lives of others," and James's own surrogate. If Coverdale "represents Hawthorne's misgivings that he himself was either too much of a Paul Pry, or too much of an onlooker, who had . . . turned away from his duty," in *The Sacred Fount* James too is dramatizing similar misgivings. And when his narrator, like Coverdale, expresses qualms about his methods, Lady John sets him right "in terms reminiscent of Zenobia's strictures upon Coverdale's prying." All of Hayne's quotations from both novels are the same as Beebe's. He also remarks that in *The Sacred Fount,* as in all his later works, James turned away from the relatively photographic realism of his earlier period to a more symbolic or idealistic presentation, "an artistic procedure directly opposite to that of Hawthorne, who sought in his old age to move" from the ideal to the real.

Stephen F. Martineau's dissertation, "Opposition and Balance: A Characteristic of Structure in Hawthorne, Melville, and James" (Columbia, 1967), contains only a parenthetical reference to *Blithedale* and *The Sacred Fount.* Martineau notes that as a first-person narrator, Coverdale "presents an interesting contrast to the Narrator of *The Sacred Fount*. . . . For Coverdale seems to remain basically untouched by his experience, and finally still unaware of the extension of his own limitations; while it is *The Sacred Fount*'s Narrator's full awareness of his isolation and the shock of that self-realization that create the balance in his character" (11n.). Martineau does not explain, however, what he means by his odd statement that Coverdale is unaware of the "extension" of his own limitations.

"Professor Fargo"

The first person to relate *Blithedale* to "Professor Fargo" was Peter Buitenhuis. In *The Grasping Imagination* (1970), pp. 71-74, Buitenhuis noted that whenever James treated businessmen in his early fiction, "he tended to associate them with fraud or grasping shrewdness." But so had Cooper, Poe, Hawthorne, and Melville; they too distrusted "commercial" characters and represented them in their fiction equivocally. In "Professor Fargo," James modeled the title character on Professor Westervelt in *Blithedale.* "Like Westervelt, Professor Fargo claims hypnotic powers and travels around . . . New England putting on his show in town and village halls." Miss Gifford too "derives a good deal from Priscilla." After further examination of the story, Buitenhuis concluded that in "'Professor Fargo,' Hawthorne's example led James, through his realistic treatment of a theme from *The Blithedale Romance,* to considerable artistic success." By employing "themes of squalor, deceit, and failure, James was able to make a fairly good use of the American environment. Perhaps, too, the schemata provided by the city scenes in *The Blithedale Romance* helped him here."

As already indicated, Martha Banta in chapter 4 of *Henry James and the Occult* (1972) finds *Blithedale,* "Professor Fargo," and *The Bostonians* closely "related in theme and matched in many details of character and plot" (90). "Professor Fargo," she explains, "throws further light over those Hawthornian attitudes toward spiritualism-cum-mesmerism that James continued to share in the 1870's." After discussing the contest of wills "waged among Zenobia, Westervelt, and Hollingsworth to see who can win Priscilla"; the many direct connections between sexual domination and mesmeric control that are made in *Blithedale;* Colonel Gifford's complaint "about the necessity to couple pure science with mongrel spiritualism"; and Professor Fargo's finally gaining control over the soul and body of Miss Gifford, Banta notes that whereas in *Blithedale* Hawthorne presented "the binding power" as partially occult, in "Professor Fargo" James depicted it "as sexual attraction alone" (96).

Howard Kerr too, in chapter 6 of *Mediums, and Spirit-Rappers, and Roaring Radicals* (1972), indicates that "James drew on his reading of Hawthorne for 'Professor Fargo'" (121), a story in which he dramatized "the sinister sexual implications which Hawthorne had feared in mesmerism." In this story, James "united elements of anti-spiritualistic satire with the mesmeric melodrama" of *Blithedale.* Kerr discusses the relation between Professor Fargo and Westervelt, the circumstances and sexual nature of Fargo's "mesmeric ravishment" of Miss Gifford, and the character of Colonel Gifford. What James presents, he observes, is "a struggle for possession of a passive young woman between her father . . . and a fraudulent medium" (146). Kerr finds also that the character of Miss Gifford, as a deaf-mute heroine, reveals the same "ethical and sexual implications of the vulnerability exhibited by Hawthorne's seeresses" (203). And the narrator of James's story too possesses "an ironic detachment like that with which Hawthorne's Miles Coverdale had distanced himself from the world" (212).

Roderick Hudson

In *The Grasping Imagination* (1970), pp. 80–81, Peter Buitenhuis points out a number of similarities between *Blithedale* and *Roderick Hudson.* Both novels have a remarkably constant point of view, and both have a "quartet of figures." In chapter 5 of *Hawthorne,* James describes Coverdale as a man "whose passions are slender, whose imagination is active, and whose happiness lies, not in doing, but in perceiving—half a poet, half a critic, and all a spectator." This description, says Buitenhuis, fits Rowland Mallet remarkably well. And James treats him in the same way as Hawthorne treated Coverdale.[14] Buitenhuis enumerates a number of similarities between these two characters: both "fall in love with the New England maiden who loves the other male member of the quartet; both are left alone in the end with the sense of having failed." But the most significant similarity between them "is in the moral ambiguity with which they are treated." Both Hawthorne and James were interested in "psychological investigation into motive and behavior," and both were concerned about the fine line to be drawn between curiosity and the unpardonable sin of violating another's personality. Although in *Roderick Hudson* this violation is not on the same scale as that in *The Scarlet Letter,* it certainly is comparable to Coverdale's prying into the lives of the other characters in *Blithedale.* "Mallet is to a degree responsible for Roderick's ultimate tragedy, just as Coverdale is guilty, to a degree," of Zenobia's suicide. Furthermore, "although both point-of-view figures . . . are spectators to the action, they are also too deeply involved in it to be sufficiently aware of their own moral culpability."

Sanford E. Morovitz too points out, in "*Roderick Hudson:* James's *Marble Faun,*" *Texas Studies in Literature and Language,* 11 (1970), 1427-43, that Rowland Mallet, "James's center of consciousness in the novel, assumes a dignity" which is similar to Coverdale's, and that Coverdale's function as an implicated observer is also comparable to that of Mallet (1435-36). He further notes that, as a personality, Mary Garland can be vaguely linked to Zenobia (1440n.). Gaillard F. Waterfall, in his dissertation entitled "The Manipulation Theme in the Works of Nathaniel Hawthorne and Henry James" (University of South Caroline, 1973), p. 105, also comments on the resemblance between Mallet and Coverdale. "James's character, like Coverdale," he writes, "acts as a stage manager, prompting the participants while remaining somewhat removed from the action. Also like Coverdale, Mallet professes to be secretly enamored of a female participant, who is, in turn, romantically devoted to a more active personality. In both cases the third party suffers great emotional harm."

The Europeans

Only Peter Buitenhuis has written on the relation between *Blithedale* and *The Europeans.* In *The Grasping Imagination* (1970), he suggests that the Arcadian schema of *Blithedale* is one possible source of *The Europeans.* "Hawthorne's novel," he writes:

> begins with Coverdale and his companions setting off from Boston in a snow-storm towards the middle of . . . April bound for the farm. James's story begins in Boston in a snow-storm on the 12th of May. Coverdale talks of setting out to begin "the life of Paradise anew." Felix, when he gets to the Wentworths' home outside Boston says: "This is Paradise." Both novels frequently refer to man's

> pre-lapsarian state. Felix compares the Wentworths to people who lived "in a mythological era, when they spread their tables upon the grass, replenished them from cornucopias, and had no particular need of kitchen stoves." Coverdale talks of an ideal Blithedale without kitchen and house work. "It is odd enough," he says, "that the kind of labor which falls to the lot of women is just that which chiefly distinguishes artificial life . . . from the life of Paradise. Eve had no dinner-pot, and no clothes to mend, and no washing-day." (90)

James's use of the pastoral mode in *The Europeans,* however, led to a different effect from that achieved in *Blithedale.* Hawthorne continually employs "Arcadian and Edenic imagery for ironic and pathetic purposes, and the irony increases as the colony is increasingly rent by the passions of its fallen inhabitants." In the end all the characters in *Blithedale,* who had been engaged in Arcadian and necromantic revelry, pursue Coverdale "through the woods, 'so that,' he thinks, 'I was like a mad poet hunted by Chimeras.'" Although James in *The Europeans* "uses Felix as Hawthorne uses Coverdale to create an imaginary new Arcadia out of the cold and unpromising materials of New England, [he] develops the analogy not for pathetic but for purely comic purposes" (91). Buitenhuis points out also that the Baroness Eugenia "has, in common with . . . Zenobia, an 'Oriental or exotic aspect'" (94).

Chapter 5

The Marble Faun

After *The Scarlet Letter* and *The Blithedale Romance, The Marble Faun* influenced the greatest number of James's works. This romance has been paired with, alphabetically, *The Golden Bowl,* "The Last of the Valerii," *The Portrait of a Lady, Roderick Hudson, The Sacred Fount, The Tragic Muse,* and *The Wings of the Dove.* Next to *The Blithedale Romance* and *The Bostonians, The Marble Faun* and *Roderick Hudson* is the pair that has been most frequently analyzed. The review below considers this pair first, and concludes with a list of James's other works which have been minimally compared with *The Marble Faun.*

In chapter 6 of *Hawthorne* (1879), James evaluates Hawthorne's years in Europe, and the works which resulted from this experience.[1] He points out that when Hawthorne came to Europe, he was almost fifty years old, and this partly accounts for the rigidity of point of view in his five volumes of notebooks. Hawthorne's experiences, he explains, had always been narrow. His fifty years had been spent largely in "small American towns," and he had led exclusively "a village life." In short, "he was exquisitely and consistently provincial." His English Note-Books deal mainly with superficial and external matters; so do his Italian Note-Books, for his contacts with Italy, its people and their customs, were those of a tourist. Italian art too bored him; what he appreciated in statues was "the smoothness and whiteness of the marble."

James felt that *The Marble Faun,* as a title, failed to characterize Hawthorne's story; thus, he always used its original title in England, *Transformation.* He found a great deal of beauty, interest, and grace in the book, but declared it less complete than its companions, and its value slighter. "Hawthorne forfeited a precious advantage in ceasing to tread his native soil," he wrote. "Half the virtue of *The Scarlet Letter* and *The House of the Seven Gables* is in their local quality; they are impregnated with the New England air." But Hawthorne knew Italy only superficially. And he was not a realist. Thus, although *Transformation* describes certain actualities of Rome closely, and expresses the character of the city eloquently, certain sections of the book seem "factitious and unauthoritative." In short, it is "a charming romance with intrinsic weaknesses."

James was struck especially by "the simple combination and opposition of the four actors": Donatello and Miriam, Kenyon and Hilda. He admired particularly the ingenious way Hawthorne unfolds the history of Donatello's "tasting of the tree of knowledge," and the way this unworldly hero, and the dark, passionate, more experienced Miriam, "are equalised and bound together" by their common, morally insulating secret. And, of course, he was deeply impressed by Hilda's confession in St. Peter's. As was indicated in the first essay, some critics have shown that James's admiration of Hawthorne became more open as he grew more sure of himself, and as his literary reputation became more established. It is also interesting to note the stylistic and structural changes in these various assessments of his predecessor. For example, in *Hawthorne* (1879), he phrased the episode of Hilda's confession thus:

> This pure and somewhat rigid New England girl, following the vocation of a copyist of pictures in Rome, unacquainted with evil and untouched by impurity, has been accidentally the witness, unknown and unsuspected, of the dark deed by which her friends, Miriam and Donatello, are knit together. This is *her* revelation of evil, her loss of perfect innocence. She has done no wrong, and yet wrongdoing has become a part of her experience, and she carries the weight of her detested knowledge upon her heart. She carries it a long time, saddened and oppressed by it, till at last she can bear it no longer. If I have called the whole idea of the presence and effect of Hilda in the story a trait of genius, the purest touch of inspiration is the episode in which the poor girl deposits her burden. She has passed the whole lonely summer in Rome; and one day, at the end of it, finding herself in St. Peter's, she enters a confessional, strenuous daughter of the Puritans as she is, and pours out her dark knowledge into the bosom of the church—then comes away with her conscience lightened, not a whit less a Puritan than before. (*Hawthorne,* chapter 6)

In his introduction to the selections from Hawthorne in Warner's *Library of the World's Best Literature* (1897), this passage appeared thus:

> A young woman from across the Atlantic, a gentle copyist in Roman galleries of still gentler Guidos and Guereinos, happens to have

> caught a glimpse, at a critical moment, of the dismal secret that unites Donatello and Miriam. This, for her, is the tree of bitter knowledge, the taste of which sickens and saddens her. The burden is more than she can bear, and one of the most charming passages in the book describes how at last, at a summer's end, in sultry solitude, she stops at St. Peter's before a confessional, and Protestant and Puritan as she is, yields to the necessity of kneeling there and ridding herself of her obsession. (*Library,* XII, 7059-60)

The writing here is smoother, more concise, but also slightly less specific. In *The Sense of the Past* (1917), this episode was squeezed into one sentence:

> He [Ralph Pendrel] recalled the chapter in Hawthorne's fine novel in which the young woman from New England kneels, for the lightening of her woe, to the old priest at St. Peter's, and felt that he sounded as never before the depth of that passage. (*The Sense of the Past,* Book 3)

On the whole, James felt there were too many "light threads of symbolism" in *Transformation,* and they remain on the surface. "The element of the unreal is pushed too far," and the action wavers between the literally sketched streets of Rome "and a vague realm of fancy." The narrative structure too is faulty; "the story straggles and wanders, is dropped and taken up again, and towards the close lapses into an almost fatal vagueness."

The Italian Experience

Before considering the efforts of critics to find the influence of *The Marble Faun* in *specific* works by James one should first review their attempts to determine how Hawthorne's and James's Italian experiences affected their work *in general.* Undoubtedly the single study which should be compulsory reading for anyone interested in this topic is Nathalia Wright's *American Novelists in Italy* (Philadelphia: University of Pennsylvania Press, 1965). Wright points out that what pervades the Italianate works of most American writers—from Washington Allston to Henry James—who visited the country is a "sense of discovery, both geographical and experiential." The characters in these works are primarily concerned with moral problems, and though most of these writers depicted the Italian scene realistically, "they tended to endow it with symbolic values." Italy is a place "where Americans may have intercourse with the world and the past, from fruitful attachments, or escape frustration." In most of this fiction one finds, first, "the innocent American girl exposed to pernicious influences on foreign soil," and, second, the Garden of Eden. In fact, the character type of the American girl abroad developed almost exclusively in an Italian setting.

In the section on Hawthorne, pp. 138-67, Wright points out that some of Hawthorne's most lasting impressions of Italy were very disagreeable. But he was also fascinated by Rome, and in *Our Old Home* "he applied the figure of the title to Italy as well." It was also in Italy that "he was most conscious of the thinness of American culture." However, his only work inspired by his Italian residence, *The Marble Faun,* "contains no essential elements which are radically different from those in his other fiction." There are references to Italy and Italian culture in many of his tales, and the theme of the Fall of Man, and that of "art versus nature and society," and the basic images of the legendary Arcadia and the Garden of Eden appear not only in *The Marble Faun* but throughout his fiction. However, his American artists in Rome are different from "his other artists and artist-scientists, who are typically solitary, at odds with society, and in fatal conflict with nature." Kenyon, Hilda, and Miriam "have a general conception of art as the expression of inner life and experience." Wright's conclusion is that although Hawthorne found in Italy "abundant confirmation of his conception of the moral weakness and the limited powers of man," his stay there "gave him a more hopeful view of human nature than he ever before maintained." In Italy, as nowhere else, he saw man's "weaknesses and limitations in perspective: beside a long series of catastrophies survived by the spirit, as recorded in beautiful and enduring works of the imagination."

In chapter 6 on James, pp. 198-248, Wright notes that before James went to Italy, "he knew and admired the work of two American writers who had been there: Hawthorne and Howells." Later, he called Hawthorne's treatment of Italy "old-fashionedly romantic" and approved Howells's as realistic. For James Italy represented the whole experience of man, past and present. Everywhere he looked he saw "the deep interfusion of the present with the past." But he was also "conscious in Italy of powerful counterforces to great life."

Most of James's fiction, Wright indicates, contains references to Italy. Essentially, these works project "the myth of the Fall of Adam and Eve in the Garden of Eden." However, the conclusion of this drama "is not the regaining of Paradise but the beginning of another cycle of life on another stage, played out by characters . . . representing the best elements in the Old and the New Worlds." Wright notes further that for many years James found it difficult to write in Italy. Thus, like Hawthorne before him, "he wrote most of his Italianate fiction outside Italy," assisted largely by memory. She finds that "the influence of *The Marble Faun* on James' treatment of Italian material [in *Roderick Hudson*] is particularly evident," but notes later that although "the influence of *The Marble Faun* on subsequent American novels and stories laid in Italy has been powerful and long-lasting," Hawthorne's novel "crystallized rather than originated a pattern." Wright comments also on several of James's prefaces, and on his non-fictional works in which he evaluated the experiences of American artists in Italy: his biographies of Hawthorne and Story, and his reviews of Hawthorne's and Howells's works. Her conclusion is that of all the works inspired by the Italian scene during the period of its discovery by American artists, "the most beautiful and original were the paintings of Allston and the fiction of Hawthorne and James."

It is unfortunate that Harry F. Arader's fine dissertation, "American Novelists in Italy: Hawthorne, Howells, James, and Crawford" (University of Pennsylvania, 1953), has not found its way into print, in some form or other, especially since it precedes Wright's *American Novelists in Italy.* The major flaw in Arader's dissertation is repetitiousness, which could easily have been minimized by a reduction and rearrangement of his numerous chapter sub-divisions.

Arader notes that the period from 1850 to 1900 "was a time of pronounced American interest in Italy," and that all the above writers "made a major literary use of their Italian experiences." In each case, however, the experience was different: "Hawthorne's was a tourist experience of a year and a half . . . toward the end of his career"; James visited Italy fourteen times "between his youth and old age." In the chapter on Hawthorne, pp. 1-102, Arader notes that although the Hawthornes had for long looked forward to visiting Italy, Hawthorne's first impressions of Rome were unfavorable. However, the charm and beauty of the city soon won him over. Arader indicates that there is a very "close relationship" between Hawthorne's Italian experience and *The Marble Faun.* Every object described in the romance "can be found similarly described in the travel notes, and many passages were transmitted without change from one to the other." Even the drift of the action in the romance follows Hawthorne's general pattern of travel. Although in the preface Hawthorne tried to justify his extensive use of descriptive material, many critics feel that an overabundance of such extraneous passages "mars the artistic quality of the work." Throughout the romance tourist impressions "delay the action and confuse the meaning" of the story.

Arader makes several other observations about the relation between Hawthorne's Italian experience and *The Marble Faun.* He explains that since Hawthorne "limited his social activity to the Anglo-American art colonies of Rome and Florence," "most of the characters [Hilda, Kenyon, Miriam] and much of the plot development and background material for *The Marble Faun*" were drawn from these artist colonies. Furthermore, "Hawthorne made no effort to learn the Italian language, nor associate with the Italian people." It is not surprising, therefore, that the only important Italian in the romance, Donatello, was evolved out of the Faun of Praxiteles; and he is "not convincing as an Italian." Undoubtedly, however, it was while in Italy that Hawthorne reached the peak of his aesthetic appreciation, taste, and judgement. Just as he frequently discussed aesthetic problems with members of the art colony, so does the "idea of an increased understanding . . . of art" play an important part in the romance. His deep interest in the idea of Beatrice Cenci's innocent suffering is also reflected in Hilda's character, and though "his knowledge of the Church was limited," his openmindedness enabled him to appreciate many aspects of Catholicism, as is shown by his dramatic use of confession in the romance. Later, Arader connects "the elements of sorrow and the theme of innocent suffering" in the story of Una's fever and the Hawthornes' illness in general while they were in Italy. He also notes that the Villa Montauto which the Hawthornes occupied in Florence was transferred to the romance "in the account of Donatello's villa, Monte Beni."

Arader interprets *The Marble Faun* as a psychological/theological debate between Miriam's liberal concept that "a mixture of good might exist in evil," and Hilda's strict view that "evil can never be anything but evil." In the end, the four characters "gain in understanding and strength through suffering." Arader points out that although Hawthorne's experiences "revealed to him an ugly and treacherous Rome beneath the exterior charms and beauties," he "chose to present an idealized Italy, rather than a realistic one." He "sacrificed the real for the ideal," and "altered factual material to embody a moral." Paradoxically, the moral that developed defended the realistic view. In both the romance and in his personal experiences, "the romantic land of Italy was rejected in favor of the realities of life and work at home."

In the chapter on James, pp. 243-381, Arader observes that "James's response to the European heritage differed" from Hawthorne's. His understanding of Italian culture was deeper, and though he eventually made England his permanent residence, Italy continued to serve him "in bringing the 'flower of art' to bloom." His attitude toward Italy was "a mingling of love and fear." He loved its picturesqueness but feared its distractions. In general, his travel writing reflects his romantic appreciation of the country, while most of his Italian fiction reflects his conviction that a realistic view should limit and balance this romantic enjoyment. Like Hawthorne before him, he got acquainted with Story and the Anglo-American colony in Rome. But he "failed to gain an entrée into the sort of European society that he believed would stimulate his work." Throughout his life he remained "the casual tourist," never the well-informed "interpreter of Italian life." That is why the characters in his Italianate fiction are mostly "American expatriates or travelers, rather than Italians."

Arader analyzes many of James's works set entirely or in part in Italy: "Travelling Companions," "At Isella," "Adina," *The Portrait of a Lady, The Aspern Papers, The Golden Bowl,* and several others. He also discusses James's biography of Story. In works like "The Madonna of the Future," Arader indicates, James illustrated the theory that beneath the charm and beauty of Italy is concealed a danger to the artist; in others like *Roderick Hudson,* he contrasted the ideal with the real; and in those like *Daisy Miller,* he dramatized "the essential differences between a genuine American girl and an artificial, Europeanized society." Arader's comparison of "The Last of the Valerii" with *The Marble Faun* is discussed in the last section of this essay. Turning once again to the Anglo-American artist colony in Rome, Arader writes:

> In their creative work both Hawthorne and James had drawn upon the artist colony for character and background, and . . . for a basic theme. Both writers had found a moral . . . in the experience of the expatriates: the artist should give up the life of a romantic enjoyment and should return to reality and hard work. In *The Marble Faun* Kenyon and Hilda returned before it was too late, but James's expatriates had remained in Italy to languish and to fail.
>
> Looking at them in Rome and Florence, Hawthorne and James had observed that their fellow American artists who remained in "the golden air," surrounded by the glories of the picturesque and the great triumphs of past art, did not themselves accomplish work of permanent distinction. (362)

That is why most of James's fictional American artists in Italy fail. In his conclusion, Arader remarks again that James "never gained an understanding of the Italian character, Italian literature, the Catholic Church, or the contemporary political scene." He was interested mainly "in the grandeur of the past, in the beautiful countryside, in the great artistic achievements." His only major Italian fictional character is Prince Amerigo in *The Golden Bowl.*

Many observations similar to Arader's were later made by Van Wyck Brooks in *The Dream of Arcadia: American Writers and Artists in Italy, 1760–1915* (New York: E. P. Dutton, 1958). Brooks points out, for example, that it was Story's studio which Hawthorne described as Kenyon's; that if Story himself did not appear in *The Marble Faun,* his Cleopatra did, as did a number of Americans then in Italy; that Hawthorne's villa at Bellosguardo is the one described as Monte Beni in the romance; and that the portrait of Beatrice Cenci, which profoundly affected Hawthorne as a symbol of the existence of evil in the world, was also used in the romance. Brooks quickly points out, however—as Wright did later—that even before *The Marble Faun,* Hawthorne had in "Rappaccini's Daughter" associated Italy with evil. (Brooks, pp. 102–144)

The sections on James, pp. 155–75, also repeat many of Arader's observations. Brooks too indicates that James's appreciation of Italy was deeper than Hawthorne's; that the only Italians James knew were "washer-women and waiters"; and that the artist colony in Rome supplied James with many of his fictional characters. Lastly, Brooks finds the theme of "Adina" vaguely suggesting Hawthorne, Conte Valerio in "The Last of the Valerii" recalling

Donatello in *The Marble Faun,* and "The Madonna of the Future" saturated with Hawthorne.

Many other published studies which discuss James's Italianate fiction—down to Carl Maves's *Sensuous Pessimism: Italy in the Works of Henry James* (Bloomington: Indiana University Press, 1973)—include references to Hawthorne, and vice versa. For instance, in *The Grasping Imagination: The American Writings of Henry James* (Toronto: University of Toronto Press, 1970), pp. 81-82, Peter Buitenhuis observes that one "striking example of the difference between Hawthorne's and James's response to Europe was in their estimation of . . . Story." Hawthorne's estimation "was just this side of idolatry, as his fulsome description of *Cleopatra* in [*The Marble Faun*] shows." James, on the other hand, called Story "a case of *prosperous* pretention[sic]"; later, he said it would have been better if Story "has stayed at home in Boston and worked his imagination and his material in that cold northern air."

Thomas H. Pauly's dissertation, "The Travel Sketch-Book and the American Author: A Study of the European Travelogues of Irving, Longfellow, Hawthorne, Howells, and James" (University of California at Berkeley, 1970) does not discuss any similarities or differences between Hawthorne's and James's "European Travelogues." The chapter on Hawthorne, pp. 140-90, looks at *Our Old Home* and Hawthorne's other sketches, short stories, and unfinished romances; that on James, pp. 235-81, examines *Italian Hours* and *Transatlantic Sketches.*

Of the twenty-three dissertations reviewed in this text, two add practically nothing to our understanding of Hawthorne and James. The first is Miller's "Representative Tragic Heroines," which is reviewed at the end of the second essay. The second is "American Romance and Italian Reality in the Nineteenth Century" (University of Pittsburgh, 1973), by John E. Pyron, Jr. Pyron relies considerably on Wright's study, but some of his statements are almost offensive. Several others are stereotypic, and some are so obvious they need no mention. He finds it ironic that many American writers went to Italy, "this land of bad food, bad weather, damp climate, dirt and disease for their health!" The main reason they flocked to the country, however, was because nineteenth-century Italy "offered a sharp contrast to the American way of life." "To most Italians," Pyron points out, "life is for living and . . . leisure is for loafing." Pyron notes also that Daisy Miller's mother "has many characteristics still recognizable today as those of a typical American tourist." As for the Italians themselves, "these colorful people," he observes that perhaps "no other people are at once so simple and so complex." But he is surprised that "little appeared in nineteenth-century literature of one highly visible fixture of the Italian scene, the beggar."

The American writers Pyron discusses include Irving, Longfellow, Cooper, Emerson, Stowe, Melville, Hawthorne, Howells, Twain, and James. Lest one might think otherwise, Pyron points out in his last chapter, pp. 114-18, that since for the most part nineteenth-century American fiction overlooked Italy's blemishes and depicted the country as "a virtual paradise," for one to "understand what Italy really was like in the nineteenth-century, one must look to the non-fiction of the period."

Roderick Hudson

Roderick Hudson and *The Marble Faun* have been compared almost as frequently as *The Bostonians* and *The Blithedale Romance.* The most detailed study of the similarities between this Italianate pair is Sanford E. Morovitz's "*Roderick Hudson:* James's *Marble Faun,*" *Texas Studies in Literature and Language,* 11 (1970), 1427-43. Morovitz suggests that *Roderick Hudson* "should be considered a companion piece to *The Marble Faun.*" Although the works of other authors may have been inspirational, "it is *The Marble Faun* which had the most direct and immediate impact on James's novel." The setting, the structure, several of the main characters, and numerous secondary features of both novels are "strikingly similar." Both books, of course, are set amid the artist colony in Rome. Their themes too are "almost identical":

> Whereas the sin of Donatello is clearly allegorical, however, Roderick's "fall" is an allusion to his tragically aborted career, an acknowledgement of innocence corrupted by the influence of Europe. Nevertheless, the similarity of themes is manifest when Roderick . . . tells his mother, "If I hadn't come to Rome I shouldn't have risen, and if I hadn't risen I shouldn't have fallen." The only element missing from *Roderick* is the bond of guilt that inextricably unites Miriam with Donatello; but . . . its omission did not necessitate James's altering the theme of his own novel, for the idea of falling from innocence–largely through succumbing to the spell of an enchantress–is central in both. (1433)

In *The Marble Faun,* the theme of the Fall of Man is interfused with the concept of "suffering into life," and the two ideas together constitute the central moral issue of the novel. "The same theme–the need to suffer in order to live–is also central in *Roderick Hudson.*" Although Hawthorne "probed the depths of the soul to grapple with the taint of original sin in every man," and James dealt ostensibly with "sin" of a less serious nature–"the sin against social convention"–"both authors clearly explored a moral dilemma that evolves as their characters–Hilda and Mary, Donatello and Roderick, even Miriam and Christina–grow increasingly aware of guilt and its effects . . . upon their companions and particularly upon themselves."

The pattern of characters in *The Marble Faun* is also repeated in *Roderick Hudson.* "Rowland Mallet takes the place of Kenyon," and Roderick himself occupies the position of Donatello. "As Donatello is to the Faun of Praxiteles, so is Roderick to the small bronze which he himself has created." Although the animal element in Roderick is not stressed as it is in Donatello, it is nevertheless there, and in both characters "it connotes a definite sense of innocent liveliness uninhibited by moral restraint." Both figures are also tragic, although Donatello does become a total human being and does not resign himself to suffering, "whereas Roderick cannot accept the responsibility of living in a continuous state of insatiable longing . . . and presumably takes his own life" (1437).

Miriam and Christina Light are also alike. Miriam's beauty clearly matches Christina's, and her Semitic elements parallel Christina's seemingly "Hebraic appearance." Even their very names are linked. "Miriam's name is a variant of Mary, the Mother of Christ, which suggests her close kinship to the enchanting Christina, Roderick's 'goddess.'" In name, features, and character, the two heroines are thus very much alike. The blood of each is mixed, their backgrounds are left vague, they both suffer from a past sin, and "suicide is suggested as a possible means for both women to escape from their oppressive bondage to the past" (1439).

James admired Hilda so much that he transposed her physically into his own novel; "for if 'this pure and somewhat rigid New England girl' and Miss [Augusta] Blanchard are not identical twins, they are . . . sisters with few disparate features to distinguish one from the other." As with Christina and Miriam, "Augusta's name suggests an immediate affinity with Hilda," and the two women are so similar physically that their portraits must be considered complementary. However, Augusta's role in *Roderick Hudson* is only secondary, whereas Hilda's place in *The Marble Faun* is a prominent one. Mary Garland too "has no definite correlate in Hawthorne's fiction." Of course, James's scope in *Roderick Hudson* was "wider than Hawthorne's, for, whereas Hawthorne portrayed but four individuals, James presented a society."

One of the scenes James admired most in *The Marble Faun* was "the murder committed by Donatello under Miriam's eyes." Hawthorne used Miriam's glance to fuse her own will with Donatello's action and to initiate a bond between them. Hilda too noted the look, "and at once recognized its moral significance to both of her companions. James, of course, is known for his subtle use of the meaningful glance":

> Using terms similar to Hawthorne's, he developed the relationship between Roderick and Christina Light. . . . Brought to the girl by her mother, Prince Casamassima asks Christina to dance; upon his invitation, "Christina and Roderick exchanged a single glance—a glance caught by Rowland and which attested on the part of each

> something of a new consciousness. She passed her hand into his arm; he tossed his ambrosial locks and led her away." . . . Here, in two brief sentences, James included the desire, the glance, the observer, the link, and the action. Further, the "new consciousness" of Roderick and Christina in regard to their association—"attested" by the glance—can be directly paralleled with the awakening of both Donatello and Miriam, not only to the dramatic transformation in their relationship as a consequence of her glance and his action, but also to the Faun's immediate conversion into a human being with a new sense of moral awareness. Ultimately, too, it is the recently married Princess' final distant glance toward Roderick that leads to his fatal plunge . . . from a Swiss mountainside. (1441)

In addition to the themes and the characters, the technical devices of the two novels are also similar. "Sculptures and paintings are symbolic keystones in the construction of *The Marble Faun,* and James's use of Hawthornesque symbols in *Roderick Hudson* was extensive." Donatello's temperament is similar to that of the Faun of Praxiteles, just as Roderick's is similar to that of the youth represented by the Grecian statuette. Roderick's varied busts also recall the many heads of clay and marble in Kenyon's studio, and, like Kenyon's, they too are symbolic.

Despite all these striking similarities, however, "the differences between the works are greater and far more crucial than any of their similarities":

> Hawthorne focused on one fundamental moral problem—guilt—with all its ramified effects; James explored the virtues and vices bred by any unbending adherence to convention and tradition. Hawthorne plunged to the soul of Everyman; James examined and reflected upon the expanding consciousness of individual characters caught in a web of circumstance. Hawthorne's ambiguities force us to leap back and forth over the boundary of possibility that separates appearance from reality; James's labyrinthine suggestions seldom transcend the world of probability. Hawthorne's characters ultimately turn inward for answers; James's search for hints and clues outside. (1442)

All these major differences are "obvious." But unquestionably Hawthorne was James's earliest model, and James "absorbed Hawthorne's tales and romances in such a way that many of their most apparent features and qualities were woven into his own writing."

Many other people have written on the relation between *Roderick Hudson* and *The Marble Faun.* Since none of their contributions is as comprehensive as Morovitz's, they will be reviewed chronologically. In "The Hawthorne Aspect," *Little Review,* 5 (August, 1918), 47-53, T. S. Eliot termed *Roderick*

Hudson the novel of a promising young writer "just coming out to a self-consciousness where Hawthorne never arrived at all." Nonetheless, he admitted that *The Marble Faun* has "a kind of solid moral atmosphere" which *Roderick Hudson* never achieves. "James in *Roderick Hudson* does very little better with Rome than Hawthorne," Eliot declared. He found the "generic resemblance" of *Roderick Hudson* to *The Marble Faun* to be "in the occasional heavy facetiousness of the style, the tedious whimsicality . . . the verbalism." The main difference between the two books, he said, lies in James's "instinctive attempt to get at something larger."

In *American Renaissance* (New York: Oxford University Press, 1941), F. O. Matthiessen noted that many of Hawthorne's characters have artistic traits. In *The Marble Faun* there is Kenyon, a young American sculptor in Rome, "a type that James was to endow with passion in Roderick Hudson, but not even then to make very convincing." Matthiessen observed further that James cast *Roderick Hudson* in the American art colony in Rome only fifteen years after Hawthorne had laboriously broken the ground, and that "James' somewhat vague discussion of aesthetic problems there might have been even worse if Hawthorne had not already occupied all the most damaging pitfalls." In *The James Family* (New York: Alfred A. Knopf, 1947), Matthiessen observed again that when "James set himself to dramatizing, in *Roderick Hudson,* the problems encountered by a young American artist in Rome, he also dwelt on the weight of the past there–as Hawthorne had in *The Marble Faun."* F R. Leavis, however, stated in *The Great Tradition* (1948; reprinted Garden City, New York: Doubleday, 1954) that although "the influence of Hawthorne is very apparent in some of James's earliest stories," the influence one notes "in *Roderick Hudson* is not that of Hawthorne"; it is rather the influence of Dickens, especially the Dickens of *Martin Chuzzlewit* (Leavis, pp. 160, 162).

In his introduction to *Roderick Hudson* (New York: Harper and Brothers, 1960), Leon Edel noted that when James started to write this novel, he

> seemed to be taking up where Hawthorne had left off in *The Marble Faun.* That novel had carried Hawthorne from Salem and Boston to Rome; and in Rome he had sketched an American artist-group. But it was the work of a man who discovered the Eternal City late in life, too late, and who saw it with rural eyes. Hawthorne was both enchanted and ill-at-ease in Papal Rome. James seemed to have asked himself: what if a younger American, as sensitive as Hawthorne, had come to Rome from the same provincial horizons–younger . . . looking with the brazen eyes of his youth rather than those of tired middle age upon the Forum and the Capitol . . . (ix-x)

Edel found that "James's Rome (and Hawthorne's) is everywhere in the pages of *Roderick Hudson.*" He also indicated that whereas Hawthorne took Story seriously as an artist, "James saw him for the figure of 'prosperous pretention' that he was—a second-rate artist with a first-rate reputation." In *Henry James,* University of Minnesota Pamphlets on American Writers, no. 4 (Minneapolis: University of Minnesota Press, 1960), Edel again observed that in substance and setting *Roderick Hudson* "seems to take up where Hawthorne left off in *The Marble Faun.*" But while Hawthorne tried to write "a characteristic 'romance,' reworking, in terms of the real and the mystical, the Puritan struggle between guilt and goodness in a Roman setting," James "wrote a novel romantic in theme . . . yet realistic in its painting of the American art expatriates in the Holy City." Lastly, while discussing James's "The Great Good Place," Edel explained in *Henry James: The Treacherous Years, 1895-1901* (New York: J. B. Lippincott, 1969)[2] that the great good place was a very old fantasy of Henry James's. In *Roderick Hudson*

> he had depicted a similar place, near Fiesole, where Rowland Mallet finds peace within a cool cloister, and lays his hand on the arm of a Brother to whom he speaks of the temptations of the devil. James had always been fascinated by the moment in Hawthorne's *Marble Faun* when Hilda . . . filled with the horror of the crime she has accidentally witnessed, goes to confession—though a Protestant—to ease herself of her burden. In a monastery the world's burdens drop away . . . The craving for a great good place and the touch of a Brother's hand had existed for years. (241)

F. J. Masback's dissertation, "The Child Character in Hawthorne and James" (Syracuse, 1960), was reviewed in the second essay. Masback too points out that both *The Marble Faun* and *Roderick Hudson* deal with American artists in a foreign environment, delineate a disastrous fall from innocence, but maintain that "such a fall can also produce wisdom and enlightenment." Furthermore, both novelists symbolize one of their themes "by describing a piece of sculpture early in the novel." *The Marble Faun* has the statue of the child with the dove and the snake; *Roderick Hudson* has the statue of a naked youth drinking from a gourd. (Masback, pp. 151-52)

In *The Novels of Henry James* (New York: Hafner Publishing, 1961), Oscar Cargill remarks that James's first novel, *Roderick Hudson,* has a "greater naturalness" than Hawthorne's last novel, *The Marble Faun.* But he admits that *The Marble Faun* did influence *Roderick Hudson,* particularly "in the grouping of characters and in the final tragedy." Both novels are about Americans in Rome, "and in each tale one of the Americans is an artist and one a 'spectator' to the events. In each narrative tragedy comes in a fall from a great height." Cargill is convinced that Donatello must have been in James's mind as he created the character of Roderick. But he finds Hawthorne's "set descriptions" impeding the flow of the novel; James, by contrast, "concentrates on producing 'atmosphere.'" Cargill's conclusion is that "if *The Marble Faun* suggested the general subject matter, it was not the immediate source of *Roderick Hudson*"; that source was *L'Affaire Clemenceau* by Dumas. (Cargill, pp. 19-23, 33n.)[3]

Tanner's 1967 introduction to James's *Hawthorne* was reviewed in the first essay. In "A Tanner in the Works," *Cambridge Review,* 89A (May, 1968), 430-31, P. R. Grover disagreed with Tanner's "exposition of the essential and lasting connections between Hawthorne and James," and remarked that "the best thing that can be said for *The Marble Faun* is that it made possible *Roderick Hudson.*" Tanner too, of course, had related *Roderick Hudson* to *The Marble Faun.*

Peter Buitenhuis's "Henry James on Hawthorne," *New England Quarterly,* 32 (June, 1959), 207-25, was also reviewed in the first essay. Buitenhuis too noted that *Roderick Hudson* has as its inspiration and setting the Rome of *The Marble Faun.* Just as Hawthorne in this romance dwelt on the situation of the expatriated American artist, so did James make this the theme of his novel, and develop "ideas and conflicts that Hawthorne had merely suggested." In *The Grasping Imagination* (1970), Buitenhuis again noted that one of the main sources of *Roderick Hudson* is *The Marble Faun.* Both novels are set largely in Rome. Like Hawthorne, James uses "a quartet of figures to organize the structure of the novel, three of them similar in occupation or function." Kenyon is transformed into Roderick; Miriam becomes Christina Light; and Hilda becomes Mary Garland. "The typically Hawthornesque fantasy figure, the Faun, however, is transformed into the solidly realistic American, Rowland Mallet." As should be obvious, Buitenhuis pairs six of his eight figures differently from Morovitz. Morovitz paired Kenyon with Rowland, Donatello with Roderick, and Hilda with Augusta; he further indicated that Mary Garland "has no definite correlate" in *The Marble Faun.* Buitenhuis does admit that Roderick is "a far less phlegmatic figure than Kenyon," but he maintains that with the figure of Rowland James departed radically from the example of *The Marble Faun;* here "James drew on his own experience with Roger Lawrence in *Watch and Ward* and created in Rowland Mallet another meticulous bachelor of independent means." After discussing the similarities between *Roderick Hudson* and *Blithedale* (see fourth essay), Buitenhuis concludes that it is the schemata of *Blithedale* and *The Marble Faun* that "were the most powerful determinants of [*Roderick Hudson*'s] location, subject, and technique"; in writing this novel James "began, in a real sense, where Hawthorne left off in . . . *The Marble Faun.*" (*The Grasping Imagination,* pp. 78-81)

With respect to the influence of *The Marble Faun* on *Roderick Hudson,* Paul A. Newlin's "The Development of *Roderick Hudson:* an Evaluation,"

Arizona Quarterly, 27 (Summer, 1971), 101-23, has virtually nothing new to say. Newlin's aim is to "synthesize and comment upon the prevailing theories concerning the sources of influence on *Roderick Hudson,*" and to "elaborate upon a neglected source of influence—that of William Wetmore Story and the Roman artist-circle he headed." Curiously, Newlin discusses Matthiessen's "theories" as if they were elaborations on Edel's findings; he also terms Matthiessen's "Henry James and the Plastic Arts" (1943) "an earlier essay" than *American Renaissance* (1941).

In the preface to *The Marble Faun,* Hawthorne complained about "the difficulty of writing a Romance about a country where there is . . . [nothing] but a common-place prosperity . . . as is happily the case with my dear native land." It was "the same feeling," Newlin states, "or lack of feeling, for America" which made James set *Roderick Hudson* "amongst the 'romance,' 'poetry,' and 'ruin' of Rome." Hawthorne,

> whose New England heritage gave him a vigorous rural society of another century for material, felt the need for growth; similarly, James's need for a firmly based cultural heritage called for more sophisticated and complex groundings than those provided by the still youthful, cultureless United States. Therefore, both men turned to Italy and Rome for the settings of *The Marble Faun* and *Roderick Hudson* because these settings provided the artistic atmosphere they similarly sought, and answered . . . James's questions as to his place in the scheme of artistic reconciliation between Europe and America. (114-15)

Thus James, "a young man of thirty-one," took up where Hawthorne, "an older man at fifty-six, had left off fifteen years before." *Roderick Hudson,* then, became "James's effort to frame the American art colony in Rome—the same colony, revolving around . . . Story, which Hawthorne had treated earlier in *The Marble Faun.*" One of Hawthorne's pitfalls which James managed to avoid, says Newlin, echoing Matthiessen, was the vagueness in the discussion of art in *The Marble Faun.* After commenting on "Hawthorne's aesthetic views on sculpturing" as expressed in chapter 13 of this novel, and relating them to "the development of Roderick Hudson as a sculptor," Newlin observes that the "similar aesthetic views of art" in *The Marble Faun* and *Roderick Hudson* are among the major "connecting links" between these two works.

Another "outstanding" link between Hawthorne and James, says Newlin, is Story. Story's Italy, Story's *Cleopatra,* and Story himself appear in *The Marble Faun,* and in *Roderick Hudson* the sculptor Gloriani "is at least a partial portrayal of Story . . . . But if Story himself does not appear in *Roderick Hudson,* the Rome of Story permeates the novel to the extent of being its main essence." Story's Italy, therefore, stands as "an indirect link between these two novels of Italian settings." Newlin discusses four other people who influenced the development of James's novel: Regnault, Dumas, Balzac, and Turgenev.

The Portrait of a Lady

The first person to relate *The Portrait of a Lady* to *The Marble Faun* was Bliss Perry, who, in *A Study of Prose Fiction* (Boston: Houghton Mifflin, 1904), p. 231, declared *The Marble Faun* superior to *The Portrait.* This, according to Perry, is proof that "Hawthorne is a better story-writer than Henry James." Three other people have written about this pair. In "The Houses that James Built–*The Portrait of a Lady,*" *Texas Quarterly,* 1 (Winter, 1958), 176-96, Robert W. Stallman examines the influence of *The Marble Faun* on *The American* and *The Portrait.* In *The Portrait,* Stallman argues, James uses the metaphors of houses and gardens to render symbolically the nature and plight of his characters. This novel, together with *The American,* shows how James "refined upon Hawthorne's symbolic devices. Midway through *Roderick Hudson"* James deposited his hero in the Villa Pandolfini, the same villa that Osmond inhabits in *The Portrait.* It is in fact the Villa Mercede, which James had once visited. From its gardens–as James explains in *Roderick Hudson*– "can be seen 'the crenelated tower of a neighboring villa.'" This is Villa Montauto, where Hawthorne once lived. It figures as the crenelated tower that Kenyon visits in chapter 24 of *The Marble Faun.* According to Stallman, James had not read *The Marble Faun* when he wrote *Roderick Hudson.* (The items just reviewed above, of course, indicate otherwise.) "He had read it, however, by the time he wrote" *The American.* Hence the technical differences between these two novels. Whereas *Roderick Hudson* is devoid of symbolism, in *The American* James "employs the same symbolic devices as in *The Portrait.*" The Villa Mercede, for example, "has a lovely *cortile*":

> In *Roderick Hudson* it is described as "a great cool *cortile,* graced round about with light arches and heavily-corniced doors of majestic altitude and furnished on one side with a grand old archaic well." *The Portrait,* employing Hawthorne's chiaroscuro style, presents it as a "high court, where a clear shadow rested below and a pair of light-arched galleries, facing each other above, caught the upper sunshine upon their slim columns and the flowering plants in which they were dressed." (181)

"It is here that Isabel first visits Osmond"–chapter 24 of *The Portrait*–"and the setting as rendered with its shadow-sunlight is therefore appropriate symbolically." Roderick Hudson's villa, on the other hand, "has no metaphoric import; it is simply a villa." In *Roderick Hudson* all the objects "remain unused, symbolically, and merely picturesque." In *The Portrait,* however, "nothing is *merely* picturesque. Here realism is extended into symbolism by metaphors of designed purpose."

Jay Bochner's "Life in a Picture Gallery: Things in *The Portrait of a Lady* and *The Marble Faun,*" *Texas Studies in Literature and Language,* 11 (1969), 761-77, considers the difference between Hawthorne's and James's concern for "real things." Bochner finds that Hawthorne cares little for tangible objects; "objective reality is much more a matter of symbols. A rose . . . is more symbolic than it is real and almost always more important for the reader than for the fictional character." Furthermore, "symbolic meaning in Hawthorne is general, even cosmic," and most often "it is moral in a social or religious sense." Symbolic meaning in James, on the other hand, "is particular and human, a matter of personal, not of social or religious, morality. Things seen by Hilda and Miriam point *through* them to us, but things seen by Isabel point always to Isabel." Frequently Hawthorne's characters fail to materialize because they are merely representatives of "'symbolic action,' not real people living actions both real and symbolic." James, however, never instructs the reader to pay attention to some moral lesson; for him "the question is rather what reality means to Isabel."

Everything in *The Scarlet Letter,* Bochner points out, functions on a symbolic level: "the wild roses, the scaffold, the armor, the 'A,' the sunlight." Some of these symbols are also in *The Marble Faun,* and they are hardly things at all; "they are barely concretized ideas. But there *are* things in *The Marble Faun* . . . and in a way Hawthorne has come into James's world." Italy gave Hawthorne "the items of high civilization" James enumerated in *Hawthorne,* and they affected him so profoundly that he tried to make them the foundation of a novel that never needed them. What went wrong in *The Marble Faun* can be illustrated by contrasting Hawthorne's use of things and houses in this novel with James's use of similar items in *The Portrait.*

All the houses in *The Portrait* are different from each other. James is concerned not only with the *idea* of a house, but with the *actuality* of houses as well, "because he is concerned with the reality of his characters." As Madame Merle tells Isabel in chapter 19 of *The Portrait,* "one's house, one's furniture, one's garments . . . these things are all expressive" of one's "self." Bochner argues that Isabel's character can be discovered through what she thinks and feels about different houses. Gardencourt, of course, is the most important, and its different meanings for her are the measure of the changes she undergoes. But Gardencourt is not merely a symbol; it is also meaningful to her as a distinct place. "The point is that a house is always particular and made real enough to be used as the objective correlative for a person's outlook." James's mistake in *Roderick Hudson* was to attempt to "do" a real town, Northampton, "when a kind of town was what he wanted." In *The*

Portrait, Gardencourt, Lockleigh, and even the house in Albany "partake a definite reality" because they are presented in terms of things known. When Hawthorne uses real houses in *The Marble Faun,* on the other hand, the effect is entirely different. James appeals to our sense of things *in general.* He is not concerned with giving information.

Bochner examines also James's "use of *objets d'art* in the relationship between Isabel and Osmond"–Osmond, the collector, sees Isabel as a choice object worth adding to his collection; she is both "a real little passionate force" (chapter 7) and a painting in a gallery–and in the scene in the gallery of the Capitol in Rome where Isabel turns down Lord Warburton for the final time (chapter 28). In this scene, Isabel first meets Lord Warburton standing before the statue of the Dying Gladiator, and "when he leaves, defeated, 'Isabel looked a moment at the vanquished Gladiator,' an interesting subtlety . . . when we consider that Kenyon's objection to the statue is that it never manages to die."

In *The Marble Faun,* Bochner observes, Hawthorne gives us "an appreciable chunk of Italy along with the story." But the novel is not "actual travelogue." Everything Hawthorne sees tempts him to symbolic interpretation, and the characters themselves "are eternally moralizing upon everything they see." Italy furnishes Hawthorne "with a plethora of symbols, but in such richness lie serious problems for his story." Hilda's tower is one example. The building as a place for her to live in "vanishes almost entirely under the burden of symbolic import." And this is where the different between the two writers becomes very distinct. "Hawthorne gives us the real place, though like James he was not . . . writing of the social scene. James presented a particular kind of re-creation which was supposed to 'generalize itself' in the reader's perception. But in Hilda's tower Hawthorne presents a place which is quite generalized already in its function as a purely symbolic building, yet which is as well absolutely and verifiably real." And yet, for Hawthorne much more than for James, "it was of the utmost importance that the tower exist nowhere at all except in the novel." What one expects from a romance is a "faithful portrayal of a place of the mind . . . 'where actualities would not be so terribly insisted upon'"; what one gets in *The Marble Faun* is a world which actually exists and "is forever reminding us of that fact. The world of *The Marble Faun* has its own life outside of the novel, and that is the novel's major fault."

Bochner examines also Hawthorne's uses of paintings and sculpture in *The Marble Faun.* He feels that in general the novel would have done better with fewer works of art. In the preface to *The Marble Faun,* Hawthorne admitted that he was "surprised to see the extent to which he had introduced descriptions of various Italian objects." Bochner agrees:

> These objects indeed flow out upon th page and vie with the fiction for our attention. Hawthorne was thoroughly overwhelmed by Europe, by the place which held in itself sin and guilt and beauty in so many forms, just as he was overwhelmed by . . . Miriam, and the faun was overwhelmed by Miriam and Rome. . . . James, familiar with Europe, in need of surfaces from the start, used them to get to his characters and to present us with substantial human beings in conflict and trouble, acting out life among the surfaces of life in different places. But Hawthorne was so caught up with the brilliant, meaningful surfaces that he was not able to distil from them the unified meaning which can make for art. Innocent, he fell for the picture gallery like a ten-year-old let loose in a candy store, and, in mistaking a picture gallery for life, made the same mistake as Isabel Archer. (776-77)

Another fine essay which includes a discussion of *The Portrait* and *The Marble Faun* is Linda R. Pratt's "The Abuse of Eve by the New World Adam," in *Images of Women in Fiction,* revised edition, edited by Susan K. Cornillon (Bowling Green, Ohio: Bowling Green University Popular Press, 1973), pp. 155-74. Sections of Pratt's essay were reviewed in the second and fourth essays. Pratt disagrees with those critics who assume that Hawthorne's and James's "light-dark women characters represent a rigid dualism of good and evil." Her thesis is that Hawthorne uses the pure and impure women to represent the pre- and post-lapsarian Eve. "The pre-lapsarian Eve can never enter the world of experience and be humanized by worldly contact," while the post-lapsarian Eve is "humanized by the experience of evil," but is as a result "rejected by the Adamic hero who must protect his innocence." Perhaps because Hawthorne was attracted by naive innocence, it is his Hildas, the pre-lapsarian Eves, who find happiness in life, although his Miriams, the post-lapsarian figures, earn the "higher innocence." According to Pratt, Hilda and Miriam are "Hawthorne's most direct treatment of the pale-dark dichotomy within the terms of the fortunate fall." Hilda rejects Miriam in order to preserve her white-robed innocence, but the rejection places her outside humanity. Although Kenyon argues for a mixture of good in things evil, Hilda's insistence on "only one right and one wrong" frustrates the wisdom he might have won from knowing the fallen Miriam. "As a weak and unsure Adam, Kenyon disavows belief in the fortunate fall and turns to his pre-lapsarian Eve to guide him back to the Edenic world." It is the character of Donatello which illustrates the "moral and intellectual transformation possible through embracing the post-lapsarian Eve." Miriam's passions prove to be the redemptive force for both herself and Donatello, her Adamic companion, and the extent to which society rejects the fallen pair is a measure of its lack of wisdom and compassion, a theme Hawthorne develops more emphatically in *The Scarlet Letter.*

At the end of her discussion of *Blithedale,* Pratt turns to Zenobia's suicide. Coverdale, she points out, is only half right when he says, in chapter 28, that it is "a miserable wrong . . . that the success or failure of woman's existence should be made to depend wholly on . . . one species of affection; while man has such a multitude of other chances, that this seems but an incident." It is true, Pratt notes, that

> the very existence of a fallen Eve depends "on one species of affection," but Hawthorne's novels repeatedly suggest that man's existence is equally dependent on his ability to offer that affection. Coverdale is wrong when he claims that men have a multitude of other chances, as the cases of Hollingsworth, Coverdale, Kenyon, Donatello, and Dimmesdale must illustrate. None of the Adamic figures were ever truly innocent . . . all they accomplish in rejecting such post-lapsarian Eves as Zenobia, Miriam, and Hester is their own damnation.
>
> In refusing the reality of women who are touched by the world, these false Adams condemn themselves to a life of self-deception and moral infancy. Their lives become a series of repeated refusals of the truth. (165)

Thus Kenyon rejects the obvious lesson in the fall "for the life of a washed-out artist with a simpleton wife." It is Hawthorne's men, Pratt emphasizes, who are morally timid and intellectually shallow, and the women's "beauty, wisdom, and vitality are finally inadequate to shake the men from their fearful dependence on the male illusion."

Of the major nineteenth-century American authors, Pratt finds James the one who most completely rejected the validity of an Adamic American, and thus created women characters who are fully human. For illustration, she analyzes in detail the last chapter of *The Portrait,* where Isabel refuses Caspar in order to return to Osmond. Isabel's character, Pratt argues, is a combination of both pre- and post-lapsarian Eve figures. "If viewed in the perspective of the dual nature of Eve . . . her choice is analogous to that made by Miriam. . . . As the post-lapsarian Eve, Isabel's rejection of Caspar, the 'American Adam,' frees her to grow while it incapacitates him in a static illusion. Her qualified acceptance of the role of wife to Osmond . . . imposes on the fallen world the knowledge of sin and redemptive wisdom which is the essential function of Eve." In returning to Rome, Isabel moves "out of the garden (literally Gardencourt) into the world of experience." What she fears in Caspar is not his "hard manhood," or his passion, but his violent possessiveness. Caspar tells her to desert Osmond because "a woman deliberately made to suffer is justified in anything in life," a rationale which, Pratt notes, "virtually suggests that the pain of life in the world justifies a private morality to protect one's emotional ease. Such a position approximates Hilda's rejection of Miriam in order to wear back to God her white robe of inhuman innocence." What Caspar offers Isabel is a return to a pre-lapsarian state, an escape from life. "If she is to make any meaning out of her life, her fall from innocence to wisdom must move her back to the world of experience," and that means the world of Osmond. Although social freedom from Osmond is as impossible for her as Caspar's naive promise of a new beginning, "her understanding of Osmond's nature . . . frees her from Osmond's moral and spiritual influence." When she returns to Rome, she will certainly continue to insist on her moral and intellectual integrity. Thus, in her final choice she rejects both the role of pre-lapsarian Eve which the Adamic Caspar wishes her to play, and the restrictions of obedient effacement wich Osmond demands. "In the figure of Isabel," Pratt concludes, "James rejects the limits imposed on women by such Americans as Cooper and Hawthorne. . . . Uncommitted to the preservation of innocence and unambiguous as to the educational value of sin, James has no necessity to force women into pre- and post-lapsarian dichotomies. His women characters are more fully human because they are less abstract and less symbolic." But neither was Hawthorne a consistent advocate of the Adamic stance. If the works of these writers are re-evaluated in the light of social and sexual realities, one discovers that their "women characters often surpass the so-called heroes in moral complexity and human veracity" (170).

The Wings of the Dove

The first person to relate *The Wings of the Dove* to *The Marble Faun* was F. O. Matthiessen in *Henry James: The Major Phase* (New York: Oxford University Press, 1944), pp. 59-65. While considering the contrast between Kate Croy and Milly Theale, Matthiessen noted that, "as was the usual practice of Hawthorne and Melville, the innocent heroine is fair, and the dangerous worldly girl is dark." Matthiessen also discussed the image at the end of chapter 5 of the novel, where Mrs. Stringham finds Milly seated on the edge of a precipice. Through this pictorial image James indicates that "the menace of death is always near her." Milly was not, of course, meditating a jump; rather, she "was looking down on the kingdoms of the earth," " in a state of uplifted and unlimited possession":

> On thing notably absent from such a compelling image is any apparent awareness by James of its full religious implications. When Hawthorne had Miriam and Donatello reenact the fall of man, he

> was thoroughly conscious of the root of his scene in the Bible, and especially in Milton. But James is concerned only with the beautiful sweep of the possible kingdoms at Milly's feet. At no point . . . does he . . . suggest that she is tempted by the devil in her choice of this world. (64)

Similarly, when James suggests that Kate is attracted to Merton Densher because he has tasted of the tree of knowledge, and is "thereby prepared to assist her to eat," he forgets that "such an image is inescapably one of temptation, since it is certainly not Kate who is led into evil by Densher. Such carelessness or obliviousness on James's part shows how far he had drifted from the Christian knowledge that Hawthorne possessed."

Marius Bewley's "*The Marble Faun* and *The Wings of the Dove*" first appeared in *Scrutiny,* 16 (Winter, 1949), 301-17, and was later reprinted in *The Complex Fate: Hawthorne, Henry James and Some Other American Writers* (New York: Chatto and Windus, 1952), pp. 31-54. Bewley finds the influence of *The Marble Faun* on *The Wings of the Dove* not as laudable as that of *Blithedale* on *The Bostonians:* here James is less critical, the relation more tenuous, and the influence, though less extensive, was unfortunate in its effect on James's art.

Both *The Wings of the Dove* and *The Marble Faun,* Bewley notes, deal with the theme of the American woman. Although James was far more successful than Hawthorne with this theme, the two had a common ground. In his idealization of the American woman in his late work, James was looking back to the "positive apotheosis of New England girlhood that Hawthorne had provided for the general edification many years before." Bewley disagrees with Matthiessen's observation in *American Renaissance* (1941), p. 296, that James's heroines, like Isabel Archer and Milly Theale, mark his greatest advance beyond Hawthorne. With characters like Milly, Bewley says, James drew very near Hawthorne; and it was near Hawthorne's "sorriest aspects." *The Marble Faun,* although the worst of Hawthorne's four major novels, impressed James deeply, and it was the most forceful influence on the conception of Milly's character and function. James, of course, had always admired Hilda. It is not surprising, therefore, that the symbolism with which Milly and Hilda are presented is similar. The passage in chapter 6 of *The Marble Faun,* where Hilda is called "The Dove" and her apartment "The Dove-cote," looks directly towards the central image of *The Wings of the Dove;* possibly the very title of James's novel was suggested by this passage. Many critics have also correctly indicated that James had his cousin Minny Temple in mind when he conceived Milly Theale. Thus, although in characterizing Milly James maintained his usual critical stance toward the American woman, he also tried—since he was commemorating Minny—not to violate the sentimental memory. The end result is an imperfectly realized character:

some of the metaphors James uses are inappropraite to her, and in general she lacks animation and wit. "In the days when James had dealt with . . . heroines with whom he felt satirically, critically free (having no personal reasons to feel otherwise)," he had delved deeper into their psyche than he does with Milly.

Faced with these difficulties, James welcomed eagerly "the hints that he found in *The Marble Faun* on how to canonize an American girl in a novel." In additon to the central dove symbol in both novels, Milly's moral quality is one with Hilda's, and both women are characterized from the outside: they are both set against "suggestive backgrounds" and decorated with "symbols of universally acknowledged value." Even the scene of Hilda's confession in chapter 39 of *The Marble Faun* is recalled by Milly's speech to Kate Croy in chapter 12 of James's novel: "I feel–I can't otherwise describe it–as if I had been, on my knees, to the priest. I've confessed and I've been absolved. It has been lifted off." The situations and natures of both women resemble too. Both are "incorruptibly pure" and "positively purifying in their effect on others." Hilda loses her innocence by proxy, and just as her knowledge of Miram's guilt induces a grave psychological crisis, so does Milly's knowledge of the extent of Kate's treachery kill her. "Both the Doves are personally stainless, but the guilt of others is unbearable to them."

Bewley discusses also James's frequent use of "Hawthorne's device of endowing ancient portraits with extraordinary resemblances to the living." In *The Marble Faun,* he notes, no less than four such resemblances are introduced, and for purposes similar to James's in his novel: to emphasize the sinlessness of both women. Both Milly, the "Princess," and Hilda, the "Saint," are out to improve the past. In their names are deposited "gilt-edged metaphors" which enable them to draw lavishly on dividends which they have done little to earn. In this respect, says Bewley, James was "'taken in' by Hilda in a way he hadn't been 'taken in' by Priscilla and Zenobia." In *The Bostonians* James profited in a sharper manner from Hawthorne's art than he did in *The Wings of the Dove.* His memory of Minny Temple personalized his conception of Milly's character, and his commemorative intentions inhibited him. A similar thing may have contributed to the failure of Hilda, for in his letters Hawthorne usually addressed his wife as his "Dove." Bewley agrees with Quentin Anderson's analysis of *The Wings of the Dove* in "Henry James and the New Jerusalem" (*Kenyon Review,* Autumn 1946, pp. 515-66), an analysis he says helps to reveal an "inherited" weakness in Milly.

The Marble Faun, Bewley notes, is an allegory on the Fall of Man. Donatello, a descendant of a faun, inherited both the innocence and some of the physical characteristics of his ancestor. He falls in love with Miriam, a wholly European product who bears some secret guilt with her. By getting involved in her guilt, "he loses his original innocence." In addition to these two

Europeans are two Americans, Kenyon and Hilda, who are "keenly aware of the good vibrations from the past," but are immune to the malign influences which have corrupted the two Europeans. Hilda acts as a symbol of absolute good; not only has she not fallen, she is literally incapable of falling, and Hawthorne seems to wish her to appear more than human. Kenyon too has exalted sentiments, and his manner of speech is very similar to Hilda's. But he is not an incorruptible fountain of grace like Hilda, and he is practical. As a married couple, the two can live only in America, for their moral tone and achievement "can only be permanently sustained in the pure New England air." Hence the "dismal failure" of Hilda as a character. "The moral reality that she is supposed to embody . . . has no counterpart in reality. It is as impossible in the world of imagination as it is in life. By the time Hawthorne got round to creating Hilda," Bewley concludes, "he was irrevocably ruined as an artist." And yet, James admired Hilda's characterization. In her he thought he had discovered a method:

> The guilt of the past, so largely European, is revealed . . . by the contrasting purity of a young girl who, being an American, has no part in that heritage of crime and misery that belongs to the Old World. This girl is a "saint" . . . who purifies by her mere presence. Hawthorne erred, of course, by making her apotheosis so complete that no one except Kenyon . . . can rise to the rarified levels where her regenerative influence might be effective. But the sanctifying force that is implicit in the Dove image is to be taken just as seriously in Hilda's case as it is in Milly's. She has a mystic sympathy with everything good in the past . . . but she is so sensitive to evil that the mere presence of a guilty person in the universe is terrible torture to her. (*Complex Fate,* p. 53)

She seems to exist merely as "an impossible example in moral perfection unattainable by ordinary and non-American mortals. Everybody defers to Hilda in the same way that everybody defers to Milly." The two are "sisters under the symbol, and it is a symbol that fails to convince one that its value is valid in either novel."

In his review article in *American Literature,* 26 (January, 1955), 580-83, Randall Stewart points out a major flaw in Bewley's interpretation. Bewley believes Hilda's repulsive purity was an unfortunate influence on the creation of Milly, who is too ideal, with no criticism in her portrayal. He blames "a 'failure' by Hawthorne for a comparable 'failure' by James, though some readers may not be entirely convinced that there *is* failure in either case." Even if there were a failure, Bewley does not suggest why, in *The Bostonians,* James profited from the mistakes in *Blithedale* (*Complex Fate,* pp. 11-30), and yet succumbed in *The Wings of the Dove* to the faults in *The Marble Faun.* "Hawthorne was a good deal more than Henry James's forerunner,"

Stewart concludes; "he had an autochthonous force which James, as great as he was, could scarcely compass."

Two dissertations have included a discusson of Hilda and Milly. In chapter 3 of "The Faces of Eve: A Study of Women in American Life and Literature in the Nineteenth Century" (University of Minnesota, 1973), Judith J. Fryer notes several similarities between these two "American Princesses"; both are associated with doves, "and James surely intends this association to be felt when Milly's first two dove-like acts of deviousness lead her to the National Gallery to watch the lady-copyists"; "both are 'impossibly without sin'; both are ready to give themselves up . . . to the masculine mind . . . both experience alienation"; and "both through 'the wisdom of the serpent' seek absolution." But Hilda accepts the word *dove* as descriptive of her purity, whereas Milly accepts it as "prescriptive." Ultimately, says Fryer, Milly is a richer and more complex character than Hilda. "Hilda is not only not doomed; she is so 'spotless' . . . that one artist portrays her as 'Innocence Dying of a Bloodstain.'" Milly, on the other hand, "is physically doomed by her illness, spiritually doomed by her alienation and doomed, too, through her entanglement with Kate Croy," Aunt Maud, Merton Densher, and even Susan Stringham. (Fryer, pp. 139-64)

Gaillard F. Waterfall comments on Hildaand Milly in chapter 9 of his dissertation, "The Manipulation Theme in the Works of Nathaniel Hawthorne and Henry James" (University of South Carolina, 1973), pp. 78-99. He too finds the two heroinces similar, but notes that Milly has "more depth and compassion than the cold, aloof, and austere Hilda," and that she is also "far less of an abstraction." Nonetheless, both heroines cannot "endure the guilt of others or the evil that exists in the real world from which they insulate themselves."

The Golden Bowl

Six people have written on the relation between *The Golden Bowl* and *The Marble Faun*, but none in great detail. In *The Romance in America* (Middletown, Connecticut: Wesleyan University Press, 1969), pp. 215-26, Joel Porte indicated that *The Golden Bowl* "is at once a rewriting of Poesque explorations and an infinitely subtle reworking of *The Marble Faun*, in which the mysteries of art again provide a terminology and a touchstone for the varieties of human experience." In the works preceding *The Golden Bowl*,

> James seems to have paid careful attention to Hawthorne's advice, in the preface to *The House of the Seven Gables*, that it is the part of wisdom in a romancer "to mingle the Marvellous rather as a slight, delicate, and evanescent flavor, than as any portion of the actual

> substance of the dish offered to the Public." But the major imaginative extravagance in James's book clearly ignores this caveat, requiring—as do most of the works of Hawthorne—the further license provided by Hawthorne's next sentence: "He can hardly be said, however, to commit a literary crime, even if he disregard this caution." The device of the gold bowl itself represents, if not a literary crime, at least a novelistic misdemeanor, for by continually violating the boundary between fantasy and reality . . . it distinctly casts an aura of the marvellous and the preternatural over the "actual substance" of the whole book, providing a range of applications and implications scarcely less ample than that suggested by the scarlet letter. (220)

The golden bowl "speaks many meanings, one of which, like that of the Cenci portrait in *The Marble Faun,* concerns the universal relevance of *flaws* in a fallen world." James's theme here is "man's inhumanity to man, to himself as well as to others." At the end of the novel Maggie, having "doomed" Charlotte to the sterile aesthetic vacuum of an American city, is left alone with Prince Amerigo; similarly, at the end of *The Marble Faun* "Miriam, we might say, has been packed off with Kenyon and Donatello left to Hilda, each relegated to a world he neither understands nor enjoys."

Before Porte, F. O. Matthiessen had remarked, in *American Renaissance* (1941), p. 292, that Hawthorne "is the direct ancestor of *The Golden Bowl.*" But he did not draw any specific parallels between James's novel and any of Hawthorne's works. His comments on Hawthorne and *The Golden Bowl* in *Henry James: The Major Phase* (1944), pp. 89-104, are also not focused exclusively on a single work by Hawthorne. He notes a connection between Mrs. Assingham's "saying that Maggie 'wasn't born to know evil, she must never know it,'" and Hawthorne's world of Hilda and her doves in *The Marble Faun,* but finds James's view of the relation between Maggie and her father a puzzling limitation. James regards the intimacy between them as perfectly natural and naively innocent, without any pathological fixation which modern novelists would see in it. The point is, Matthiessen writes, "James occupies a border line between the older psychologists like Hawthorne or George Eliot, whose concerns were primarily religious and ethical, and the post-Freudians." Although, as in *The Bostonians,* he could understand lesbianism without naming it, he was oblivious to many sexual deviations which "seem an almost inevitable concomitant of the situations he posits."

Matthiessen notes further that the Ververs, unlike most of James's other Americans in Europe, are in the end completely triumphant. Maggie gets initiated into evil, and she wins the prince's love and respect. But since she keeps her innocence intact, one may feel that, again like Hilda, she "both has her cake and eats it too." According to Matthiessen, one reason the positive values in *The Golden Bowl* are unsatisfactory and unconvincing is because James tried "to invest his triumphant Americans with qualities they could hardly possess." Love alone cannot redeem a world like Maggie's; she and the prince will continue to lead a futile existence. In *The Scarlet Letter,* adultery "brought out a festering growth of hypocrisy and pride and vengefulness through which Hester Prynne had to struggle alone towards her redemption. And even if Hawthorne's narrative, like James', concentrated upon the personal relations of a very few characters, Hawthorne gave, through the depth of his moral perception, a sense of the larger society of which his characters were part." In this respect, *The Golden Bowl* is inadequate because it substitutes a part for the whole. Matthiessen goes on to discuss the similarities between James's definition of romance in the preface to *The American* and Hawthorne's discussion of his own works, and concludes that "despite the conventional classification, James was very little of a realist." His test for the romance was that, although it deals with "experience liberated," it must "make its events correspond to our sense 'of the way things happen,'" a dictum that is similar to Hawthorne's in the preface to *The Seven Gables.* But *The Golden Bowl* has "too many flagrant lapses in the way things happen." With all its magnificence, it is "hollow of real life."

Marius Bewley, in "'The Marble Faun' and 'The Wings of the Dove'" (*Complex Fate,* pp. 31-54), noted that James's remark in chapter 6 of *Hawthorne,* that "there is a great deal of interest in the simple combination and opposition of the four actors" in *The Marble Faun,* "makes one think of *The Golden Bowl*" (*Complex Fate,* p. 34). In *The Novels of Henry James* (1961), p. 390, Oscar Cargill indicated that Prince Amerigo is not corrupt but amoral, and that he reminds one of Count Donatello, whom James in *Hawthorne* called a "simple, joyous, sensuous young Italian"–until he discovers evil. But James also wished that Hawthorne had made Donatello "more definitely modern, without reverting so much to his mythological properties and antecedents . . . which belong to the region of picturesque conceits, much more than to that of real psychology." On the score of realistic psychology, Cargill suggested, Prince Amerigo should be looked upon as a corrective to Count Donatello. In his introduction to James's *Hawthorne* (1967), Tony Tanner also commented on James's praise of *The Marble Faun* "for its close study of the moral relationship between 'four people.'" Of Hilda, James wrote: "she has done no wrong, and yet wrongdoing has become a part of her experience, and she carries the weight of her detested knowledge upon her heart." It is possible, Tanner observed, to discern in James's praise and in his comment on Hilda "the outlines of the situation in *The Golden Bowl* and the plight of Maggie Verver." (Tanner, pp. 15-16)

Deanna Collingwood Nash's dissertation, "The Web as an Organic Metaphor in *The Marble Faun, Middlemarch: A Study of Provincial Life,* and *The*

Golden Bowl: The Growth of Contexualism as an Aesthetic Theory in the Nineteenth Century" (University of North Carolina at Chapel Hill, 1971), does not discuss the question of influence. Nash finds that each of the above novels "enmeshes a group of interrelated characters in a web of life." In terms of nineteenth-century aesthetics, she explains, "the web becomes an analogue for the media of consciousness, narration, and human interaction." As James explained in "The Art of Fiction": "Experience is never limited, and it is never complete; it is . . . a huge spider web . . . suspended in the chamber of consciousness. . . . It is the very atmosphere of the mind." In the above three novels, "the web is used explicitly to show the interrelations of men in a given community"; it also "functions as an analogue for the mind, for the work of art, and for the society."

In chapter 1 on Hawthorne and *The Marble Faun*, pp. 24–41, Nash considers the question of whether Donatello's transformation is "an emblem of ruin or an emblem of salvation." Her argument is that "one of the major factors in this deliberate ambiguity is Hawthorne's use of *web*, along with" related nouns and verbs. Through the spider web, Hawthorne conveys the thesis that "the actions of one person determine the circumstances affecting other individuals," and the result of his "use of the web . . . is that the four characters . . . realize the bonds, the intricate relationships of each to all." In chapters 4 and 5 on James and *The Golden Bowl*, pp. 118-89, Nash shows that in *The Golden Bowl* "James used the web as a medium for the mind, the artistic structure, and social relationships." Her conclusion is that Hawthorne, George Eliot, and James all "believed that a man is an inextricable part of his surrounding medium." Hawthorne used the web in the form and content of *The Marble Faun* "to indicate the interconnectedness of his characters in a web of society." James, who believed in "the complexity of contexts . . . put more emphasis than did Hawthorne or Eliot on the mind as a web." In *The Golden Bowl*, "the web is a medium for the interrelations of human beings in society." And all three authors "envisioned a work of art as a web-like structure which reflects the web-like configuration of society itself."

The Sacred Fount

In "*The Marble Faun* and *The Sacred Fount*: A Resemblance," *Studi Americani*, 8 (1962), 21-33, Robert L. Gale discusses a "specific parallel between pictures symbolically employed" in chapters 15, 20, and 21 of *The Marble Faun* and in chapter 4 of *The Sacred Fount*. In chapter 15 of Hawthorne's novel, Miriam, Hilda, Kenyon, and Donatello go to an apartment of an eminent member of the aesthetic body in Rome where they examine "a large portfolio of old drawings." Hilda asserts that one of them is Guido Reni's "original sketch for the picture of the Archangel Michael setting his foot upon the demon." Gale discusses at length how Hilda continuously urges Miriam to examine the sketch closely and commend it, and how Miriam uncooperatively holds back. When Kenyon enters the discussion, he states that he has seen the demon's face "on the shoulders of a living man!" Hilda concurs, and Donatello declares that it is the face of Miriam's model. But Miriam denies it all. Hawthorne at the same time invites us "to consider that present evil is not unique but rather is partly a consequence of past evil."

Gale next turns to Miriam's and Kenyon's perplexing discussion of Guido's painting in chapter 20 of *The Marble Faun.* In chapter 15 of the novel, the disagreement had centered on the resemblance of the devil in the original sketch to Miriam's model. "And it was only Miriam who refused to acknowledge this resemblance. Hilda, Kenyon, and Donatello saw it quickly." In chapter 20, however, Kenyon says that, except for Hilda, "we were all agreed in our recollection of the picture." Miriam not only seconds this statement, but adds that they were all wrong, "and Hilda right, as you perceive." Gale examines the various alternatives in which Hilda might be said to have been right and Miriam wrong, but they all present difficulties or conflicts. His conclusion is that "we have here a lapse in consistency by Hawthorne," a kind of "unintentional confusion." James too must have been puzzled by this incident. But he rather liked *The Marble Faun,* and even remembered the innocent and dove-like Hilda when he adumbrated the character of his innocent and dove-like Milly Theale. Gale feels that James might have thought back to the confusion surrounding Guido's painting when he wrote *The Sacred Fount.* In chapter 4 of that novel, the narrator, May Server, Gilbert Long, and Ford Obert "meet by pairs in 'one of the rooms' of the estate at Newmarch which has 'some pictures.' After they come together, they exchange comments on one portrait in pastel": a young man holding in his hands a representation of a human face modeled in some substance not human. May Server suggests that it is the mask of death, but the narrator contends that the mask symbolizes life while it is "the mask's own face that's Death." After some discussion as to whose face among them the mask resembles, Gilbert Long declares that it resembles the absent Guy Brissenden. Obert and the narrator agree, and May acquiesces "for harmony." "James does not allude to the portrait again."

Gale finds the significance of the picture of the man with a mask obscure because only the "strange" narrator tells us what it looks like, and "James does not follow through and make of the picture an explicit allegorical representation of the relationships of specific characters." Gale is aware, however, that James, "taking a Hawthornean portrait for slight allegorical purposes, would merely touch upon its implications and then change the subject, in the light of what he said of symbolism in Hawthorne's fiction." In his interpretation of the picture, Gale further notes that "James's occasional preoccupation with the smiles of his deceptive characters"–May Server's smile is repeatedly described as a painted and mechanical grimace–"indicates another possible influence from Hawthorne."

Gale discovers many similarities between the "circumstances surrounding the Guido painting in *The Marble Faun* and the pastel portrait in *The Sacred Fount*." In each novel the work of art is introduced rather early: in chapter 15 of Hawthorne's 50-chapter novel; in chapter 4 of James's 14-chapter novel. In *The Marble Faun* four characters "look at a sketch in a studio and then agree to meet and consider the painting purportedly based upon it." They consider "whether the devil's face in the sketch resembles that of the absent model." Donatello is the first to say that it does, but only after Kenyon and Hilda have said that it resembles some living man. Miriam strongly denies it all, but the others seem not to agree with her. "The four walk away, generally in pairs; later three of them meet at the church containing the painting, but the talk does not concern identifications." In *The Sacred Fount,* four characters examine a pastel portrait in a gallery and "consider whether the unmasked face in the picture resembles that of the absent Guy Brissenden." Long is the first to say it does, "but only after the narrator has said that he knows but will not tell whose face" it resembles. Obert agrees to the resemblance, but May concedes only for harmony. After that, the four do not meet again as a group. Gale concludes that "each picture polarizes an opposition":

> the one, that of an archangel and the devil, hence good and evil; the other, that of a livid face and an elaborate mask, hence perhaps life and death, or appearance and reality. Each picture seems to be symbolic, but only vaguely so. The details of the treatment of neither picture can endure analysis without revealing some weakness in writing: Miriam's remarks are confused, and the Jamesian narrator's remarks hide rather than shed light. But in both novels the action is advanced by the puzzled, puzzling responses of the characters to the picture, and as those persons seek resemblances they to a degree characterize themselves. Both novelists, then, use challenging pictures, hung in deceptive light, to elucidate character and implement plot, while the postures within the frames are themselves symbolic. (33)

"The Last of the Valerii"

"The Last of the Valerii" was first related to *The Marble Faun* by W. D. Howells, who, in his review of *A Passionate Pilgrim and Other Tales* in the *Atlantic Monthly,* 35 (April, 1875), 490-95, noted that James's story, like the figure of Donatello in *The Marble Faun,* is a poetic study of the remaining paganism in the Italian character. In *The Early Development of Henry James* (Urbana: University of Illinois Press, 1930), pp. 153-54, Cornelia Pulsifer Kelley likewise remarked that in sketching Conte Valerio, James "recalled Hawthorne's Donatello and tried to make his count more probable." However, says Kelley, James took the hint from, and modeled his story after, Mérimée's *La Venus d'Ille.*[4] For F. O. Matthiessen in *American Renaissance* (1941), pp. 292-93, James's story shows "how James found himself through Hawthorne's methods," for the story's "allegorical theme of an Italian count who falls in love with a pagan statue . . . can hardly have been developed without backward glances at *The Marble Faun.*" Marius Bewley, in "*The Marble Faun* and *The Wings of the Dove,*" was more specific and detailed in his observations on "The Last of the Valerii" and *The Marble Faun* (*Complex Fate,* 1952, pp. 34-36). Bewley found the only resemblance between James's story and *La Venus d'Ille* to be in their parallel plot constructions: in both stories "pagan statues of goddesses are disinterred . . . [and] interfere in the marriages of the two heroes." But even here, in Mérimée the interference is supernatural, in James psychological. Without the Hawthornean overtone, James's story "would be a piece of lifeless clap-trap. Conte Valerio derives from the pagan-Christian Donatello. . . . Just as Donatello resembles the Faun of Praxiteles, Conte Valerio 'had a head and throat like some of the busts in the Vatican. . . . He was like a statue of the Decadence.'" Martha, the heroine, is also characterized by "dove-like glances." Many descriptive passages and plot details in the two stories are also similar. Donatello, for example, discovers an antique statue of a beautiful goddess. Hawthorne's and James's scenes in the Pantheon are also related. But the closest and most significant resemblance between the two stories "is in the moral tone—the simultaneous love and fear of the past which was so characteristic of both men." James's story is a subtle "analysis of the conflict between the past and the present"; it "shares its central moral meaning with Hawthorne, and its indebtedness to him is at the very centre of its life."

Harry F. Arader makes similar observations in his dissertation, "American Novelists in Italy" (1953), pp. 314-17. He argues that "The Last of the Valerii" was influenced by both *The Marble Faun* and *La Venus d'Ille,* but finds James's thematic treatment more subtle and psychological than Mérimée's. These three works, he notes, share the basic idea of "the unearthed statue symbolizing the echoes of an ancient past that could break violently through to the present." Count Valerio was at least partially based on Donatello; James even compares him to an antique statue. But Valerio "is identical only with the *early* Donatello. James made no effort to treat the development of a soul or conscience in Valerio, as Hawthorne had in Donatello." James also "borrowed from Hawthorne the episode of the marble hand which the count keeps in his cabinet." Hawthorne had recorded a similar episode in both his Italian notebooks and *The Marble Faun.*

Three other people have commented on "The Last of the Valerii" and *The Marble Faun.* In *Henry James: The Conquest of London 1870-1881* (New York: J. B. Lippincott, 1962), pp. 102-103,[5] Leon Edel notes that in James's story, "a Roman count, a kind of sleepy, well-fed Donatello, marries a young American girl. In the grounds of the Valerio Villa, a statue is disinterred, much in the manner in which Hawthorne describes the digging up of a Venus, or as Mérimée recounts a similar occurrence" in *La Venus d'Ille.* However, if "the tale is thus an amalgam of Hawthorne and Mérimée, its denouement is pure James." In "*Roderick Hudson:* James's *Marble Faun*" (1970), p. 1142, Sanford E. Morovitz writes that one of "the most illuminating examples of James's use of Hawthornesque symbols occurs in the marble hand which Kenyon modeled from Hilda's." In "The Last of the Valerii," this hand reappears as Juno's missing hand, and Count Valerio adores it "exactly as Kenyon does in *The Marble Faun.*" And, in *Sensuous Pessimism* (1973), Carl Maves hears "the creak of Hawthorne's supernatural-allegorical machinery in the background" of "The Last of the Valerii":

> American purity confronts Old World "evil," a statue exerts sinister power on the heir of a tainted race: perhaps it is right to note here some regression, something of a backward glance, in James's art. Still, Hawthorne's treatment of Rome in *The Marble Faun* was not only a conspicuous precedent but an unavoidable influence. The younger author had not yet rethought the city on his own terms, and given a common American bias, many of his first impressions naturally coincided with those of a literary predecessor who . . . claimed to know Rome "better than my birth place." (34-35)[6]

The Tragic Muse

Only two people have connected *The Tragic Muse* with *The Marble Faun.* While discussing the similar types of character that both Hawthorne and James conceived, F. O. Matthiessen in *American Renaissance* (1941), pp. 296-97, observed that in his heroines Hawthorne often "stressed . . . a 'voluptuous, Oriental' taste for the gorgeous." In *The Marble Faun* he accounted for the touch of exotic splendor in Miriam's "full-blooded, almost majestic appearance . . . by the hint that she is partly Jewish. It can hardly be altogether fortuitous that James' Miriam Rooth, whose magnificent presence separates her so signally from all the other characters in *The Tragic Muse,* is similar in her beauty and her race, if not her fate, to her earlier namesake." And Alexander Cowie, in *The Rise of the American Novel* (New York: American Book, 1948), pp. 704, 853n., observed that Hawthorne's use of art as a motif in *The Marble Faun* "must have appealed to James, who occasionally worked out rather intellectualized Gothic effects in connection with portraits"—as in *The Wings of the Dove, The Tragic Muse,* and *The Sense of the Past.* Echoing Matthiessen, Cowie noted that it "is perhaps no accident that in *The Tragic Muse* the chief female character is not only given the name of Hawthorne's heroine in *The Marble Faun* (Miriam) but also has like Miriam a tincture of Jewish blood."

"Adina" and Other Works

As is indicated in the second essay, "Adina" and *The Marble Faun* were analyzed in some detail by James R. Bashore, Jr., in his dissertation, "The Villains in the Major Works of Nathaniel Hawthorne and Henry James" (University of Wisconsin, 1959), II, 115-19. Bashore finds parallels between Sam Scrope and the Spectre of the Catacombs, and between Angelo and Donatello. Both works also share "the innocence-fall theme," and James's story too has frequent "references to 'the Capuchin convent at the edge of the Alban Lake.'" However, as Bashore points out, the denouement of "Adina" is different from Hawthorne's. Carl Maves too, of course, comments on this pair (*Sensuous Pessimism,* 1973, p. 44).

Many other works by James have been marginally compared with *The Marble Faun,* as is indicated in various essays in this text. These works include *The Aspern Papers* and *The Sense of the Past* (Matthiessen, *American Renaissance,* 1941, pp. 298, 363-64 respectively); "The Great Good Place" and "Guy Domville" (Edel, *The Treacherous Years,* 1969, pp. 240-41); *The Ambassadors* (Buitenhuis, *New England Quarterly,* 32, June, 1959, p. 218); and "Daisy Miller" (Fryer, 1973, p. 151).

Chapter 6

Hawthorne's Other Works

The House of the Seven Gables

Although in chapter 5 of *Hawthorne* (1879) James called *The House of the Seven Gables* Hawthorne's "most elaborate" work, much "larger and more various than its companions, and full of all sorts of deep intentions, of interwoven threads of suggestion," he nevertheless found it less rounded and complete than *The Scarlet Letter.* It seemed to him "more like a prologue to a great novel than a great novel itself." Its "expansive quality . . . never wholly fructifies," so that one has the sense of reading "a magnificent fragment." But it is still Hawthorne's most successful attempt at creating "a picture of contemporary American life." It has "more literal actuality than the others."

James found Hawthorne's characters to be "pictures rather than persons," "types, to the author's mind, of something general, of something that is bound up with the history . . . of families and individuals." Hepzibah's picture is descriptive; it is not dramatically exhibited, and Clifford, although a more remarkable creation, is not as vividly depicted. Even Judge Pyncheon is "a picture rather than a character." Holgrave too is intended to be "a kind of national type," and his lack of traditions, his democratic stamp, and his "genial and enthusiastic view of the future" all contrast with "the desiccated prejudices and exhausted vitality" of the Pyncheons. But Hawthorne should have "painted a lusty conservative to match his strenuous radical." Evidently he did not intend to represent a struggle between an old society and a new one, but simply "the shrinkage and extinction of a family." Hawthorne mistrusted "old houses, old institutions, long lines of descent," and the whole "idea of long perpetuation and survival." In this "he was more American than many of his countrymen, who . . . have often a lurking esteem for things that show the marks of having lasted." After praising "the soft, bright, active presence of Phoebe," her relations with Hepzibah, and her influence on Clifford, James concludes that in general *The Seven Gables* "is a large and generous production . . . a great work of fiction."[1]

Although as early as 1870 William James, after reading *The Seven Gables,* had noted a "resemblance of Hawthorne's style" to Henry James's, and although Henry had expressed, in his reply, a desire "to write as good a novel one of these days (perhaps) as *The House of the Seven Gables*,"[2] very few people have compared in detail a specific work by James with *The Seven Gables.* William James did not specify which of his brother's stories resemble *The Seven Gables* in style. Twenty years later, he wrote to Henry praising *The Tragic Muse* as "a most original, wonderful, delightful and admirable production. . . . The only thing I positively find to object to in the book is the length of the chapter on Mr. Nash's portrait, which is a little too much in the Hawthornian allegorizing vein for you."[3] Probably here William had in mind Hawthorne's use of Colonel Pyncheon's portrait in *The Seven Gables.* As is indicated in the first essay, Henry James does refer to Hawthorne directly in book 8 in volume 2 of *The Tragic Muse.*

Most critics who discuss the resemblance of James's works to Hawthorne's usually refer to *The Seven Gables* only in passing. Thus T. S. Eliot in "The Hawthorne Aspect"[4] stated that "James in *Roderick Hudson* does very little better with Rome than Hawthorne [in *The Marble Faun*], and as he confesses in the later preface, rather fails with Northampton" (Dupee, *Question,* p. 131). "Was Hawthorne at all in his mind here?" Eliot wondered:

> In criticising *The House of the Seven Gables* he says "it renders, to an initiated reader, the impression of a summer afternoon in an elm-shadowed New England town," and in the preface to *Roderick Hudson* he says "what the early chapters of the book most 'render' to me to-day is not the umbrageous air of their New England town." (131n.)

While discussing Hawthorne's use of the portrait—particularly Colonel Pyncheon's in *The Seven Gables*—to analyze character and probe beneath conventional appearance, F. O. Matthiessen noted, in *American Renaissance* (New York: Oxford University Press, 1941), p. 300, that James too used this device in *The Sense of the Past.* Matthiessen further observed that "Hawthorne suggested the helplessness of [Clifford's] aesthetic temperament before the ruthless energy of [Judge Pyncheon] by saying that any conflict between them would be 'like flinging a porcelain vase, with already a crack in it, against a granite column.'" Hawthorne here, Matthiessen noted, used a "symbolic, almost Jamesian image" (327). In "James and the Plastic Arts," *Kenyon Review,* 5 (Autumn, 1943), 533-50, Matthiessen repeated that one of the many devices Hawthorne taught James was "the use of a portrait to bring out character, as Holgrave's daguerreotype pries beneath Judge Pyncheon's smooth appearance and shows his real kinship to his hard and grasping ancestor" (535). James used "this device in stories at both the beginning and the end of his career": in "A Passionate Pilgrim," and again in *The Sense of the Past.* "But one ground of James's dissatisfaction with Hawthorne was that in his hands such devices remained naked allegories."Lastly, in *Henry James: The Major Phase* (New York: Oxford University Press, 1944), p. 65, Matthiessen again discussed James's "device of using a portrait to bring out character," a device he had learned from *The Seven Gables.* In *The Wings of the Dove,* he developed it into "one of his supreme recognition scenes," where the Bronzino looks so much like Milly that she is transformed into a Renaissance princess.

In addition to James's five works mentioned above–*The Tragic Muse, Roderick Hudson,* "A Passionate Pilgrim," *The Sense of the Past,* and *The Wings of the Dove*–four others have also been tentatively related to *The Seven Gables: The Portrait of a Lady,* "The Romance of Certain Old Clothes," "De Grey: A Romance," and "Poor Richard." In "The Houses that James Built–*The Portrait of a Lady,*" *Texas Quarterly,* 1 (Winter, 1958), 176-96, Robert W. Stallman notes that the houses in *The Portrait,* like the Pyncheon house in *The Seven Gables,* "serve to interpret their inhabitants metaphorically" (181). But Stallman's other references are to *The Marble Faun.* Paul A. Newlin, in his dissertation entitled "The Uncanny in the Supernatural Short Fiction of Poe, Hawthorne and James" (University of California, Los Angeles, 1967), observes that "The Romance of Certain Old Clothes" is often considered "as being highly derivative of Hawthorne in its content and structure" because of its "emphasis upon a colonial New England setting and the involvement with a family curse" similar to Maule's curse in *The Seven Gables.* Newlin finds such a view "no compliment to Hawthorne," since in James's story "the setting in the past is not fully exploited," and since the unseen ghost "is an inartistic and unbelievable creation." "De Grey: A Romance," he observes, carries the family curse "even deeper into the Hawthorne tradition," and couples it with the theme of inherited sin. Peter Buitenhuis's comments on "The Romance of Certain Old Clothes" and *The Seven Gables* in *The Grasping Imagination: The American Writings of Henry James* (Toronto: University of Toronto Press, 1970), pp. 33-44, are similar to Newlin's, although more detailed. Buitenhuis notes that James's story "is set in one of Hawthorne's favourite milieux, colonial Massachusetts, 'toward the middle of the eighteenth century.'" The description of the scene in which Lloyd finds Viola dead "compares not unfavourably with Hawthorne's description" of Colonel Pyncheon's corpse in *The Seven Gables.* Buitenhuis points out also that when "Poor Richard" was first published, "Richard's second name was Clare. In the revision, James, apparently . . .

seeking to strike the American note more firmly, changed it to Maule, perhaps in order to recall the curse placed on the Pyncheon family" in *The Seven Gables* "as an analogy of Richard's betrayal of Severn." But Buitenhuis does not relate "Poor Richard" to *The Seven Gables* beyond that one suggestion. Lastly, in *Happy Rural Seat: The English Country House and the Literary Imagination* (New Haven, Connecticut: Yale University Press, 1972), p. 289n., Richard Gill notes that some "of the motifs that attend the house symbol in James might . . . be traced to Hawthorne's influence. The garden imagery, for instance, may have its source in the Pyncheon garden, whose Edenic attributes Hawthorne elaborately describes" in chapter 10 of *The Seven Gables.*

THE SENSE OF THE PAST

Four of James's works, however—including one already mentioned above—have been compared in some detail with *The Seven Gables: The Sense of the Past, The Bostonians, The Europeans,* and *The Spoils of Poynton.* T. S. Eliot in "The Hawthorne Aspect" (1918) observed that James's "sympathy" with Hawthorne is most felt in the last of his novels, *The Sense of the Past.* By then James had been through "a much more elaborate development than poor Hawthorne ever knew," and the fact that he nevertheless returned to Hawthorne makes more certain the genuineness of the relation (Dupee, *Question,* p. 131). Ralph Pendrel, Eliot pointed out, belongs to the same race as the Pyncheons, and if one compares James's novel with *The Seven Gables,* one finds that Hawthorne's situation,

> the "shrinkage and extinction of a family," is rather more complex, on the surface, than James's with . . . fewer character relations. But James's real situation here, to which Ralph's mounting the step is the key, as Hepzibah's opening of her shop, is a situation of different states of mind. James's situation is the shrinkage and extinction of an idea. The Pyncheon tragedy is simple; the "curse" upon the family a matter of the simplest fairy mechanics. James has taken Hawthorne's ghost sense and given it substance. (132)

At the same time he has made the tragedy much more ethereal. After noting "the Hawthorneness of the confrontation of the portrait," Eliot remarked that throughout his career James took "talents similar to Hawthorne's and made them yield far greater returns than poor Hawthorne could harvest from his granite soil."

F. O. Matthiessen, as indicated above, noted in *American Renaissance* (1941), p. 300, that "James' introduction of the likeness between Ralph Pendrel and the young man in the portrait of a century ago" is related to

Hawthorne's use of Colonel Pyncheon's portrait. Later in the book, Matthiessen observed that Hawthorne's "continual effort to suggest the symbolic equivalence . . . of human traits in different ages"—as when, in *The Seven Gables,* he saw mesmerism as a modern manifestation of the evils of witchcraft—links him to the James of *The Sense of the Past* (355). Matthiessen repeated his remarks about the use of the portrait in *The Seven Gables* and *The Sense of the Past* in his "James and the Plastic Arts" (1943), p. 535, and in *Henry James: The Major Phase* (1944), pp. 134-35.

Three other people have commented on *The Sense of the Past* and *The Seven Gables.* In *The Novels of Henry James* (New York: Hafner Publishing, 1961), pp. 487-88, 492n., Oscar Cargill rejected the relation Eliot and Matthiessen drew between these two works. "One is not inclined to see much of Hawthorne in *The Sense of the Past,*" Cargill wrote, and then went on to relate James's novel to Walpole's *The Castle of Otranto.* In "Images of Value and the Sense of the Past," *New England Quarterly,* 35 (March, 1962), 3-26, Allen Guttmann discusses, among other things, how the Pyncheon house in *The Seven Gables* "stands as a token of the Pyncheon's [evil] past." Henry James, he notes, "shared many of Hawthorne's concerns. In James we find the correlation of the house and the sense of the past—and the most labyrinthine elaboration of domestic symbolism" (15). After narrating how Pendrel returns to his inherited "old house" in England, and how, by entering the house, "Pendrel moves, magically, into the past," Guttmann contrasts Hawthorne's and James's house imagery with Howells's and Faulkner's. "James and Hawthorne," he writes, "are conservatives in that they sought a sense of the past; Faulkner . . . is much more like Howells in that he is interested not in the rediscovery but in the *creation* of social order. Ralph Pendrel and Isabel Archer and Phoebe Pyncheon *find* houses; Flem Snopes and Thomas Sutpen and Silas Lapham *build* them" (18-19). Richard Gill, in *Happy Rural Seat* (1972), p. 289n., also notes that "the device of the portrait in *The Sense of the Past* may have been suggested by the portrait of Colonel Pyncheon." But Gill is quick to point out that "mysterious portraits play their part in the Gothic fiction with which James was also highly familiar."

THE BOSTONIANS

The Bostonians and *The Seven Gables* have been related only by R. W. B. Lewis in "The Tactics of Sanctity: Hawthorne and James," *Hawthorne Centenary Essays,* edited by R. H. Pearce (Columbus, Ohio: Ohio State University Press, 1964), pp. 271-95.[5] Lewis finds the Hawthorne aspect of *The Bostonians* to be so pervasive "that James's novel seems at times to be composed largely of cunning rearrangments and inversion . . . of ingredients taken over from Hawthorne." After showing that *The Bostonians* shares with *The Scarlet Letter* "an interest in revolutionary ideas about the condition of women" (see the third essay in this text), Lewis next argues that "those ideas palpitate in *The Bostonians* within a general atmosphere of decline oddly similar to that of" *The Seven Gables.* In both *The Bostonians* and *The Seven Gables,* "almost every item participates in a pattern of diminution. The historical distance spanned in" James's novel is not as vast as that in Hawthorne's; it is at most eighty years, and

> James's impressionistic and allusive evocation of even so short a stretch of history illustrates perfectly the remark of T. S. Eliot that Hawthorne's sense of the past "exercised itself in a grip on the past itself," but that "in James it is a sense of the sense." . . . James had in particular a sense of Hawthorne's sense; and this made it possible for James to include in his own pattern of decay a much larger variety of elements than Hawthorne, and to cover a great deal more of the national landscape. (288)

Lewis finds Basil Ransom "a deliberate inversion" of Holgrave. He also observes that the spells and webs used to characterize Olive Chancellor's and Verena Tarrant's relationship carry us back "to the story of enchanted Alice Pyncheon in *The Seven Gables."* Further, he indicates that "as a dramatic construct" the scene between Ransom and Verena in Central Park (chapter 33) derives "from the long scene between Holgrave and Phoebe that extends from Ch. XII through Ch. XIV in *The Seven Gables."* Essentially, James is here "carefully revising Hawthorne":

> It is not only that all of [Ransom's] eloquence goes toward getting rid of the present in the name of the past, rather than, as with Holgrave, the other way round. It is also that Holgrave, for all his temptation to acquire "empire" over Phoebe's spirit, does have the high quality of reverence for her individuality, and releases the girl from her momentary enslavement. Ransom persists in his imperial design to the end of the . . . novel.
>
> That kind of reversal characterizes the relation consciously aimed at . . . and achieved between *The Bostonians* and the novels of Hawthorne. (293)

"There is no one in *The Bostonians,*" Lewis continues, "like Hester or Dimmesdale . . . or Holgrave, who has or acts upon a clear sense of the heart's sanctity." Lewis's conclusion is that "James, in *The Bostonians,* is exploiting Hawthorne to suggest a view opposite to Hawthorne's about the fundamental *course* of human affairs. . . . James saw the American character moving away from, not toward, a belief in the sanctity of the human heart; away from, not toward, relationships consecrated by that belief." Thus in *The Bostonians* he "made his comment upon the American scene . . . by reassembling themes and motives and devices and language from Hawthorne and then by twisting and reversing them" (295).

THE EUROPEANS

The possible relation between *The Europeans* and *The Seven Gables* was first mentioned by F. O. Matthiessen, who, in *American Renaissance* (1941), p. 293, noted that "the setting of *The Europeans* (1878) in an old house near Boston suggests more than a little of the atmosphere of *The Seven Gables*." "James' book," he continued, "is much slighter but much more fully 'done,' as in the exquisitely fresh picture of his house [in the first paragraph of chapter 2 of the novel]—the scene, like Hawthorne's, is about 1850." In his dissertation entitled "The Short Novel in Hawthorne, Melville, and James" (University of Wisconsin, 1952), pp. 256-57, Charles G. Hoffmann found it "difficult . . . to agree with F. O. Matthiessen's opinion." Although both novels are set in New England, Hoffmann observed, their tone "is entirely different. The somber, guilt-ridden atmosphere of Hawthorne's old house has little in common with the Wentworth house in Boston." The tone of *The Europeans* "is light, almost frivolous; the sobriety and seriousness that characterizes the New England moral nature is satirized rather than presented seriously." *The Europeans,* Hoffmann found, "is much closer in both theme and tone" to James's *An International Episode* "than to any of Hawthorne's works." Paul A. Newlin, however, echoes Matthiessen. In "The Development of *Roderick Hudson*: an Evaluation," *Arizona Quarterly,* 27 (Summer, 1971), 101-23, Newlin notes that one of the many "romantic traces of Hawthorne" in James's early work is "the old house setting of *The Europeans* (1878) with its *House of Seven Gables* atmosphere" (113). But the work by Hawthorne which Newlin discusses in detail is *The Marble Faun* (see the fifth essay).

THE SPOILS OF POYNTON

In addition to *The Spoils of Poynton,* Marius Bewley contrasts *The Seven Gables* with *Washington Square.* In *The Eccentric Design: Form in the Classic American Novel* (New York: Columbia University Press, 1959), pp. 175-79, Bewley terms *The Seven Gables* "a study of guilt transmitted through time, from generation to generation." The novel presents a debate between the respective claims of "the past, inherited wealth, and aristocratic status," and those of the present, and "of democratic equality, both financial and social." However, "the debate does not come off successfully." This is because when "he was dealing with ideas, Hawthorne was inferior. His mind lacked the intellectual rigor, consistency, and logical courage of Cooper's," for example. The conflict in attitudes, the tension between past and present, "is nowhere absorbed into a more comprehensive viewpoint." In *The Spoils of Poynton,* James too built up "an attitude around the same theme, but with a subtle complexity" which is absent in *The Seven Gables.* Mrs. Gereth's house becomes a symbol of what can happen when the values of the past are substitued for human values. But the whole matter is stated from several conflicting points of view. In *The Seven Gables,* by contrast, the "sudden transition which occurs in Holgrave's character in the final chapter" is heavy and embarrasing. Unlike Hawthorne, James "retained a wonderful control of tone." In *Washington Square,* for example, this tone is very effective in Arthur Townsend's speech about "the virtues of the perennial New York habit of tearing down the city every few years for the sake of putting up something equally unsure of itself." The playful irony that permeates Townsend's speech in chapter 5 of the novel is itself a "commentary on this exhibition of the tension between past and present in the American mind." But Townsend is no more of a featherbrain than the solemn Holgrave whom Hawthorne takes so seriously. This kind of tension, Bewley concludes, can be resolved in art only in terms of finely controlled tone; it "is not amenable to the sort of intellectual solemnity into which Hawthorne falls so disastrously."

Other Works

James's evaluation of Hawthorne's shorter works in chapters 2 and 3 of *Hawthorne* is not always consistent. Although he praises the originality and the "infinite grace and charm" of such "masterpeices" as "Roger Malvin's Burial," "Rappaccini's Daughter," and "Young Goodman Brown," for example, and terms them "glimpses of a great field, of the whole deep mystery of man's soul and conscience," he nevertheless belittles them as "small things," "little sketches," "such trifles" of which it "would be a mistake to insist too much upon." He divided these works into three groups: "the stories of fantasy and allegory," like "The Great Carbuncle"; "the little tales of New England history," like "The Maypole of Merrymount"; and the "sketches of actual scenes and of the objects and manners about him," like "A Rill from the Town Pump." James had read all these works many times and admired them greatly.

James was amazed by Hawthorne's preoccupation with the Puritans' strong sense of sin, which, James noted, Hawthorne tried to transmute into the very substance of his art. What is most curious, James observed, is "this almost exclusively *imported* character of the sense of sin in Hawthorne's mind; it seems to exist there merely for an artistic or literary purpose." His relation to the Puritan conscience was not moral; it was intellectual, and he treated it objectively. He took liberties and played tricks with its elements and judged them "from the poetic and aesthetic point of view."

James found some of Hawthorne's stories more fanciful than imaginative, and the more metaphysical ones allegorical, a mode which, to James, "is quite one of the lighter exercises of the imagination," and one "apt to spoil two good things—a story and a moral, a meaning and a form." In such stories as "The Snow-Image" and "Dr. Heidegger's Experiment," one is struck with "the ingenuity and felicity of Hawthorne's analogies and correspondences," but in others like "The Birthmark" and "The Bosom Serpent," one is conscious of "something stiff and mechanical, slightly incongruous." Nevertheless, they are all charming, "and their interest is moral . . . . The fine thing in Hawthorne is that he cared for the deeper psychology, and that, in his own way, he tried to become familiar with it." This is what constitutes the originality of his tales. He so easily and regularly dwells "in the moral, psychological realm." James praised also Hawthorne's historical sketches, which are "full of a vivid and delightful sense of the New England past." "Hawthorne was at home in the early New England history," James wrote. Hungry for the picturesque, which he could not find around him, he turned back into the past and converted "the somewhat meagre and angular facts of the colonial period . . . into impressive legends and pictures."

James's first consideration of Hawthorne's European experiences was in his review of the *French and Italian Note-Books* in the *Nation,* 14 (March 14, 1872), 172-73, which was summarized in the first essay. In chapter 6 of *Hawthorne,* he once again considers Hawthorne's years in Europe, and the works which resulted from this experience. He points out that when Hawthorne came to Europe, he was almost fifty years old, and this partly accounts for the rigidity of point of view in his five volumes of notebooks. Hawthorne's experience, James explains, had always been narrow. His fifty years had been spent largely in small American towns, and he had led exclusively "a village life." He was, in short, "exquisitely and consistently provincial." The *Note-Books* are provincial, but although this is slightly true of the sketches in *Our Old Home,* the author's "being remotely outside of everything he describes" gives them an added significance. James believed that Hawthorne greatly enjoyed his residence in England. As consul in Liverpool, he probably met more Americans than he had ever done at home, and "Consular Experiences" in *Our Old Home* is indicative of how much material he might have found, as a novelist, in his office as consul. James once again seems embarrassed to praise *Our Old Home.* Hawthorne's touch is light, fine, felicitous, and admirable, although his judgement is not always sound, for it often rests on narrow observation. His perception is keen and excellent, although it is frequently partial and incomplete. The book has especially one serious defect: "It is the work of an outsider, of a stranger, of a man who remains to the end a mere spectator . . . and always lacks the final initiation into the manners and nature" of the people he describes. Hawthorne mistrusted and was always suspicious of the society which surrounded him, but since he came to England late in life, with his habits, tastes and opinions already formed, it is not surprising that he remained thus detached and critical. Nevertheless, he was a singularly intelligent and discriminating individual, and *Our Old Home* contains numerous pages of his best writing.

In chapter 7 of *Hawthorne,* James reiterated that although *Our Old Home* has less value than Hawthorne's fiction, "the writing is singularly good, and it is well to remember . . . that it was produced at a time [that is, during the Civil War] when it was painfully hard for a man of Hawthorne's cast of mind to fix his attention." Of *The Dolliver Romance,* James said it is too brief to elicit a detailed evaluation. Nevertheless, "the few pages which have been given to the world contain a charming picture of an old man and a child." "*Septimus Felton,* as it stands, with its . . . mere allusiveness and slightness of treatment, gives us but a very partial measure of Hawthorne's full intention." In general, James felt "the idea and intention of the book" were rather feeble, and even if Hawthorne had completed it, "it would have occupied a very different place in the public esteem from the writer's masterpieces."

There has not been much detailed discussion of the influence on James of Hawthorne's shorter fiction. Most of the comments, like those on the influence of *The Seven Gables,* have not been elaborated upon. As indicated in the second essay, Rebecca West in *Henry James* (New York: Henry Holt, 1916), pp. 24-26, found little substance in James's "first stories that appeared in *The Atlantic Monthly* and *The Galaxy* . . . . Where there is any richness of effect, as in *The Romance of Certain Old Clothes,* it comes from the influence of Nathaniel Hawthorne." "The plot of *The Passionate Pilgrim*," West continued, "with its American who comes to England to claim a cousin's estate . . . is very clumsy Hawthorne, but in those days Mr. James could not draw normal events and he had to have some medium for expressing his wealth of feeling about England."

Fred Lewis Patte, in *The Development of the American Short Story* (1923; reprinted New York: Biblo and Tanner, 1966), pp. 199-200, noted that the early James was greatly influenced by Hawthorne. He even wrote "in the Hawthorne manner with Hawthorne materials, as in "The Romance of Certain Old Clothes' and 'De Grey: A Romance,' but not for long," for Hawthorne was a romancer and James a realist. Hawthorne, "with his problems of New England Puritanism and his constant dwelling upon the deeper concerns of the moral and the religious, had little in common with the later James." James's native bent was critical and scientific, but his early environment and training "had made him romantic. *He* was Benvolio," living in two different chambers. "Benvolio" "is allegory and it savors of Hawthorne, but it reveals the soul of Henry James." As he mastered his art, he progressively "turned away from the garden of romance and centered his attention . . . upon real life, real men and women living their real lives." But just as Hawthorne had been solitary and detached, James too viewed life from his solitary window. "He studied life without contacts with life and recorded what he saw, himself . . . totally detached from his material."

According to Cornelia Pulsifer Kelley in *The Early Development of Henry James* (Urbana: University of Illinois Press, 1930), pp. 73-82, 252-55, Howells was largely responsible for "the entrance of romantic elements in James's work." James had considered romanticism "not quite the thing" for a serious artist, but when Howells, who acclaimed romanticism and praised Hawthorne, became assistant editor of *Atlantic Monthly* in 1866, James tried "to supply his editor-friend with a story ['The Romance of Certain Old Clothes'] as much as possible like Hawthorne's without being a direct imitation. He took his own theme, but went back to the past" to conjure up the setting and the scenes. Kelley also observed that although in *Hawthorne* James called allegory one of the lighter exercises of the imagination, he himself had used it before 1879, and was to use it again, especially in the stories of the 1890's which deal with authors and authorship. However, with James "allegory, especially as he used it later, was never over prominent as with Hawthorne. It was often hidden deeply." Similarly, although he occasionally returned to romanticism, his emphasis was different; "in such things as his ghost stories, his interest was in the psychological effect of imagination upon his characters rather than in any romantic aspects of his plots."

Carl Van Doren in *The American Novel* (New York: Macmillan, 1931) found that many of the short stories James excluded from the New York Edition of his works "betray a strong influence of Hawthorne":

> *The Romance of Certain Old Clothes,* with its dusky scene laid in eighteenth-century America and its ghostly, inconclusive conclusion; *De Grey: A Romance,* the study of an ancestral curse dubiously inherited by a New York family from its European forebears; and *The Last of the Valerii,* wherein a young Roman nobleman digs up a statue of Venus from his garden and fatally reverts to the worship of her pagan loveliness. No such dominant magic as Hawthorne's, however, quite invests these tales; Henry James belongs to a different universe, with a different heaven and hell. Nor could he even as well as the Hawthorne of *The Seven Vagabonds,* for instance, succeed with little adventures into the picaresque like *Professor Fargo,* with its tawdry traveling showmen. (192)

Van Doren noted also that "*The Passionate Pilgrim* carries an overwrought American to England to claim a fortune, as Hawthorne's *Ancestral Footstep* had done. The plot is nearly as romantic as Hawthorne would have made it; the chief concern is the sensation of the ardent traveler in the presence of that charm which maddens, in Henry James, the 'famished race'" (193).[6] The same concern is found in *Roderick Hudson,* and although Rowland Mallet "does not speak in the first person, [he] renders the narrative something the same service that Miles Coverdale renders in *The Blithedale Romance"* (194).

C. Hartley Grattan's observations in *The Three Jameses* (New York: Longmans, Green, 1932), pp. 232-33, are similar to Kelley's. Grattan explains that at the beginning of his writing career James was faced with two choices: to become a romancer or a realist. "The principal American influence upon him was Hawthorne and this turned him toward romance," but his "natural drive was toward realism and conscience, analysis and form." George Sand too was an early influence; so was Howells, who had not yet turned to realism. "It was from Howells that encouragement came to write romances and James continued his debate by writing romances for *The Atlantic* and realistic stories for . . . *The Galaxy.*" In *New England: Indian Summer* (1940; reprinted New York: E.P. Dutton, 1965), pp. 253-54, Van Wyck Brooks emphasizes the influence of French writers on James. He finds that the family curse in such stories as "Poor Richard," "De Grey," "Crawford's Consistency," and "Eugene Pickering" "is very different in accent from Hawthorne's curse, the good old convincing curse of Salem. It is a Frenchified curse, as the young men are Frenchified." But James tried also to follow "the only American model that he felt as germane," and the influence of Hawthorne can be felt in such stories as "The Last of the Valerii," "The Romance of Certain Old Clothes," "A Passionate Pilgrim," and "The Madonna of the Future."

Carl Van Doren had noted a similarity between "A Passionate Pilgrim" and *The Ancestral Footstep.* F.O. Matthiessen in *American Renaissance* (1941) observed that the germ of *The Ancestral Footstep,* "the return of an American to rediscover the older European life, bears a curious resemblance to that of . . . *The Sense of the Past*" (268). Hawthorne often tried "to suggest the symbolic equivalence . . . of human traits in different ages." He always sensed "the past in the present"; this was especially true of his experiences in Italy. "But as an American he resented the massiveness of antiquity that made his moment seem less real in Rome than it did elsewhere. This attitude towards Europe was operating" in *The Ancestral Footstep,* where the American hero's conclusion is: "'Let the past alone.' This is a conclusion more incisive than what would probably have emerged from . . . *The Sense of the Past,* where what is uppermost . . . is the contrast between the vulgar vitality of the London Midmores and the finer consciousness . . . in their American descendant of a century later" (355). Matthiessen also observed that some of James's early stories follow very closely "Hawthorne's model. Indeed, you can hardly see anything else in 'The Romance of Certain Old Clothes'" (292). In chapter 3 of *Hawthorne,* James had said that the charm of Hawthorne's allegories is that they are glimpses of "the whole deep mystery of man's soul and conscience. They are moral, and their interest is moral." How inwardly they had spoken to James, Matthiessen wrote, "is attested by the theme of 'The Beast in the Jungle' (1903), whose hero is finally crushed by realizing that he is 'to have been the one man in the world to whom nothing whatever was to happen.' That statement could very well have come from Hawthorne's notebook" (295). In *Henry James: The Major Phase* (1944), pp. 70-71, Matthiessen once again indicated that in several of James's "earlier stories, as in *The Romance of Certain Old Clothes* and *Benvolio,* he had depended on allegory in the manner of Hawthorne." But as he mastered "the skills of realism, he grew dissatisfied with allegory's obvious devices; and yet, particularly towards the end of his career, realistic details had become merely the covering for a content that was far from realistic." "A Round of Visits," for example, did not start "from a concrete anecdote, but as a Hawthornesque abstraction" (133).[7] While analyzing James's revisions in *The Portrait of a Lady,* Matthiessen discussed also James's

> conception of the discipline of suffering. It is notable that his kinship here to Hawthorne becomes far more palpable in the final version. Take the instance when, at the time of Ralph's death, Isabel realizes how Mrs. Touchett has missed the essence of life by her inability to feel. . . . The view of suffering adumbrated [in chapter 54 of the novel], even the phrasing, recalls Hawthorne's *The Christmas Banquet,* where the most miserable fate is that of the man whose inability to feel bars him out even from the common bond of woe. (183-84)[8]

Matthiessen went on to show how the "common bond of sin, so central to Hawthorne's thought, was also accentuated [in *The Portrait*] through James' retouching" (184).

Matthiessen had related *The Sense of the Past* to *The Ancestral Footstep;* Marius Bewley related James's novel to *Dr. Grimshawe's Secret.* In "The American Problem" in *The Complex Fate: Hawthorne, Henry James and Some Other American Writers* (New York: Chatto and Windus, 1952), pp. 55-78,[9] Bewley argued that in *Dr. Grimshawe's Secret* what Hawthorne suggested as a resolution of the conflict between Europe and America was a "fusion" that would ultimately be intolerable. As Hawthorne put it: the English character "must assimilate itself to the [American], if there is to be any union." But Hawthorne offered, "to qualify this, pre-Jamesian hints of the possibilities of the international marriage as a more workable solution." If one reads *Dr. Grimshawe's Secret* together with *The Sense of the Past,* one notices a striking "similarity between the preoccupations of the two men. On the basis of these studies alone, one might say that Hawthorne's interests had shifted on to grounds from which only James's art could provide the saving issue. Hawthorne had raised problems that were technically beyond his solution, but they lead American literature directly into the work of Henry James." (*Complex Fate,* pp. 69-70n.)[10]

Matthiessen had further related "The Beast in the Jungle" to Hawthorne in general; Allen Tate related James's story specifically to "Egotism" and "Young Goodman Brown." In "Three Commentaries: Poe, James, and Joyce," *Sewanee Review,* 58 (Winter, 1950), 1-15, Tate saw "The Beast in the Jungle" as a study of "the isolation and frustration of personality," a subject that goes back to Hawthorne in "Egotism" and "Young Goodman Brown" (5). Hawthorne was the first American writer "who was conscious of the failure of modern man to realize his full capacity for moral growth." In an August 1837 entry in *American Note-Books*—some sixty years before James's story was written—Hawthorne actually stated the theme of "The Beast in the Jungle":

> A young man and girl meet together, each in search of a person to be known by some particular sign. They watch and wait a great while for that person to pass. At last some casual circumstance discloses that each is the one that the other is waiting for. Moral—that what we need for our happiness is often close at hand, if we knew but how to seek for it. —*Passages from the American Note-Books* (1868; reprinted Boston: Houghton Mifflin, 1910), p. 86.

After considering the structure of James's story, its point of view, and the characterization, Tate concluded that in "the long run its effect is that of tone, even of lyric meditation; and it is closer to the method of Hawthorne than one might at a glance suppose; for in the last scene it is very nearly allegory" (Tate, pp. 9-10).

Four other people have commented briefly on the influence on James of Hawthorne's shorter fiction, three of them very briefly indeed: Oscar Cargill in *The Novels of Henry James* (1961), p. 33n., noted that the situation of Owen Warland in "The Artist of the Beautiful" suggests that of Roderick Hudson in Northampton; Quentin Anderson in his introduction to James's *Hawthorne* (1962; reprinted New York: Collier Books, 1966), pp. 7-12, called Hawthorne the "man who had been the strongest discernible influence in [James's] early fiction." Even in "Benvolio," Anderson observed, "James was laying the Hawthorne ghost in his own work—rather consciously ridding himself of his baggage of Hawthorne devices and attitudes." And in his dissertation entitled "The Manipulation Theme in the Works of Nathaniel Hawthorne and Henry James" (University of South Carolina, 1973), pp. 59-69, Gaillard F. Waterfall noted that in "The Author of Beltraffio," as in "The Gentle Boy," it is Dolcino, the child, "who suffers and dies as a result of the parents' radical beliefs and behavior."

Laurence B. Holland's comments are less brief. In the chapter on *The Portrait of a Lady* in *The Expense of Vision: Essays on the Craft of Henry James* (Princeton, New Jersey: Princeton University Press, 1964), Holland discusses the American writers' obsession with the "movement of the plot which shifts the ambitions and opportunities for experience from one generation to another." Frequently, the American writer "sharpens the distinctions among the generations even when cultivating the connections among them" (19). "There is in American literature," Holland observes, "one image of this disturbed, this labored concern for history which is . . . grotesque":

> "the charming picture," as James called it, in Hawthorne's *The Dolliver Romance,* of a great-grandfather . . . cut off from "the entire confraternity of persons whom he once loved" and unable to follow them in death because he is held back by the clutched "baby-fingers" of his three-year-old great-granddaughter. The girl's name, Pansy, is echoed in *The Portrait.* More enchanting in its juxtaposition of past, present, and future is a description that is echoed in the *Portrait*'s opening setting in the "perfect middle of a splendid summer afternoon," the description of what Hawthorne found to be a typically English summer day with "positively no beginning and no end," where "Tomorrow is born before Yesterday is dead. They exist together in a golden twilight where the decrepit old day dimly discerns the face of the ominous infant; and you, though a mere mortal, may simultaneously touch them both, with one finger of recollection and another of prophecy." . . .
>
> James quoted this description admiringly and referred to "the charming picture of the old man and child" in the critical work on Hawthorne which he published . . . the year before he began work in earnest on the *Portrait.* (20)

Hawthorne's description of an English summer day occurs in "A London Suburb," *Atlantic Monthly,* 11 (March, 1863), 306-21, reprinted in *Our Old Home* (1863; reprinted Columbus: Ohio State University Press, 1970), pp. 213-42. James quoted the passage in chapter 6 of *Hawthorne;* his remark about *The Dolliver Romance* appears in chapter 7. Holland's passage quoted above contains a few minor inaccuracies: James refers to "*a* charming picture of *an* old man and *a* child"; Hawthorne's "Tomorrow is born before *its* Yesterday is dead" (emphases mine). And, of course, Hawthorne's child is called *Pansie;* James's, Pansy.

These, then, are some of Hawthorne's other works which have been marginally compared with James's: *The Ancestral Footstep* with "A Passionate Pilgrim," *Roderick Hudson,* and *The Sense of the Past;* "The Christmas Banquet" with *The Portrait* and "The Beast in the Jungle"; *Dr. Grimshawe's Secret* with *The Awkward Age* and *The Sense of the Past;* "The Artist of the Beautiful" with *Roderick Hudson;* "The Gentle Boy" with "The Author of Beltraffio"; and *The Dolliver Romance* with *The Portrait.* Many othe works by James, of course, have been related to Hawthorne *in general:* "Benvolio," "The Madonna of the Future," "The Romance of Certain Old Clothes." These and others have been indicated in the second essay and in this one. Eight other works by Hawthorne, however, which have been compared with James's in more detail than the above, are reviewed in the next section.

"Rappaccini's Daughter"

THE TURN OF THE SCREW

Four people have written on *The Turn of the Screw* and "Rappaccini's Daughter." In "Giovanni and the Governess," *American Scholar,* 37 (Autumn, 1968), 655-78, Charles Thomas Samuels notes many parallels between James's tale and "Rappaccini's Daughter." Each tale "concerns a young impressionable provincial away from home for the first time": Giovanni in Hawthorne; the governess in James. In each tale the hero finds himself amidst rich, Edenic, and sinister surroundings. And in both tales evil "has transformed and blighted innocence": that of Beatrice in Hawthorne, and that of Miles and Flora in James. "Determined to rescue innocence, both Giovanni and the governess attempt to vanquish evil. Giovanni poisons Beatrice," and the governess causes Miles's death. The meaning of Hawthorne's story, Samuels argues, adumbrates the meaning of James's. Hawthorne's "art, so different in style, provided James with a classic example of oblique expression demanding the reader's rapt scrutiny." The changes he made on the theme of Hawthorne's story gave his own tale a power to fascinate that Hawthorne's tale does not possess. First, he "gave earthliness to Hawthorne's theme by grounding it in the ordinary":

> From Hawthorne's vague, exotic Padua with its luxuriant garden and ceremonial Italians speaking archaisms . . . James moves to an English country house whose terrors . . . [are] domesticated by James's absolute mastery of colloquial speech and English mannerism. Whereas . . . Hawthorne could not keep from stating his ideas, James hides behind a mask so that the reader is forced to fear and interpret. And whereas Hawthorne depicts evil as a potion and some

> poisonous blooms, James knew that truly to appall evil must be blank. (660)

James gave his story a natural frame, left his terrors vague, removed himself from the action, and, finally, quite unlike Hawthorne, he made "the victim of good and evil not a young, articulate girl but younger, sheltered children":

> Beatrice confesses her evil as she proclaims her innocence, thereby indicating both Rappaccini's pride and Giovanni's prurience. Miles and Flora proclaim nothing, so that readers have seen them as vessels of ghostly wickedness cracked inadvertently despite the governess' good intentions, or as innocent victims of her delusionary fears. When we recall Hawthorne's parallel, however, the story argues against both notorious views.
>
> Its central character is more quickly and pointedly defined than he is in Hawthorne. Like Giovanni sighing "heavily" as he looks round the room whose former occupant "had been pictured by Dante . . . [in] his Inferno," the governess "had expected, or had dreaded, something . . . melancholy" at Bly. (660)

In his characterization of the governess James, like Hawthorne, uses "self-examination to suggest egotism." She is proud, conceited, and has a childish imagination.

On the controversy over James's ghosts, Samuels's position is that the ghosts at Bly "are no less real than Rappaccini's poisonous plants." What they let the governess prove is "the lesson of Giovanni: that good, like evil, is an abstraction threatening the shaded substance of humanity," and what is revealed by her "ruthless pursuit of indivisible virtue is the doubleness of her own nature. For her, as for Giovanni, allurements are simultaneously snares." At the beginning, for example, "she awaits Miles's return from school with . . . the same frightened longing with which Giovanni pursued" Beatrice. And, just as Giovanni pursues Beatrice with a mixture of revulsion and desire, so does she pursue "the ghosts with a mixture of enmity and pleasure." Samuels continues:

> Like Rappaccini and Giovanni, the ghosts and the governess fight to possess the life that lies between them. Like Rappaccini, the ghosts seek to give their charges the knowledge and power belonging to evil, while the governess, like Giovanni, wishes to claim them for good. But she is no less exploitive than the ghosts and far more deadly. Like Giovanni's, her story speaks an awful irony: the means of virtue are indistinguishable from those of vice when virtue declares itself inexorable. (666)

In both stories, "ordinary human virtue is insufficient, and its relentless pursuit is, ironically, a vice." By reading James's tale with Hawthorne in mind, "we exit from the notorious controversy that has surrounded" the story and "can insist that the governess is essentially flawed without having to judge her an hallucinating neurotic."

Samuels finds, however, that the Hawthorne parallel fails to answer a number of serious questions raised by James's text. In the prologue, James prepares the reader "for a creepy horror story." Soon after that, however, the focus shifts from horror to love. One is tempted to believe that James imitated "Rappaccini's Daughter" as much as he did because he wished to prepare us for a tale of love. But the parallel does not lead to that extreme. "The governess, like Giovanni, lacks measure and compassion, but her involvement with the children, unlike his with Beatrice, is in no literal sense erotic." What the Hawthorne parallel does is to account "for the governess' disease as her virtue's dark underside." More serious problems are revealed by a scrutiny of the language and form of James's story. And it is here that "the Hawthorne parallel is really instructive. Because the stories are so similar, their differences are revealing." The first of these is James's use of the first person narrative, which Hawthorne seldom used. And when he did, as in *The Blithedale Romance,* he laid himself open to questions similar to those raised by *The Turn of the Screw.* If James, "mindful of Hawthorne's error, played the detached and . . . hostile narrator in *The Bostonians* to clarify his intentions," why did he revert to first person narrative in *The Turn of the Screw*? (672)

According to Samuels, another difference between James's story and Hawthorne's "is the difference between Mrs. Grose and Baglioni." Although they both occupy similar confidential roles, "Baglioni encourages, even initiates, Giovanni's fears, while Mrs. Grose, with great reluctance," merely confirms the governess' surmises. And since Baglioni's motives are suspicious, he merely "increases our sense that Giovanni is both premature and overzealous in his doubts." Mrs. Grose, however, "works rather to suggest that the governess will browbeat anyone . . . [who] can be made to feed her suppositions." Furthermore, "what little corroboration she provides for the governess' theories is overwhelmed by the new doubts she raises about the governess' investigative methods." The example of Baglioni, says Samuels, "indicates that James needn't have so conceived Mrs. Grose; that he did suggests either that the story . . . has not theme or that he did not quite know what its theme was." The latter possibility is made especially plausible when one compares the use of ambiguity in each tale. "In Hawthorne, ambiguity is finite and . . . temporary. He teases the question of Beatrice's evil only long enough to establish the haste and arbitrariness with which Giovanni forms an answer." By the story's end we know just how evil Beatrice is, and we easily "shift our attention to the moral, which is not ambiguous at all." Hawthorne's ambiguity, in short, "is a means toward *gradually* unfolding meaning." At the end of James's tale, however, the question of Miles's and Flora's evil is still open. "Since we cannot know certainly that they are tainted, we cannot estimate the degree to which the governess' behavior was justified." What all this reveals is this:

> When James is creating idiom, gesture and milieu . . . he is immeasurably superior to Hawthorne, who either could not or would not so naturalize the surface. But in expressing the meaning of what he so finely creates, although his meanings are frequently Hawthornesque, they are seldom presented with Hawthorne's firmness and comprehension. His ambiguity is an evasion of final statement. . . .
>
> Hawthorne raises questions in the manner of a man who knows the answers. . . . Mysterious as he can be, he usually baits his hook with riddles to catch paradoxes. James, on the other hand, frequently seems so overwhelmed by his questions as to be writing to gain time. (674)

Thus he hides "behind narrative masks, ambiguous finales and impersonal dramaturgy." He found it difficult to make moral judgements, "although he yearned for them." We cannot finally say whether the governess is heroic or arrogant, "because James himself could not tell us." He was, metaphysically, a relativist.

What relevance the last section of Samuels's essay has to "Giovanni and the Governess" is hard to find. He writes of "the myth of Henry James," "the tone of James criticism," "all the indiscriminate idolatry"—and then curiously concludes his essay thus:

> The truth is that James is a greater writer because he is a poorer one than we have been told. . . . Only when you begin to understand the number of his confusions can you measure the scope of his achievement. . . . For each problem there is a success and many failures. Yet we are told that James seldom failed.
>
> The standard James, the James who . . . wrote about his vision so lucidly as to damn as irrelevant any further questioning—this James is a foolish joke. James suffered his perceptions and did not always master them. His *oeuvre* is not the edifice that . . . he tried to sell as real estate. His house of fiction is cracked. Some rooms have faulty heating, others were drawn to faulty plans; some have tilting floors, and the plumbing leaks.
>
> It isn't a house at all. We have taken James's word for it and have lost its reality. We have tried to live in it and have lost our taste. . . . James's most popular work can have no meaning and . . . half its power is the way it drives us mad. (678)

What motivates this vengeance is hard to find. It seems irresponsible to make such supercharged allegations, and then apply them to James's fiction *in general,* when one has examined only a single work by the author. These charges may be justifiable as a conclusion to a general study of James's fiction, but not as a conclusion to "Giovanni and the Governess." But then, as Matthiessen remarked in *American Renaissance* (1941), p. 362, "James is always easier to ridicule than to understand."

Another comparison of *The Turn of the Screw* with "Rappaccini's Daughter" appears in Hans-Joachim Lang's "How Ambiguous is Hawthorne," *Geist Einer Freien Gesellschaft* (Heidelberg: Quelle and Meyer, 1962), pp. 195-220. Lang analyzes five of Hawthorne's stories: "Young Goodman Brown," "The Minister's Black Veil," "The Wives of the Dead," "The Birthmark," and "Rappaccini's Daughter." He strongly objects to those critics who maintain that the theme of "Rappaccini's Daughter" is "'the dual nature of humanity', 'man's radically mixed, his good-and-evil being' . . . pronouncements that remind us of what has been said about the children in 'The Turn of the Screw', who are in Beatrice's position in the garden at Bly" (214). Lang agrees with Nathan B. Fagin (see below) that it is not Freud, but Hawthorne, who furnishes a more likely clue to the interpretation of James's tale. But he feels that Fagin "misunderstands the [Hawthorne] tradition." Lang's own interpretation of "Rappaccini's Daughter," however, is not radically different from many others. Beatrice, he argues, is not ambiguous; "she is ambivalent." And the story has no ethical ambiguity whatsoever. Giovanni, an average man and a drifter, meets an angel, Beatrice, but does not know how to live with her. He distrusts her, mistakes the physical for the spiritual, "sees sin where it is not, and does not see it where it is (in himself)." His vision of the world is colored by the peculiar atmosphere of Rappaccini's garden, and the upshot of his doings is Beatrice's death. But before she dies she condemns him, expatiates on her own worth, and becomes "slightly insufferable thereby" (219).

To make his point clearer, Lang turns to *The Turn of the Screw.* "The children are innocent, just as Hawthorne's women are" in four of the above five stories. "The governess has a gloomy vision, such as Hawthorne's heroes have; but James does not let her down. It is a story about 'seeing ghosts'—and going to them for knowledge." The identification of Peter Quint by Mrs. Grose—the stumbling block to many interpretations—"will bother us less once we know how Hawthorne, too, e.g. in 'The Wives of the Dead,' made it impossible to separate the artfully mixed planes of reality and dream." The physical details in these stories may be deceptive, and

> James called "The Turn of the Screw" an "irresponsible little fiction" just for that. He had possibly reread Hawthorne when he wrote "The Turn of the Screw"; anyway, he had just published an

> essay on Hawthorne in 1879, and in his later preface he said his demons were "as loosely constructed as those of the old trials of witchcraft." From the traumatic experience of the witchcraft trials in 1692 over the witch-judge's descendant to James's "irresponsible little fiction" there is a chain of events and causations no link of which can be neglected. Of the three–the trials, Hawthorne and James–Hawthorne, with his firm sense of values, was the least ambiguous. (220)

Lang's conclusion is that despite James's "fantastic" statements in his "amazing and exasperating" introduction to the Hawthorne section in Warner's *Library* (see the first essay in this text), he consciously imitated Hawthorne's technique when writing *The Turn of the Screw.*

In "Another Reading of *The Turn of the Screw,*" *Modern Language Notes,* 56 (March, 1941), 196-202, Nathan Bryllion Fagin calls James's tale "a simple allegory of the type which fascinated Hawthorne." But James considered allegory "one of the lighter exercises of the imagination," and he himself "never valued *The Turn of the Screw* higher than as 'one of the lighter exercises of the imagination.'" But he praised Hawthorne's preoccupation with sin, "this heavy moral burden" which seems to exist in the romancer's mind "merely for an artistic or literary purpose." "In simple terms," Fagin states, *The Turn of the Screw* "is an allegory which dramatizes the conflict between Good and Evil." All the action and characters in this story are "reminiscent of Hawthorne, of 'Young Goodman Brown' and 'Rappaccini's Daughter.'" "The purposes for which Quint seeks to meet little Miles are the same old purposes for which the Devil met Young Goodman Brown in the woods near Salem. And little Flora is another Beatrice Rappaccini, outwardly marvellously beautiful, but inwardly corrupted by the poison of evil." As the governess battles for the souls of her charges, it is "almost as if Hawthorne's Salem ancestors were writing about little Flora: 'She was not at these times a child, but an old, old woman.'" In the end the Agent of Good almost succeeds, but little Miles dies, "like Beatrice Rappaccini, exhausted by the ordeal." He is probably "too corrupted to live without evil," just like Georgiana in "The Birthmark."

The first and slightest correlation of *The Turn of the Screw* with "Rappaccini's Daughter" was by Henry A. Beers while he was commenting on the various parallel interpretations of Hawthorne's tale. "The lure of the symbolic and the marvellous tempted Hawthorne constantly to the brink of the supernatural," Beers wrote in *Four Americans* (1919; reprinted Freeport, New York: Books for Libraries, 1968), p. 44. But Hawthorne's old-fashioned ghost "is too robust an apparition for modern credulity"; the modern ghost is rather a "clot on the brain," just a suspicion of evil presences, as in James's ghosts in *The Turn of the Screw.* However, Hawthorne too was just as ambiguous. "His apparently preternatural phenomena always admit of a natural explanation": the water of Maule's well in *The Seven Gables,* for example, or the furry, leaf-shaped ears of Donatello in *The Marble Faun.*

Washington Square

The relation of *Washington Square* to "Rappaccini's Daughter" was first suggested by Gerald Willen in his preface to James's novel. Willen observed that one of the critical issues in *Washington Square* which might be "profitably explored is the Puritanism represented by Dr. Sloper and threatened by Morris." "Somewhat related to the question of Puritanism," he continued,

> is the extent to which James might have been influenced in the rendering of the father-daughter relationship by "Rappaccini's Daughter." (James's *Hawthorne* appeared in 1879, the year he wrote *Washington Square*.) If there is, indeed, a connection between Hawthorne's short story and James's novel, an extremely interesting comparison of the father(scientist)-daughter-suitor relationships may be drawn.[11]

Robert Emmet Long's "James's *Washington Square:* The Hawthorne Relation," *New England Quarterly,* 46 (December, 1973), 573-90, explores this very connection between Hawthorne's story and James's novel. Long points out that the *donnee* of *Washington Square* was furnished by Frances Anne Kemble, and that James's treatment of Mrs. Kemble's story "was almost certainly indebted to Balzac": there are many similarities between *Washington Square* and *Eugenie Grandet.* But while James "admired Balzac's skill, he placed himself in another tradition—with novelists such as Eliot and Hawthorne, who 'care for moral questions' and 'are haunted by a moral ideal.'" And although he complained of "the lack of 'paraphernalia' which his New World setting in *Washington Square* imposed," he nevertheless "found American sources from which to draw . . . in Hawthorne and the convention of the gothic tale." Long too notes that James's *Hawthorne* was completed "just before he began to write *Washington Square*." And in this biography James picked "Rappaccini's Daughter" and "Young Goodman Brown" as perhaps the best of Hawthorne's "stories of fantasy and allegory." "Rappaccini's Daughter," Long writes, "belongs to a distinctive mode of Hawthorne's gothicism; its dominant character, the doctor and scientific investigator, overwhelmingly proud of intellect, who cruelly destroys the soul of his daughter, is a recurring figure in Hawthorne." This character type "is developed most richly in 'Rappaccini's Daughter,' which in turn bears upon *Washington Square*." Each of these tales has "a triangle of forces, with the heroine caught between her father and lover," who consciously use her for their purposes.

Catherine and Beatrice are not identical twins, but they are similar. They are both violated by the figures who surround them. Beatrice is betrayed by her father, by Giovanni, and by Dr. Baglioni. Although Catherine does not perish like Beatrice, at the end of the novel "her life faces in death's direction." Mrs. Penniman uses her to indulge in a vicarious romance with Townsend, and both Dr. Sloper and Townsend deny her any inner being or self. Dr. Sloper and Dr. Rappaccini are also similar. Both are "men of science," but in their thwarted natures "egotism and pride of mind have replaced their capacity for love." Rappaccini uses his daughter for a scientific investigation in which he is figured as God, and Dr. Sloper "too uses his daughter for an experiment to gratify his own egotism." And in the end, Dr. Sloper's ingenuity is as futile as Rappaccini's. He loses his daughter's love, as well as his ability to dominate her.

Long emphasizes that "*Washington Square* is not an exact, modern equivalent of 'Rappaccini's Daughter'"; for one thing, its climate is more contemplative than tragic. Nevertheless, Hawthorne's archetypes do loom in its background, "suggesting and reinforcing moral connotations and meanings." James's imagination brought Hawthorne's situations into "greater clarity on a level of psychological realism." Dr. Sloper's actions are convincingly motivated, and this "more plausible motivation is part of the great difference between 'Rappaccini's Daughter' and *Washington Square.* What one sees, in comparing the two works, is the movement from the romance to the novel of manners; Hawthorne's gothic situations are now treated from a cosmopolitan point of view and with a precise social observation." In *Washington Square* James was consciously trying to adapt the romance to the requirements of the novel. Long's conclusion is that "*Washington Square* stands perhaps as another instance . . . in which James turned to Hawthorne in composing a novel with an American setting." This is not surprising, for "James considered himself Hawthorne's heir as well as his 'corrector.'" Thus one cannot really say that "James lacked American sources from which to draw in composing *Washington Square.* These sources were not of New York, where the novel is set, but of New England, where James's own roots lay deeply buried."

In addition to "Rappaccini's Daughter," Harold Schechter's "The Unpardonable Sin in 'Washington Square,'" *Studies in Short Fiction,* 10 (Spring, 1973), 137–41, has references to "Dr. Heidegger's Experiment," "The Birthmark," "Ethan Brand," *The Scarlet Letter,* and *The Seven Gables.* "A recurrent character in Hawthorne's fiction," Schechter writes, "is the man who sacrifices his humanity by spiritually isolating himself from the rest of mankind. Choosing the life of the mind over that of the heart," such men as Aylmer, Rappaccini, and Ethan Brand commit the Unpardonable Sin; "they allow their intellects to become ascendant, their emotions to wither and die; and they eventually come to regard other human beings" as mere objects "to be manipulated for the sake of either scientific investigation or . . . sheer amusement." Since Hawthorne's genre was the Romance, most of these characters' pursuits are highly fantastic and symbolic. Rappaccini, for example, "brings up a daughter who derives nourishment from the toxic atmosphere of her father's garden." James's artistic methods and goals were different from Hawthorne's. Hence, Dr. Sloper is not engaged in any bizarre allegorical pursuits; he is protrayed realistically. Nevertheless, allowing for the differences in style, Dr. Sloper is "quite similar to Hawthorne's Unpardonable Sinners. He suffers from that gross defect that Hawthorne . . . defines as 'the complete separation of the intellect from the heart.'" Hawthorne's Unpardonable Sinners are usually scientists, and quite often physicians: Heidegger, Chillingworth, Rappaccini, among others. It is no coincidence, therefore, that James makes Austin Sloper a renowned physician. He is physically and intellectually "a Jamesian analogue to Hawthorne's man of the mind." With one or two exceptions, "all of Hawthorne's men of the mind use young [impressionable] females as the primary subjects for their experiments." Rappaccini uses his daughter Beatrice, Aylmer his wife Georgiana, and Ethan Brand had used Esther. The situation in *Washington Square* is similar. From the moment Townsend shows an interest in Catherine, Dr. Sloper prepares himself for "some entertainment from the little drama." As he puts it in chapter 21 of the novel: "Catherine and her young man are my surfaces; I have taken their measure." Schechter finds this notion of "cold-bloodedly measuring a human being's soul for the sheer intellectual enjoyment of it" reminiscent of Holgrave in *The Seven Gables,* except that Holgrave is saved from becoming an Unpardonable Sinner by Phoebe's love. At the end of *Washington Square,* Dr. Sloper of course dies, but "it is too late for Catherine." Like Hawthorne's heroines, "she has fallen prey to the machinations of a heartless man and perishes spiritually."

"DE GREY: A ROMANCE"

Two other works by James have been related to "Rappaccini's Daughter": "De Grey: A Romance," and "Benvolio." In *The Grasping Imagination* (1970), pp. 38-44, Peter Buitenhuis points out that the theme of "De Grey: A Romance" "is enhanced by a variation that James probably derived from . . . *Rappaccini's Daughter.* Margaret has a suspicion that Paul has begun to dislike her, as if 'a dim perception of her noxious influence had already taken possession of his senses.' It is the poisoned garden of her will that has begun to destroy his organism, and she is now powerless to prevent the outcome, as Beatrice was powerless to prevent the poisoning of the system of her lover." Earlier, in his dissertation entitled "The Uncanny in the Supernatural Short Fiction of Poe, Hawthorne and James" (1967), pp. 247-52,

Paul A. Newlin too had found the passage in which Margaret, convinced that she is having a baleful effect on her lover, lapses into despair, "clearly reminiscent of Hawthorne's use of Beatrice Rappaccini as a carrier of organic evil." Beatrice's evil, Newlin noted, "is an organic poison that draws the life out of those who come in contact with her; Margaret's suggested evil is in the uncanny realm of omnipotence of thought" which allows or causes someone to perform evil acts.

"BENVOLIO"

Only Leon Edel has marginally related "Benvolio" to "Rappaccini's Daughter." In *Henry James: The Conquest of London* (New York: J. B. Lippincott Co., 1962), p. 190,[12] Edel found James's tale to be "frankly like one of Hawthorne's allegories, and the old philosopher and his daughter in it might . . . [be] Rappaccini and Beatrice; only there was no evil in the Jamesian garden and there is none in the tale."

"The Prophetic Pictures"

"THE LIAR"

In "Hawthorne's 'The Prophetic Pictures' and James's 'The Liar,'" *Modern Language Notes,* 65 (April, 1950), 257-58, Robert J. Kane points out that although James's *Notebooks* show that Daudet's *Numa Roumestan* was the source of "The Liar," James does not mention Daudet's novel in his preface to the story. Kane suggests that probably there was "another unconscious and unacknowledged debt . . . to Hawthorne's 'The Prophetic Pictures'":

> In this tale the husband is not a liar but a potential murderer, a fact which grimly confronts his wife (the future victim) in his portrait, though he is blissfully unaware. The painter has deliberately revealed the murderer in him just as James's painter was later to bring out the lying quality in obtuse Colonel Capadose, much to the dismay of the latter's wife. In both stories the painter is an unsparing analyst of souls, but the significance of his analysis is appreciated only by the sensitive and fine. (258)

Edward H. Rosenberry too, in "James's Use of Hawthorne in 'The Liar,'" *Modern Language Notes,* 76 (March, 1961), 234-38, mentions James's prefatory description of the genesis of "The Liar," and the entry in his *Notebooks* which attributes the story to *Numa Roumestan.* Rosenberry finds that although these two sources "satisfactorily account for the setting of 'The

Liar' and for its title character," they do not account for three other important features in the story: "the introduction of a painter as narrative mediator," "the progressive shift of focus from the liar to his wife and ultimately to the painter himself," and "the reversal of Daudet's denouement of marital alienation." Of course James could have invented all these additions and alterations, but their existence in Hawthorne's "The Prophetic Pictures," which James knew early in his career, "argues a conscious or unconscious literary borrowing." And certain ideas and images in Hawthorne's tale reappear in James's. The figure of the painter is one. Both Hawthorne and James were fascinated by the role of the observer of life, the artist who is blessed with insight but carries the curse of detachment. Hawthorne's prophetic painter reads other people's bosoms, but fails to see the disorder of his own. He perfectly reproduces Walter Ludlow's latent madness and Elinor's consequent suffering, but his only interest is to learn whether the events will justify his vision. James's painter, Oliver Lyon, also penetrates and exposes Colonel Capadose's weakness, but only for the selfish purpose of testing Everina's reactions. "That the touching of hidden nerves may be agonizing to their subjects seems to both painters beyond their concern." Hawthorne's Unpardonable Sin of violating the human heart "is inherent in the attitude of both artists," and the two writers dramatize it in identical ways.

Rosenberry further observes that both Walter Ludlow and Colonel Capadose are static characters; the focus of interest is rather on Elinor and Everina. Both husbands are obtuse and their wives discerning, and in developing their dramatic climax both writers use the tensions between husband and wife in a similar way: they both have "the painter come upon his man and wife in contemplation of the revelatory work of art at the moment of total apprehension." And what follows the recognition scene in each case is an act of violence: Walter Ludlow turns a concealed knife against his wife; Colonel Capadose seizes a knife and slashes the painting "in a gesture of symbolic suicide." And each painter sees the tragic picture as the creation of his genius. Thus in each story "the artist finally displaces his subjects as the central figure in the drama he manipulates."

Lastly, Rosenberry notes that the ending of "The Liar" is very different from the way James originally conceived it in his *Notebooks.* He suggests that James may have got the hint he needed to convert the ending of *Numa Roumestan* into that of "The Liar" from the concluding scene of "The Prophetic Pictures." Although Ludlow's portrayer is driven not by jealousy but by pride, he wishes, no less than James's disappointed suitor, to be able to say "I told you so." But just as he attains the peak of his power, Elinor brings him down by the greater power of the simple words: "But–I loved him!" Oliver Lyon too wants desperately to hear Everina confess the inferiority of her marital judgement. But, like Elinor, she confounds his complacent indignation with a deeper wisdom than his own: "For you, *cher maître,* I'm very sorry. But you must remember I possess the original." This reproving of the painter in both stories, says Rosenberry, illustrates more decisively than the particulars "the deeper psychology" which both authors shared. "The Prophetic Pictures," of course, is not the best instance of "the deeper psychology" in Hawthorne's art. "But the problem of the artist is all there . . . head versus heart, pride versus humility, detachment versus sympathy," and it is doubtful "whether James could have made so fine a tale out of Daudet's liar had he not added to his ingredients the point of view and the interior drama of Hawthorne's painter."

"THE STORY OF A MASTERPIECE"

"The Story of a Masterpiece" was also possibly derived from "The Prophetic Pictures." Thus writes Peter Buitenhuis in *The Grasping Imagination* (1970), pp. 38-44. The name of Hawthorne's hero, Ludlow, was earlier used by James in "A Day of Days." But Hawthorne's emphasis in "The Prophetic Pictures" is on "the painter's ability to discover and portray characteristics invisible to unskilled eyes and on the almost magical aspects of this kind of gift." James's emphasis, by contrast, is on the psychological aspects of this theme, not the magical.

Our Old Home

"A PASSIONATE PILGRIM"

Several people have related "A Passionate Pilgrim" to *Our Old Home.* In *Henry James* (1916), pp. 25-26, Rebecca West did not mention *Our Old Home* by name, but she did indicate that "the plot of *The Passionate Pilgrim,* with its American who comes to England to claim a cousin's estate . . . is very clumsy Hawthorne, but in those days Mr. James could not draw normal events and he had to have some medium for expressing his wealth of feeling about England." Christof Wegelin too, in *The Image of Europe in Henry James* (Dallas: Southern Methodist University Press, 1958), p. 37, noted that the figure of the American claimant to an English estate in "A Passionate Pilgrim" symbolizes the same traditional home-feeling for England which Hawthorne expressed in *Our Old Home.* In "Locksley Hall Revisited: Tennyson and Henry James," *Review of English Literature,* 6 (October, 1965), 9-25, Giorgio Melchiori recounts how, while visiting the great country house of his ancestors, Clement Searle in "A Passionate Pilgrim" "recognizes his own features in the portrait of a young man in eighteenth-century costume" and identifies himself so completely with the young man that "from this moment [he] lives simultaneously in both past and present." One source of James's story, says Melchiori, is *Our Old Home,* "in which the author recounts his experiences as American consul in Liverpool and quotes many cases of Americans who laid claim to property in England, grounding it on the slightest and most fanciful evidence." Melchiori mentions one previous study, and I quote verbatim: "V. Sanna, 'I primi racconti di Henry James: 1864-1872,' AION (Annali dell'Instituto Orientale di Napoli) Sezione Germanica, V (1962), pp. 213-48." Melchiori writes:

> Vittoria Sanna has studied the links between *Our Old Home* and *A Passionate Pilgrim* with great penetration, drawing attention to many points of contact, not the least of which is the story told by Hawthorne of the claims of an American who, when visiting one of the seats of the English aristocracy, discovered there a portrait greatly resembling himself.
>
> While it is true that Hawthorne provided the starting point of the story, James's method of composition is always highly complex, involving a constant and closely woven network of references, allusions and reminiscences forming the very tissue of the tale. What matters in *A Passionate Pilgrim* is the 'sense', the 'tone' . . . of old England as discovered by the visitor from overseas . . . . The very air, says the narrator, 'had blown from the verses of English poets.' The poets are indeed very much present in the story . . . Shakespeare is the *genius loci,* present in frequent allusions and hidden quotations. (14-15)

In addition to Shakespeare, Tennyson too "makes himself felt in this story." Thus, although the idea of James's story was suggested by Hawthorne, it was "immediately enriched by the deep feeling for the position of an American with regard to Europe and for the author's personal experiences in Europe." Melchiori goes on to show how in "A Passionate Pilgrim" the "Hawthornian suggestion and the Shakespearian echoes are submerged by the Tennysonian references."

Before Melchiori, Peter Buitenhuis had also noted in "Henry James on Hawthorne," *New England Quarterly,* 32 (June, 1959), 207-25, that "A Passionate Pilgrim" is based on an incident Hawthorne relates in "Consular Experiences." Buitenhuis recalled how, as consul in Liverpool, Hawthorne was approached by many American claimants to rich English estates, and how one of these Americans "had discovered in the . . . country house to which he laid claim 'a portrait bearing a striking resemblance to himself.'"[13] "Starting with these incidents," Buitenhuis wrote, James created "A Passionate Pilgrim," "in which the implications of what Hawthorne called this 'blind pathetic tendency' in his countrymen are . . . skilfully worked out" (Buitenhuis, p. 210). Tony Tanner too, in his introduction to James's *Hawthorne* (1967), pp. 1-3, related James's story to *Our Old Home.*

In *The Grasping Imagination* (1970), pp. 49-51, Buitenhuis once again writes on "A Passionate Pilgrim" and *Our Old Home.* He asserts that in "A Passionate Pilgrim" James must have been comparing his European experience with that of Hawthorne, "for the story is based on two incidents which appear in 'Consular Experiences'": that of the American claimant who discovers a portrait resembling him, and that of the shopkeeper from Connecticut with no evidence to prove his claim (*Our Old Home,* p. 16). "Combining these two incidents," Buitenhuis once again observes, James created "A Passionate Pilgrim." After indicating the similarities between Rawson and Clement Searle, and how, before he dies, Searle aids Rawson in his plans to go to America, Buitenhuis notes that "James was in this way careful to balance the hopeless pathos that Hawthorne found in the situation of the deluded American claimant to an English inheritance with the eagerness that [Rawson] feels for the opportunities offered by a land unencumbered by class, privilege, and tradition."

THE AMBASSADORS

Alan R. Shucard's "Diplomacy in Henry James's *The Ambassadors,*" *Arizona Quarterly,* 29 (Summer, 1973), 123-29, is not about *Our Old Home* and *The Ambassadors;* neither does Shucard mention *Our Old Home* in his article. But he does relate Lambert Strether to Hawthorne as American consul in Liverpool. After analyzing "the intricate web of diplomacy" as a major structural device of *The Ambassadors,* Shucard observes that there is "in James's sense of Lambert Strether a reflection of his feeling toward Hawthorne expressed in his 1879 monograph on Hawthorne, in the section . . . concerning the period Hawthorne spent abroad *as a representative of his government.*" In chapter 6 of *Hawthorne,* James wrote:

> The tone of his European Diaries is often so fresh and unsophisticated that we find ourselves thinking of the writer as a young man, and it is only a certain final sense of something reflective and a trifle melancholy that reminds us that the simplicity which is . . . the leading characteristic of their pages is, though the simplicity of inexperience, not that of youth. . . . Hawthorne's experience had been narrow. His fifty years had been spent . . . in small American towns . . . and he had led exclusively . . . a village life. . . . He was exquisitely and consistently provincial. I suggest this fact . . . in support of an appreciative view of him. I know nothing more

> remarkable . . . than the sight of this odd, youthful-elderly mind, contending so late in the day with new opportunities for learning old things, and . . . profiting by them so freely and gracefully.

"This, after all," says Shucard, "is in great measure Lambert Strether, an unprofessional emissary on a diplomatic mission among other unprofessional diplomats, 'learning old things' in an unfamiliar setting that will permit him to live in the living out of his life" (Shucard, p. 128).

"Egotism; or, The Bosom Serpent"

In "Hawthorne's 'Egotism' and 'The Jolly Corner,'" *Emerson Society Quarterly,* 63 (Spring, 1971), 13-18, Mildred K. Travis points out that both "Egotism" and James's "The Jolly Corner" feature "solipsistic characters with gnawing secrets in their breasts"; both "contain the concept of the alter ego, where the other self is seen as a hostile beast of prey termed in serpent imagery"; and both have a happy ending, "reflecting the redemptive power of love." In order to show these elements, Travis offers a close reading of the two stories. She notes that in chapter 3 of *Hawthorne,* James praised such stories as "The Snow Image" and "Rappaccini's Daughter," but detected "something stiff and mechanical" in others like "The Birthmark" and "Egotism." It is very likely, Travis suggests, that in "The Jolly Corner" James "was consciously trying to improve upon those facets of Hawthorne's fiction which he found vulnerable to criticism," while at the same time drawing upon those others which he admired.

In "Egotism," Roderick Elliston's "withdrawal from Herkimer reflects social alienation. The refuge into the family residence signifies retreat into past and privacy. The imagery of subtle motion and gliding," as well as the serpent imagery, is "a reference to the gnawing secret in his breast." But his alienation alternates with a kind of compulsion to mingle with people. Whereas previously the sight of people and the sunshine was a horror to him, now he forces himself upon the notice of everybody. In "The Jolly Corner," Spencer Brydon too "retreats from the world into his family residence to combat and nurse a tormenting and tormented inner self, a gnawing secret." Like Roderick, "his alienation from both human intercourse and daylight is alternated by a strong desire for signs of human beings." Both Hawthorne and James describe the gnawing secret as "egotism" and evil; both see the secret obsession as "a second consciousness or alter ego"; and both "ascribe to the 'egotism' the characteristics of a beast of prey. In Hawthorne's tale, the obsession is allegorized as serpent. In James' story it is symbolized generally as beast; but occasionally and specifically, as snake." Spencer's final encounter with his alter ego is also similar to Roderick's. In each story, once "the self faces its alter ego . . . it is rendered temporarily insensible." Furthermore, the final scenes of both stories "detail similar redemptive qualitites of love," and each scene "involves the protagonist, a kind of interlocutor, and the loved one of the opposite sex." Hence, one might say that both stories "have in common–at least in part–the phenomenon of 'triadic structure.'"

Travis finds "The Jolly Corner" generally more realistic, and thus less allegorical, than "Egotism." James is also "much more subtle with snake imagery and more sophisticated in his rendition of the idea of the alter ego" than Hawthorne. "Yet the idea of how a deeply guilt-beleaguered conscience becomes purified is made pervasively clear in analogous terms." James in "The Jolly Corner" "seems to try to improve upon Hawthorne, while he illustrates his indebtedness to him."

"The Beast in the Jungle," *The Portrait of a Lady,* and *Roderick Hudson* have also been mentioned in connection with "Egotism." In "Three Commentaries" (1950), pp. 5-10, Allen Tate called "The Beast in the Jungle" a study of "the isolation and frustration of personality," a subject which Hawthorne had treated in "Egotism." In fact, in an August 1837 entry in *American Note-books*–some sixty years before James's story was written–Hawthorne had actually stated the theme of "The Beast in the Jungle":

> A young man and girl meet together, each in search of a person to be known by some particular sign. They watch and wait a great while for that person to pass. At last some casual circumstance discloses that each is the one that the other is waiting for. Moral–that what we need for our happiness is often close at hand, if we knew but how to seek for it. –*Passages from the American Note-Books,* (1868; reprinted 1910), p. 86.

After analyzing various elements in James's story, Tate concluded that in the long run "its effect is that of tone . . . and it is closer to the method of Hawthorne than one might at a glance suppose; for in the last scene it is very nearly allegory."

The Portrait of a Lady was first related to "Egotism" by Randall Stewart. In *American Literature and Christian Doctrine* (Baton Rouge: Louisiana State University Press, 1958), p. 104, Stewart indicated that both Hawthorne and James were concerned with the insidiousness of egotism. In "Egotism," Hawthorne "used a snake as a symbol of self-involvement," and Elliston "goes about crying, 'It gnaws me, it gnaws me!'" Although in *The Portrait* Osmond "does nothing so melodramatic as that . . . James (remembering Hawthorne's tale, very likely) says of him, 'His egotism lay hidden like a serpent in a bank of flowers.'" Oscar Cargill too, in *The Novels of Henry James* (1961), p. 33n., notes that in *The Portrait* "James uses the figure of a serpent, curiously, to describe the egotism of Osmond." And in his dissertation entitled "Societal Definitions of Individualism and the Critique of Egotism as a Major Theme in American Fiction" (Brown, 1972), pp. 195-214, David J. Thompson writes on how Isabel Archer the egocentric manipulator tries to possess Osmond but ends up being possessed by him irrevocably. In the end, Thompson explains, Isabel comes to realize that her sole means of salvation lies in devoting her life to serving others. Thus, by accepting responsibility toward Pansy, she "exorcises the serpent of egotism much as Roderick Elliston exorcises his bosom serpent by forgetting himself in the thought of another."

While comparing *Roderick Hudson* with *The Marble Faun* in *The Novels of Henry James* (1961), Oscar Cargill refers to Roderick Elliston and his sculptor friend George Herkimer in "Egotism" (33n.). But Cargill never says what connection he sees between *Roderick Hudson* and Hawthorne's "Egotism."

"The Maypole of Merrymount" and The Europeans

In chapter 3 on Hawthorne and James in *A World Elsewhere: The Place of Style in American Literature* (New York: Oxford University Press, 1966), pp. 93-143, Richard Poirier discusses, among other things, James's *Hawthorne.* He finds that some of James's characterizations of Hawthorne in this biography indicate the "essential differences between the two writers and between the world to which each belonged." For illustration, he contrasts "The Maypole of Merrymount" with *The Europeans.* "Thematically," he writes:

> "The Maypole of Merrymount" and *The Europeans* are much alike. Each is about a contest between . . . "jollity and gloom" for dominion in New England; each is enacted in a New England dominated either by Puritanism or, in James's novel, by some later modified form of it. But the *way* in which the contending forces are defined and in which the narrator sounds in each work is radically different. The characters and James himself as narrator of *The Europeans* are wholly defined by their tones of voice, by their conduct in dialogue and in social relations, and by the extent to which they can deal with the phenomenon of the Baroness Eugenia, confronting her American relatives with her "large element of costume." Everyone in the novel is revealed through verbal, social, and sexual manners, and the differentiations are extremely delicate and exacting. By contrast, nothing can be inferred from the way the characters sound in Hawthorne's story; they have no existence in the social and sexual world where James's characters come to life. As a narrator, Hawthorne . . . projects no social or class type; he never observes social conduct, but only the degree to which

> his characters are submissive to allegorical definition. James is accurate enough when he complains that Hawthorne "had certainly not proposed to himself to give an account of the social idiosyncrasies of his fellow citizens." (104-105)

According to James, Hawthorne is "thin" because America is "thin." In *The Europeans,* James

> wrote a novel about Hawthorne's own time and place which Hawthorne himself presumably could not have written. He literally brings into that "thin" environment an element of contrast— the Europeans—without which the sweet but essentially silent American could have no novelistic existence.
>
> Missing from James's account is the ample evidence from Hawthorne's fiction and especially from his prefaces that, far from feeling deprived by what James thinks is lacking in his society, Hawthorne was usually anxious to escape from what it did offer. Nearly every novel and story is about his own and his characters' entrapment in . . . "artificial systems," the control exerted over consciousness not only by social organization but by literary conventions. (105-106)

Poirier's verdict is that "James was unable to see either the genius of Hawthorne or the extent to which Hawthorne's concern for the self and its environment resembled what were to be his own later preoccupations" (115).

"The Birthmark" and The Turn of the Screw

In "How Ambiguous is Hawthorne" (1962), Hans-Joachim Lang had related *The Turn of the Screw* to "Rappaccini's Daughter"; in "The Turns in *The Turn of the Screw,*" *Jahrbuch fur Amerikastudien,* 9 (1963), 110-28, he relates James's tale to "The Birthmark" in particular, and to several of Hawthorne's other tales in general.[14] Most details in James's story, he explains, can be interpreted in a double sense, but instead of supporting each other, the two possible meanings are incompatible. This he calls "disjunctive ambiguity," and notes that the first specimen of such ambiguity in American literature is probably Hawthorne's "The Wives of the Dead," which can be read as reality or as a wishful dream, all because of the grammatical ambiguity of the last sentence: "But her hand trembled against Margaret's neck, a tear also fell upon her cheek, and she suddenly awoke," which is very much like the possible double construction of Miles's cry: "Peter Quint— you devil!" Hawthorne, by some physical details, absolutely forbids the reader to think that the action is only a dream until the very last sentence. Although one cannot prove that James studied this story's technique, he did know "Young Goodman Brown" and "The Minister's Black Veil," two stories in which "the sinister construction of facts or supposed facts leads to unfortunate results. The dark forest in 'Young Goodman Brown' is for the protagonist what Bly is for the governess, the locale of trial by apparitions," and the "veil in 'The Minister's Black Veil' stands for the somber vision, of which the governess herself is so very conscious." These two stories present a perfect historical context for *The Turn of the Screw.* A third story, "The Birthmark," is even more relevant for James's tale:

> "The Birthmark" is an early psychoanalytic story. The alchemical paraphernalia hide from the alchemist's sight the true nature of his art, which is clearly revealed to him in a dream, in which he brutally operates with a knife on the birthmark of his wife's cheek, until he cuts away at her heart. The analytic insight and the ethical doctrine of the tale—idealism commended—militate against each other and make the story a doubtful success. But the technique of the story in certain other respects is an unmitigated triumph. . . . Hawthorne brilliantly uses the technique of inversion: Aylmer believes that the mark symbolizes the grip death has on everybody, but what his wife suffers from is exactly the grip he has on her. (120-21)

The Turn of the Screw presents a similar situation: "what the ghosts do to the children is problematical, potential, speculative; what the governess does to them can be demonstrated by results." Hawthorne's stories, Lang emphasizes, "can be read in two ways: one general, 'allegorical,' the other specific, personal and dramatic. There is no doubt where James stands," and we should not be content with only an allegorical or generalized interpretation of *The Turn of the Screw.*

Lang finds the technique of James's story to be "a refinement on Hawthorne and his contemporaries." He discusses the Gothic elements in the story, and the question of whether it is the house or the governess who is haunted. His conclusion is that the governess "is not a prisoner in a castle . . . but finds—or creates—tragedy there." Just as the evil in "Young Goodman Brown" "is perhaps only 'a monster of his own making', so the Evil at Bly, and the whole drama is perhaps the creation of her own imagination." But if the riddle cannot be solved by an investigation of the *what* of the story, the only recourse is to the *how,* and for this Lang turns to "the general movement of technique from the Gothic Novel via Poe and Hawthorne to James":

> Abstract formulations of the law of terror, sublime landscapes and gruesome buildings were kept distinct in the Tales of Terror. Poe and Hawthorne pictorialized their stories, but not completely. There is moralizing in Hawthorne and philosophizing in Poe. The outside (nature, landscape, castles) stands for inside. It is Young Goodman Brown himself who is the chief horror of the scene. What James does is to pictorialize and dramatize further quite ruthlessly. . . . It is tempting to say that the ghosts are simply the objective correlative of the governess' insanity. But . . . a theory of *The Turn* should be developed which does not contradict James's own pronouncements in his letters and Preface. (126-27)

He himself interpreted the ghosts as agents of a sort. They are emblematic of a particularized evil. On the one hand, they "belong to the house in the sense that they are emblematic of the former situation at Bly"; on the other, they "belong to the governess in the sense that she makes them active. . . . She acts like Aylmer in 'The Birthmark' in that she interprets a mere possible symbol and acts on this interpretation until she has all her proofs and the symbols become a reality" (127-28).

"The Threefold Destiny" and "The Beast in the Jungle"

Only Terence Martin has related "The Beast in the Jungle" to "The Threefold Destiny." In *Nathaniel Hawthorne* (New Haven, Connecticut: College and University Press, 1965), Martin points out that in many tales by Hawthorne—for example, "The Minister's Black Veil: A Parable," or "Fancy's Show Box: A Morality"—the subtitles are not elaborations of the main title but rather "descriptions of the *form* of the tale. They tell not what the tale is about, but what the tale is. They are explicit indications of the *kind* of fiction Hawthorne is endeavoring to write." Martin continues:

> "The Threefold Destiny," for example, Hawthorne's "Fairy Legend," presents the story of Ralph Cranfield, who, "from his youth upward, had felt himself marked out for a high destiny." This, in James's terms, is the *donnée* of the tale; indeed, it is virtually the *donnée* of James's "The Beast in the Jungle" in which John Marcher, too, feels that he is marked out for a special destiny. But the difference in form between the two stories is immense, and crucial. John Marcher waits and watches for years with May Bartram to see what special destiny fate has reserved for him; with a subtle twist, James makes the waiting itself Marcher's destiny. He has

> missed life thoroughly, utterly . . . he has become the man . . . to whom nothing ever happened, as he realizes when he throws himself face downward in a futile embrace of May Bartram's grave. Hawthorne's Ralph Cranfield feels, very much in the style of a hero of fairy legend, that his destiny is threefold. (53)

Martin goes on to discuss Ralph's "threefold destiny," and how in each case his destiny is to be "fulfilled only after the appearance of a special sign."

"Ethan Brand" and "The Beast in the Jungle"

The antecedents of "The Beast in the Jungle," says F. W. Dupee in *Henry James* (1951; reprinted New York: William Morrow, 1974), pp. 155-56, are to be found in Hawthorne and in James's earlier work. In characters like Ethan Brand, Hawthorne portrayed sinister men who are committed to the unpardonable sin of inhuman isolation. James's Marcher, however, "is an Ethan Brand who has . . . read Walter Pater if not James himself; in him the Romantic ego has turned inward and become pure sensibility; *his* unpardonable sin consists in his refusing common life under the impression that he is being reserved for 'something rare and strange.'" Charles G. Hoffmann, in his dissertation entitled "The Development of the Short Novel in Hawthorne, Melville, and James" (1952), pp. 325-26, explains that when in the preface to "The Beast in the Jungle" James calls his story a fantasy, the term is to be taken in somewhat the same sense in which some of Hawthorne's short stories, like "Ethan Brand," are called fantasies: "an anecdote or idea is . . . illustrated through a narrative with emphasis on psychological or spiritual patterns rather than on surface realism":

> Thus the donnee for *The Beast in the Jungle* as found in James's notebooks parallels the idea of "Ethan Brand" as expressed in Hawthorne's notebooks. The idea . . . that an investigator searching for the Unpardonable Sin finds it after a life-time of seeking in his own heart and practice is strikingly similar to the idea that a man fearing something horrible will happen to him finds it after a life-time of waiting in his own impotence and lack of passion. However, the method of treatment is different in the two stories. One is allegorical, the other symbolic and imagistic; one is moralistic in tone, the other ironic.

Hoffmann makes the same observation in *The Short Novels of Henry James* (New York: Bookman Associates, 1957), p. 99.

Conclusion

In his forword to *American Literary Scholarship: An Annual/1972* (Durham, North Carolina: Duke University Press, 1974), p. vii, J. Albert Robbins lamented "the proliferation of published mediocrity" and cited some of the *ALS* contributors' complaints which "attest to substantive naivete, carelessness, unoriginality—and ignorance of published scholarship" on the part of the authors. If work on the James-Hawthorne relationship in 1973 is indicative of future trends in this area, it is likely that many dissertations whose subject includes a consideration of Hawthorne and James will continue to "discover" relationships which have already been widely discussed. Of the thirteen 1973 items reviewed in this study, nine are dissertations, but only a few contain any substantially new insights as far as Hawthorne and James are concerned. Of the three articles, two concentrate on Hawthorne's tales: "Rappaccini's Daughter," "Dr. Heidegger's Experiment," "The Birthmark," and "Ethan Brand." It is the influence of these shorter works—as well as that of *The Seven Gables*—which has not as yet received as much *detailed* critical attention as that of *The Scarlet Letter, The Blithedale Romance,* and *The Marble Faun.* There might also be some possibilities in an interdisciplinary approach to the James-Hawthorne relation. Above all else, it is hoped that the essays in this text will make it less excusable to duplicate already available scholarship.

Appendix Chronological List of James's Writings on, and References to, Hawthorne

The first essay in this study examined James's published items in which he wrote about, or directly referred to, Hawthorne and/or his works. The list below gives the publication in which each item first appeared. Some of the items that first appeared in periodicals were revised when collected in book form. Where the revision affected the specific reference to Hawthorne, this fact was indicated in the first essay. The compilation of this list was greatly facilitated by Leon Edel's and Dan H. Laurence's *Bibliography of Henry James,* second edition, revised (London: Rupert Hart-Davis, 1961).

1865 "Miss Braddon." *Nation,* 1 (November 9, 1865), 593-94. Unsigned.

1868 [William Dean Howells's] "Italian Journeys." *North American Review,* 106 (January, 1868), 336-39. Unsigned.

1870 Letter to William James, February 13, 1870. *The Thought and Character of William James,* 2 vols., by Ralph Barton Perry. Boston: Little, Brown, 1935, I, 316-19.

1872 "Hawthorne's French and Italian Journals." *Nation,* 14 (March 14, 1872), 172-73.

1873 "A Roman Holiday." *Atlantic Monthly,* 32 (July, 1873), 1-11.

1874 "A Chain of Italian Cities." *Atlantic Monthly,* 33 (February, 1874), 158-64.

_____. "Frühlingsfluthen. *Ein Konig Lear des Dorfes.* Zwei Novellen. Iwan Turgéniew. Mitau. 1873." *North American Review,* 108 (April, 1874), 326-56.

1875 "Mr. Tennyson's Drama." *Galaxy,* 20 (September, 1875), 339-402.

1876 "Charles Baudelaire." *Nation,* 22 (April 27, 1876), 279-81.

_____. "Daniel Deronda: A Conversation." *Atlantic Monthly,* 38 (December, 1876), 684-94.

1877 "George Sand." *Galaxy,* 24 (July, 1877), 45-61.

_____. "In Warwickshire." *Galaxy,* 24 (November, 1877), 671-80.

1879 *Hawthorne.* English Men of Letters Series. London: Macmillan, 1879.

1880 Letter to William Dean Howells, January 31, 1880. *The Letters of Henry James,* 2 vols., ed. Percy Lubbock. New York: Charles Scribner's Sons, 1920. I, 71-74.

_____. Letter to Elizabeth Boott, February 22, 1880. *The Notebooks of Henry James,* ed. F. O. Matthiessen and Kenneth B. Murdock. New York: Oxford University Press, 1947, p. 29n.

1881 Notebook entry, following that dated November 25, 1881. *The Notebooks of Henry James,* pp. 24-33.

1883 "The Correspondence of Carlyle and Emerson." *Century Magazine,* 26 (June, 1883), 265-72.

_____. "The Impressions of a Cousin." *Century Magazine,* 27 (November and December, 1883), 116-29; 257-75.

1884 "The Art of Fiction." *Longman's Magazine,* 4 (September, 1884), 502-21.

1887 "The Life of Emerson." *Macmillan Magazine,* 57 (December, 1887), 86-98.

1888 "London." *Century Magazine,* 37 (December, 1888), 219-39.

1889-1890 *The Tragic Muse. Atlantic Monthly,* 63-65 (January, 1889-May, 1890).

1892 "James Russell Lowell." *Atlantic Monthly,* 69 (January, 1892), 35-50.

1897 "Nathaniel Hawthorne." *Library of the World's Best Literature,* 30 vols., ed. Charles Dudley Warner. New York: R. S. Peale and J. A. Hill, 1896-1897. XII, 7053-61.

_____. "James Russell Lowell (1819-1891)." *Library of the World's Best Literature,* XVI, 9229-37.

1898 "The Story-Teller at Large: Mr. Henry Harland." *Fortnightly Review,* 69 (April 1, 1898), 650-54.

_____. "American Letter." *Literature,* 3 (July, 1898), 17-19.

1899 Letter to Mrs. Humphry Ward, July 1899. *The Letters of Henry James,* I, 320-23.

1902 "Honoré de Balzac." *The Two Young Brides.* London: William Heinemann, 1902, pp. v-xliii.

1903 *William Wetmore Story and his Friends,* 2 vols. Boston: Houghton Mifflin, 1903.

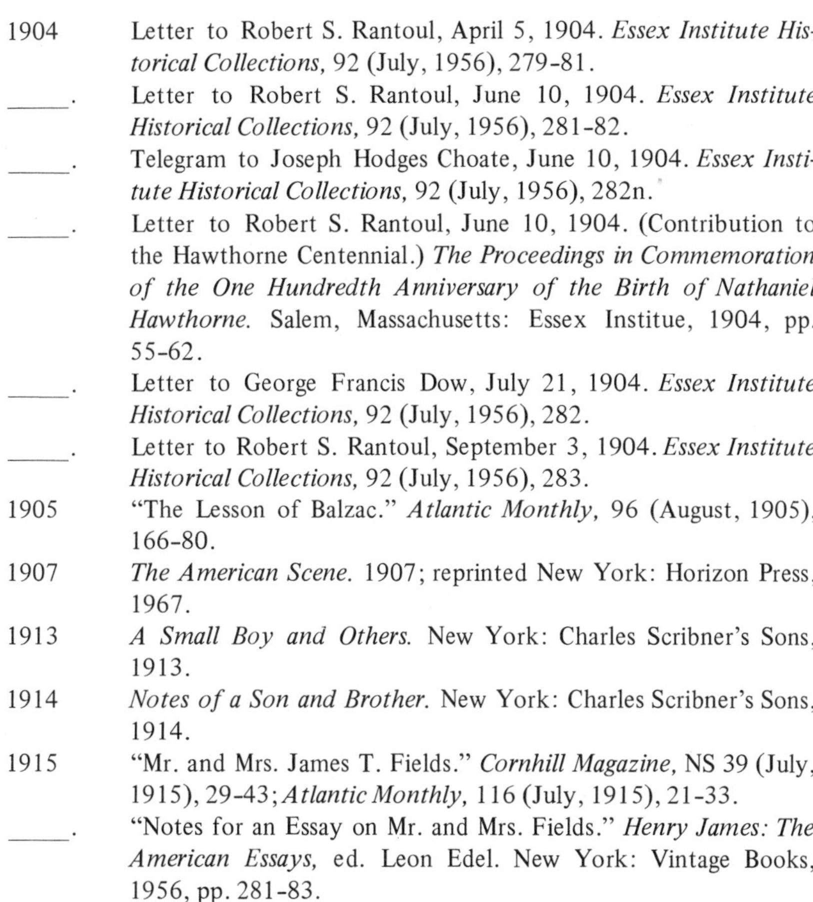

1904 Letter to Robert S. Rantoul, April 5, 1904. *Essex Institute Historical Collections,* 92 (July, 1956), 279-81.

_____. Letter to Robert S. Rantoul, June 10, 1904. *Essex Institute Historical Collections,* 92 (July, 1956), 281-82.

_____. Telegram to Joseph Hodges Choate, June 10, 1904. *Essex Institute Historical Collections,* 92 (July, 1956), 282n.

_____. Letter to Robert S. Rantoul, June 10, 1904. (Contribution to the Hawthorne Centennial.) *The Proceedings in Commemoration of the One Hundredth Anniversary of the Birth of Nathaniel Hawthorne.* Salem, Massachusetts: Essex Institue, 1904, pp. 55-62.

_____. Letter to George Francis Dow, July 21, 1904. *Essex Institute Historical Collections,* 92 (July, 1956), 282.

_____. Letter to Robert S. Rantoul, September 3, 1904. *Essex Institute Historical Collections,* 92 (July, 1956), 283.

1905 "The Lesson of Balzac." *Atlantic Monthly,* 96 (August, 1905), 166-80.

1907 *The American Scene.* 1907; reprinted New York: Horizon Press, 1967.

1913 *A Small Boy and Others.* New York: Charles Scribner's Sons, 1913.

1914 *Notes of a Son and Brother.* New York: Charles Scribner's Sons, 1914.

1915 "Mr. and Mrs. James T. Fields." *Cornhill Magazine,* NS 39 (July, 1915), 29-43; *Atlantic Monthly,* 116 (July, 1915), 21-33.

_____. "Notes for an Essay on Mr. and Mrs. Fields." *Henry James: The American Essays,* ed. Leon Edel. New York: Vintage Books, 1956, pp. 281-83.

1917 *The Sense of the Past.* New York: Charles Scribner's Sons, 1917.

Notes

Chapter 1

1. Henry James, "The Lesson of Balzac," *Atlantic Monthly,* 96 (August, 1905), 170.
2. Caroline Ticknor, *Hawthorne and His Publisher* (Boston: Houghton Mifflin, 1913), p. 141.
3. Ralph B. Perry, *The Thought and Character of William James,* 2 vols. (Boston: Little, Brown, 1935), I, 316.
4. ibid., p. 319.
5. Percy Lubbock, ed., *The Letters of Henry James,* 2 vols. (New York: Charles Scribner's Sons, 1920), II, 490.
6. Twelve years before Buitenhuis, F. O. Matthiessen had made the same observation. In *The James Family* (New York: Alfred A. Knopf, 1947), p. 481, Matthiessen noted that Hawthorne never entertained the thoughts contained in the preface to *The Marble Faun* until he went to live in Europe.
7. Morris Shapira, ed., *Henry James: Selected Literary Criticism* (1963; rpt. New York: Horizon Press, 1964), p. 59. A further explanation is necessary here. What James rejected in "The Art of Fiction" was any complete separation, in terms of "execution," between the novel and the romance. He never implied, however—and F. O. Matthiessen clearly shows this in *Henry James: The Major Phase* (New York: Oxford University Press, 1944), p. 103—that the two modes are identical. In the preface to *The American,* reprinted in *The Art of the Novel: Critical Prefaces* (New York: Oxford University Press, 1944), pp. 20-39, his test for the romance was that although it deals with "experience liberated"—and is thus different from the novel—it must make its events correspond to "our general sense of the way things happen"

(pp. 33, 34), a definition that is similar to Hawthorne's in the preface to *The House of the Seven Gables.*

8. Hamlin Garland, *Roadside Meetings* (New York: Macmillan, 1930), p. 461.
9. Shapira, p. 59.
10. In his 1881 essay on Emerson, reprinted in *The James Family,* pp. 434-38, James's father had also written that Emerson "did not know the inward difference between good and evil" (435), and that he appeared to him "utterly unconscious of himself as either good or evil. He had no conscience, in fact, and lived by perception" (437).
11. In the biography, James had found one fault of *The Scarlet Letter* to be "an abuse of the fanciful element—of a certain superficial symbolism," which was overdone at times and became mechanical, with the images seeming to stand for nothing more serious than themselves. *The Marble Faun* too contains "a great many light threads of symbolism." Likewise, the people in *The Scarlet Letter* struck James "not as characters, but as representatives . . . of a single state of mind," and those of *The Seven Gables* as figures rather than characters, pictures rather than persons.
12. Shapira, p. 192. (*The Two Young Brides,* of course, is a translation of Balzac's *Deux Jeunes Mariées.*)
13. In his reply to Robert S. Rantoul's invitation to contribute an essay for the centennial celebration of Hawthorne's birthday, James identified this critic as Guillaume Guizot (*Essex Institute Historical Collections,* 1956, p. 280).
14. Frederick W. Dupee, ed., *Henry James: Autobiography* (New York: Criterion Books, 1956), pp. 479-80.
15. Edward Sandford Martin, *The Life of Joseph Hodges Choate,* 2 vols. (London: Constable, 1920), II, 258.
16. "New England: An Autumn Impression" was first published, in three parts, in the *North American Review,* 180 (April-June, 1905), 481-501, 641-60, 801-16.
17. "Boston" was first published in the *North American Review,* 182 (March, 1906), 335-55, and in the *Fortnightly Review,* 85 (March 1, 1906), 439-59.
18. With respect to *The Marble Faun,* James had earlier objected to this title in chapter 6 of *Hawthorne.* "Hawthorne's choice of this appellation," he had written then, "is rather singular, for it completely fails to characterise the story, the subject of which is the living faun, the faun of flesh and blood, the unfortunate Donatello. His marble counterpart is mentioned only in the opening chapter."
19. This passage was also quoted at length in the section on James's letter to the Hawthorne Centenary.

Chapter 2

1. Ralph B. Perry, *The Thought and Character of William James,* I, 316, 319. Longer excerpts from both letters may be found in the first essay in this text.
2. ibid., I, 413.
3. Part 1 of Eliot's article first appeared, entitled "In Memory of Henry James," in the *Egoist,* 5 (January, 1918), 1-2.
4. Henry James, *The Art of the Novel: Critical Prefaces* (New York: Charles Scribner's Sons, 1934), p. 32. In *Henry James: The Major Phase* (New York: Oxford University Press, 1944), pp. 103-104, Matthiessen used this definition of romance to suggest that "despite the conventional classification, James was very little of a realist."
5. In the epilogue to *The James Family,* Matthiessen again explained that Eliot penetrated to the deepest spiritual level in James when he emphasized the novelist's profound sensitiveness to good and evil, for this clearly indicates that James's "real progenitor" was Hawthorne.
6. Eliot had remarked, in his review of *The Cambridge History of American Literature,* Vol. II, which was published in the *Athenaeum,* April 25, 1919, pp. 236-37, that Hawthorne "was a real observer of the moral life," and that his work is truly a criticism of the Puritan and the Transcendentalist morality, and of the world which he knew. "It is a criticism as Henry James's work is a criticism of the America of his times" (237).
7. In his essay entitled "*The Marble Faun* and *The Wings of the Dove*," Bewley once again blames a "failure" in *The Wings of the Dove* on a similar "failure" in *The Marble Faun*–*Complex Fate,* pp. 53-54.
8. For a similar view see Edwin Fussell's "Hawthorne, James, and 'The Common Doom,'" *American Quarterly,* 10 (1958), 438-53, which is reviewed in the fourth section of this essay.
9. For an elaboration on this observation, see the section entitled "The Italian Experience" in the fifth essay.
10. Buitenhuis, of course–echoed by Tanner–arrives at a rather different conclusion: that the later James believed that Hawthorne was a successful artist precisely because he remained true to his New England environment (*New England Quarterly,* June 1959, pp. 220-21).
11. In *Henry James,* University of Minnesota Pamphlets on American Writers, No. 4 (Minneapolis: University of Minnesota Press, 1960), p. 11, Edel notes that although "James's models were largely French: Balzac, Mérimée, George Sand," his early writing "shows also an attentive reading of Hawthorne. There is a touch of Hawthorne in 'The Romance of Certain Old Clothes' (1868), first of the many ghostly tales James

was to write." This story, published in the *Atlantic* in February 1868, is probably one of the "two rather Hawthorne-like tales" Edel refers to in *The Untried Years.* The second could be "The Story of a Year," or "Poor Richard," or "De Grey: A Romance," all published in the *Atlantic* before 1870, and all rather Hawthornesque.

12. For other similarities between "The Last of the Valerii" and *The Marble Faun,* see the fifth essay.
13. For a more detailed comparison of *The Seven Gables* with *The Sense of the Past,* see the sixth essay.
14. For Hawthorne's and James's views on the relation of the artist to society, see the fourth section of this essay.
15. As indicated above, Masback reached the opposite conclusion with regard to the child character. He found that Hawthorne tries "to make the child's death meaningful to the adults who have caused it," whereas James's adults are usually unaffected by the child's death (Masback, pp. 7–8).
16. Many of Bashore's remarks are taken, with due acknowledgement, from published scholarship.
17. For other people who have discussed the relation between "Professor Fargo" and *Blithedale,* see the fourth essay.
18. In the main, Bashore discusses James's novels chronologically. They are reshuffled above in order to minimize the additional disjointedness resulting from brevity.
19. Later, Hoffman explains that the terms "short story" and "short novel" "are generic rather than mutually exclusive categories," and that it is not "necessary to distinguish categorically between" them (329). This seems merely to minimize the primary purpose and distinctive value of Hoffmann's 405-page exercise.
20. Hoffmann's *The Short Novels of Henry James* (New York: Bookman Associates, 1957) grew out of part of this dissertation, although this fact is not mentioned in the book. The book contains the same comments on Hawthorne's and James's use of anecdotes from real life, and the same comparison of *The Scarlet Letter* with "Madame de Mauves," *The Spoils of Poynton,* and *The Turn of the Screw,* and of "Ethan Brand" with "The Beast in the Jungle."
21. This rather contradicts Hinchliffe's concluding observation quoted previously. In his conclusion Hinchliffe states that not only is the bowl in *The Golden Bowl* "mechanical" and "a nuisance," but it is indicative of the difference between Hawthorne's, Melville's, and James's use of symbolism. Hawthorne's and Melville's symbols are exploratory; James's are explanatory (674).
22. F. W. Dupee, ed. *Henry James: Autobiography* (New York: Criterion Books, 1956), p. 415.
23. ibid., pp. 424–25.
24. Lewis also points out, as others have done,that even before Hawthorne and James lamented the lack of artistic materials in the New World, Cooper had noted the absence in America of "annals," "manners,"

"obscure fictions," and "gross and hardy offences" for the artist to work with.

25. Martin's essay is reprinted in *The American Sisterhood: Writings of the Feminist Movement from Colonial Times to the Present,* ed. Wendy Martin (New York: Harper Row, 1972), pp. 257–72.
26. Leon Edel, in *Henry James* (Minneapolis, 1960), also observes that during James's lifetime his reputation rested "upon his 'studies' of young American girls encountering Europe . . . like Hawthorne's young heroes, these Americans have to discover that the world is not as innocent as it seems, and that behind the smiling facades of castles and picturesque ruins lurk centuries of wrongdoing and the dark and evil things of the human spirit" (18).
27. As indicated in the section on *The Golden Bowl* in the fifth essay, Matthiessen had earlier connected James's phrase with *The Marble Faun* in his *Henry James: The Major Phase* (1944), p. 90.
28. In "Images of Woman in the American Novel," *Aphra,* 2 (Winter, 1970), 56–68, Kimberley Snow traces "the broad outlines of the evolutionary process which turned" the earlier image of woman as "the hand-wrought creation of the gods" into "the witch of the Industrial Revolution." However, the article contains no discussion of Hawthorne's or James's heroines, although Snow does point out that Hester Prynne and Isabel Archer are two obvious examples of "individual characterization of women . . . which transcend the usual pattern," and that Hawthorne is the only major American author of the romantic movement who "delves into the psychology of women."
29. John E. Pyron, Jr., "American Romance and Italian Reality in the Nineteenth Century" (University of Pittsburgh, 1973). This dissertation is reviewed at the end of the section entitled "The Italian Experience" in the fifth essay.

Chapter 3

1. Edith Garrigues Hawthorne, ed., *The Memoirs of Julian Hawthorne* (New York: Macmillan, 1938), pp. 127 ff.
2. Quentin Anderson, Introduction to *Hawthorne,* by Henry James (New York: Macmillan, 1962), pp. 11–12.
3. James's other extended evaluation of *The Scarlet Letter* appears in his introduction to the selections from Hawthorne's works in *Library of the World's Best Literature,* 30 vols., ed. Charles Dudley Warner (New York: R. S. Peale and J. A. Hill, 1896–97), XII, 7053–7061.
4. This essay is retitled "Hawthorne and James: the Matter of the Heart," in Lewis's *Trials of the World: Essays in American Literature and the Humanistic Tradition* (New Haven, Connecticut: Yale University Press, 1965), pp. 77–96.
5. What Bewley actually said, while commenting on what happens to Oliver Lyon's consciousness in the course of his painting Colonel Capadose's portrait, is that Oliver gets on the verge of committing "the crime which for both Hawthorne and James was the worse possible: of

violating the integrity of another man's personality"–*The Complex Fate: Hawthorne, Henry James and Some Other American Writers* (New York: Chatto and Windus, 1952), p. 86. Bewley never suggested any similarity between "The Liar" and *The Scarlet Letter* or any other specific work by Hawthorne.

6. It is actually chapter 18, and is entitled "A Flood of Sunshine," not, as Gottschalk has it, "Hester in the Forest."
7. Peter Buitenhuis made the same observation when he wrote, in "Henry James on Hawthorne," that "Even *What Maisie Knew* can be traced to some of the things that Pearl knew in *The Scarlet Letter*"–*New England Quarterly,* 32 (June, 1959), 216.
8. Masback's observations on Pearl and Maisie may be found on pp. 113–19, 143–50, 217–25, 260–61, and 280–84 of his dissertation.

Chapter 4

1. The selections from Hawthorne are on pp. 7061–96, and include four from *The Scarlet Letter* ("Salem and the Hawthornes"–from "The Custom-House" sketch–"The Minister's Vigil," "The Child at the Brook-Side," and "The Revelation of the Scarlet Letter"), and one each from *The House of the Seven Gables* ("Hepzibah and Pyncheon"), *Mosses from an Old Manse* ("The Old Manse"), and *The Marble Faun* ("The Faun's Transformation").
2. Percy Lubbock, ed., *The Letters of Henry James,* 2 vols. (New York: Charles Scribner's Sons, 1920), I, 115–17 [14 Feb. 1885].
3. F. O. Matthiessen and Kenneth B. Murdock, eds., *The Notebooks of Henry James* (New York: Oxford University Press, 1947), p. 47.
4. This essay is retitled "Hawthorne and James: the Matter of the Heart," in Lewis's *Trials of the World: Essays in American Literature and the Humanistic Tradition* (New Haven, Connecticut: Yale University Press, 1965), pp. 77–96.
5. The "bit of strange business used between Zenobia and Priscilla" occurs at the end of chapter 13 of *Blithedale;* the James passage Banta misquotes is from chapter 18 of *The Bostonians.* In both the Modern Library and the Bodley Head editions of *The Bostonians,* the passage reads: Olive "prepared to throw a fold of her mantle, as she had *done* before, over her young friend" (emphasis mine). From Banta's subsequent quotations, probably the other "gesture of symbolic unfolding" she refers to is that in chapter 42 of *The Bostonians.* One wishes authors would keep to a minimum such imprecise references as "on leaving a party," "towards the middle of the novel," "at one point" . . .
6. Martha Banta too notes that in the end Hollingsworth "finds himself drained of vitality and virility by the not-so-helpless Priscilla" (*Henry James and the Occult,* p. 91).

7. Fryer's *The Faces of Eve: Women in the Nineteenth-Century American Novel* was published in 1976 by Oxford University Press.
8. In "The American Galatea," *College English,* 32 (1971), 890–99, Judith H. Montgomery too considers, among other things, the question of whether nineteenth-century American female authors were able "to create heroines more successfully human and independent" than those by male authors (896). Her conclusion rather contradicts Fryer's assertion. In a note on p. 898, for example, she writes: "Nineteenth-century authors of the 'domestic' novel, for instance, were often women; yet they subjected their heroines to the same strictures as those imposed by male novelists."
9. Lucke points out also the two "unconscious" revisions James made in Hawthorne's passage: where Hawthorne had written that "Hollingsworth hardly said a word," James wrote "Hollingsworth scarcely said a word"; where he had written "by perpetrating some huge sin," James wrote "by committing some huge sin."
10. Monteiro notes, further, that both Hawthorne and James related "this lust for power over others to impotence"—a connection that is corraborated by psychology.
11. Poirier finds also that Coverdale's "position" in chapter 12 of *Blithedale,* after his "retreat from society into an 'ideal' community and from there into sequestered landscape," is comparable to Milly Theale's in chapter 5 of *The Wings of the Dove,* where she is seen seated on the edge of a cliff.
12. In "The Dark Lady of Salem," *Partisan Review,* 8 (September–October, 1941), 362–81, reprinted in *Image and Idea: Fourteen Essays on Literary Themes* (Norfolk, Connecticut: New Directions, 1949), pp. 22–41, Philip Rahv saw Zenobia as "an earlier and cruder version of Madame de Vionnet," and Coverdale as the ancestor of Lambert Strether (*Image and Idea,* p. 38).
13. As indicated in the second essay, Randall Stewart had earlier connected Roderick Elliston in "Egotism" with Gilbert Osmond. In *American Literature and Christian Doctrine* (Baton Rouge: Louisiana State University Press, 1958), p. 104, he noted that the "insidiousness of egotism was James's great concern, as it was Hawthorne's." In "Egotism," Hawthorne "used a snake as a symbol of self-involvement," and Elliston "goes about crying, 'It gnaws me, it gnaws me!'" Although in *The Portrait* Osmond does nothing so melodramatic as that, "James (remembering Hawthorne's tale, very likely) says of him, 'His egotism lay hidden like a serpent in a bank of flowers.'" Oscar Cargill too, in *The Novels of Henry James* (New York: Hafner Publishing, 1961), p. 33n., noted that "James uses the figure of a serpent, curiously, to describe the egotism of Osmond."
14. Carl Van Doren, in *The American Novel* (New York: Macmillan, 1931), p. 194, had earlier observed that although Rowland Mallet "does not

speak in the first person, [he] renders the narrative something the same service that Miles Coverdale renders in *The Blithedale Romance*."

Chapter 5

1. James had earlier written on Hawthorne's European experiences in his review of Hawthorne's *French and Italian Note-Books* (*Nation,* March 14, 1872, pp. 172–73). He later wrote on these experiences again in his introduction to the selections from Hawthorne in Warner's *Library of the World's Best Literature* (1879), and in his letter to the Hawthorne centennial (1904). All these three items are reviewed in the first essay in this text.
2. This is Vol. IV of Edel's 5-vol. biography of James (1953–1972).
3. Cargill finds also that the situation of Own Warland in "The Artist of the Beautiful" suggests that of Roderick in Northampton, and that "in its unusual emphasis so far as 'the other woman' is concerned," *Roderick Hudson* reminds one of "the dislocation of emphasis in Hawthorne's treatment of the human triangle in *The Scarlet Letter*." But Cargill does not explain what connection he sees between *Roderick Hudson* and Roderick Elliston and his sculptor friend George Herkimer in "Egotism." His remark about James's "curious"use, in *The Portrait of a Lady,* of the figure of a serpent to describe Osmond's egotism was previously made by Randall Stewart in *American Literature and Christian Doctrine* (1958); and his observation, in response to Philip Rahv, that Mary Garland suggests Hilda more than she does Priscilla or Zenobia is not new either, for Rahv himself had stated, both in his *Partisan Review* article (May-June 1943, p. 234) and in the 1949 edition of *Image and Idea,* p. 49, that "Mary is essentially a figure from a novel such as *The Blithedale Romance* or *The Marble Faun* brought forward into a later age." Morovitz, p. 1440, says Mary "can be vaguely linked to Hester Prynne and Zenobia."
4. Kelley's book appeared first as a dissertation (University of Illinois, 1930), and was also published in vol. 15, nos. 1 and 2 of the *University of Illinois Studies in Language and Literature.*
5. This is Vol. II of Edel's 5-vol. biography of James (1953–1972).
6. Like most other works on James's Italianate fiction, *Senuous Pessimism* has a few other references to Hawthorne. "Travelling Companions," for example, is "a comparatively primitive effort"; it was composed "in the manner of the Hawthorne who transferred long descriptive passages from his Italian notebooks into *The Marble Faun* with only minor adjustments" (10). In "Adina" James tried "to equip the topaz with a 'curse,' but such pseudo-Hawthornean gloom seems forced and insignificant alongside the 'natural desire' of Angelo and Adina" (44). Both this story and "The Madonna of the Future" "are presumably set in the Italy of the 1840s or 50s–the Italy of Hawthorne, an Italy James never saw, never directly knew" (63).

Chapter 6

1. James's other extended evaluation of *The Seven Gables* appears in his introduction to the selections from Hawthorne in Warner's *Library of the World's Best Literature* (1897). This introduction is reviewed in the first essay in this text.
2. Ralph B. Perry, *The Thought and Character of William James* (Boston: Little, Brown, 1935), I, 316, 319; see also the first essay.
3. ibid., p. 332.
4. T. S. Eliot, "The Hawthorne Aspect," *Little Review,* 5 (August, 1918), 47–53; reprinted in *The Question of Henry James,* ed. F. W. Dupee (London: Allan Wingate, 1947), pp. 127–33.
5. This essay is retitled "Hawthorne and James: The Matter of the Heart," in Lewis's *Trials of the World* (New Haven, Connecticut: Yale University Press, 1965), pp. 77–96.
6. As indicated later in this essay, "A Passionate Pilgrim"has also been compared with "Consular Experiences" in *Our Old Home.*
7. See *The Notebooks of Henry James,* ed. F. O. Matthiessen and Kenneth B. Murdock (New York: Oxford University Press, 1947), p. 151.
8. Tony Tanner, probably remembering this passage by Matthiessen, wrote: "Other critics have noted significant thematic resemblances between" Hawthorne's works and James's. Thus "The Beast in the Jungle" "may be compared with Hawthorne's 'The Christmas Banquet,' for both are studies of men whose tragedy is that they never suffer because they are incapable of genuine human feeling"–Introduction to James's *Hawthorne* (London: Macmillan, 1967), p. 16.
9. Bewley's "The American Problem" first appeared in *Scrutiny,* 17 (Spring, 1950), 14–37.
10. As indicated in the second essay, Yvor Winters observed, while discussing the "excessive subtlety" with which the characters in *The Awkward Age* "scrutinize each other and the whole situation," that these characters "remind one–and James . . . likewise reminds one–of Hawthorne scrutinizing Dr. Grimshaw's spiders with insanse [sic] intensity, but with no illumination" (*In Defense of Reason,* 1937, p. 321).
11. Gerald Willen, preface to James's *Washington Square* (New York: Thomas Y. Crowell, 1970), p. vii.
12. This is Vol. II of Edel's 5-vol. biography of James (1953–1972).
13. Nathaniel Hawthorne, *Our Old Home* (1863; reprinted Columbus: Ohio State University Press, 1970), p. 23.
14. As indicated previously, in "Another Reading of *The Turn of the Screw,*" N. B. Fagin had noted that Miles in James's story is probably "too corrupted to live without evil," just like Georgiana in "The Birthmark" (*Modern Language Notes,* March 1941, p. 201).

Bibliography

One of the basic sources of reference for this study has been Beatrice Ricks, Joseph D. Adams, and Jack O. Hazlerig's *Nathaniel Hawthorne: A Reference Bibliography, 1900–1971* (Boston: G. K. Hall, 1972). An obvious caution in using this bibliography is not to substitute its annotations for the reading of the items themselves.

Ricks lists item 679 on p. 67 as a dissertation by I. W. Finch: "A Study of the Relationship Between Hawthorne and Henry James" (Harvard, 1939). There is no record of this dissertation at Harvard. F. O. Matthiessen too, in *American Renaissance* (1941), p. 292n., mentions a book, "under preparation by John Finch," on the James-Hawthorne relation. I have failed to trace such a book. James Woodress, in *Dissertations in American Literature, 1891–1966* (Durham, North Carolina: Duke University Press, 1968), lists as item 1232 a dissertation by Donald C. Summerhayes: "The Relation of Illusion and Reality to Formal Structure in Selected Works of Fiction by Nathaniel Hawthorne, Melville, and James" (Yale, n.d.). Possibly this dissertation was dropped. Item 1574 lists a dissertation by John W. Switzer: "Henry James's Debt to Hawthorne" (University of Missouri, n.d.). This dissertation was never completed. I am grateful to the University of Wisconsin for lending me a copy of the dissertation by Charles G. Hoffmann (1952).

The list below does not include any of Hawthorne's or James's works. Where these are discussed in the essays, the reference is usually to their chapters, since this form of reference seems the most useful for users of different editons. The few exceptions are clealy indicated either in the text or in the notes.

Anderson, Charles R. "Person, Place, and Thing in James's *The Portrait of a Lady*." In *Essays on American Literature in Honor of Jay B. Hubbell.* Ed. Clarence Gohdes. Durham, North Carolina: Duke University Press, 1967, pp. 164–82.

Anderson, Quentin. "Henry James and the New Jerusalem." *Kenyon Review,* 8 (Autumn, 1946), 515–66.

_____. *The American Henry James.* New Brunswick, New Jersey: Rutgers University Press, 1957.

_____. Introuction to *Hawthorne,* by Henry James. New York: Macmillan, 1962.

Arader, Harry F. "American Novelists in Italy: Nathaniel Hawthorne, Howells, James, and F. Marion Crawford." Diss. University of Pennsylvania 1953.

Banta, Martha. *Henry James and the Occult: The Great Extension.* Bloomington: Indiana University Press, 1972.

Bashore, James Robert, Jr. "The Villains in the Major Works of Nathaniel Hawthorne and Henry James." 2 vols. Diss. University of Wisconsin 1959.

Baxter, Annette K. "Independence vs. Isolation: Hawthorne and James on the Problem of the Artist." *Nineteenth Century Fiction,* 10 (1955), 225–31.

Beebe, Maurice. *Ivory Towers and Sacred Founts: The Artis as Hero in Fiction from Goethe to Joyce.* New York: New York University Press, 1964.

Beers, Henry A. *Four Americans: Roosevelt, Hawthorne, Emerson, Whitman.* 1919; rpt. Freeport, New York: Books for Libraries, 1968.

Bewley, Marius. *The Complex Fate: Hawthorne, Henry James and Some Other American Writers.* New York: Chatto and Windus, 1952.

_____. "Correspondence." *Scrutiny,* 17 (Spring, 1950), 56–60.

_____. *The Eccentric Design: Form in the Classic American Novel.* New York: Columbia University Press, 1959.

Bochner, Jay. "Life in a Picture Gallery: Things in *The Portrait of a Lady* and *The Marble Faun*." *Texas Studies in Literature and Language,* 11 (1969), 761–77.

Bowden, Edwin T. *The Dungeon of the Heart: Human Isolation and the American Novel.* New York: Macmillan Co., 1961.

Brooks, Van Wyck. *New England: Indian Summer.* 1940; rpt. New York: E. P. Dutton, 1965.

_____. *The Dream of Arcadia: American Writers and Artists in Italy. 1760–1915.* New York: E. P. Dutton, 1958.

Buitenhuis, Peter. "Henry James on Hawthorne." *New England Quarterly,* 32 (June, 1959), 207–25.

_____. Introduction to *Twentieth Century Interpretations of "The Portrait of a Lady."* Englewood Cliffs, New Jersey: Prentice-Hall, 1968.

_____. *The Grasping Imagination: The American Writings of Henry James.* Toronto: Univeristy of Toronto Press, 1970.

Cargill, Oscar. *The Novels of Henry James.* New York: Hafner Publishing, 1961.

Cohen, B[enjamin] Bernard. "Henry James and the Hawthorne Centennial." *Essex Institute Historical Collections,* 92 (July, 1956), 279–83.

Cowie, Alexander. *The Rise of the American Novel.* New York: American Book, 1948.

Crews, Frederick C. "A New Reading of *The Blithedale Romance.*" *American Literature,* 29 (May, 1957), 147–70.

Dean, Sharon Welch. "Lost Ladies: The Isolated Heroine in the Fiction of Hawthorne, James, Fitzgerald, Hemingway, and Faulkner." Diss. University of New Hampshire 1973.

Dupee, F[rederick] W[ilcox]. *Henry James.* American Men of Letters Series. 1951; rpt. New York: William Morrow, 1974.

Edel, Leon. Introduction to *The Ghostly Tales of Henry James.* New Brunswick, New Jersey: Rutgers University Press, 1948.

_____. "Correspondence." *Scrutiny,* 17 (Spring, 1950), 53–55.

_____. *Henry James.* 5 vols. New York: J. B. Lippincott, 1953–1972.

_____. *Henry James.* University of Minnesota Pamphlets on American Writers, No. 4. Minneapolis: University of Minnesota Press, 1960.

_____. Introduction to *Roderick Hudson,* by Henry James. New York: Harper and Brothers, 1960.

Eliot, T[homas] S[tearns]. "In Memory" and "The Hawthorne Aspect." In *The Question of Henry James: A Collection of Critical Essays.* Ed. F. W. Dupee. London: Allan Wingate, 1947, pp. 123–33.

_____. Review of *The Cambridge History of American Literature,* Vol. II. *Athenaeum,* April 25, 1919, pp. 236–37.

Fagin, Nathan Bryllion. "Another Reading of *The Turn of the Screw.*" *Modern Language Notes,* 56 (March, 1941), 196–202.

Fiedler, Leslie A. *Love and Death in the American Novel.* Rev. ed. New York: Stein and Day, 1966.

Fryer, Judith J. "The Faces of Eve: A Study of Women in American Life and Literature in the Nineteenth Century." Diss. University of Minnesota 1973.

Fussell, Edwin. "Hawthorne, James, and 'The Common Doom.'" *American Quarterly,* 10 (1958), 438–53.

Gale, Robert L. "*The Marble Faun* and *The Sacred Fount:* A Resemblance." *Studi Americani,* 8 (1962), 21–33.

Garland, Hamlin. *Roadside Meetings.* New York: Macmillan, 1930.

Gill, Richard. *Happy Rural Seat: The English Country House and the Literary Imagination.* New Haven, Connecticut: Yale University Press, 1972.

Gleckner, Robert F. "James's 'Madame de Mauves' and Hawthorne's *The Scarlet Letter.*" *Modern Language Notes,* 73 (December, 1958), 580–86.

Gottschalk, Jane. "The Continuity of American Letters in *The Scarlet Letter* and *The Beast in the Jungle.*" *Wisconsin Studies in Literature,* 4 (1967), 39–45.

Grattan, C. Hartley. *The Three Jameses: A Family of Minds.* New York: Longmans, Green, 1932.

Grover, P. R. "A Tanner in the Works." *Cambridge Review,* 89A (May, 1968), 430–31.

Guttmann, Allen. "Images of Value and the Sense of the Past." *New England Quarterly,* 35 (March, 1962), 3–26.

Hawthorne, Edith Garrigues, ed. *The Memoirs of Julian Hawthorne.* New York: Macmillan, 1938.

Hayne, Barrie S. "The Divided Self: The Alter Ego as Theme and Device in Brockden Brown, Hawthorne, and James." Diss. Harvard 1964.

Hinchliffe, Arnold P. "Symbolism in the American Novel, 1850–1950; an Examination of the Findings of Recent Literary Critics in Respect of the Novels of Hawthorne, Melville, James, Hemingway and Faulkner." Diss. Manchester 1963.

Hoffmann, Charles G. "The Development of the Short Novel in Hawthorne, Melville, and James." Diss. University of Wisconsin 1952.

_____. *The Short Novels of Henry James.* New York: Bookman Associates, 1957.

Holland, Laurence Bedwell. *The Expense of Vision: Essays on the Craft of Henry James.* Princeton, New Jersey: Princeton University Press, 1964.

Howe, Irving. Introduction to *The Bostonians,* by Henry James. New York: Modern Library, 1956.

_____. *Politics and the Novel.* New York: Avon Books, 1957.

Howells, William Dean. "James's Hawthorne." *Atlantic Monthly,* 45 (February, 1880), 282–85.

Kaman, John Michael. "The Lonely Hero in Hawthorne, Melville, Twain and James." Diss. Stanford 1973.

Kane, Robert J. "Hawthorne's 'The Prophetic Pictures' and James's 'The Liar.'" *Modern Language Notes,* 65 (April, 1950), 257–58.

Kelley, Cornelia Pulsifer. *The Early Development of Henry James.* Urbana: University of Illinois Press, 1930.

Kenton, Edna. "Henry James in the World." In *The Question of Henry James: A Collection of Critical Essays.* Ed. F. W. Dupee. London: Allan Wingate, 1947, pp. 144–50.

Kerr, Howard. *Mediums, and Spirit-Rappers, and Roaring Radicals: Spiritualism in American Literature, 1850–1900.* Urbana: University of Illinois Press, 1972.

Kornfeld, Milton H. "A Darker Freedom: The Villains in the Novels of Hawthorne, James, and Faulkner." Diss. Brandeis 1970.

Kraft, Quentin G. "The Central Problem of James's Fictional Thought: From *The Scarlet Letter* to *Roderick Hudson.*" *Journal of English Literary History,* 36 (1969), 416–39.

Krier, William John. "A Pattern of Limitations: The Heroine's Novel of the Mind." Diss. Indiana University 1973.

Lang, Hans-Joachim. "The Turns in *The Turn of the Screw.*" *Jahrbuch fur Amerikastudien,* 9 (1963), 111–28.

_____. "How Ambiguous is Hawthorne?" *Geist Einer Freien Gesellschaft.* Heidelberg: Quelle and Meyer, 1962, pp. 195–220.

Leavis, F[rank] R[aymond]. *The Great Tradition: A Study of the English Novel.* 1948; rpt. Garden City, New York: Doubleday, 1954.

Lewis, R[ichard] W[arrington] B[aldwin]. *The American Adam: Innocence, Tragedy, and Tradition in the Nineteenth Century.* Chicago: University of Chicago Press, 1955.

_____. "The Tactics of Sanctity: Hawthorne and James." *Hawthorne Centenary Essays.* Ed. Roy Harvey Pearce. Columbus: Ohio State University Press, 1964, pp. 271–95.

Long, Robert Emmet. "The Society and the Masks: *The Blithedale Romance* and *The Bostonians.*" *Nineteenth Century Fiction,* 19 (September, 1964), 105–22.

_____. "'The Ambassadors' and The Genteel Tradition: James's Correction of Hawthorne and Howells." *New England Quarterly,* 42 (March, 1969), 44–64.

_____. "James's Washington Square: The Hawthorne Relation." *New England Quarterly,* 46 (December, 1973), 573–90.

Lucke, Jessie Ryon. "The Inception of 'The Beast in the Jungle.'" *New England Quarterly,* 26 (December, 1953), 529–32.

McElroy, John. "The Hawthorne Style of American Fiction." *ESQ: A Journal of the American Renaissance,* NS 19 (2nd quarter, 1973), 117–23.

Martin, Terence. "Adam Blair and Arthur Dimmesdale: A Lesson from the Master." *American Literature,* 34 (1962–63), 274–79.

_____. *Nathaniel Hawthorne.* Twayne United States Authors Series. New Haven, Connecticut: College and University Press, 1965.

Martin, Wendy. "Seduced and Abandoned in the New World: The Image of Woman in American Fiction." In *Woman in Sexist Society.* Ed. Vivian Gornick and Barbara K. Moran. New York: Basic Books, 1971, pp. 226–39.

Martineau, Stephen F. "Opposition and Balance: A Characteristic of Structure in Hawthorne, Melville, and James." Diss. Columbia 1967.

Masback, Frederick Joseph. "The Child Character in Hawthorne and James." Diss. Syracuse 1960.

Matthiessen, F[rancis] O[tto]. *American Renaissance: Art and Expression in the Age of Emerson and Whitman.* New York: Oxford University Press, 1941.

_____. "James and the Plastic Arts." *Kenyon Review,* 5 (Autumn, 1943), 533–50.

_____. *Henry James: The Major Phase.* New York: Oxford University Press, 1944.

_____. *The James Family, Including Selections from the Writings of Henry James, Sr., William, Henry & Alice James.* New York: Alfred A. Knopf, 1947.

_____. *The Achievement of T. S. Eliot.* 2nd ed., rev. New York: Oxford University Press, 1947.

Maves, Carl. *Sensuous Pessimism: Italy in the Works of Henry James.* Bloomington: Indiana University Press, 1973.

Melchiori, Giorgio. "Locksley Hall Revisited: Tennyson and Henry James." *Review of English Literature,* 6 (October, 1965), 9–25.

Miller, Raymond A., Jr. "Representative Tragic Heroines in the Work of Brown, Hawthorne, Howells, James, and Dreiser." Diss. University of Wisconsin 1957.

Miner, Earl Roy. "Henry James's Metaphysical Romances." *Nineteenth Century Fiction,* 9 (June, 1954), 1–25.

Monteiro, George. "Hawthorne, James and the Destructive Self." *Texas Studies in Literature and Language,* 4 (1962), 58–71.

Montgomery, Judith H. "The American Galatea." *College English,* 32 (May, 1971), 890–99.

Morovitz, Sanford E. "*Roderick Hudson:* James's *Marble Faun.*" *Texas Studies in Literature and Language,* 11 (1970), 1427–43.

Nash, Deanna C. "The Web as an Organic Metaphor in *The Marble Faun, Middlemarch: A Study of Provincial Life,* and *The Golden Bowl:* The Growth of Contextualism as an Aesthetic Theory in the Nineteenth Century." Diss. University of North Carolina at Chapel Hill 1971.

Newlin, Paul A. "The Uncanny in the Supernatural Short Fiction of Poe, Hawthorne and James." Diss. University of California at Los Angeles, 1967.

_____. "The Development of *Roderick Hudson:* An Evaluation." *Arizona Quarterly,* 27 (Summer, 1971), 101–23.

Pattee, Fred Lewis. *The Development of the American Short Story.* 1923; rpt. New York: Biblo and Tanner, 1966.

Pauly, Thomas H. "The Travel Sketch-Book and the American Author: A Study of the European Travelogues of Irving, Longfellow, Hawthorne, Howells, and James." Diss. University of California at Berkeley 1970.

Perry, Bliss. *A Study of Prose Fiction.* Boston: Houghton Mifflin, 1904.

Poirier, Richard. *The Comic Sense of Henry James: A Study of the Early Novels.* New York: Oxford University Press, 1960.

_____. *A World Elsewhere: The Place of Style in American Literature.* New York: Oxford University Press, 1966.

Porte, Joel. *The Romance in America: Studies in Cooper, Poe, Hawthorne, Melville, and James.* Middletown, Connecticut: Wesleyan University Press, 1969.

Pratt, Linda Ray. "The Abuse of Eve by the New World Adam." *Images of Women in Fiction: Feminist Perspectives.* Rev. ed. Ed. Susan Koppelman Cornillon. Bowling Green, Ohio: Bowling Green University Popular Press, 1973, pp. 155–74.

Pyron, John E., Jr. "American Romance and Italian Reality in the Nineteenth Century." Diss. University of Pittsburgh 1973.

Rahv, Philip. *Image and Idea: Fourteen Essays on Literary Themes.* Norfolk, Connecticut: New Directions, 1949.

Reynolds, Gordon Duncan. "Psychological Rebirth in Selected Works by Nathaniel Hawthorne, Stephen Crane, Henry James, William Faulkner, and Ralph Ellison." Diss. University of California at Irvine 1973.

Rose, Harriet. "The First-Person Narrator as Artist in the Works of Charles Brockden Brown, Nathaniel Hawthorne, and Henry James." Diss. Indiana University 1973.

Rosenberry, Edward H. "James's Use of Hawthorne in 'The Liar.'" *Modern Language Notes,* 76 (March, 1961), 234–38.

Ross, Maude Cardwell. "Moral Values of the American Woman as Presented in Three Major American Authors." Diss. University of Texas 1964.

Rovit, Earl. "James and Emerson: The Lesson of the Master." *American Scholar,* 33 (1964), 434–40.

Samuels, C[harles] T[homas]. "Giovanni and the Governess." *American Scholar,* 37 (1968), 655–78.

Schechter, Harold. "The Unpardonable Sin in 'Washington Square.'" *Studies in Short Fiction,* 10 (Spring, 1973), 137–41.

Shelden, Pamela Jacobs. "American Gothicism: The Evolution of a Mode." Diss. Kent State University 1972.

Shucard, Alan R. "Diplomacy in *The Ambassadors.*" *Arizona Quarterly,* 29 (Summer, 1973), 123–29.

Snow, Kimberley. "Images of Woman in the American Novel." *Aphra,* 2 (Winter, 1970), 56–68.

Stallman, Robert W. "The Houses that James Built—*The Portrait of a Lady.*" *Texas Quarterly,* 1 (Winter, 1958), 176–96.

Stewart, Randall. *American Literature and Christian Doctrine.* Baton Rouge: Louisiana State University Press, 1958.

Stone, Albert E., Jr. Introduction to *Twentieth Century Interpretations of "The Ambassadors."* Englewood Cliffs, New Jersey: Prentice-Hall, 1969.

Stone, Edward. *The Battle and the Books: Some Aspects of Henry James.* Athens, Ohio: Ohio University Press, 1964.

Tanner, Tony. Introduction to *Hawthorne,* by Henry James. London: Macmillan 1967.

Tate, Allen. "Three Commentaries: Poe, James, and Joyce." *Sewanee Review,* 58 (Winter, 1950), 1–15.

Thompson, David J. "Societal Definitions of Individualism and the Critique of Egotism as a Major Theme in American Fiction." Diss. Brown 1972.

Tintner, Adeline. "The Spoils of Henry James." *PMLA,* 61 (March, 1946), 239–51.

Travis, Mildred K. "Hawthorne's 'Egotism' and 'The Jolly Corner.'" *Emerson Society Quarterly,* 63 (Spring, 1971), 13–18.

Tytell, John. "Henry James and the Romance." *Markham Review,* 5 (May, 1969), 1–2.

Van Doren, Carl. *The American Novel.* New York: Macmillan, 1931.

Ward, J. A. "Henry James and the Nature of Evil." *Twentieth Century Literature,* 6 (July, 1960), 65–69.

Warren, Austin. *Rage for Order: Essays in Criticism.* Ann Arbor: University of Michigan Press, 1948.

Waterfall, Gaillard FitzSimmons. "The Manipulation Theme in the Works of Nathaniel Hawthorne and Henry James." Diss. University of South Carolina 1973.

Wegelin, Christof. *The Image of Europe in Henry James.* Dallas: Southern Methodist University Press, 1958.

_____. "The Rise of the International Novel." *PMLA,* 77 (June, 1962), 305–10.

West, Rebecca. *Henry James.* New York: Henry Holt, 1916.

Willen, Gerald. Preface to *Washington Square,* by Henry James. New York: Thomas Y. Crowell, 1970.

Winters, Yvor. "Maule's Curse: Hawthorne and the Problem of Allegory." *American Review,* 9 (September, 1937), 339–61.

_____. "Maule's Well, or Henry James and the Relation of Morals to Manners." *In Defense of Reason.* Denver: Allan Swallow, 1937, pp. 300–43.

Wright, Nathalia. *American Novelists in Italy: The Discoverers.* Philadelphia: University of Pennsylvania Press, 1965.

Index of Authors, and Works of Hawthorne and James